Broken Republik

Broken Republik

The Inside Story of Germany's Descent into Crisis

Chris Reiter and Will Wilkes

BLOOMSBURY PUBLISHING
LONDON • OXFORD • NEW YORK • NEW DELHI • SYDNEY

BLOOMSBURY PUBLISHING
Bloomsbury Publishing Plc
50 Bedford Square, London, WC1B 3DP, UK
Bloomsbury Publishing Ireland Limited,
29 Earlsfort Terrace, Dublin 2, D02 AY28, Ireland

BLOOMSBURY, BLOOMSBURY PUBLISHING and the Diana logo are trademarks of
Bloomsbury Publishing Plc

First published in Great Britain 2025

Copyright © Chris Reiter and Will Wilkes, 2025

Chris Reiter & Will Wilkes have asserted their right under the Copyright, Designs and Patents
Act, 1988, to be identified as Authors of this work

Every reasonable effort has been made to trace copyright holders of material reproduced in
this book, but if any have been inadvertently overlooked the publishers would be glad to hear
from them

All rights reserved. No part of this publication may be: i) reproduced or transmitted in any form,
electronic or mechanical, including photocopying, recording or by means of any information
storage or retrieval system without prior permission in writing from the publishers; or ii) used
or reproduced in any way for the training, development or operation of artificial intelligence
(AI) technologies, including generative AI technologies. The rights holders expressly reserve
this publication from the text and data mining exception as per Article 4(3) of the Digital Single
Market Directive (EU) 2019/790

Bloomsbury Publishing Plc does not have any control over, or responsibility for, any third-party
websites referred to in this book. All internet addresses given in this book were correct at the
time of going to press. The author and publisher regret any inconvenience caused if addresses have
changed or sites have ceased to exist, but can accept no responsibility for any such changes

A catalogue record for this book is available from the British Library

ISBN: HB: 978-1-5266-7914-7; TPB: 978-1-5266-7918-5; EBOOK: 978-1-5266-7916-1;
EPDF: 978-1-5266-7917-8

2 4 6 8 10 9 7 5 3 1

Typeset by Newgen KnowledgeWorks Pvt. Ltd., Chennai, India
Printed and bound in Great Britain by CPI Group (UK) Ltd, Croydon CR0 4YY

To find out more about our authors and books visit www.bloomsbury.com
and sign up for our newsletters

For product safety related questions contact
productsafety@bloomsbury.com

Contents

Introduction: For Friends and Neighbours ... 1

One The House is Crumbling ... 5
A brief overview of deficiencies ... 6

Two Coddled Child ... 29
Protective uncle ... 30
Sins of the father ... 40
Sibling rivalry ... 47
Mutti ... 52

Three Myth Busting ... 65
Myth of efficiency ... 66
Myth of diligence ... 73
Myth of the progressive nation ... 80
Myth of moral clarity ... 85

Four Cracked Pipes ... 93
Deep trouble ... 94
Faustian pact ... 99
Green shoots ... 103
Ashes to ashes ... 107

Five Busted Boiler ... 113
Sunset in Autoland ... 115
End of the line ... 126
Clocking out ... 131
Barren frontiers ... 135

Six	Neighbourhood Decay	143
	Cracks in the pavement	144
	Wobbly bridge	155
	End of the road	160
Seven	Broken Ladder	169
	Heir apparent	171
	Hard ceiling	177
	Empty promises	186
Eight	House Divided	193
	False friends	196
	Public enemy	208
	Day X	215
Nine	Angst and Isolation	223
	Trouble with 'you'	224
	Culture clash	231
	Closing the gates	241
Ten	Patchwork	249
	Repair and reset	251
	Habitat for Heimat	257
	Digital leapfrog	261
	Power to the people	263
	Zusammenfeiern!	266
	Closing Remarks: Ein Haus für Alle	271
	Acknowledgements	277
	Notes	281
	Index	323

Introduction: For Friends and Neighbours

'We humanise what is going on in the world and in ourselves by speaking of it, and in the course of speaking of it we learn to be human.'

Hannah Arendt

Ernst Müller was born in the small German city of Düren and rose to prominence as a boxer in the 1970s (competing in the Olympics and winning a European championship in his heyday). At the time, Germany was in the midst of the post-war economic miracle, full of promise and purpose. Half a century later, his home town – located midway between Cologne and the Dutch border – faces decline like so much of the country, and anxiety and suspicion have become evident. The open-cast lignite mines surrounding the city once provided abundant and affordable energy, supporting a cluster of paper mills. But the mines are due to close and the certainties that once existed here and elsewhere in Germany have crumbled, opening the door to divisive nationalistic sentiment.

In his own small corner of the country, Müller, who's over seventy years old, had taken on the fight to help keep German society from falling apart. Along with his wife Yvonne, he runs a modest boxing gym tucked away in a primary school. Together, they train a few dozen youngsters for a few cents a day. Some have genuine athletic ambitions, whereas for others, jabbing and sparring is an escape from troubled homes. While Ernst motivates them, Yvonne provides care, including handing out gloves and equipment to the kids who don't have the resources. Ernst and Yvonne offer a counterpoint to the martial-arts events where right-wing movements regularly recruit frustrated young men, and the former boxing champion might be one of the last role models preventing these kids from drifting into darkness. Although his office is decorated with photographs and memorabilia from his competitive feats, Müller points with pride to an award from Düren's town hall. It recognises his achievements in integrating migrants into German society. It's an accolade he values more than his collection of medals and belts. 'Boxing teaches you respect,' he said amid the thud of gloves hitting pads. 'It doesn't matter what you look like, what language you speak, or where you come from.' This book is for people like the Müllers, the unsung heroes trying to keep the dream of a new Germany alive.

In all honesty, when we started exploring the idea of writing about our years of experience living in and reporting on Germany, the focus was on the hidden crisis behind the country's deceptive stability. At the time in early 2023, our adopted homeland had made it through a tense winter without energy rationing after Vladimir Putin sought to weaken Europe's anchor by cutting off gas supplies in retaliation for Berlin's support of Ukraine. Despite what looked like more evidence of German resilience, we thought it was important to draw back the curtain and show that the country is far more fragile than the world thinks. Since then, though, its vulnerabilities have burst into the open. Crises have tumbled into one another and revealed deep-seated issues that were only hinted at before. The collapse of Olaf Scholz's coalition on 6 November 2024, just hours after the re-election of Donald Trump, was a poignant warning of how fragile and unpredictable Germany had become.

But the root causes are still misunderstood. This is not simply a cyclical hiccup and it goes beyond structural issues. There is a fundamental weakness in the idea of Germany itself. The core of national solidarity is based around prosperity and that makes its gradual economic decline so much more destabilising than in other countries, because the fallback sense of identity is divisive ethnic nationalism. The political class is ill-suited to recognise the underlying problems, as it throws together piecemeal reforms rather than articulating visions of what Germany can and should become. That's because there's little frame of reference for the concept of nation-building, and the country's own self-mythologising creates blind spots to its own deficiencies. The idea that a German identity

INTRODUCTION

can be shaped and nurtured is foreign to a country that believes in legends of a *Volk* which has endured over epochs and regime changes.

The helplessness was hard to ignore in September 2024. During a town-hall event in Berlin, a childcare worker voiced the frustration of millions of Germans, when he asked the chancellor why his government resembled 'a bunch of fussy toddlers'. In a rare moment of honesty, Chancellor Scholz didn't try to deflect or soften the criticism, but acknowledged the lack of unity in the three ruling parties. He then effectively shrugged his shoulders and asked the childcare worker what his patent formula to fix the problem would be, adding with a smirk 'I'm asking for a friend.'

That's where we come in, an American and a Brit, respectively, but with deep roots in Germany. And we bring the perspective from our own experiences with decline and division in our birth countries. For the United States, the polarisation of Trump is chilling, while the UK is still grappling with the deep divides exposed by Brexit. Germany feels like it's heading in that direction and maybe worse. While our account might seem forthright at times, writing too reverently would be more disrespectful. That would accept decline as inevitable. Of all the troubles ailing Germany at present, perhaps the most dangerous is a creeping fatalism. It's a tide we hope the book will push against, by writing about the country's faults with empathy while also sketching out a few ideas that could chart a way forward.

We believe it's a fundamentally optimistic endeavour, imploring German citizens to recover a sense of boldness and togetherness similar to when it forged a path out of the destruction of Nazism and tapped into German creativity before the demons of ethnic nationalism took hold. And if the German people can find a way to rally together and face the future, there will be lessons to be learned for other countries as well.

1
The House is Crumbling

'Often, the outward and visible material signs and symbols of happiness and success only show themselves when the process of decline has already set in.'

Thomas Mann

On an overcast spring morning in 2024, a jolt shook the tenants of an apartment building in Berlin's prosperous Schöneberg district. Cracks marred the façade, hinting at the rot within. Restored following World War II, the building in a prime location was at risk of collapse, plunging the lives of the people who lived and worked there into turmoil. The damage was the result of years of neglect and warning signs going unheeded. Emergency measures were taken to shore up the building, but it wasn't clear how deeply unstable its internal structure had become. The incident is bitterly symbolic of Germany's current condition.

In the prime period of industrialisation during the late 1800s, Germany developed rapidly in what's known as the *Gründerzeit* (founders' period). Buildings from that time – like the one in Schöneberg that nearly collapsed – had imposing and decorative fronts facing the street, and behind them were arrayed utilitarian structures for living space, production facilities, storage, as well as keeping livestock. It was effectively a microcosm of the country sharing the same address. In between were courtyards (sometimes several, and the former Meyers Hof in Berlin had eight). The spaces between buildings had to be big enough for a horse-drawn fire engine to be able to turn around, which in Prussian precision was determined to be an area at least 5.34

metres long and wide. The elegant residences in the front were marked by ornate decoration, high ceilings, and they often featured separate entrances and bare-bones quarters for servants. There were also the infamous *Mädchenkammern* (maid's chambers), which were little more than sleeping cubbies in crawl space built beneath the towering ceilings.

The *Gründerzeit* style consisted of generally backward-looking revivals of extravagant Renaissance and Baroque design, as the up-and-coming industrial bourgeoisie sought to preserve the pomp and privilege of the aristocracy. In short, life was good for a select few, but mostly miserable for the rest. This, in essence, is the way the country is increasingly heading, and to help illustrate Germany's issues we'll return periodically throughout the book to the metaphor of a crumbling *Gründerzeit* building and its polarised inhabitants. We'll call it simply the 'House of Germany'.

Indeed, although the country is still intact and impressive, the veneer of stability is starting to crack and profound fissures are being laid bare. There's anger over foreigners, there are attacks on politicians, and a spreading economic gloom that tears at the social fabric. After decades of resilience and sleepwalking past structural issues, Germany's gathering problems loom large and will demand attention and action both at home and abroad. In some ways, the country's situation is unique, but there are commonalities with other liberal democracies. Germany's problems are very much linked to the decaying post-war order. As in other Western countries, politics has become influenced and infiltrated by corporate interests and wealthy power players at the expense of everyday people. Growing inequality has in turn provided fertile ground for populists to sow seeds of doubt and frustration. But there are reasons why Germany is more vulnerable than other countries. Defusing the threat of populism requires a fresh perspective, and the goal of this book is to outline Germany's risks as precisely as possible and draw lessons from what ails the country in order to help patch things up.

A brief overview of deficiencies

Germany clearly has its strengths. Its well-engineered industrial goods are still in demand across the world, underpinned in many ways by world-class vocational training. Its system of collaboration between employees and management, known as *Mitbestimmung* (co-determination), forces companies to consider perspectives that extend beyond quarterly results and annual bonuses, bringing a form of democratic power-sharing to boardrooms. Although the system is under threat, it offers the prospect of offsetting the helplessness felt by workers in other countries, especially as artificial intelligence and other technologies force sweeping changes on the workforce. The German constitution – the *Grundgesetz* (Basic Law) – has created a political system that requires compromise between parties, traditionally defusing polarising rhetoric. On a social level, Germans are ready to welcome refugees, send aid to victims of natural disasters around the world, as well as challenge government actions.

But despite decades of resilience and its solid foundation, cracks in the House of Germany have become apparent. The issues have become deeper than many recognise and more acute than most want to believe. That's been the case for people inside and outside the country. There's often wishful thinking that slumping economic performance is cyclical rather than structural, that political tension is merely a bumpy patch after a series of crises, and that social polarisation isn't really worse than anywhere else. Germany can navigate this stormy period like it has many times before, optimists argue.

That narrative is appealing in part because the prospect of the country straying from the liberal order raises disturbing echoes and would risk destabilising the West. But dismissing the risks would be short-sighted. Although its problems might not be vastly different from other developed countries, there are peculiarities that threaten to send Germany again careening down a dark, unpredictable path faster than others. The good news is that Germany still has plenty of economic substance and a vibrant civil society, and there are opportunities to change the current dynamic (we'll present some ideas in chapter 10).

There's a lot to cover here, so we'll be deliberately superficial at times to allow for depth elsewhere. Much of the perspective, especially before reunification, will be West German, a somewhat unavoidable shortcut but also defensible considering how the East was incorporated and subsequently marginalised.

One of our key observations is how little there is holding the country together. Displaying the country's black, red and gold colours was considered nationalistic and unacceptable for the mainstream until Germany hosted the FIFA World Cup in 2006. That was a stark (and to be fair, refreshing) contrast to the zealous flag-waving in the United States and the cheap commercialisation of the Union Jack in Britain. As we know all too well from our home countries, national pride can go overboard, but a basic feeling of togetherness does have its uses. A sense of belonging can help rally people around a common purpose or at least maintain a sense of community in times of hardship, which is the reality for many Germans and risks getting worse for Europe's powerhouse economy. The country may have wanted to avoid the uncomfortable task of nation-building after instigating two world wars, but not addressing the issue would be dangerous neglect.

Outlets for living an inclusive sense of German identity are lacking. The bread is probably the best in the world, but it's not a public enjoyment. The same goes for eating white asparagus in the early spring. There are a smattering of local traditions like Karneval in the Rhineland and Oktoberfest in Bavaria which bring people together, but few national rallying points. The final of the DFB football cup is the climax of the domestic season, but hardly resonates beyond the two teams involved. By contrast, the Super Bowl in the United States is a national event for which an American football game is just the backdrop. In Germany, most holidays are Christian, while national commemorations obviously have a sombre tone and are marked by political speeches rather than public participation. There are few traditions or customs that cut across religious, ethnic and socioeconomic boundaries, making the bonds linking the country's 84 million people thin.

Germany does have its so-called *Verfassungspatriotismus* (constitutional patriotism), which upholds the Basic Law as a national unifier. Its importance stems from Germany's relatively late unification. It wasn't until 1871 that the German Empire came into being, and it took war with France to make that happen. That victory provided Germany with national pride as well as war reparations to invest, helping it to become an industrial power alongside its military might. Those German traditions combined disastrously, though, in further war and the ethnic nationalism of the Nazis. So the country's emergence as a constitutional democracy after World War II occupies an important place in the national psyche.

The Basic Law indeed sets up a robust structure for the institutions of the state, establishes an independent people's court to resolve differences, and expresses aspirational values like the protection of human dignity. It was designed to ensure Germany never again could or would devolve into a fascist, authoritarian power. 'The mothers and fathers of the Basic Law wanted to build a better Germany,' President Frank-Walter Steinmeier said on the 75th anniversary of the constitution, 23 May 2024. 'They left us a free, democratic and good Germany. Let us preserve the legacy that has been entrusted to us.'[1]

But at the end of the day, it's a legal text. There's little opportunity to get together with friends and toast the power-sharing between federal and state administrations and cheer as a parade of the articles march by. And as noble as the ideas in the Basic Law are, everyday reality has departed from those principles. Expecting people to think about democratic piety when they're angry over a job loss or anxious about soaring rents is a stretch even for the most ardent constitutional patriot. Something with more emotional appeal is needed to connect people.

As in many other Western countries, the state and the public have drifted apart in Germany, and the political class has shown little capacity to come up with answers to counter social fragmentation. Party rosters are filled with people who have worked their way through internal structures. There are competent speakers and well-meaning technocrats, but the process promotes networking skills over new ideas. People who move up do so often because they show commitment to the cause rather than individual ability. Bogged down in process, the big picture gets subsumed in poll results and tactical positioning between parties.

The growing disconnect was evident in 2024, when the *Bundestag* lawmakers gave themselves a 6 per cent salary increase despite budget austerity that compromised much-needed investment in economic competitiveness to safeguard people's future. The extra

€635.50 a month was more than what the government expects people on *Bürgergeld* (citizen's money, or long-term welfare) to live on. At the same time as granting themselves a generous increase, many right-leaning politicians use welfare recipients as scapegoats for fiscal constraints, blaming the spending on supporting 'lazy Germans' and 'freeloading refugees' for why schools are in poor condition and roads and bridges can't be fixed.

That level of dissonance and the lack of viable solutions have opened a gap for anti-establishment movements, above all the *Alternative für Deutschland* (AfD). The far-right party has tapped into frustration by reviving ethnic tropes to appeal to disaffected Germans, a common playbook across much of the West but with deep roots in Germany and with only a weak counter-narrative to set against it. Re-migration, a euphemism for mass deportation of unwanted foreigners (and maybe even some non-White Germans), has gone from provocation to an openly discussed proposal by the far-right.[2] Whether Germany likes it or not, xenophobic nationalism is back, and the country needs to face it.

European identity is often cited as a point around which Germans can rally. The number who feel they're European Union citizens is indeed relatively high compared to the numbers in other countries on the continent, but those feelings are more prevalent among educated urbanites and less so in groups prone to nationalist sentiment such as the working class and people living in rural areas. A clear majority of those without degrees would rather Germany prioritise its own interests over EU integration.[3]

During the sovereign-debt crisis, it became all too evident that European identity couldn't serve as a surrogate. Popular right-wing media organisations stoked nationalistic backlash by portraying Greeks as lazy and living off the backs of hard-working German taxpayers. The *Bild* tabloid, Germany's most widely read daily, called for the Hellenic republic to be kicked out of the eurozone, imploring Angela Merkel in July 2015 to be the 'Iron Chancellor' and reject bailouts for Athens. *Focus* magazine ran a front cover that depicted the famous ancient Greek statue *Venus de Milo* with an extended middle finger and the headline: *Betrüger in der Euro-Familie* (Frauds in the Euro Family). Animosity cut both ways, with

Greek newspapers regularly depicting Merkel and Finance Minister Wolfgang Schäuble as Nazis, and public protests accompanying the chancellor's visit to Athens in 2012.

Such scenes intensified internal German divisions over the European project. Conservatives resented the money flowing towards imprudent neighbours, while chipping away at the progressive appeal of a pan-European identity. Such concerns over Europanisation have, in turn, been used by the far-right to counter multiculturalism in the Fatherland. In a 2019 poster campaign called 'learning from Europe's history', the AfD's Berlin chapter featured a nineteenth-century painting of a naked Caucasian woman being inspected by dark-skinned, turban-wearing slave traders. The slogan was 'so that Europe doesn't become "Eurabia"'.

While outright euroscepticism remains confined to populist fringes, there are signs that enthusiasm for the European project is waning. A study by the Konrad Adenauer Stiftung (Foundation) revealed that only a third of Germans were enthusiastic supporters of the EU and that nearly one in five distrust the bloc's bureaucrats in Brussels.[4] Although Germany is highly unlikely to ever leave the bloc, it's another dividing line that can hobble efforts to bolster European integration at a time of geopolitical instability. Underscoring the growing animosity towards the European project, a 14-metre-high sculpture of the euro symbol in Frankfurt, home to the European Central Bank, has been targeted by vandalism so often that the city's authorities have floated the idea of removing it unless a sponsor can be found to help cover the clean-up costs.[5]

With the bonds of togetherness limited, growing frustration and deepening inequality has stoked volatility and a level of fragmentation akin to the Weimar Republic (1918–33). But despite the experience of Nazism, there's little to patch those fissures. The country's post-war development was stunted, leaving it with a view of itself that's fragile and focused on what should never be again rather than looking forward to what could be.

As a result, Germany hardly qualifies as a modern nation. It's more of a joint economic area. That means it's held together by cash and a lot of it: €1.2 trillion a year, to be precise. That's the annual budget for total social spending (from welfare and health services to daycare and pensions) and effectively the cost of national cohesion. It's a hefty burden when the underpinnings of the country's competitiveness are wobbling and budget pressures are tight. But it's also a specious way to keep a community of millions together.

Money may indeed make the world go round, but there's more to a nation than collecting and distributing taxes. A sense of commonality bonds people together and that shared sense of purpose can help bridge turbulent periods. The United States remains convinced it's the world's greatest country despite debilitating internal divisions, while Britons can still rally behind their monarchy and bridge the messiness of Brexit with their sense of humour, and the French would go back to the barricades to defend the republic. But what can Germans agree on that doesn't veer dangerously back to 'blood and soil' nationalism?

For obvious reasons, nation-building was an impossible undertaking after World War II and so the outline of a new, civil identity was left vague. Even in its pre-war incarnations, Germany relied on an 'other' to define itself, because of tensions between regions like Prussia and Bavaria after a long history of conflict. During unification in the 1800s, it took wars with France to bring the country together, and then the Third Reich targeted Jews to help define itself. In the post-war period, the 'other' is often within.

At its most basic level, Germany's modern sense of self stems from not being Nazis (which doesn't necessarily rule out ethnic nationalism under a different brand name). But it's been generations since the end of the war, and the power of Nazism as a national foil is fading. As a result of that void, the space available for internal 'others' such as migrants and Muslims has grown.

Germany's practice of affirming itself by projecting what it isn't stems from cultural factors that make bridging internal divisions difficult. This includes the subtle fissures that come from distant and impersonal interaction, which is part of the language and makes showing solidarity as compatriots hard to express. On a daily basis, mutual mistrust is more pronounced than camaraderie. Public interactions are rarely positive, and so speaking with strangers on the street and in supermarket checkout lines generally evokes a defensive reflex.

Suspicion of one another in turn promotes a reliance on structure to manage interpersonal relations. That includes an array of rules to regulate bad behaviour. For instance, failing to clean up after a picnic can lead to fines of as much as €1,500, and particularly serious cases of *Wildpinklen* (urinating in public) can even get you a year in jail (we're not quite sure what that entails and don't really want to find out).[6]

Another manifestation of obsessions with structure is *Haftpflichtversicherung* (personal liability insurance) – one of the first complex German words with which foreigners will likely be confronted when coming to the country. The policies are intended to insure against damage caused to others, such as breaking a friend's vase during a dinner party. German authorities recommend coverage of at least €10 million per person – and €50 million to be on the safe side. Effectively, that means you're covered if you knock over a candle and burn down a friend's flat. While personal liability isn't required, such protection is almost ubiquitous.* Widespread insurance coverage, which goes beyond *Haftpflichtversicherung*, speaks to latent distrust, an obsession with money as well as a deeply ingrained desire for security. The latter can become a vulnerability when applied to a nation heading for a marked period of instability, especially in a country where the economy plays an inordinately important role in creating a national sense of well-being.

After emerging as an Allied enclave following World War II, the formative event for West Germany was the *Wirtschaftswunder* (economic miracle). Aided by geopolitical circumstances, the revival of commercial life gave the country a renewed sense of forward-looking pride (we'll deal with the historical underpinnings of modern Germany in more depth in the next chapter). The approach was crystallised in the 1957 rallying cry of the then economics minister and vice-chancellor Ludwig Erhard: *Wohlstand für alle* (prosperity for all). Germany is indeed good at making things, and for decades that engineering prowess (as well as some

---

*According to the German insurance association GDV, 83 per cent of all German households have a policy.

excellent World Cup football teams) was enough for the country to consider itself a nation.

As long as Germany was upwardly mobile, there was a sense of cohesion, backstopped by a protective and generally expanding social-welfare system. The country didn't need to wave the flag like the fanatical Americans or kowtow to an outdated monarchy like the Brits. Germany had fast cars and Autobahns and a growing bank account. That was sufficient and yielded decades of stability, albeit with episodes of extremist violence.

Although still regularly repeated, Erhard's promise of prosperity looks irreparably broken for millions of Germans. Social inequality is among the worst in Europe. While affluent Germans cruise around major cities in hulking Porsche or Mercedes-Benz SUVs, others face mounting anxiety from rising rent and utility bills. The widening gap between rich and poor is out of step with the egalitarian aspirations enshrined in the country's post-war constitution and its effort to give capitalism a conscience in what's known as the 'social market economy'. Instead of holding to those ideals, welfare recipients and asylum seekers have been blamed for lack of money for roads and schools and had their benefits squeezed.

But bashing the weakest in society distracts from the fact that wealth is well-protected for the elite. So despite the objective affluence of the world's third-largest economy, a growing number of people are in precarious situations, with worsening job prospects and exposure to the fraying social safety net.

More than one in five Germans are classified as poor, meaning they struggle to pay rent and utility bills and don't have enough money to go out to eat or drink with friends once a month. The numbers of those at risk of poverty and social exclusion, though, is certainly higher than the 17.7 million who fell into this category in 2023. That's because most Germans are tenants and wage earners, and have few assets to fall back on. So when the economy starts to wobble livelihoods can be quickly threatened. It wouldn't take long for a job loss to lead to an existential crisis for those living from pay cheque to pay cheque. That's a big group that has no hope of aspiring to Germany's cherished stability and are prone to being lured away from the democratic establishment.

In large part, the country's vulnerability stems from a housing model that creates hurdles to home ownership through high up-front costs. That as well as a historically conditioned avoidance of risk, which makes many people shy away from taking on the responsibility of owning their own home, has led to most Germans being tenants, with no assets besides a rapidly depreciating car. So as the economy stumbles, affecting traditionally stable blue-collar manufacturing jobs, a large proportion of Germans are faced with declining opportunities and fragile living standards, just as the government tightens its belt on social spending – the traditional path towards German cohesion. This combination creates a toxic mix. In a country where the government is supposed to be constitutionally obligated to take care of its citizens, anger and frustration risk fomenting anti-establishment sentiment and rocking what's supposed to be an anchor of stability in Europe.

To sum it up, it doesn't matter as much where you are but how you feel about where you're going, and for many in Germany the trajectory is precipitously downhill. The sensation of falling leads to a reflexive search for something to hold on to. That's evident across much of the West with the rise of right-wing populism. But unlike elsewhere, Germany doesn't have robust civic traditions to absorb these tensions. Instead, the fallback sense of German identity is ethno-nationalist, and reviving the appealing legend of the 1,000-year *Volk* has increasingly found fertile ground.

Over the past decade, the surge in legal and illegal migration as well as the mass arrivals of refugees provided fodder that has intensified feelings of ancestral alienation. Economic malaise deepens the gloom and adds a sense of urgency to take action to protect the homeland. Right-wing movements, with the anti-immigrant, anti-euro AfD as the leading political arm, have taken advantage, with the emotional appeal of repackaged 'blood and soil' patriotism (more on the political situation in chapter 8). The establishment alternative has been to appeal to the electorate's good conscience to defend democracy. But for what? What does political freedom mean when economic opportunities are unfairly distributed and people are worried about their way of life? If the system isn't working for them, why stay loyal to it?

An openness to regime change fits in with the myth that the German people have endured for epochs and withstood different forms of government. In the most messianic interpretation, the country even awaits the reawakening of a legendary king to lead it back to glory.* Set against that kind of lore, the mainstream's pitch of more of the same is pretty feeble. It effectively boils down to 'we've got a great constitution, and we're not Nazis'.

The fissures in society risk widening as the economy stumbles and opportunities for the working class grow even scarcer. Germany's traditional strengths in metal-bashing industries are under threat, adding to the unease and pressure in blue-collar households. Competition from China is intense and has spilled over threateningly to the auto industry, where Germany once thought it had an unassailable advantage. Value has shifted away from old-school engineering towards digital technologies, which Germany has neglected for years. The energy system, the lifeblood of manufacturing, has been poorly managed and is in the midst of an unsettling shift, forced on the country abruptly by Russia going from false friend to imperialist aggressor.

Revamping the energy system is just one of the many *'Wende'* (transformations) the country has been attempting. Alongside the *Energiewende*, there's a *Wärmewende* for heating, a *Verkehrswende* for transport, and those are linked to an *Infrastrukturwende* for highways and other economic interconnectors as well as a *Technologiewende* for the country's sputtering shift towards digitalisation (more on industrial issues in chapter 5). The multiple unfinished transformations reflect the complexity looming over Germany's future. They've all become urgent because of years of hesitant leadership, piecemeal reforms and tight-fisted investment. But for the population, the scope, scale and uncertainty are disorienting, especially in a country uncomfortable with change at the best of times.

---

*According to the legend of Barbarossa, Kaiser Friedrich I of the Holy Roman Empire sleeps in a cave in the Kyffhäuser hill range in northern Thuringia. With his red beard growing around a table, he waits for a time when the ravens cease circling the peak to restore Germany to a Golden Age. The AfD's radical right 'Flügel' had regularly met near a monument dedicated to the myth.

On top of economic adjustments, there's Chancellor Scholz's *Zeitenwende*, targeted at shaking the country out of its desire to disconnect from geopolitics (more on this in chapter 6). In practical terms, it has meant investing €100 billion into modernising Germany's decrepit defence forces, but it's also about preparing the nation to become a more assertive player on the international stage. That's a pressing concern with the United States threatening to withdraw its security umbrella and after open warfare returned to Europe in the form of the Russian invasion of Ukraine in 2022 – a volatile mix for Germany's export-driven economy. But domestic resistance to the approach is widespread and unites post-war pacifism, leftist traditions of appeasement with Russia and right-wing nationalism. There's no clear path ahead for Germany on foreign policy, which has struggled to adjust. Unfortunately for Germany, history did not end with the fall of the Berlin Wall. Russia's war in Ukraine shows that global power politics is back and has brought the steady expansion of globalisation to a screeching halt. That's bad news for Germany, and it adds another layer of uncertainty to the country's outlook.

Germany is a trading nation unlike any other and it was proudly *Exportweltmeister* for years before falling behind China in 2009. Despite losing the title, it's even more reliant on trade deals than ever. The country is relatively resource poor and so needs to buy materials and fuel for its factories, which make goods that are shipped out to customers around the globe. The domestic market is almost an afterthought. According to World Bank data, trade has risen steadily and was equivalent to exactly 100 per cent of GDP in 2022, nearly three times the exposure of China and four times that of the United States. The imbalance extends to similarly sized countries. France, Britain and Japan are all less reliant on imports and exports than Germany.[7]

But that strength has become a vulnerability. Germany's wide-eyed reliance on foreign partners nearly led it to disaster in the winter of 2022, after Russia halted gas deliveries in retaliation for sanctions over its invasion of Ukraine (more on energy in chapter 4). The Kremlin had prepared the move by slowly draining Germany's reserves, a chunk of which were controlled by state-run Gazprom. The country weathered that scare due to adept crisis management, a relatively warm winter, as well as a drop-off in industrial output, which has to a degree become permanent. But Germany had almost ground to a halt because it handed significant leverage to an autocratic government. It wasn't the first time and it won't be the last.

For all of Germany's much-heralded restraint, its diligence breaks down when it sees an opportunity to make money. It's a mercantilist approach to foreign policy that's dubbed *Wandel durch Handel* (change through trade), which is a thinly veiled rationale for doing deals with despots and autocrats. The self-serving theory is that liberal values will be transported along with an exchange of goods. The concept has failed. And while Germany wriggled out of its energy dependence on Moscow, the bigger threat is China.

The Asian superpower can produce many of the goods in which Germany once specialised, but it charges less (fairly or unfairly). Although China once looked to Germany for inspiration and expertise, the apprentice has become the master, resulting in massive trade deficits in recent years. In 2023 every German effectively purchased about €1,900 worth of goods and materials from China, while selling less than €1,200 to the country's biggest trading partner – a subtle but not insignificant drain on pocketbooks and the national psyche.

In the aftermath of the implosion of the *Wandel durch Handel* myth, Germany has sought to cautiously edge back from China. The buzzword has been 'de-risking', a deliberate distinction from the more rigorous 'decoupling', which could be catastrophic because of Germany's deep exposure, especially in the auto industry. The country may feel soothed by the semantic difference, but that's for its own sense of comfort. Because of the billions of euros of assets that companies like Volkswagen and BASF have tied up in China, Germany has lost what leverage it may have once had. In the meantime, Beijing has given up most of the pretence about open markets and level playing fields. Attempts to prod China to refrain from unfair pricing and to protect human rights are greeted with little more than polite indifference.

Germany is ill-equipped to respond to China or almost any other country with a strong executive. It's not entirely a function of personal leadership. The central government is weak by design.

As the Cold War started to take shape in the immediate aftermath of World War II, the Allies wanted to integrate Germany into the liberal democratic system, but they were still wary and made sure power was decentralised. So the Federal Republic of Germany was born, splitting authority between the central government and the *Länder* (states). The *Grundgesetz* (Basic Law) makes backing away from the federal system 'inadmissible'.* In practical terms, the states control functions such as regional planning, health policy and public safety, but it goes beyond that. When in doubt authority is delegated, Article 30 lays out that 'the exercise of state powers and the discharge of state functions is a matter for the *Länder*', unless explicitly stated otherwise. The separation means Bundestag legislators are removed from the complexities of implementing the laws they pass. To some extent, it's like having an engineer design a car without working with people on the assembly line. There are risks that all the pieces won't fit together quite so smoothly. It's a disconnect that has contributed to the country's bloated bureaucracy.

States have a say in the federal legislative process via the *Bundesrat*, the upper house of parliament, which has to sign off on many bills. Adding to the complexity the fact that states also have their own legislatures that pass their own laws, creating layers of rules that aren't always aligned. Since Germany was long divided into various kingdoms, duchies and principalities, and there was more than a little distrust between the various parts of the country, strong regional power centres developed and were staunchly defended. The most obvious example of this is that Bavaria has its own conservative party, the Christian Social Union, which is affiliated but separate from the national CDU.

The division of powers worked perfectly in the eyes of the Allies, with the German state evolving into a ponderous behemoth. Every step requires organising majorities on the federal level as well as securing support from the states (numbering sixteen since reunification in 1990). Germany's federal system creates duplicate structures that add cost and complexity. For instance, securing permissions from various authorities means that the process of

---

*See Article 79, paragraph 3, of Germany's Basic Law.

moving a crane from one building site to another across state lines could get stalled for weeks and arranging the transport of wind turbines can take as long as six months.*

Federalism also plays a role in Germany's hardening social strata. When it comes to the life chances of children, the country's federal system is particularly failing the most vulnerable. Unlike in many countries, education policy and spending in Germany is decided by each state, with the federal government providing just one-tenth of the funding. The differences between the haves and have-nots are even starker when it comes to general schooling, where almost all funding is provided by local authorities.[8]

In Bremen in the north, the number of children leaving school without qualifications is twice the rate of that in Bavaria, a wealthy region in southern Germany.[9] The proportion of 14-year-olds who fail to meet basic reading standards in Berlin and Bremen is almost twice the rate seen in the best-performing states of Bavaria and Saxony.[10] It's the same story for basic maths and writing skills. Bremen's poor performance can be partly blamed on a high share of children from first-generation immigrant families where German isn't spoken, but the coastal city state also lags behind others in structures that can offset such disadvantages.

In Germany, many primary schools also operate only from 8 a.m. to 12 p.m., when kids go home for lunch and to do homework – a system that complicates life for families with both parents working. The practice perpetuates gender inequality (a problem for German labour participation), as mothers often end up working part-time to be at home for their kids, hampering earning and career opportunities. While that still might work for well-off families, kids from disadvantaged backgrounds have it much tougher, and all-day supervision at school, especially ones that provide meals, can have health and educational benefits. Although almost all schools in wealthy Hamburg have all-day instruction, only 60 per cent of children in struggling Bremen attend such institutions.[11] These kinds of gaps also further erode opportunities for national solidarity, as fissures form on regional levels alongside the social

---

*ESTA, the European association for abnormal road transport and mobile cranes, has warned that Germany's heavy-transport sector risks collapsing due to permit delays. https://estaeurope.eu/news/growing-heavy-transport-crisis-in-germany-impacting-wider-economy-warns-esta.

stratification that the educational system intensifies rather than bridges.

Defenders of Germany's federal system laud the separation of powers, and strong states have indeed kept the federal government in check to a degree. But there's a dark side when it comes to national security. Fighting espionage and extremism is split among no fewer than eighteen federal and regional agencies, each with their own officers, headquarters and administrative staff.[12] The system was intended to prevent the emergence of a force like the Nazis' feared Gestapo, but is struggling to keep pace.

While the Cologne-based *Bundesverfassungsschutz* (federal domestic intelligence service) has a coordinating function, each state counterpart acts independently and isn't legally required to share information. As with schools, the resources vary dramatically. Bavaria, more populous than Sweden and home to juicy corporate espionage targets like BMW, has an intelligence service with around 575 staff, going up against organisations like China's Ministry for State Security, a spy service with over 110,000 employees. But Bavaria is relatively well-staffed, compared to Brandenburg, a hotbed for Germany's right-wing. The relatively poor state has only around 140 staff to keep tabs on some 3,000 right-wing extremists, alongside other duties such as protecting Berlin's airport and Tesla's German factory.[13]

The set-up weakens Germany's defences and the Kremlin has played havoc with it. In 2019 a Russian hitman shot and killed a Chechen dissident in broad daylight in a popular Berlin park. In December 2022 a hacker group linked to Russia's GRU secret service was blamed for cyberattacks, including on the ruling Social Democratic Party.[14] In 2023 a high-ranking Russian double agent was discovered in Germany's foreign-intelligence agency, thanks to a tip-off from the FBI.[15] In April 2024 two alleged German-Russian saboteurs were arrested for photographing critical infrastructure and military installations and preparing for attacks.[16] These are just the cases that have been uncovered, and suggest more activity has taken place in the shadows, exploiting the gaps in the system. Ben Wallace, a former British defence secretary, has described Germany as 'pretty penetrated by Russian intelligence'.[17]

Local empowerment and checks on national authority might be well-meaning, but German federalism in practice has created an overregulated and impenetrable structure. Instead of solving problems, decisions get caught up in a tangle of competing jurisdictions and authorities, and the institutional bias is towards avoiding mistakes rather than getting things done. This is another example of how Germany's structure has opened a rift in society and undermined its own legitimacy.

Aside from the federalist system, the *Grundgesetz* establishes the government as a social state with an obligation to ensure that people can live with *Würde* (dignity). For the growing ranks of impoverished Germans, the state hasn't been fulfilling its duty in various ways, but especially in terms of the basic need for shelter. Like most Western countries, Germany has delegated housing to investors. The laws of the market are supposed to create supply, where there's demand. But it doesn't work like that in the highly regulated world of real estate. For property owners, scarcity is a good thing because it drives up prices, but that only benefits a minority of Germans. When housing is constructed, incentives are to maximise the value of the land, which means more expensive rather than affordable homes. The result is that the supply of rental accommodation is tight and prices are soaring. That's more of a problem in Germany than many other countries, because it has one of the lowest rates of home ownership in the Western world and a middle class that lacks the personal financial cushion as in the United States. This means that there are even fewer chances to move up the socioeconomic ladder, while many are just a layoff away from slipping down it.[*]

At the same time, the state-pension system faces an unsustainable financing dilemma, driving further wedges through society. Rather than a reservoir of cash, the system is funded by current contributions from employers and employees. As Baby Boomers retire, the ratio of workers to pensioners is dropping fast. In the Netherlands, for

---

[*] According to the OECD, about one in every three Germans would slip into poverty if they didn't receive a pay cheque for three months, based on data from 2018. Since then, the level of poverty has increased to record levels. See the Paritätischer Armutsbericht 2024 at https://www.der-paritaetische.de/fileadmin/user_upload/Schwerpunkte/Armutsbericht/doc/Paritaetischer_Armutsbericht_2024.pdf.

example, a greater share of pensions is invested, meaning they're able to grow in value and rely less on the contribution of current workers. Whereas pensions in France are funded in a similar way to Germany, its working-age population is expected to grow over the coming decades. By contrast, Germany with the ninth-highest median age in the world – four years older than France and six older than the UK – is set to lose roughly 5 million workers (nearly the combined population of Berlin and Munich) by 2035.*

Pensions also play an important role because of the preponderance of tenants, meaning few have a home as a safety net and the elderly stay exposed to rising rents and threats of ending up on the street. For instance, Manfred Moslehner in 2023 was threatened with eviction from the house where the 84-year-old Berliner was born. The new owners wanted to modernise the building, leading to costs that the tenant couldn't afford from his meagre pension, so they cancelled his rental contract and threatened him with fines and jail time.[18]

Germany's pension crisis adds to anxiety for the old and burdens the young, who are already struggling with uncertainty over a changing working world and the risks posed by the unfolding climate crisis. Cutting pension benefits is obviously an unsavoury option for politicians, which would plunge more of the elderly into poverty, so their response has been temporary patches of financial assistance that do little to calm both young and old.

Systemic problems intensify Germany's existing identity issues. That was evident in the rocky road it took to accepting migration. As the *Wirtschaftswunder* started taking off, the economy was growing so fast that it needed help. In 1955 the first *Gastarbeiter* (guest worker) agreement was signed with Italy, followed by pacts with Spain, Greece, Turkey, Morocco, Portugal, Tunisia and the former Yugoslavia. Millions of hired hands came to help fuel the boom and so were welcomed for the growing affluence they represented, but for nothing more. One of them was Armando Rodrigues de Sá.

---

* Figures from Germany's Federal Statistics Offices are compared with 2018 levels, when 51.8 million people were of working age. That's a drop of roughly 10 per cent.

The Portuguese carpenter arrived on 10 September 1964 and was unexpectedly bestowed a place in post-war German history as the one-millionth guest worker. Without warning, the perplexed 38-year-old was greeted at a train station in Cologne and presented with a certificate, a bouquet of carnations and a Zündapp moped.[19] He was briefly celebrated as a milestone for Germany and then quickly forgotten. He bounced around various cities, but struggling with the language and the bureaucracy (something many foreigners still wrestle with), he was taxed for years at a higher rate because of missing documentation about his wife and children who stayed in Portugal. On a visit to his native village in 1970, he fell ill and was later diagnosed with cancer. He never returned to Germany. As an employee paying into the healthcare system, he would have been entitled to treatment in Germany, but because he wasn't aware, he had pension benefits paid out early to fund medication privately in Portugal. Most of the earnings from his five years as a guest worker were used up in fighting the disease. Abandoned by Germany, Armando Rodrigues de Sá died in 1979.

That same year, Heinz Kühn, the first federal commissioner for foreigners, issued a memorandum calling for efforts to integrate the people who Germany had recruited for labour. 'It must be recognised that an irreversible development has occurred here,' the Social Democrat wrote in September 1979, calling for citizenship and voting rights and the end of segregation in schools.[20] For the establishment, that was a step too far. In 1981 a group of fifteen university professors issued what's known as the *Heidelberger Manifest*, which denounced the 'infiltration of the German people' and the 'alienation of our language, our culture and our nationality' by immigrants.[21] That type of xenophobia became official policy with the 1982 coalition agreement between the Christian Democratic Union and the Free Democrats. The ruling parties bluntly stated that Germany was not a migration country. In the document that laid the groundwork for Helmut Kohl's first term as chancellor, they wrote that 'all humanitarian measures must therefore be taken to prevent the influx of foreigners'.[22]

It would take two decades for Germany officially to change its position. In 2001, Gerhard Schröder's government acknowledged the reality that millions of migrants who had answered the recruitment ads and subsequently raised families in the country were indeed part of Germany.[23] Four years later, in 2005, the country started compiling official statistics on people with 'migration backgrounds', a broad-brush term that deliberately sidesteps uncomfortable ethnic and religious categories. That was exactly half a century after the first deal to exploit the labour of foreign workers.

On top of the challenge of immigration, reunification has deepened the complexity of forming a cohesive nation. East and West Germany had completely different post-war experiences. The East suffered through an authoritarian police state that the people succeeded in overthrowing. That victory was then eradicated by the widespread upheaval that followed. Nearly all East Germans had their lives disrupted by reunification, losing jobs and seeing towns and communities decimated as young people moved away to seek better opportunities elsewhere. This suffering was often underappreciated in the more affluent West Germany, where reunification hardly registered.* Its pathway to liberty and prosperity, by contrast, was paved by the Allied powers, which needed a thriving West Germany as a bulwark against the spread of Soviet influence. After the fall of the Berlin Wall in November 1989, the country was stitched together administratively and economically, but a common community was neglected. East Germany was in many ways the 'other' through which West Germany defined itself and made itself feel 'good'. And so it was ill-equipped to offer a sense of solidarity, which the country had never fully developed itself.

More than three decades after reunification, signs of the complex undercurrents of modern Germany are evident on a walk through modern Berlin. Along the main thoroughfare of Unter den Linden – the stately tree-lined boulevard connecting the UNESCO-recognised *Museumsinsel* (Museum Island) and the symbol-laden Brandenburg Gate – the kiosks improbably still sell little bits of the Berlin Wall, along with postcards, T-shirts and coffee mugs adorned with East Berlin's iconic *Fernsehturm* and the *Ampelmännchen* (the perky hat-wearing icon of East German

---

* Katja Hoyer's 2023 book *Beyond the Wall* is a recent and well-received effort to humanise East German history.

pedestrian signals), presenting reunification as a joyous event. With more than a hint of *Ostalgie* (longing for the old East Germany), the DDR Museum next to the Prussian-era Berlin cathedral reveals examples of daily life in the former Communist police state as well as the sense of constant surveillance, and features a driving simulator of the adorable, but dirty Trabant (the people's car of the East). The combination gives the misleading impression that the culture and the people of the two Germanies have taken their place equally following reunification.

The reality is that there is a schism in the country. Angela Merkel herself has said that her East German background was seen as 'ballast' that needed to be thrown overboard to advance her political career after the Wall fell. The dismissive attitude towards the East became clear in the decision to tear down the *Palast der Republik*, the former parliament building of the one-party state, in favour of a €700-million homage to Germany's imperial past. The destruction of a building, which also functioned as a community centre with bars, dance clubs and a bowling alley, marked a lost opportunity to engage with East Germany and the lives of its 16 million citizens in a more nuanced way. East–West divisions have become more complex over time, but disorientation is a common thread uniting disaffected Germans.

Without a positive sense of national unity, the innate reaction for many Germans has been to hold to the concept of the *Volk*, even after the horrors of the Nazi death machine. Enduring racism and structural hurdles for minorities have raised questions over the degree to which Germany has really overcome its troubled past. And notions of exceptionalism have been alive and well even in the reflective world of Holocaust memory.

In early 2024 a firestorm was kicked up by a proposal from Claudia Roth, the federal commissioner for culture and a Green politician, over broadening the way Germany approaches its past. Previously, state funding and official policy had focused on two pillars: the Holocaust and the former East German police state. Both are self-serving. The ugly Nazi past is admirably showcased in an unvarnished way. Publicly displaying national shame projects the idea that contemporary Germans are rehabilitated.

Similarly, historical memory that focuses on state repression in East Germany validates the messy and rapid approach to reunification. The message is that sacrifices needed to be made in order get rid of the Communist regime and extend freedom and democracy to all of Germany, but it's a one-sided view that presents West Germans as the liberators of the East. In the same way that Jews should be grateful for Germany's open guilt over the Holocaust, East Germans should be thankful for being freed from an authoritarian system, even if they were the ones that toppled a police state.

In the reform of memory culture, Roth sought to include the perspectives of migrants and not just ancestral Germans, because victimised groups and the descendants of perpetrators have become intertwined as the generations go by. The Green politician also wanted to add colonial atrocities including the German Empire's genocide committed on the Herero and Nama people in the early 1900s in what is now Namibia. That spurred a bitter pushback, especially from those involved in preserving concentration camps. Some charged that such a break from memory orthodoxy would relativise the Holocaust.[24] But that's needless polemic.

Memory isn't a zero-sum game. Multiple victims can be honoured in different ways without reducing the value of one another.[25] We can pay homage to a dead friend without belittling past relatives. What a broader memory culture would really do is force Germans to recognise that mass killings had a tradition before Adolf Hitler came to power. That would force the country to reflect and take a more active approach to 'Never Again'.

Similarly, Germany's anti-antisemitism authorities have been cracking down on views that deviate from official positions such as criticising Israel's repression of Palestinians. Jewish intellectuals have been prime targets. Despite the eerie echoes, German authorities have assumed the right to pass judgement over how Jews view the state of Israel (more on this in chapter 9). It's a disturbing trend at a time when Germany should be open to new perspectives. At the very least, the country needs to abandon the idea that it has earned moral authority just because it hasn't carried out a genocide in eighty years. A reckoning with itself is overdue, not just in terms of its Nazi past but also with how it treats migrants and handles other internal divisions.

Not all is lost though. When Germany's prowess in science and engineering is combined with energy and creativity, world-changing innovations can result. BioNTech is a recent shining example. Founded by Turkish migrants, the Mainz-based start-up helped defuse the Covid-19 pandemic with the world's first mRNA vaccine – a breakthrough technology that teaches cells how to fight off disease. And while the political class appears ever more distanced from the voting public, it's hard to find another country where citizens are so engaged. From holding the government to account on climate goals and bailing out people in jail for unpaid bus tickets to plugging gaps in the social safety net and opening homes to Ukrainian war refugees, Germans get involved. That's a powerful resource waiting to be harnessed for renewal, if only Germany's institutions would allow and encourage this more. It's a sign that the will of the people is there, and a refreshing departure from the apathy evident in many other Western countries.

Given the dynamics that are tearing at the social fabric, patching things up won't be easy. But it could involve more touchpoints to build a greater sense of community and a little self-belief and optimism to help temper the country's tendency towards morose introspection. Part of the solution needs to be better access to shared opportunities and widening the group that gets to participate in Germany's success. To make this happen, the political class has to empower people and tap the energy that's there. This involves unwinding bureaucratic systems that thwart initiative and stifle change. That in turn requires humility from the political class and coming to terms with their own self-perpetuated myths. To start that process, we need to take a look at how Germany got here.

2
Coddled Child

'Spare not grace nor effort
Not passion nor understanding
So a good Germany flourishes
Just like other good lands.'

Bertolt Brecht

To understand Germany's deepening malaise, we must return to the zero hour of the modern nation after the collapse of Nazism. In May 1945, the Third Reich's armies lay defeated, its cities reduced to ruins, and its people left to sift despondently through the rubble.

The European theatre of war had claimed 40 million lives, including over seven million Germans – soldiers, civilians, and 300,000 victims of racial persecution. In addition, six million Jews, along with countless others, were systematically murdered in the Holocaust by the Nazis and their collaborators, leaving an enduring scar on humanity. At Nuremberg, 22 prominent Nazis were put on trial; 10 were hanged as tokens of retribution. Amid this desolation, the story of modern Germany – the House of Germany – begins.

The victorious Allies crafted the people's fate, with the two sides shaping the territory to suit their respective agendas in the ideological standoff of the Cold War. In the West, Germany was pushed and prodded to be a shining example of capitalism and what happened is often hailed as a saga of remarkable recovery, with the country emerging as an industrial titan and a model of liberal democracy. But obscured by the gleaming facade of the so-called economic miracle and the image of resilience and renewal, unresolved traumas and buried tensions festered quietly.

Factories hummed, German goods became hallmarks of excellence, and democratic institutions promised a new beginning. But the nation's role in the horrors of the Holocaust were sidelined, overshadowed by a narrative of progress and shared prosperity. The Nazi era became the 'other' through which post-war Germany defined itself, but fundamental questions over its fractured identity were left unanswered.

Often celebrated as the culmination of Germany's post-war journey, reunification in 1990 questioned the certainty of the national narrative of the reformed Volk and exposed fault lines in its muddled and fragile image. By integrating the East, the West was faced with other dilemmas and traumas that it was ill-suited to resolve. While the country flourished commercially and was hailed as an anchor of stability in a fragmented world, its outward success obscured inward fault lines.

The much-vaunted image of German exceptionalism rested on a brittle foundation of historical amnesia and deferred reckoning, issues that are coming home to roost after decades of avoidance. Beneath the veneer of success, there's a fractured society, increasingly unable to escape the truths it had long suppressed.

Protective uncle

The war in Europe has just ended. Across Germany, once-thriving cities lie in ruin, wrecked by Allied bombing raids and house-to-house fighting. After the smoke and gunfire have subsided, survivors try to make their way through the destruction. A photograph taken in 1945 poignantly captures the country's defeat. Staring into the distance, two men sit alone among the shattered remains of a building in Frankfurt. It was the birthplace of Johann Wolfgang von Goethe, Germany's greatest poet.

The older man is Ernst Beutler, head of the literary society that owned the Goethe Haus, a memorial to one of the driving intellects of German Romanticism. It was at this address in the city's Große Hirschgraben Street that Goethe started work on *Faust*, a play in which the protagonist makes a fateful bargain with the devil before angels intervene to save him. For Germans who'd made a pact with the Nazis to escape the disorder of the interwar era, hopes for such redemption looked forlorn. As if to underscore the descent of a country that claimed to be the *Land der Dichter und Denker* (land of poets and thinkers), a bust of what looks like Friedrich Schiller, the great poet, playwright and philosopher, lies at Beutler's feet. It's cracked and covered in debris, transformed into just another piece of rubble.

Adolf Hitler had lured the masses with fiery promises to change Germany. He more than came through with his pledge. After twelve years of Nazi rule and nearly six years of war, much of the country was indeed unrecognisable. Frankfurt's famed half-timbered centre was largely flattened. The elegant townhouses of Cologne, the charming metropolis on the Rhine, were gone forever. In Berlin, the Tiergarten park was stripped of trees as residents scavenged for fuel to stay warm. Dresden, dubbed Florence on the Elbe for its pre-war beauty, had been reduced to ash. The human cost was similarly immense. Aside from the millions of dead, millions more were prisoners of war.[1] Groups of women known as *Trümmerfrauen* (rubble women) were left to clean up the devastation by hand. The country's political map was changed, a quarter of its land annexed by Poland and the Soviet Union. Königsberg, the lifelong home of the Enlightenment philosopher Immanuel Kant, became Kaliningrad.

Across Europe other peoples were counting their losses from Germany's latest war of aggression. The Germans had murdered around two-thirds of the continent's pre-war Jewish population in an industrialised campaign of death. Where German culture had once stood for Enlightenment, reason and science, it was now associated with murder, destruction and mass hysteria. In a poem published in 1948 the poet Paul Celan's words spoke for a harrowed continent, '*Der Tod ist ein Meister aus Deutschland*' (death is a master from Germany).[2]

Occupying Germany at the end of the war, the victorious Allies moved swiftly to denazify the country and prevent it from threatening peace again. Active suppression of the enemy was the order of the day. According to a directive issued to American forces, Germany in its zone of occupation was to be treated as a 'defeated enemy nation', its living standards prevented from exceeding those in neighbouring states.[3] The German industrial machine should only be able to produce enough to provide for a basic standard of living for the German population and no more. In the east of the country, factory machinery and railroads were dismantled and sent to the Soviet Union. Captains of industry were imprisoned. Former SS members such as the automotive pioneer Ferdinand Porsche and grocery magnate Rudolf-August Oetker were incarcerated by the Allies. As an American directive to occupying forces read: 'the Germans cannot escape responsibility for what they have brought upon themselves'.[4]

But a change of heart came surprisingly quickly, altering Germany's course forever. As early as 1946, the American approach to its zone of occupation started to soften. Reducing Germany to an agricultural backwater made little sense. With Europe in ruins and its people impoverished and exhausted by years of war, preventing Germany from rebuilding its factories would only deprive the continent of the efforts of its most productive workers. Meanwhile, the United States faced competition with the Soviet Union for global influence. Communists were marching through cities like Paris, Rome and Vienna, their movements building and gathering strength.

The realities of the emerging Cold War prompted an about-turn in Washington. Speaking in Stuttgart in September 1946, US Secretary of State James F. Byrne formally changed course on the vengeful approach. The United States would work towards the political and economic reconstruction of the country and steadfastly stay the course. The American people, he said, wanted Germans to retake their 'honourable' place in the world.[5] For a country preparing for uncertain years in the wilderness, the speech rekindled hope. Just like in Goethe's *Faust*, redemption was unexpectedly at hand. America followed up its encouraging words with the Economic Recovery Act of 1948, better known as the Marshall Plan, an aid package that would supply Germany and other European nations with the materials needed to speed reconstruction. For German society that hadn't even begun to address the collective trauma and guilt of war, the reconstruction task ahead would prove a welcome distraction.

CODDLED CHILD

There was much to do. Most urgently, millions of people were homeless or living in the bombed-out hulks of buildings. New roads, schools, hospitals were also needed. Yet the foundations for a sustained recovery were absent. Germany's currency, the Reichsmark, had been discredited by years of overspending on war, leading to runaway inflation and a thriving black market where desperate citizens traded items like cigarettes for food. Price controls introduced to prevent hunger meant that there was no incentive for Germans to produce new consumer goods. Germany's hobbled banks were in no position to finance the necessary construction work.

West German and Allied officials started working through the problems. Using funds from the Marshall Plan, the proto-West Germany established the *Kreditanstalt für Wiederaufbau*, a state bank that made cheap loans to help finance reconstruction (it remains a key actor to this day). Facing another ruinous wave of inflation, officials introduced a new currency in the American, British and French areas of occupation in June 1948. Called the Deutsche Mark, the new currency was issued to each citizen in two instalments totalling DM60. While this effectively destroyed the savings that people had in the old Reichsmark, it restored faith in the means of exchange, helping to revive economic activity. Just weeks later, administrators led by Ludwig Erhard, a man who would later become finance minister, vice-chancellor and then chancellor of West Germany, lifted price controls, stimulating the production of much-needed goods. As reconstruction gathered pace, the stage was set for the *Wirtschaftswunder* (economic miracle).

Efforts to rebuild West Germany hadn't gone unnoticed in the Kremlin, where Soviet premier Joseph Stalin harboured ambitions to create a united Germany allied to the eastern bloc. In particular, Stalin saw the currency reforms as a dangerous affront. Although the Deutsche Mark wasn't initially introduced in West Berlin – an Allied-controlled enclave surrounded by the Soviet zone of occupation – the city would become the target of the dictator's wrath.

Barely a week after the new currency was introduced, Red Army soldiers blockaded rail, road and river access to West Berlin, a move aimed at forcing a rethink in Washington. Overnight, 2 million people became trapped without supplies of food and fuel as Stalin sought to crush the resolve of the Allies and take full control of Berlin.

Breaking the blockade by force was impossible. Just 20,000 American, British and French servicemen in West Berlin were up against 1.5 million Soviet troops stationed around the capital.[6] Open conflict would also surely mean another ruinous war. With the attention of the world focused on Berlin, letting Stalin win wasn't a viable option either. Failure to stand up to the Kremlin would show teetering governments across the world that the United States was an unreliable partner. Ernst Reuter, mayor of Berlin, appealed to the Western powers for intervention: 'People of the world, look at this city and realise that you must not and cannot abandon this city and this people!'[7]

Allied planners started work on a miracle. With ground access severed, the only way to supply West Berlin was through air corridors agreed with the Soviets before the end of the war. Keeping the people fed and warm by plane presented an intractable challenge. Several thousand tons of food and fuel would need to be flown in each day to keep citizens fed and warm. Demobilising since the war, Allied air forces were short on aircraft and pilots. The only way to make it work would be to fly in continuous shifts, a burden that would push airmen and aircraft to their limits, and the skies above Berlin were prone to storms, rain and buffeting winds. Still, doing nothing wasn't an option. After hurried preparation, aircrews were ordered aloft.

Following a tentative start, the Berlin Airlift gathered pace. With Nazi-built Tempelhof Airport in West Berlin as the hub, cargoes of coal, fuel and food were flown in and then rushed out to the city on trucks. The operation was so intense that the airport's lone runway became potholed, and another one was hurriedly built.[8] In the process, legends were born. The American pilot Gail Halvorsen dropped chewing gum for children waiting at the airstrip's perimeter to boost the morale of impoverished and isolated West Berliners. Known as the 'Candy Bomber' or 'Uncle Wiggly Wings' (because he wobbled the plane before landing so the kids could identify him), Halvorsen became a symbol of American support for its new dependent state. 'Without hope, the soul dies,' he said. 'The airlift was a symbol that we were going to be there – service before self.'[9]

The Berlin Airlift proved so successful that by spring 1949 Stalin realised the blockade was futile. Barriers were lifted and West Berliners returned to normal life. Washington had faced down the Kremlin and won. Recalling later that the Berlin Airlift had risked plunging the world back into war, US President Harry Truman said he was undeterred. 'I had made the decision that we would stay in Berlin come hell or high water.'[10]

Meanwhile, Britain, France and the United States were intensifying efforts to usher West Germany into the global family of liberal democracies. Shortly after the airlift concluded, on 12 May 1949, the Federal Republic came into being. Operating under guidelines from the Allies, German officials had written the *Grundgesetz* (Basic Law) that established West Germany as a parliamentary democracy with protection of minorities and a clear separation of executive powers. With its capital in the sleepy, unimposing town of Bonn, the Federal Republic was meant as a bulwark against a slide back into totalitarianism and as an example of liberal democracy. Fearing the new constitution might make the division between East and West Germany permanent, its German drafters insisted that it be a temporary document until the country was again reunited. 'We must be sure that what we construct will someday be a good house for all Germans,' said Karl Arnold, premier of North Rhine-Westphalia in the British occupation zone.[11]

In response, the Soviets established the *Deutsche Demokratische Republik* (German Democratic Republic). East Germany was democratic in a Soviet sense. At its first election in 1950, its citizens could only choose candidates from an approved list. After the vote, Walter Ulbricht, from the Marxist *Sozialistische Einheitspartei Deutschlands* (Socialist Unity Party of Germany), became leader. Forged by Bismarck in 1871 and kept together through the fires of two world wars, Germany was again divided.

For West Germany at least, it was a cosy existence. The Bonn republic continued to benefit from the indulgence of its new protectors. In 1953 a group of over twenty countries agreed to forgive over half of Germany's external debts, freeing the country to spend more on its accelerating reconstruction. Corporate Germany also got a helping hand. Volkswagen was kept afloat with orders from the British Army. I. G. Farben, the chemicals company that had built the Auschwitz concentration camp, was carefully split into Bayer and BASF, which remain essential cogs in Germany's industrial machine. Migrant agreements with Italy, Turkey and other nations allowed Germany to offset its lack of manpower with immigrants from abroad. These *Gastarbeiter* would play a key role in the country's reconstruction, manning everything from coal mines to steel plants to construction sites. Germany was once again becoming Europe's economic engine, thanks mainly to the support of countries it had recently called foes.

Another milestone came in 1955 when West Germany was admitted to the North Atlantic Treaty Organisation (NATO). Its membership in the military alliance was a formality as there were already vast Western forces stationed in the country, but it meant West Germany's place in the world order was secured, allowing its leaders to focus time and resources on reconstruction. Speaking about Germany's accession to NATO, Chancellor Konrad Adenauer said the alliance was in full harmony with 'the German nation which, after a dreadful experience gained in two world wars, is longing as ardently as any other nation in the world for security and peace'.[12]

Although German economic life recovered swiftly from the war, the uniquely German culture that burned bright during the Weimar period did not. Many prominent artists had gone into exile during the Nazi period and chose not to return. Fritz Lang, director of *Metropolis*, a pioneering science-fiction film made in 1927, settled in Hollywood. Similarly, Thomas Mann, the acclaimed author of *The Magic Mountain* and *Death in Venice*, emigrated to the United States, where he became a vocal critic of the Nazi regime and an influential figure in American literary circles.

Others that the Nazis had deemed degenerate remained in Germany, but they struggled to recapture the prominence they'd had before Hitler seized power. Jeanne Mammen was a painter who played a leading role in the *Neue Sachlichkeit* (New Objectivity) movement that rejected expressionism and sought to engage with social conditions in the country. She was banned from publishing or exhibiting art by the Nazis and returned to Germany after the war, but she was unable to replicate her success during the Weimar period. Others maintained a prodigious output, but it was no longer German. Billy Wilder, an Austrian-born Jewish screenwriter and director who'd been working in Berlin when the Nazis came to power, escaped to Paris and then on to the United States. He became a Hollywood stalwart, directing hit films such as *Some Like it Hot* with Marilyn Monroe and winning seven Oscars.

The cultural void was filled by mounting prosperity in West Germany. The country was rapidly turning into a consumer society with its own particular quirks, with an emphasis on solidity rather than excitement. Firms targeting newly affluent West Germans noted that consumers had a penchant for goods perceived as high-quality.[13] There was a tonic called *Frauengold* (Women Gold) that was marketed as a drink to calm the nerves of busy West German housewives, an effect achieved by its relatively potent alcohol content. Other cultural movements also seemed to reassure Germans. So-called *Heimatfilme* (homeland films) became popular in the 1950s. They were typically set in pastoral settings and contained plots where traditional values would triumph through adversity. Hitting cinemas in 1955, *Die Mädels vom Immenhof* (The Immenhof Girls) told the story of three girls who fled Prussia after World War II and went to live with their grandmother on a horse farm in Schleswig-Holstein, near the Danish border. Faced with the threat of financial ruin, the family sang their way through their troubles before eventually being bailed out by a wealthy man who purchases Immenhof horses. The film was a major commercial success, leading to two sequels.

Life was tougher in East Germany. Angered by declining living standards and intensifying Sovietisation of the economy, construction workers led mass demonstrations that spread throughout East Germany's major cities. On 17 June 1953, in a vicious crackdown, Soviet troops killed 125 demonstrators, a move that went unanswered by West Germany. While the protests managed to slow Sovietisation, it showed East German dissidents that they were alone in their struggle against totalitarianism. The state's grip on its citizens came through the ironclad machinery of a vast surveillance apparatus. Founded in 1950, the *Ministerium für Staatssicherheit* (Ministry for State Security) became an omnipresent force, infiltrating nearly every corner of daily life. More commonly known as the Stasi, its sprawling network of agents spied on East Germans to root out any whisper of dissent. From tapping phones to sabotaging careers, even twisting and undermining personal relationships, the Stasi proved ruthless at preventing subversion. After the 1953 uprising, it would be another generation before mass disobedience was attempted again.

Back in West Germany, the 1950s saw the mood brighten further. Triumphalism over the *Wirtschaftswunder* was starting to spread. The VW Beetle became a hit, realising the vision Hitler had when his regime commissioned Ferdinand Porsche to develop a people's car. In 1955 the millionth rolled off the production line at the Nazi-built plant in Wolfsburg, Lower Saxony. Painted gold and its bumper studded with rhinestones, the VW Beetle embodied all the ostentation and glitz of Western capitalism. In 1957, Finance Minister Ludwig Erhard published a book titled *Wohlstand für Alle* (Prosperity for All), celebrating the higher standard of living delivered by the *Wirtschaftswunder* and coining a phrase that endures as a substitute for national solidarity.

The transformation of German society was indeed remarkable. Through the 1950s, the West German economy grew at around 8 per cent a year, faster than almost everywhere in Europe. The rapid growth doubled living standards within a decade. At the start of the 1950s, hundreds of thousands of Germans were still housed in refugee camps. By 1956 the country was building well over half a million new homes each year.[14] At the start of the 1950s, there were around 600,000 cars in the Federal Republic. By 1960 the number had increased sevenfold to over 4.5 million.[15] And beer consumption almost quadrupled. It wasn't the only miracle to bolster the mood of West Germans. In 1954 its national football team overcame the favourites Hungary to win the football World Cup, rekindling a sense of national pride that was almost exclusively reserved for sport.

It was during the 1950s that economic prowess became a pillar of post-war solidarity. In Frankfurt, emerging as the centre of German economic power, the Goethe Haus was rebuilt exactly as it had stood before, as if nothing had happened. Not far away, the artist Wilhelm Geissner celebrated Germany's recovery with a three-storey-high mosaic of a phoenix rising from the ashes. For many Germans, it was time to forget and move on.

For East Germans, however, the totalitarian grip was tightening. It would soon take the form of an imposing wall. For years, citizens had been fleeing to the freedom and rising prosperity of West Germany. The exodus represented a severe brain drain. Of the 3.5 million people who had fled by 1960, many were young and among the best educated in society. While the East German regime had tightened controls at many border crossings, it was still relatively easy to slip out via West Berlin. In 1961, fearing a collapse of his state, Ulbricht, the East German leader, decided something had to be done.

Construction of the Berlin Wall began on 13 August 1961, a day that became known as Barbed Wire Sunday. Officially called the *Antifaschistischer Schutzwall* (anti-fascist protective barrier), East Germany's propaganda justified the barricade as a shield from a fascist regime that it claimed persisted in West Germany. Stretching for 155 kilometres around West Berlin, it was manned by armed guards who had orders to shoot anyone crossing the no-man's-land called the 'death strip'. Twelve people would die trying to cross the border during the Wall's first year alone. Constructed almost overnight, the Wall would separate Berlin families from each other, making West Berlin a bizarre island and isolating East Germans for almost thirty years.

Although US President John F. Kennedy travelled to West Berlin to deliver his 'Ich bin ein Berliner' speech in June 1963, the words meant little to East Germans, especially as he'd elsewhere said the division was preferable to war.[16] Instead, these Germans were left to make the best of life behind the Iron Curtain.

As the 1960s dawned in West Germany, few would have reckoned with the trauma and division that the new decade would bring. For fifteen years after the war, the herculean task of reconstruction had consumed the mental and physical efforts of society. The economic miracle had underpinned a political miracle whereby a totalitarian state had become a thriving democracy in a matter of years. Having twice sought to overthrow the European order, West Germans were instead settled into the liberal, democratic fold. The Allies gave the country a generous helping hand with reconstruction and paved the way back to democracy, but a nation is more than that. Coming to terms with the Nazi past still loomed, along with even harder questions of what bound Germans together beyond the task of rebuilding and the materialism of *Wohlstand für Alle*. It was a reckoning that couldn't be put off forever.

Sins of the father

The Frankfurt Christmas Market of 1963 looked like any other. People flocked to drink *Glühwein* and admire craft stalls in the square outside the Römer, the town hall destroyed in the same bombing raids that claimed the Goethe Haus. Like many other buildings, the Römer was rebuilt much as it had been before, then ceremoniously opened by German President Theodor Heuss in 1955. Among its various functions, the building hosted the regional law court for Frankfurt's home state of Hesse. As choirs sang carols outside, inside the courtroom a thunderclap was gathering that would resound through German society for decades to come.

Starting on 20 December 1963, the *Auschwitz-Prozess* (Auschwitz Trial) in Frankfurt sought to establish the guilt of twenty-two low- or middle-ranking officials who had worked at the concentration camp.[17] Senior officials had been tried immediately after the war. In 1947 camp commandant Rudolf Höss was hanged for his role in the killing of 1.1 million people sent to Auschwitz. But this would be the first time that functionaries from the camp faced justice in West Germany. Defendants at the trial included Oswald Koduk, the camp's roll-call leader who had been freed by the Soviets and was working as a nurse in post-war West Berlin.

For Fritz Bauer, *Generalstaatsanwalt* (state prosecutor) for Hesse, the trial marked the culmination of years of forensic work and an even longer struggle against fascism. Born into a Jewish family in Stuttgart in 1903, Bauer had worked as a judge in that city until Hitler came to power in January 1933. Dismissed by the Nazis for being a Jew and a Social Democratic activist, Bauer was sent to Heuberg concentration camp in southern Germany where he was beaten and forced to clean the camp's latrine. Released after signing a document of submission to the regime, he fled to Denmark in 1936. When the German army swept into that country in 1940, the Danish Resistance smuggled Bauer and around 7,000 others to Sweden in fishing boats. During his time in Sweden, Bauer dedicated himself to journalistic and political work to make ends meet. He also met the future German Chancellor Willy Brandt and together they founded a newspaper for exiled Social Democrats.[18]

Returning to Germany after the founding of the Federal Republic in 1949, Bauer re-entered state legal service. In 1956 he was made Hesse's top prosecutor, a powerful position with almost 200 staff. His prominence made him a crucial figure in the hunting down of Adolf Eichmann, one of the main organisers of the Holocaust. In 1957, Bauer had received a tip that Eichmann was hiding at a specific location in Argentina. Fearing German officials would tip off the fugitive to avoid an embarrassing trial, Bauer instead informed the Israeli intelligence agency Mossad of Eichmann's whereabouts. In a daring operation, Israeli agents travelled to Argentina, kidnapped Eichmann, and smuggled him back for trial in Jerusalem where he was convicted of crimes against humanity and hanged in June 1962.

Meanwhile, Bauer had devoted himself to another project. In 1959 a journalist had sent him a list of Auschwitz guards, alleging they had shot prisoners as they attempted escape. Bauer sought to bring prosecutions. After securing permission to try the case in Frankfurt, he set about establishing evidence and securing witnesses to testify. Towards the end of 1963 the trial began.

It was the first time much of the German public had to face the horrors of Auschwitz in such vivid detail, with accounts of casual killings and systemic starvation. Previously, discussions around the death camp had more often been written up in academic publications, meaning its horrors hadn't fully penetrated civil society. Lasting two years, the trial heard harrowing accounts from people who had been kept at Auschwitz. When the defendant Wilhelm Boger was confronted with an account of his use of the 'Boger Swing', a torture device upon which inmates were hung, naked and upside down, while guards beat them to death with crowbars, he coldly refused to take the blame and said he'd simply been following orders. Another witness accused Boger of killing a young boy by dashing his head against a camp wall. The inmate who saw this was then forced to clean the resulting bloodstains from the stones. Boger initially found the trial an affront. Germany had been through denazification and he'd been cleared. But by the end, he showed at least some contrition. 'Today I see that the idea I adhered to brought ruin and was wrong,' he said towards the conclusion of the trial.[19] He was sentenced to life imprisonment.

The case was hard to ignore, even for Germans who would rather have looked the other way. Between November 1963 and September 1965 there were over 900 articles on the trial in just four major newspapers.[20] The proceeding was of particular interest for young Germans who had been stonewalled when asking about the war during the initial *Wirtschaftswunder* years. Groups of university students and high-school children regularly attended court hearings. For some Germans, Bauer's efforts were an unwelcome provocation, and the court received hundreds of letters criticising the case.

When the trial concluded, judges ruled that defendants could only be found guilty of crimes they personally committed, leading to relatively light sentences. Boger, the camp official who had killed the small boy, was one of just a few to receive life terms. Bauer, who had hoped that the German public would accept the trial as a day of judgement over themselves, was left disappointed. Just three years later, suffering from severe bronchitis that he would self-medicate with alcohol and sleeping tablets, his lifeless body was found drowned in his apartment bath.

Although Bauer died believing his life's work had failed, the case had kick-started the painful process of *Vergangenheitsbewältigung* (coming to terms with the past). Germans could no longer pretend that guilt for Nazism rested solely with high-ranking officials. West Germany had been shaken from the materialist escapism of reconstruction and the *Wirtschaftswunder*. Now clear that culpability for Nazi crimes was spread more broadly, West German youths increasingly viewed their parents and the state they had built with suspicion. The 1966 election did little to assuage those concerns. Kurt Georg Kiesinger, a former member of the Nazi Party, rose to become chancellor as the head of a Grand Coalition of Christian Democrat-led Conservatives and Social Democrats.

Distrust over West German society and the state intensified in 1967 during the Shah of Iran's visit to Berlin. As student protesters clashed with police and the Shah's security agents outside the Deutsche Oper, the student Benno Ohnesorg was killed by a policeman with a gunshot to the head. At the time of the shooting, the 26-year-old was married and his wife was expecting their first child. The policeman stood trial but was acquitted, heightening tensions so that the violence continued. In 1968 student leader Rudi Dutschke was shot by a Nazi sympathiser who had hung pictures of Adolf Hitler in his bedroom. The attack triggered major student protests against the Springer media company whose *Bild* newspaper had singled out Dutschke as a subversive. The activist had previously called for a 'long march through the institutions' to liberalise what he saw as Germany's still-authoritarian society. Although Dutschke survived the shooting, he was left with severe brain damage that contributed to his death in 1979 at the age of thirty-nine.

Germany's confrontation with its past intensified in December 1970 when Chancellor Willy Brandt of the Social Democrats visited Warsaw. Solemnly approaching the monument to the 1943 uprising in the city's ghetto, Brandt dramatically dropped to his knees in silence. Head bowed and hands clasped in front of him, it was seen as a public appeal for forgiveness for the deaths of tens of thousands of ghetto dwellers at the hands of Germans. While admired internationally, this symbolic act wasn't warmly received back home. A snap poll by *Der Spiegel* magazine found a majority of Germans aged thirty to fifty-nine thought Brandt's move was exaggerated.[21] The chancellor was in the Polish capital to make another controversial break with the past by signing a treaty that waived the Federal Republic's claims to territory lost after World War II. The move enraged groups representing Germans who'd been driven from those areas. The Treaty of Warsaw was part of a series of agreements that aimed to reset Germany's relations with Poland and the Soviet Union. But like the *Kniefall* at the ghetto monument, Brandt did not have the full support of German society. In a debate in the Bundestag to approve the agreements, conservative politicians called the treaties 'a sellout of German interests'.[22]

The 1970s would prove to be a period of mounting internal tensions. At the start of the decade, a group of young left-wing radicals formed the *Rote Armee Fraktion* (Red Army Faction), an armed group also known as the Baader–Meinhof gang after two of its founders, Andreas Baader and Ulrike Meinhof. An offshoot of the 1968 student movement, the RAF conducted attacks against American military installations and high-ranking businessmen and officials, killing over thirty people. The group believed that the Federal Republic was largely governed by the same people who had organised the Holocaust. The RAF member Gudrun Ensslin once warned fellow members: 'You know what kind of pigs we're up against. This is the Auschwitz generation.'[23]

Despite its violent spree, the RAF was popular with younger Germans, pointing to their suspicion of the West German state and the severity of divisions over Germany's past. One 1971 survey showed that one in ten Germans would be willing to hide members of the group.[24] In January 1972 the author Heinrich Böll published an article widely viewed as sympathetic to the RAF by criticising the reporting of the Springer media group. In 1974 he followed it up with *Die verlorene Ehre der Katharina Blum*, a thinly veiled attack on the way the conservative Springer press vilified left-wing activists. While other Western countries experienced student movement terrorism (such as the United States with its Weather Underground), they rarely received the same kind of sympathy that there was in Germany. Perhaps only the *Brigate Rosse* (Red Brigades) in Italy (another country struggling to face up to its fascist period) matches the division of the German experience over left-wing terrorism. Having spent most of the post-war period burying its head in reconstruction, Germany was in the midst of an inter-generational breakdown.

The RAF's campaign of violence reached its zenith in late 1977, a period known as the *Deutsche Herbst* (German Autumn). Despite its name, the violence actually started in the spring. In April of that year, members of the group ambushed the car of Siegfried Buback, West Germany's attorney general and former member of the Nazi Party, killing him, his driver and a colleague. The terror campaign escalated during the summer with the failed kidnapping and murder of Jürgen Ponto, the head of Dresdner Bank. In

September of that year, RAF members kidnapped Hanns Martin Schleyer, a former SS officer who had risen to become head of the *Bundesverband der Deutschen Industrie* (Federation of German Industries), an organisation representing businesses like Siemens, Volkswagen and Mercedes-Benz. The armed gang tried to exchange Schleyer for the release of Andreas Baader, founder of the RAF who was being held at the high-security Stammheim prison near Stuttgart. After the government refused to negotiate, the RAF along with the Popular Front for the Liberation of Palestine hijacked a Lufthansa flight flying to Frankfurt from Palma de Mallorca on 13 October, eventually forcing it to land in Mogadishu. On 19 October, Chancellor Helmut Schmidt ordered a SWAT team to storm the aircraft. The operation killed four hijackers and freed all the hostages. The next morning, three imprisoned RAF members, including Baader, were found dead in their cells. They were all ruled to be suicides, but some in the group and others in broader society suspected the state of extrajudicial killings, raising questions over the democratic veneer of Germany's political class.

The dawn of the 1980s restored relative calm to West Germany. Yet the Sisyphean tasks of reconstruction and confronting Germany's past had meant that discussions of what bound the nation together had never been truly resolved. The philosopher Jürgen Habermas claimed West Germany had replaced its traditional ethnonationalism with a *Verfassungspatriotismus* (constitutional patriotism) under which the country was united by liberal democratic values. The concept aligned with many Germans' enthusiasm for European integration, rejecting nationalistic notions in favour of an identity rooted in constitutional and civic principles. That sounded soothing, but it was never clear how deep that sentiment ran through society. It would be several decades until Habermas's claim would be tested by resurgent nationalism and was arguably found wanting.

As the 1980s came to a close, Germans remained in doubt as to who they were or what they collectively stood for. Rather than engage with those complex questions, there was an effort to separate the post-war nation from the Nazis without defining what that meant. In a speech to the Bundestag on 8 May 1985, to mark forty years since the end of World War II, President Richard von Weizsäcker referred to Germany's 'liberation' from Nazism and also called on fellow citizens to never relent in their efforts to confront the nation's past. While the speech was acclaimed for its moral clarity, it wouldn't settle the fraught task of processing collective guilt or chart a path forward. Just days earlier, during a visit to a military cemetery near the Luxembourg border, Chancellor Helmut Kohl and US President Ronald Reagan sparked international controversy by holding a commemoration ceremony intended to honour fallen American soldiers as well as their German counterparts who had been conscripted into the Wehrmacht with supposedly little choice. Yet the Bitburg cemetery where the event took place also held graves of troops from the Waffen SS, the combat branch of the Nazi Party responsible for some of the worst German atrocities of the war.

The fallout initiated the *Historikerstreit* (historians' dispute), a clash between conservative and left-wing intellectuals over how to place the Holocaust in the country's national story. On one side, Conservatives around Ernst Nolte argued that the Nazis' 'final solution' for the Jews wasn't unique, therefore Germans shouldn't bear an exceptional burden of guilt for the genocide. On the other side were figures including Habermas, who argued that the approach amounted to apologism for Nazi crimes. The argument raged in newspaper editorials and television talk shows, but a consensus remained elusive. The painter Gerhard Richter gave a visual expression to the nation's inner conflict. In 1988 he produced *Betty*, a painting of his eleven-year-old daughter in which she turns away from the viewer, redolent of West Germany's difficulties facing its post-war identity.

Separated for forty years, the two Germanies were about to be plunged into a process that would make it even harder to redefine a national identity. By the 1980s it had become clear that the East German economy wasn't working and dissatisfaction with the ruling SED was mounting. Against the backdrop of the Perestroika policy of reforms introduced by Mikhail Gorbachev in the Soviet Union, the first democracy movements emerged in several eastern bloc countries, including the GDR.

In September 1989 peaceful protesters in Leipzig started gathering outside the St Nicholas church, demanding the right to travel and vote in free elections. Known as the Monday demonstrations, the weekly protests steadily spread across East Germany. The numbers gradually increased, and on 16 October over 120,000 people marched in Leipzig, undeterred by the regime's threats to use force to disperse them. The once-feared police state looked vulnerable. Underscoring its sudden fragility, the East German premier Erich Honeker, who months earlier had vowed that the Berlin Wall would last for 50 or 100 years, was pressured to resign on 18 October. The following week, the number of demonstrators more than doubled to well over 300,000. East Germans were pushing towards freedom, with the rallying cry of *Wir Sind das Volk* (we are the people).

Sibling rivalry

Harald Jäger, an officer with the feared Stasi, was facing the unknown while on duty at the Bornholmer Straße border crossing between East and West Berlin. It was 9 November 1989 and the station commander with standing orders to shoot people who tried to flee the Communist police state just heard a functionary stumble through a change in travel policy. Pent-up East Germans had been allowed to cross into West Berlin without permission for the first time in decades. Intended as a sop to protesters amid the tumult sweeping the Warsaw Pact, news of the measure spread rapidly. By early evening, it was carried on all major West German news stations, with relay antennas broadcasting into East German homes. Thousands of GDR citizens headed to thinly manned border crossings like Jäger's. The *Friedliche Revolution* (Peaceful Revolution) was culminating, and German history was lurching towards another fateful turn.

People had been massing at the Bornholmer checkpoint in central Berlin all evening, and Jäger was faced with a restless crowd of thousands. Radioing his superiors for instructions, he was told to let provocateurs pass but turn back others. It was an impossible order to carry out. Fearing a deadly stampede, instead he opened the border and thousands of East Berliners streamed across the Bösebrücke bridge unhindered. The Berlin Wall was open, and Europe changed forever.

After thirty years of division, Germany entered a period of unbounded joy. West Germans welcomed estranged compatriots from East Germany, embracing complete strangers and handing out bananas as a token of camaraderie. In Bonn, Bundestag members rose spontaneously to sing the national anthem. East German Trabant cars rolled along West German roads, cloaked in the black, red and gold flag of the Bundesrepublik. Less than a year later, at midnight on 3 October 1990, reunification was formalised after a ceremony complete with sweeping speeches and a tremulous rendition of Beethoven's 'Ode to Joy'. Addressing the Bundestag shortly afterwards, Chancellor Helmut Kohl triumphantly said: 'Through free self-determination, we Germans were able to complete the unity of our fatherland – without violence and bloodshed, in full agreement with all our neighbours. A dream has come true.'[25]

It soon became a nightmare, especially for citizens from East Germany. For West Germans too, the rude awakening of reunification would expose Germany's deep-seated shortcomings as a nation. The Federal Republic had recovered economically from the devastation of the Nazis, but not socially and culturally. Its approach to reunification would lay bare that fact. The focus was on money and integrating the East German economy at frightening speed. The toll that would have on East Germany was underestimated by some and hidden from the public by others. The cultural shock that would rumble through the country wasn't thought through, because it wasn't really understood. The act of legal reunification was one thing, a true coming together of the two separate cultures was quite another.

Fixing East Germany's crumbling economy came first. Scrambling to close the gap between the old and new federal states, administrators from West Germany administered economic shock therapy. Where Kohl had promised to turn the East German states into *blühende Landschaften* (flourishing landscapes), East Germans got a harrowing. In July 1990 the Federal Republic's Deutsche Mark was introduced in the new states, instantly exposing East Germany's antiquated factories to competition from more technologically advanced rivals in West Germany. Thousands of workers were laid off and hundreds of production sites forced to shut down. The purge would only intensify. Founded in March 1990, the *Treuhandanstalt* (trust agency) was charged with privatising or closing state-owned industries. Effectively the bankruptcy administrator for the East German economy, its work proved so disruptive that its president, Detlev Karsten Rohwedder, was shot dead by a sniper hiding in bushes outside his house. Chancellor Kohl's celebration of unity without bloodshed had proved premature.

The rapid closure of factories and other businesses quickly pushed unemployment to 15 per cent, exceeding the rate in all other former eastern bloc countries.[26] At a vast chemical complex in Leuna, the heart of the East German chemical industry, thousands were laid off, devastating the town.[27] It was a scene repeated across the region. Economic historians likened the destruction wrought on East Germany to the 1930s Great Depression.

The ensuing social toll was similarly intense. The population of the new federal states is 2 million lower than it was at reunification. Around 1.2 million people, mainly the young, left for West Germany.[28] Others were never born. Birth rates crashed as people put their energies into scraping by, rather than starting families. Soaring unemployment fuelled a period of far-right violence, known throughout Germany as the *Baseballschlägerjahre* (baseball-bat years). Unable to function due to massive depopulation, football clubs, dance centres and schools shut down. It is a cost that continues to weigh. Surveys find that people living in East German states are considerably less happy than their counterparts in West Germany,[29] and loneliness runs at twice the rate.[30]

As Germany grappled with the economic fallout from reunification, questions of shared identity were sidestepped or ignored. Due to uncertainty over an eventual Soviet backlash, West Germany chose speed and convenience and simply subsumed East Germany. Although the Federal Republic's 1949 *Grundgesetz* was meant to be temporary until the two Germanies could write one together, in the end it was just extended to include the new states. The East German national anthem *Aufstand aus Ruinen* was ditched in favour of the *Deutschlandlied* of West Germany. Other cherished East German symbols were similarly discarded or destroyed, leaving reunification to resemble more of a conquest than a coming together of equals.

The fate of the East German *Palast der Republik* (Palace of the Republic) exemplifies the roughshod treatment. Opened in 1976, the Palast was a symbol of the socialist state's cultural life. Built to house the country's parliament, the building also contained bars, a bowling alley, a discotheque and restaurants. For many East Germans, the building had been the setting for personal memories. Young couples would gaze at each other across tables in the Palast's Milchbar, and older citizens would travel across the country to waltz at balls that recalled the glitz of imperial Vienna. While the building perpetuated the facade that the East German regime was close to the people, it was also an example of citizens coping and making the best of what was available to them under the totalitarian state. Although East Berliners were sealed off behind the Iron Curtain, something of the capital's libertine spirit lived on regardless.

The memorial of the Palast has been wiped off the map. Just before reunification, asbestos was found in its ceilings and it was closed to the public. For years, German society debated what to do with the sealed-off building. Government officials recommended it be torn down, but then what? One Hamburg millionaire had a solution: skip over the whole Communist era and rebuild the Prussian royal residence where it stood before the Palast was built over its ruins. In February 2006 bulldozers moved in and construction work on the neoclassical Berliner Stadtschloss began.

For East Germans, that connection to their past was gone. Officials pointed to elements that survived elsewhere, but it's scant consolation. Scrap steel from the Palast was reused in the towering Burj Khalifa building in Dubai, home to Giorgio Armani-designed hotel suites that cost upwards of €2,400 per night. Other bits of metal were reused in the sixth generation of the VW Golf, among the most famous symbols of West German mass consumerism. The foundations of the Palast are still there, but buried deep like hidden evidence of some unspeakable crime. For a country that's often praised for the deftness and intensity with which it treats its history, it wasn't the finest hour. The handling of the Palast shows how the focus is on preserving and revering very specific versions of the past.

East Germany isn't alone in feeling slighted by reunification. Misconceptions led to frustrations on both sides. West Germany didn't understand why East Germans were so grumpy and dissatisfied when money was flowing their way for new roads and restored town halls, while local facilities were crumbling. Since reunification, federal taxpayers have spent around €2 trillion on transfers to East Germany,[31] almost on a par with the combined value in 2024 of the hundred biggest companies listed on Britain's FTSE stock exchange, which includes the likes of Shell, AstraZeneca and HSBC.

But new highways and restored landmarks didn't make up for the combination of economic hardship and a lost sense of identity. The question of personal value and how the people in the East and the West could forge commonality was left unanswered. West Germany had never truly answered that question for itself and so was ill-suited to deal with the complexity of embracing East Germany and its trauma. West Germany's solidarity was built around *Wohlstand* and so the focus was on providing some semblance of that prosperity to East Germany, along with the great gift of political freedom. While few East Germans mourned the passing of a corrupt and oppressive regime, they lost a sense of orientation and respect in the cold and uncaring Federal Republic. The perceived ingratitude led westerners to label their compatriots *Jammer Ossis* (whining easterners).

On the other side, East Germans felt second-class and complained about the *Besser Wessis* (arrogant westerners), a feeling that wasn't unjustified. Even today, the share of East Germans in the country's elites stands at around 12 per cent, a significant shortfall when considering they make up 20 per cent of the population.[32] In both media and business leadership positions, it's as low as 8 per cent. Improvement has been slow. Olaf Scholz's ruling coalition pledged to improve under-representation, but only five out of fifty-four government positions initially went to East Germans,[33] who have also had to deal with dismissive attitudes. In 2003 football legend Günter Netzer questioned whether the player Michael Ballack, who had grown up in East Germany, had what it takes to be a proper leader on the German national football team.[34] In 2016, Armin Laschet, later Scholz's conservative challenger for the chancellorship, said the East German state had 'permanently destroyed the minds of its citizens'. In 2023, Mathias Döpfner, head of the Springer media group, reportedly said East Germans are either communists or fascists, 'there's no in between'.[35]

Back at the site of the Berliner Schloss, there are further signs that reunification has stalled. In 2007 the Bundestag commissioned a monument to the Peaceful Revolution, and the winning entry was for a 150-ton metal structure resembling a shallow bowl. It would be set on hydraulic dampers that allow it to tip to the east or the west, depending on the movement of the people in rather obvious symbolism. It was originally slated to open in 2013, but it faced delays in part due to the construction of a nearby U-Bahn station. But now it's become too awkward. 'Ultimately no one wants it,' said Olaf Zimmermann, president of the German Cultural Council.[36]

Alongside the complexities of reunification, Germany was coming to terms with the failed integration of *Wirtschaftswunder* migrants as well as the unfinished business of confronting its Nazi past. When the Berlin Wall fell, the country was like a well-shielded youth who wasn't completely aware of its own privilege or family history. It was cocky and well-meaning, but lacked the depth to handle the consequences of dealing with traumatised family members. Mahatma Gandhi said that 'a nation's culture resides in the hearts and in the soul of its people', but Germany was a torn society. By the early 2000s, the negative impacts of reunification were being felt on both sides of Germany as drastic welfare cuts risked its cosy prosperity. That was too much to bear. The country had had enough drama and was yearning for something more comforting. The personification of that attitude was Angela Merkel.

Mutti

Standing to address delegates at the CDU's annual conference in Leipzig in December 2003, Angela Merkel took a combative tone. After emerging from a party-financing scandal that brought down Helmut Kohl, she was the party's choice to try and unseat Social Democrat Gerhard Schröder as chancellor in the 2005 election. The country at that point was labouring under a sluggish economy and persistent high unemployment, leading to it being labelled the 'sick man of Europe'.[37] Merkel, who had grown up in East Germany and obtained a doctorate in physics, was a fresh face and the first woman to lead the CDU. Formerly known as Kohl's 'girl', she had helped topple her mentor who refused to identify the source of as much as 2 million Deutsche Marks in donations. To lead the party back to the chancellery, she promised her comrades that she wouldn't shy away from administering hard medicine.

Germany, Merkel said, had fallen behind on education, infrastructure, and was sleepwalking towards a demographic cliff edge. Meanwhile, its promise of *Wohlstand für Alle* was challenged by tectonic shifts like globalisation and digitalisation. An overweening bureaucracy stood in its way. In a rousing speech, Merkel said that the time had come to banish self-doubt and forge a Germany that again provided a decent standard of living for everyone. To thunderous applause, Merkel promised to set the country on the right path. 'Germany is at a crossroads,' she said. 'The alternative is clear, dear friends: either be overwhelmed by change, or shape the change.'[38]

With the campaign for the 2005 federal election reaching its climax, Merkel looked set for victory, even if her strategy hadn't gone entirely according to plan. Voters were sceptical of Merkel's vision of transforming Germany with free-market reforms. Plans to raise sales taxes and overhaul healthcare financing particularly raised eyebrows. Having seemed out of the race at the start of the summer, Schröder's party had narrowed the gap. Yet Merkel had reason to think she had done enough. Most polls had the Conservatives leading by almost ten points shortly before voting began.

Yet when the results came through, it was clear something had gone awry. Pollsters had got it wrong and the Conservatives and Social Democrats were neck and neck. Merkel's reform zeal had backfired. Rather than storm to victory, the Conservatives had actually lost support compared to the previous election, but ended up just slightly ahead of the Social Democrats, which had tumbled further. In a sign of the fragmentation that was to intensify in coming years, the three smaller parties had secured substantial shares of the vote. That ruled out a coalition with Merkel's preferred partners, the free-market FDP. For the first time since the late 1960s, Germany would need to fall back on a so-called Grand Coalition of the two largest parties. A deal with the Social Democrats meant that Merkel's free-market medicine was off the table, and her future wasn't guaranteed. Appearing on TV after the exit polls were announced, a chastened Merkel and a bullish Schröder both claimed they had a mandate to be chancellor.

After weeks of strained negotiations, Merkel prevailed and Schröder stood aside. Germany's first female chancellor was sworn in on 25 November 2005. The electorate had nonetheless dealt her an embarrassing blow. After struggling for years under Schröder, voters were hardly enthusiastic about her as a successor. It was a lesson that Merkel and her team took to heart. From then on, she would be a different politician, less about change and more about stability. That was a recipe that kept her in power for sixteen years in which the problems she had once vowed to combat were left unattended and new ones added.

Fortunately for the new chancellor, the gloom hanging over the country was lifting in 2006. In June and July, Germany hosted its first World Cup as a reunified nation, an event that would showcase Berlin, its reunified and diverse capital. For years the city had been a symbol of a divided Europe, but as Germany kicked off the tournament against Costa Rica in Munich, TV viewers around the world saw fans streaming around the Brandenburg Gate where the Wall once stood, draped in the black, red and gold of the Federal Republic. Further boosting moods, Germany's youthful team, which had stumbled into the tournament with several losses, surprised with stylish and attacking football. After Germany beat Ecuador 3–0 in the country's final group game, commentators even asked whether the country could go on to win the tournament.[39] Not only were the players performing well on the pitch, the squad also seemed representative of modern Germany, with players from its east and west as well as ethnic minorities. There was also an extraordinary upswell of public patriotism with fans from all walks of life donning the national colours and swinging the flag in solidarity.

Although the team would lose to eventual champions Italy in the semi-final, the success of the tournament represented a boon for Germany and Merkel. Under the motto 'the world as a guest of friends', Germany had hosted a raucous month-long party. The title of a documentary film that followed the team's progress through the tournament summed up the mood: *Deutschland. Ein Sommermärchen* (Germany. A summer fairy tale).

On the economic front, things were also improving. The global economy was strengthening, boosting demand for 'Made in Germany' goods like cars and factory machinery. Having remained frustratingly high for years, unemployment was falling rapidly, helped by the delayed impact of Schröder's reforms. As Germany's growth rates surged towards the highest in the developed world, the *Financial Times* asked whether the country was on the cusp of a 'new economic miracle'.[40]

Rather than using the boom as a tailwind to implement much-needed reforms, Merkel instead decided to let Germany and its crisis-weary citizens coast through stability. Aside from a gradual increase in the pension age, unveiled in 2007, she didn't attempt major changes. Germans appeared to appreciate the hands-off approach. By early summer 2007, Merkel's approval ratings had climbed to over 70 per cent. Her carefully constructed personal manner also appealed to the public. Having lived with Schröder's macho bravado, Germans now appreciated Merkel's moderate reserve.

Although largely guarded about her private life, she came across as one of the people. Merkel was photographed shopping for her own groceries in a local supermarket. She grew potatoes and made *Kartoffelsuppe* (potato soup) with a hand masher. During football tournaments, she could be seen sipping beer. For summer vacations, she went hiking in the Alps. Her plain-spoken demeanour earned her the nickname '*Mutti*' ('mummy'), reflecting Germans' desire to be cared for. Reportedly coined by a cabinet colleague in the late 2000s, the nickname swept across Germany and beyond, underscoring the yearning of a nation exhausted by reunification and years of economic grind. Although she initially rejected the label, arguing that no male leader would receive it, she eventually embraced it. The moniker, Merkel said, was 'anything but defamatory', since it 'means responsibility for the government, but also responsibility for the people in the country'.

For many Germans, her motherly aura intensified towards the end of her first term. When it came to major international crises, Merkel seemed to have a knack for sparing Germany from the worst. Her first big test started in 2007. That year, a long bubble in the American housing market burst, making it hard for people with lower credit ratings to refinance mortgages and leading to the failure of several smaller banks as loans were defaulted. German banks had invested heavily in the so-called subprime mortgage market and were among the first to be hit. Intensifying over the following year, the financial crisis exploded with the collapse of investment-banking heavyweight Lehman Brothers in September 2008. The German financial giants Allianz, Commerzbank and Deutsche Bank were caught up in the turmoil as their shares dropped over fears of exposure and contagion. Apprehensive Germans looked to Merkel to restore calm. Acting slowly initially, she eventually pushed through a €500 billion bailout of the country's financial system. Still, Germany skidded into its worst downturn in the post-war era. With exports hit by the global shock, the country entered recession towards the end of 2008, with forecasters predicting a slow and frustrating recovery.

Fortunately for Germany, help was at hand. Spooked by the worsening downturn, China's government unleashed a massive stimulus package, a move that restored demand for 'Made in Germany' goods like Siemens machinery and Volkswagen cars. While Germany was developing a dependency on the Asian autocracy, the main concern for Merkel and the rest of the country at the time was getting growth back on track. Already by mid-2009, Germany's economy was emerging from recession and starting to recover. Although Finance Minister Wolfgang Schäuble had warned the financial crisis could lead to the kind of mass unemployment that led to the rise of Hitler, in truth Germany's *Kurzarbeit* (a furlough programme, in which the state pays a major portion of wages during production disruptions) meant that most companies held on to staff. Having barely risen, Germany's unemployment rate started falling again in 2009.

It was potent fuel for the Mutti legend. In a country haunted by memories of Weimar hyperinflation, Germany's relatively smooth ride through the financial crisis reinforced the image of Merkel's government as a powerful and protective arm. To citizens watching the news, life in the *Bundesrepublik* seemed almost charmed. Britain and Ireland made deep cuts to public services to reduce deficits, riots shook Greece, and general strikes brought France to a standstill. Yet Germany cruised along, wages rose, life for many steadily improved, and the welfare state was modestly expanded. For a nation often centrally entangled in global calamities, it was a relief to sit this one out.

On top of China's spending blitz, which was particularly favourable to Germany by boosting demand for its industrial goods, Merkel's government launched a significant stimulus programme, including a cash-for-clunkers rebate programme to boost car sales (Germany's version of trickle-down economics that was supposed to benefit BMW, Mercedes-Benz, Volkswagen and their smaller suppliers). While a host of Merkel's peers got voted out of office in the wake of the crisis – including Gordon Brown in Britain, José Luis Rodríguez Zapatero in Spain and George Papandreou in Greece – Merkel not only weathered the storm but solidified her reputation as a steady hand.

But it wasn't all good for Germany. The massive bailout programme caused the second-biggest surge in government debt in Germany's post-war history. That caused grumbling among fiscal conservatives, especially those in Merkel's Christian Democrats. To maintain support (and with an eye on federal elections looming in the autumn), Merkel's administration proposed a plan that would make parsimony a constitutional obligation by setting limits on annual net new borrowing. The so-called debt brake was hard, fast rule-making to show that the financial-crisis bailout would be an exception forever and always.

On 29 May 2009 the Bundestag passed the amendment with a two-thirds majority, and the Bundesrat followed suit on 12 June. The German legend of the Swabian housewife, a frugal and prudent character from the country's southwest, had become part of the country's Basic Law, providing limits on government spending that would hamper investment in schools, infrastructure and the military for years. Under her successor Olaf Scholz, it would trigger a particularly aggressive use of so-called *Sondervermögen* (literally, 'special assets', but in practice off-budget funds) to sidestep the debt brake. Not for the first or the last time, a political expedient under Merkel would, in the name of short-term stability, make Germany less stable in the long term.

That summer, campaigning for the 2009 federal election began. Chastened by the near-loss to Schröder in 2005, Merkel and the CDU took a different tack. Rather than campaign on a platform of change, they sought to defuse political debate. Dubbed 'asymmetric demobilisation', the CDU sought to blur divisions with the SPD.

The theory went that if the Social Democrats were subdued, then Merkel would win due to her high approval ratings and incumbent status. TV duels between Merkel and her challenger (and the future president) Frank-Walter Steinmeier were thus deliberately tame, with Merkel hesitant to criticise her opponent. Questions about Germany's struggles with digitalisation and creaking infrastructure – topics she had once vowed to tackle aggressively – were dismissed with platitudes.

As election night approached on 27 September, many commentators were simply glad it was over, with one journalist describing it as the political equivalent of 'decaffeinated coffee, a blood-pressure reducer, or yoga relaxation'.[41] For Merkel, defusing debate was an effective political strategy. Even though her own party's vote share slipped yet again, the SPD fared even worse, tumbling more than ten points. Meanwhile, fragmentation intensified as the smaller parties all gained seats. But the main objective was achieved: Merkel secured a second term and this time with her preferred partner, the Free Democrats.

Much of her activity in the early 2010s was focused on dealing with the fallout of the eurozone sovereign-debt crisis. She often moralised and delayed over bailout packages for the likes of Greece, but acquiesced to German-backed support in the end. The crisis helped cement her reputation as Europe's fixer-in-chief. But often the solutions were temporary patches that allowed the continent to muddle through. Although her go-slow approach managed to keep anxious German taxpayers onside, it condemned millions to economic suffering and tarnished the dream of European unity and solidarity. She also presided over the opening of the Nord Stream 1 gas pipeline with Russia, and regularly took business delegations on almost annual trips to China to deepen commercial relations.

Domestically, German society was showing signs of widening division. In 2010 protests over the Stuttgart 21 rail project escalated into violence with more than 400 people injured in altercations with the police. That same year Thilo Sarrazin, a former board member of the Bundesbank, Germany's national central bank, published a divisive book warning that the country was destroying itself through falling birthrates, while increasing migration, especially from Muslim countries, was causing an underclass to grow.[42] Echoes of its past re-emerged with the 2011 sentencing of John Demjanjuk for his role in the murder of more than 28,000 people while serving as a guard at a Nazi concentration camp. In 2012 it was confirmed that the domestic intelligence service had destroyed files and data related to a series of murders by the neo-Nazi group National Socialist Underground. That period wasn't all grim though. In 2010, Germany finished third in the World Cup in South Africa, and Lena Meyer-Landrut won the Eurovision Song Contest.

Merkel's role in maintaining Germany's stability through the crises helped her secure the best result of her sixteen years in power at the 2013 election. After a lacklustre campaign by her opponents, the CDU/CSU boosted its vote share to 41.5 per cent, giving Merkel a deceptive aura of invincibility. While the outcome indeed stemmed the trend of declines, support for the conservatives was still weaker than at any federal ballot between the 1950s and 1980s. Meanwhile, the co-ruling FDP crashed out of the Bundestag, taking the blame for voter frustration and forcing another Grand Coalition on Germany. The election also marked the beginning of a new stage of political fragmentation, with the anti-euro AfD falling just shy of winning seats in parliament in its first national election. Although the vote was the zenith of Merkel's popularity, a new crisis would soon change German society forever and cause the Mutti legend to crack.

In 2015, after the Syrian civil war intensified, a long-simmering refugee crisis reached boiling point. By year's end, Germany's migration office was overwhelmed. Initially cautious, Merkel found herself at a crossroads: use force to turn migrants away or keep Germany's borders open. She chose the latter. Between 2015 and 2017 over 1.4 million people claimed asylum in the country. For a leader synonymous with caution and control, this appeared to many voters as a reckless leap. Instead of meticulous consensus-building, she grossly underestimated the backlash and frustration.

While many German voters felt their situation grow more precarious, the far-right pointed to taxpayer money flowing into caring for hundreds of thousands of dark-skinned foreigners. Merkel, though, placed a colossal bet on a grand humanitarian gesture, sweeping aside the public's concerns with a defiant and dismissive '*Wir schaffen das*' (we can do it). To many, it marked the moment when Merkel abandoned her role as the country's careful guardian. While some Germans did all they could to aid the new arrivals, others saw it as a chance to stoke division over Mutti's ultimate betrayal. The chief beneficiary was the AfD. Withering as it struggled to get voters to care about the euro bailouts, the refugee crisis revived the anti-establishment party (see chapter 8 for more on the refugee crisis and the AfD's rise). Merkel's approval ratings slid and once-loyal colleagues were scheming against her. In a matter of months the authority she had built up over years had broken.

As the 2017 election gradually approached, her government was mired in in-fighting and there were doubts whether Merkel would try for a fourth term to equal Kohl's tenure, but two global events pushed her to run one more time. One was the surprise result of the UK's Brexit referendum in 2016, which set in motion the country's departure from the EU – a delicate situation that threatened to permanently weaken the bloc and so put at risk Germany's export machine. The second was similarly complex: Donald Trump winning the US presidential election. Both were decisive defeats for the multilateral mainstream, and Merkel was widely seen as one of the few leaders who could serve as a standard-bearer for liberal democracy. It was at that point the Mutti cult went global.

It wasn't just Germans who found comfort in the idea of a steady motherly figure steering the broader West. Many commentators saw Merkel as the personification of a country that had become a moral leader, a shining example of the power of universal ideals. She was the embodiment of a reliable and redeemed Germany. 'The thrice-elected, soft-spoken former scientist from East Germany, armed with a doctorate in quantum chemistry, doesn't just carry the weight of Germany and Europe on her shoulders, but that of defending freedom and liberalism across the world,' Britain's *Independent* newspaper wrote in 2017.[43]

This kind of veneration ignored evidence to the contrary. Despite her reputation, Merkel maintained close ties with Russia even after it annexed Crimea and deepened relations with an increasingly autocratic China. Even at home, she was hesitant to fully defend liberal democratic principles. In 2016, the German comedian Jan

Böhmermann released a satirical poem about Turkish President Recep Tayyip Erdoğan that involved suppressing minorities as well as unspeakable acts with goats. While arguably in poor taste, the supposed leader of the free world should have been expected to uphold Böhmermann's artistic right to free speech. But not Merkel. After a phone call from Erdoğan, her chancellery intervened to ensure that the entertainer faced prosecution under antiquated German laws that criminalised insults against foreign heads of state. Although Böhmermann was eventually cleared, his disappointment in Merkel was palpable. 'She carved me up, served me to a neurotic despot for dinner, and made me become a German Ai Weiwei,' he said, referring to the dissident Chinese artist, who was jailed and then released before moving to Germany to live in exile. It was another crack in her image as Germany's steadfast matron.

Although Merkel eked out victory at the 2017 election, voters turned away in droves, handing her conservative bloc its worst result since 1949. Hobbling into her final term, Merkel was under almost constant attack from opposition figures and her own side. In the autumn of 2018, after heavy losses in regional votes, Merkel announced she would stand down as leader of the CDU, opening the door to a successor.

But fate had another crisis in store for Merkel, which offered her one more chance to shine as Mutti. Starting in China's Hubei province in late 2019, Covid-19 spread rapidly, forcing societies across the world into draconian lockdowns. For Merkel, the coronavirus pandemic played to her strengths. Whereas leaders in other countries flailed, Merkel's scientific background helped her provide a reassuring presence for German society. Her regular communications showed she understood concepts such as reproduction rates. She patiently explained the rationale for lockdowns while showing sympathy for the hardship the measures entailed, leaning into her experience in the East German police state to show that she understood the severity of limited freedoms. Her leadership was often credited with keeping Germany's fatality rates below other European countries like France and the United Kingdom. By the time she left office in December 2021, her approval ratings suggested Germans would have been quite happy had she stayed a little longer. But unlike in 2016, Merkel stuck to her retirement plans.

Her purported scientist's diligence didn't extend to planning for a successor. As Merkel edged towards the exit, it became abundantly clear to voters that her two immediate heirs weren't up to the task. Annegret Kramp-Karrenbauer, her hand-picked successor for leader of the Christian Democrats – the typical path to the chancellery – stepped down over a scandal involving an East German branch of the party breaking taboos by naively collaborating with the far-right AfD. The next candidate, Armin Laschet, was thrown almost immediately into the spotlight and floundered. As campaigning for the 2021 election got underway, he was caught giggling on the sidelines of an event to commemorate victims of flash floods, a damaging faux pas that raised questions about a lack of stature.

Despite her struggles, Merkel was still popular and Germany wanted continuity above all else. This was less about party loyalty and more about the stability that Mutti represented. That opened the door to Olaf Scholz, vice-chancellor and finance minister in her final term. The soft-spoken career politician was a technocratic centrist in Merkel's mould. His main weakness was that he was a member of the centre-left Social Democrats, who had been battered and weakened by serving as the junior partner in three of Merkel's four terms. While the chancellor took the credit for successes, she was adept at passing blame on to her partners. But the former mayor of Hamburg turned fear of change into a campaign tool by claiming the mantle as the true successor of Merkel's legacy. Like her, Scholz was seen as moderate and somewhat plodding, but calm and dependable. He even posed for a photograph with his hands positioned in the form of a *Raute* (the diamond shape that was Merkel's trademark gesture). With Germany craving stability, and alternatives in the Greens and the conservative bloc looking riskier, the gambit worked, but barely. The SPD narrowly won the election, but with the weakest support for any chancellor in post-war Germany. Scholz needed two other parties to cobble together a majority. It was further evidence that the days of reliable politics were at an end whether Germans liked it or not.

Merkel bowed out on an icy December evening in 2021. Wrapped in a black woollen coat, she sat for a ceremony outside the Bendlerblock in Berlin, where Colonel Claus von Stauffenberg had plotted to assassinate Hitler and was executed by firing squad after the plan's failure. Tears welled in her eyes as the Bundeswehr's marching band thumped through the unexpected choice for her ceremonial departure. Instead of a Beethoven symphony or the Brahms Requiem, Merkel had opted for a song from punk singer Nina Hagen about a young East German woman lamenting her abusive boyfriend's failure to bring colour film on their holiday. It was a rare nod to Merkel's roots in East Germany and broke with the usual solemnity of political farewells, reflecting her down-to-earth chancellorship. She later called the song 'a highlight' of her youth and pointed to its setting in her constituency on the Baltic Sea, 'so it all fits'. As the final notes faded into the cold Berlin air, a more fragile era was opening for Germany. Although Merkel may have represented the soothing stability that the country craved, she didn't provide the leadership that it needed and that her popularity should have given her a mandate for.

Mutti, in fact, left Germany with more problems than when she took charge. Her migration policy opened the door to a xenophobic backlash; the once-vaunted auto industry faces an existential crisis; Germany's energy sector is scarcely equipped to support an industrial powerhouse. Meanwhile, infrastructure crumbles, a sprawling bureaucracy chokes off innovation, and that demographic cliff edge looms even closer. The list of issues is long (and the coming chapters will delve into these). In short, Germany has become what Merkel warned about in her fiery reform speech to CDU delegates two decades earlier: the country is being shaped by change instead of shaping it.

Children of overprotective parents often struggle to mature or face the consequences of their actions. That's where Germany finds itself. Coddled first by post-war allies and then Merkel's deceptive calm after the turbulence of reunification, the country needs to face some harsh realities. But Merkel's successors will have a more difficult job than she did, as spreading economic malaise and a broken social contract tears at what solidarity there is.

As Merkel departed office, one apparent tribute symbolised the fragile condition in which she had left Germany. At the Etdorf Museum in Bavaria, the artist Wilhelm Koch created a statue of her sitting imperiously atop a horse. But just eighteen months after its unveiling in October 2021, the right arm fell off and then the horse's head. While Koch managed to reattach both with gaffer tape, the lurid yellow bandages clashed with the bronzed surface of the structure made with 3D printing techniques, so he painted the whole thing white – which only made it look like cheap plastic. Weakened by further wet weather, the statue eventually collapsed, leaving Merkel's once-proud image shattered. Whether intended or not, it represents an incisive commentary on her period in office.

Without a comforting parental figure to gloss over issues, the post-Merkel era has started a painful reality check for Germany. Its lost decades have left the country in desperate need of solidarity, but without the tools to rally people together. The national legends that once provided comfort and supported the belief that Germany would weather misfortune are failing as crises pile up. In short, the country needs a new narrative to start the process of really moving beyond the darkness of World War II. Escaping Germany's problems would be easier if the country openly discussed its issues with humility. Yet, many elites are slow to recognise the malaise, lulled into a false sense of comfort by the country's own self-delusions.

3
Myth Busting

'Our virtues are usually the bastards of our sins.'
Friedrich Hebbel

Although Germany's post-war history was far from a smooth march towards prosperity, it was a remarkable process that saw the ravaged nation claim a place in the liberal world order. 'Made in Germany' returned as a renowned mark of quality, while the threat of militarism had given way to ardent pacifism. On the surface, Germany was back but better. Suspicion gradually gave way to grudging respect, summed up by the English football star Gary Lineker, who after losing to Germany in penalties at the World Cup semi-finals in 1990, ruefully said: 'Football is a simple game. Twenty-two men chase a ball for 90 minutes and at the end, the Germans always win.'

Over the decades, the developments fed the legends about German *Tugenden* (virtues), such as a penchant for order, earnest industriousness and grounded logic. The traits had been honed through generations and made the country stubbornly resilient. That was underscored by Germany's economy recovering from its bout of being the 'sick man of Europe' in the early 2000s; its export and manufacturing prowess allowed for a quick recovery from the global financial crisis in 2008–9; it managed to absorb over a million refugees after the Syrian civil war; and the country even seemed to tame the Covid pandemic thanks to its rational and rule-abiding populace. The world around might change, but German characteristics would keep the country cruising along like a well-engineered Mercedes-Benz. Or so the stories of the House of Germany go.

The national myths weren't just for outside consumption, but were embraced domestically as well. Germany loves to refer to itself as the land of *Dichter und Denker* (poets and thinkers), as if Goethe, Schiller and Kant are still guiding the country today. To be sure, few countries can match Germany's canon of literature and philosophy, and national pride is important and deserved. But much of that lore has little relevance in modern Germany and has instead become a form of chauvinism that props up a fragile national identity. When the underlying assumption is that so-called German virtues are an enduring part of the national character and that they will carry the country through hardship, there's little need for substantive change. But that won't work anymore. The problems are piling up and the business-as-usual approach won't work for long. So we need to take a bit of time to poke some holes in the popular legends about Germany.

Myth of efficiency

*'Was du heute kannst besorgen,
das verschiebe nicht auf morgen.'**

Efficiency is one of the most basic German myths. But to be absolutely clear, the trains do not run on time! The entire country struggles with the dysfunction of the national rail operator Deutsche Bahn, and yet the impression that trains run like clockwork persists. It's a key part of the broader impression that things function well in the country and better than in most other places.

Like so many of Germany's unresolved issues, Deutsche Bahn's decline had its roots in reunification. The country was ill-equipped to grasp the complexities of combining disparate populations. Instead of starting afresh and forging new commonalities, it forced the West German system onto the Eastern sector, not in small part because of its conviction that the legend of German virtues are real and West Germany was the true manifestation and unadulterated by imported Communist ideals. Within Germany, the effect of the

---

* 'Don't put off until tomorrow what you can do today.' We're illustrating the myths with German proverbs, which often have English equivalents and so are less uniquely national.

myths is that order is seen as a natural outcome of the national character. Disruption is therefore temporary disturbance, allowing the country to look past underlying issues. So to chip away at this national conceit, we'll start with rail.

More than a third of German long-distance trains were late in 2023. Passengers were more likely to arrive on time in Italy, Hungary, and almost any other country in Europe. The lack of reliability is due to creaking infrastructure, ageing trains and staff shortages. It has got to the point that Switzerland blocks some Deutsche Bahn trains from its network over concerns they'll muck up the Alpine country's finely tuned schedule (Italian trains, in contrast, are welcome). It's not just daily operations, high-profile developments are a mess too. Stuttgart 21, a project that aims to rebuild the main railway hub of Germany's *Autohauptstadt* (capital of cars), is running six years behind schedule and cost estimates have more than doubled to over €11 billion.

It all started going wrong after 1994, when the debt-laden West German Bundesbahn and the Eastern sector's rickety Reichsbahn were merged and restructured as a private enterprise. The goal was to leverage the power of the profit motive to transform a bloated administration into a competitive transport company, creating a national champion in the process. Change was indeed necessary. In 1993, Germany's railway were heavily in debt and losing money. Revenue didn't even cover personnel costs. Officials were brimming with exuberance at the prospects for the move. 'The new Germany, the new Europe needs a new spirit of optimism, a new fitness programme for the good of our citizens and for the good of our country,' said Matthias Wissmann, transport minister at the time.[1]

The reorganisation did pump life into Deutsche Bahn, making it more customer- and service-oriented. Passenger traffic climbed by a third and freight has nearly doubled. But it fell short in two key areas, which hint at deeper shortcomings in political decision-making.

One is infrastructure. There hasn't been enough investment for years. Since the rail reform, more trains have been running on a network that has shrunk by nearly 12 per cent, causing greater wear and tear, and the impact has reached a critical stage. The Bahn operates 33,000 kilometres of track (the largest network in Europe) and more than a quarter of that is in need of renewal, along with one in every three switches. Deutsche Bahn estimates total network repairs would cost €90 billion.[2] And then there's outdated technology systems. Many computers still run on Windows 3.11, a product that Microsoft declared obsolete a quarter of a century ago.[3] Despite the long backlog, spending hasn't picked up. In 2022, Germany's per-capita investment in rail was a fourth of Switzerland's, and the electrification of the network (a key component to make the system more climate friendly) was behind that of Poland, Spain and Italy.[4]

Infrastructure is linked to the second problem, and that was the goal of listing Deutsche Bahn on the stock market. Appealing to investors meant a more aggressive transformation to generate profits, shifting away from public service. The strategy prompted acquisitions like the purchase of the global logistics operator Schenker-Stinnes in 2002, while unprofitable routes and services were culled and more than 2,800 train stations sold.*

There was a moment when it looked like it might work. In 2006, Berlin's new central station opened near the Berlin Wall's former death strip, symbolising the promise of reunification. As Germany hosted the 2006 FIFA World Cup that summer, Deutsche Bahn played an important part in the country's joyous *Sommermärchen* (summer fairy tale) by ferrying 15 million football fans to matches across the country. In 2007, Deutsche Bahn reported the best financial results in its history, and it expanded further by acquiring a Danish bus company, a Spanish freight-train operator, and a British passenger rail service. But soon thereafter the bubble burst.

After a rocky run-up, the long-awaited market listing was set for October 2008. The timing couldn't have been worse. The American investment bank Lehman Brothers collapsed in mid-September, intensifying the global financial crisis and prompting the German government to pull the offering. Deutsche Bahn attempted to maintain its ambitions, buying the British transport company Arriva in 2010 and wasting more money in the process.†

---

* As of 2021, Deutsche Bahn had fewer than 700 train stations, compared with 3,500 in 1999. Data from Allianz pro Schiene, https://www.allianz-pro-schiene.de/themen/infrastruktur/bahnhoefe.
† Arriva was sold in 2023 for an undisclosed sum. According to media reports, the price was about €1.6 billion. It was bought in 2010 for around €2.7 billion, including its debt.

But back in Germany, the rail networks continued to decay, service and finances declined, and the listing of Deutsche Bahn quietly disappeared from the agenda. The savings and expansion plans under Chief Executive Hartmut Mehdorn may have briefly made the Bahn appealing for investors, but at a high cost for the country. Echoing conditions from when rail reform started, Deutsche Bahn's revenues were failing to cover spending and the state-owned company has borrowed the equivalent of €5 million every single day since 2016.[5] The crisis at Deutsche Bahn has become 'chronic' and 'jeopardises the entire railroad system', according to a report from the *Bundesrechnungshof*, Germany's public-spending watchdog. 'Nothing works any more,' said Karsten Ulrichs, head of the train drivers' section of the EVG labour union. 'Politics and management have more than failed and brought the once-proud and reliable Bahn to the brink of collapse. The railway reform that was supposed to bring DB out of the red 30 years ago has flopped, and a new start is more necessary than ever.'

The Deutsche Bahn debacle bears hallmarks of other failures, namely a crisis of accountability. There was little benefit in bringing another state-owned entity onto the market after the questionable track record from Deutsche Telekom and Deutsche Post. But once a decision is made by the elite, there's little capacity for course correction. That would mean acknowledging mistakes, which would in turn raise questions about the country's diligence (more on that myth shortly).

There's a particularly German difficulty in accepting or acknowledging *Schuld* ('guilt', but also 'debt'). It's all bad, and the national complex arises often. On playgrounds, for instance, if one kid falls down and starts to cry, the reflex of others is to insist 'I didn't do it', rather than to comfort or help their playmate. It's similar with adults. When a problem arises at work or among a group of parents, the knee-jerk reaction is to focus on who and what caused the problem rather than a solution. German structures similarly get bogged down over issues of accountability. The point is to avoid getting blamed if and when things go wrong. Even when mistakes have clearly been made, the response is more often than not to point the finger elsewhere. The Bahn boss Mehdorn is emblematic of this attitude. Rather than reflecting after more than a decade since the failed listing and the growing evidence that Germany's rail system was in decline, he rejected responsibility for Deutsche Bahn's problems as 'false and baseless'.[6]

Mehdorn also had links to another German transport tragedy: Berlin's BER airport. The long-delayed new hub was a prime example of the new German inefficiency. After failing to attract private investors,* the project was led by the city of Berlin, the state of Brandenburg, and the federal government. There was, however, little expertise and it showed. Fire-safety systems didn't work, escalators were too short, doors inoperable, and pipes mismatched. There were tens of thousands of issues in total.[7] Meanwhile, the airport boss was paid half a million euros a year.[8] Costs rocketed and the world moved on. During the nine-year delay, China built and opened Beijing Daxing International Airport. In 2013, Mehdorn was brought in to try to get BER up and running, but he only lasted two years and missed the eventual opening in 2020. During his stint he addressed a key cause of Germany's sluggishness: 'Laws are laws, but there's also a lot of nonsense involved.'[9] In a word, bureaucracy.

Instead of an effective implementation of state power, bureaucracy has descended into a system of institutionalised responsibility avoidance. Despite years of political promises to streamline administration, the tangle of red tape has continued to grow. For businesses, public services and citizens, the total cost for fulfilling government regulations jumped by €9.3 billion in 2023 to €26.8 billion.[10] To get a grip on the scale of the problem, the Federal Statistics Office has been putting together a monthly bureaucracy cost index for businesses since 2012. But there have been initiatives like allowing digital (instead of paper) sick notes, electronic invoices for businesses, and abolishing mandatory X-ray passes.

The thicket of rules includes requiring truck drivers to receive annual instruction about the vehicles they use on a daily basis, bakers to keep paper records of when mixers were cleaned, and wooden stalls for open-air summer markets to be strong enough to withstand snowfall. To clear all the regulatory hurdles, a wind

---

* The losing bidder won a lawsuit over claims the tender was biased. A subsequent effort to get the two groups to work together collapsed.

turbine might require a period of six years and a bike lane seven years for them to be operational. A few concrete examples just from the city of Tübingen: for the construction of a hotel, a protective fence was needed to protect lizards (just during construction, while leaving them to their own devices thereafter), a requirement that can run to €10,000 per lizard; concerts in the courtyard of the fortress of Hohentübingen are banned because the dukes of Württemberg neglected to consider escape-route guidelines during construction 500 years ago; during the 2022 energy crisis, the Swabian university town was thwarted in efforts to conserve power by turning off street lamps between 1 a.m. and 5 a.m. because of regulations that require lighting throughout the night.[11]

The micromanagement of daily life stems from the German inclination to avoid risk, including the risk of taking the blame for something. This approach in turn creates layers of responsibility, which separate rule-makers from implementation. The federal level generally sets the rules, but so too do states and municipalities. There are also health, safety and environmental watchdogs, which all want a say lest they get called out if something goes wrong. It creates a systemic tangle that's disconnected from the people it's supposed to serve and the issues it's supposed to help resolve. 'The core of many problems is that responsible authorities generally only have to look after their own interests and never need to concern themselves with sensible, result-oriented, efficient and citizen-friendly solutions,' wrote the mayors of three Swabian towns, including Tübingen, in a letter to Chancellor Olaf Scholz.

Although bureaucracy has a role to play in protecting consumers and maintaining order, Germany's has grown into a behemoth. As of 2024, federal legislation had created over 52,000 rules, while related ordinances tacked on an additional 44,000 regulations, an almost continual increase since at least 2010.[12] But little attention is paid to whether the means justify the ends. Do trade jobs need health and safety certifications for pregnant women even if none is working at the site? Does it improve security to require IDs for kids to be renewed every year (rather than every six years as was the case until 2023)? Does it help transport to restrict cities from deciding where they're allowed to lower speed limits? Does it help integrate migrants when they have to report job changes in person? Germany's federal system is designed to delegate to regional authorities so as to avoid the creation of a dominant central authority as under the Nazis, and while that may have made sense at the time, it has created inefficiency and lengthened the chain of authority between decision-makers and the public.

Beyond gumming up the economy and sucking up resources, bureaucratic excess harbours darker threats. Rules veer into regulating personal behaviour and codify a sense of mutual distrust – between Germans as well as between Germans and the government. Rather than ensuring public orders, state power becomes a force of control to be resisted or scoffed at. Almost every second person in Germany admits to having ignored or not fully complied with regulations, according to a February 2024 survey of some 5,000 adults.[13] That attitude is a departure from the traditional view of Germans as a law-abiding and rule-bound folk, and gnaws at the state's legitimacy.

The good news is there's a lot of potential for improvement. Germany is still a fax- and paper-based country. In 2023 the federal administration's use of more than 750 million sheets of paper was equivalent to felling fifty-two trees a day.[14] To reduce that kind of waste and streamline administration, a little effort could go a long way. That is if the country finally gets serious about digitalisation. So far it hasn't. In digital government, Germany ranks below Chile, Italy and Brazil as coming in twenty-fifth out of thirty countries, according to the OECD.[15] For instance, an online process for issuing residential parking permits stumbled on guidelines that mandate the thickness of the paper to be used, which all but rules out printing the permits at home. To restore efficiency, Germany needs more than yet another *Bürokratieentlastungsgesetz* (bureaucracy relief act) – as of 2024 there have been four.

For a more systematic way to cut regulation, Germany could look no further than across its western border at the Netherlands. Faced with a similar breakdown in its economic model in the 1980s, officials there introduced a concerted series of measures aimed at driving progressive reduction in bureaucracy and fostering innovation. The country set targets for reducing regulation and consulting more with businesses and associations on what supports innovation and what doesn't. In 2023 the Netherlands ranked fifth in a competitiveness ranking that focuses on quality of infrastructure and efficiency of governance, whereas Germany lagged behind in twenty-second place.[16]

For Germany to reclaim its grasp on efficiency, its political class needs a shift in mindset. That means less top-down control and more empowerment of the grass roots. The state needs to become a facilitator and otherwise get out of the way, if it really believes in the nation's innate virtues. More of the same won't work. As Albert Einstein once said: 'Insanity is doing the same thing over and over again and expecting different results.'

Myth of diligence

'Wer den Pfennig nicht ehrt, ist des Talers nicht wert.'*

Reputedly sober and rational, Germany has become a land where €1.9 billion can appear out of nowhere – and then vanish even quicker. Wirecard, a once high-flying tech company with backing from within the highest ranks of Germany, pulled off this sleight of hand and in the process showed just how credulous the country can be.

The failure of the electronics payments company reflects a variety of German ills such as narrow views on accountability and blind faith in the country's own structures. Close links between business and the government alongside the longing for a home-grown tech champion fed institutional bias. As a result, Germany's answer to PayPal got the benefit of the doubt from authorities when detractors – above all the *Financial Times* – raised questions over Wirecard's accounting and business practices. The German establishment circled the wagons to protect one of its own rather than take a close look at what was going on behind the scenes at the mysterious shooting star of corporate Germany. The scandal represented an abject failure of the type of calm and careful diligence that the country is supposed to represent.

---

* Literally, 'Anyone who doesn't honour a penny isn't worth a thaler.' It's effectively the same as 'A penny saved is a penny earned.'

Wirecard collapsed when a third of its assets proved to be pure fantasy. Even before the *Financial Times* revealed details of false accounting and phantom deals, there were red flags that something about the company's rapid ascent didn't add up.* And yet a company with roots in online porn and gambling, and an origin story including stolen laptops,† was allowed entry into the DAX index of Germany's biggest listed companies, a seal of approval that offered legitimacy and access to power. Guardrails not only didn't work, they were cast aside in the hopes that Wirecard was the tech champion Germany so desperately wanted. There was a collective suspension of disbelief that captured Chancellor Angela Merkel's inner circle, financial watchdogs and Munich prosecutors. All in all, over €20 billion in value disappeared. But the bigger blow was to Germany's reputation for prudence.

The Wirecard scandal was especially damaging because there was widespread complicity in the fraud, even if it was unwitting. Such things aren't supposed to happen in Germany. The nation is supposed to be about solidity, about rules and about structure, all of which are designed to secure the steady accumulation of affluence and above all guard against disruption. Whereas the United States very much embraces Gold Rush-like frenzy and all-in swagger, boom and busts are not the German way, not least because of historical trauma including 1920s hyperinflation. But when the test came, the system failed.

The moment Germany went from being a negligent bystander to active participant occurred on 18 February 2019. That was the day BaFin (the country's financial regulator) issued an unprecedented ban on short sales of Wirecard stock, prohibiting investors from betting that the company's shares would drop. It was effectively a rejection of critical views of the company. The move was an intervention into the normal workings of the financial market aimed at heading off a feared attack from speculative investors, or 'locusts' as Germany sometimes likes to call them. This was a

---

* In 2008 the head of a German shareholder association raised concerns about Wirecard's accounting practices and was later prosecuted for market manipulation. In 2016 short sellers under the name Zatarra alleged money-laundering. For the inside story on the unravelling of Wirecard, see Dan McCrum's book *Money Men* (English) and *House of Wirecard* (German).
† Wirecard's predecessor filed for insolvency in 2001 after laptops belonging to the leadership duo of Markus Braun and Jan Marsalek were stolen, allowing the company to re-emerge with a new backer.

very weighty step for a country that is very much about business. The implication was that German officials knew the full truth and that Wirecard's doubters had got it wrong. BaFin underscored that impression by filing a criminal complaint against Dan McCrum, the main reporter on Wirecard at the *Financial Times*. It seemed decisive at the time, but that assumption proved premature.

What became clear later was how little BaFin needed to throw its weight behind Wirecard, and that was only part of a broader institutional breakdown. The regulator's seal of approval was based on three things: an indirect witness of alleged market manipulation; talk that a hedge fund was flying a whistleblower from Singapore to London as part of an assault on Wirecard's shares; and a bizarre tale of extortion and collusion involving the *Financial Times* and its rival *Bloomberg* (the authors' employer).[17] The strands all led back to Wirecard's Chief Operating Officer Jan Marsalek, who even at the time boasted of links to Russian spies and has been a fugitive since the company's collapse.[18]

Even without that knowledge at the time, the evidence in support of the move was thin. The witness account was an unsigned written statement from an individual who had been convicted of handling drug money. It was relayed by a Wirecard lawyer and wasn't independently verified by German officials before BaFin acted. The physical presence of a Wirecard insider in London is irrelevant for stock trading. Also, the alleged whistleblower was treated like an incoming threat, rather than as a potentially valuable source of information. But the most outlandish claim was that reporters and editors from *Bloomberg* were ready to join the *Financial Times* in a campaign against Wirecard unless they received €6 million. That's an absurd amount of money for journalists. And the idea that two bitter media rivals would collude is like suggesting that Adidas and Puma were plotting a joint shoe design. But for Munich prosecutors, which relayed the information to BaFin, scheming between non-German media outlets was evidently deemed more plausible than fraud at a home-grown blue-chip company. It was classic us versus them and Wirecard neatly exploited that innate German bias, especially in the upper echelons of society.

Throughout its development and especially after entering the DAX in September 2018, Wirecard nurtured relations with Germany's elite including former Hamburg Mayor Ole von Beust and Klaus-Dieter Fritsche, a chancellery official under Angela Merkel. The company played the role of smart local boys grateful for help from the seasoned establishment. Ego-pandering secured a protective shroud against uncomfortable scrutiny. And for those who dared peak behind the curtain, they experienced hard-line tactics ranging from surveillance and hacking to intimidation. 'Independent newspapers, slick bankers, rich investors, expensive auditors, professional regulators and feared prosecutors observed the imbalanced fight and came to the conclusion that I was the one who was wrong and possibly corrupt,' said Dan McCrum of the *Financial Times*.

One of Wirecard's unwitting stagehands was Karl-Theodor zu Guttenberg. The aristocrat was briefly the country's most popular politician and was eager to be a player again. He's also an example of Germany's enduring fascination with its aristocratic past. And like Wirecard, he had a meteoric rise and a spectacular fall. In 2009 zu Guttenberg became the youngest cabinet minister in post-war Germany and was greeted with gushing enthusiasm. Alongside his wife Stefanie, a statuesque countess who is a descendant of Otto von Bismarck, Karl-Theodor was celebrated as a blend of modern sensibilities and national tradition.* It didn't last long, and he resigned after a plagiarism scandal in 2011 at the tender age of thirty-nine.

Despite the Weimar Republic having abolished aristocratic privileges in 1919, lineage still means something in Germany. Having a 'von' or 'zu' in your last name (a sign of nobility) opens doors. And so for zu Guttenberg, whose family line and crest can be traced back hundreds of years, there was always a way back and Wirecard offered a tantalising chance. Following his self-imposed exile from politics,† zu Guttenberg had used his contacts to build up a consulting business and got an initial commission from Wirecard in 2016 to facilitate contacts in the United States. That was small relationship-building stuff, but a big deal was pending in 2019. Wirecard wanted to buy a company in China and needed an operating licence to pull it off. There were millions in fees at stake, and helping to crack open the

---

* The pair separated in 2023.
† Zu Guttenberg published a book in 2011 about his resignation called *Vorerst Gescheitert* (Failed for Now), a confessional that could have set the stage for forgiveness and rehabilitation.

Chinese financial market for Germany would have been a feather in zu Guttenberg's cap politically.

Despite his fall from grace, zu Guttenberg had met regularly (about once a year) with his former boss Angela Merkel. In September 2019 he had managed a meeting just days before the chancellor was scheduled to travel to Beijing. Seizing the moment, he pushed for a bigger payout from Wirecard, likening the value of his personal engagement with that of former US Secretary of State Henry Kissinger.[19] During the chat with Merkel, zu Guttenberg mentioned Wirecard's plans and how the up-and-coming DAX member could use a little help, notably without mentioning his relationship with the company. Since the German government's key foreign-policy approach is to act as a trade delegation, it wasn't a tough sell. Merkel delegated the details to her staff, which reviewed whether a recommendation from Merkel would be in Germany's national interest. 'Wirecard was a DAX company and fitted in here 100 per cent,' said Lars-Hendrik Röller, the chancellor's economic advisor. 'We had no evidence of irregularities.'[20]

At the time there was already a steady drumbeat of damaging reports about Wirecard as well as a criminal investigation in Singapore, but nothing from Germany – and that was what mattered. That was precisely the problem, the country's officialdom didn't see any wrongdoing because they didn't want to. A few months later, the whole facade collapsed when false accounting and dubious deals were exposed following a failed special audit. In June 2020, Wirecard filed for insolvency. Instead of resurrection, zu Guttenberg stumbled again and issued a guileless excuse for his support: 'If we had known that the business activities were based on fraud, we never would have advised the DAX company.'[21] It was classic German avoidance of blame.

A catastrophe of that scale requires a commensurate response, and a parliamentary investigation produced a report longer than *War and Peace*, at more than 2,300 pages. Changes were made to financial oversight, and the independent Financial Reporting Enforcement Panel (FREP), which was supposed to be the first line of defence against accounting fraud, was disbanded, and complete oversight was put under BaFin.

The corrections were positive, but really girding against a Wirecard sequel may require adjustments that aren't easily written into law. For one, government and business are generally too close for comfort in Germany. The FREP is a case in point. In response to earlier accounting scandals, the entity was initiated in 2004 by business associations to avoid direct regulatory oversight. The FREP's audits were random and cooperation could be dragged out as it wasn't empowered to impose sanctions. The worst case was having concerns referred to BaFin, creating institutional rivalry and giving companies plenty of opportunities to avoid being caught. The unwritten code in Germany is that deceit is basically accepted as long as it doesn't get out of hand. Wirecard took it too far, even though public officials were all too keen to become advocates for the up-and-coming national champion. Further issues were created by the German obsession with *Zuständigkeit* (area of responsibility). Because of its highly structured system and the wariness of getting blamed for something, German officialdom rarely strays from well-defined bailiwicks to look up at the big picture. Situated somewhere between a tech company and a financial-services provider, Wirecard took advantage of those gaps. Plugging this loophole requires empowerment that transcends process and procedure.

A lack of accountability and basic blame-dodging was evident in the hearings by the Bundestag's investigative committee. One official after another defended their actions. That included Olaf Scholz, who was finance minister at the time and consequently in charge of overseeing BaFin. While the head of the regulator was forced out in the aftermath of the scandal, Scholz said the watchdog acted 'within the scope of its possibilities'.[22] He was also at the centre of another major breakdown in German diligence: a shell game with taxpayer money.

Scholz and his Social Democrats narrowly won the 2021 election and needed two partners to have enough support in the Bundestag for a majority government. It was the first time since 1949 that this was necessary and a signal of the political fragmentation that has since gathered steam.* The three parties – the centre-right Social Democrats, the climate-friendly Greens and the pro-business Free Democrats – have

---

* A three-party ruling coalition had only happened once before in post-war Germany, under its first president, Konrad Adenauer, between 1949 and 1957. Since then, two parties had always been enough.

extremely disparate supporters and policy priorities. The crudest way to get them all on the same page was to give everyone what they wanted, and certainly easier than forcing a shared vision. For the SPD, it meant protecting the welfare state and raising minimum wages; for the Greens, it meant climate investment and expanding renewable power; and for the FDP, it meant not raising taxes and sticking to debt restrictions. So how do you square that circle? The answer was financial engineering, euphemistically called *Sondervermögen* (special assets). These off-budget funds (a relatively common ruse even before Scholz's government) allow federal authorities to borrow money without breaching constitutional limits.

Germany cherishes frugality and its government debt levels are indeed in much better shape than almost every other major economy. But this particular fiscal fudge, which involved repurposing Covid-related funding for climate investment, was sloppy. And on 15 November 2023 the country's top court ruled that a €60 billion fund was unconstitutional.[23] In so doing, the judges also raised questions over the legality of hundreds of billions of euros of other financing.* Once lauded for fiscal prudence like a thrifty Swabian housewife (a stereotype often cited in German political and economic debate as an ideal of careful household financing), the court decision was the moment that legend died.

The ruling also started the clock ticking on the end of Scholz's self-described 'progress' coalition, which collapsed just under a year later. Money was the glue that held the government together and when that was gone so was the solidarity. That's the risk of basing a community too much on commercial success, and the fate of Scholz's coalition serves as a disturbing morality tale for the country.

Germany has viewed budgetary restraint as a goal in its own right and pats itself on the back for having lower debt levels than all other Group of Seven countries – notably less than half of what it is in the United States. But the government's job is to think and plan ahead. And the rules, which were slapped together after bank bailouts following the global financial crisis, don't distinguish between funding

---

* In a report in August 2023, the Federal Audit Office counted twenty-nine special funds at the federal level with a total financial volume of around 869 billion euros. https://www.bundesrechnungshof.de/SharedDocs/Kurzmeldungen/DE/2023/sondervermoegen.html.

for regular government programmes and investment in the future. There's nothing prudent about letting bridges decay, technology to fall behind and schools to fail, and the country missed opportunities in the era of ultra-low interest rates when Germany could have raised money for free. Demands for investment are pressing and failing to act risks making structural issues even worse. Sacrificing the future in the name of fiscal principle is not very diligent at all.

Berlin is the epicentre of the country's descent. The capital's local administration failed to properly carry out an election in 2021, leading to a re-run that toppled the mayor and cost the FDP a seat in the Bundestag. These lapses and others chip away at Germany's image for rigour, especially in the political class, which is populated with people removed from the cares and concerns of everyday Germans.

Reviving credibility starts with humility and stepping outside of fragmented party politics to understand the problems that people are facing. If officials would accept that they don't have all the answers, it could encourage a broader search for solutions and being brave enough to make mistakes and honest enough to change course, which means accepting blame when needed – a big ask in Germany. That entails risk, but also empowerment and a little more optimism. Like in the quote by the American painter Erin Hanson: 'What if I fall? But oh darling, what if you fly?'

Myth of the progressive nation

*'Eine Schwalbe macht noch keinen Sommer.'**

On top of the breakdown of traditional traits of efficiency and diligence, pillars of Germany's post-war self-image as an enlightened nation struggle to hold up on closer inspection. But on a superficial level, things do look positive. For sixteen years, Germany was run by Angela Merkel, a physicist with understated charisma who asserted herself in the male-dominated Christian Democratic Union, the centre-right party

---

* Literally, 'One swallow doesn't make a summer.' It's effectively the same as 'Don't count your chickens before they hatch.' Merkel cited the proverb to describe her role in gender equality in Germany.

that has more often than not fielded the chancellor. During her tenure, the former cabinet minister Ursula von der Leyen, a trained physician and mother of seven, became president of the European Union's executive. Merkel's successor as head of the Christian Democratic Party was Annegret Kramp-Karrenbauer, the former premier of the state of Saarland, who stepped down before getting the chance to challenge Olaf Scholz for chancellor. During the 2021 campaign one of his chief rivals was Annalena Baerbock of the Greens, who then became foreign minister squaring off with Russia's Sergey Lavrov and visiting war zones in Ukraine and Israel. In Scholz's government, half of the sixteen cabinet members were women until Christine Lambrecht resigned as defence minister following an awkward New Year's Eve video address, when she praised meeting 'great people' in the course of Russia's war in Ukraine. Saskia Esken beat Scholz to be elected co-leader of the Social Democrats in 2019, and Ricarda Lang was her counterpart with the Greens. Even the far-right AfD has a female co-leader in Alice Weidel, who also happens to be a lesbian. With so much political influence in the hands of women, Germany has gained a reputation for gender balance, but that's deceptive.

Even in political representation (with about a third of Bundestag representatives being women), Germany isn't a leader, trailing European peers Spain, Finland and Sweden in the share of women in parliament. And fewer than one in every ten mayors is female.[24] It gets even tougher in the working world. Traditional gender roles mean women spend more time caring for their family and consequently have fewer financial resources, earning about 18 per cent less than men in 2023 and consequently ending up with pensions that are about half as much.[25] Although the wage gap has narrowed since 2006 when it was nearly 23 per cent, other countries have done better in terms of improving balance in the workforce. According to the World Economic Forum's Gender Gap Report, Germany went from thirty-second in terms of economic opportunity and participation in 2006, to eighty-eighth in 2023 (ten ranks below Sierra Leone, thirty below Cambodia, seventy below Albania).[26] In other measures, Germany is generally flatlining at a modest level. The Gender Equality Index from the European Institute for Gender Equality sees the country particularly trailing in terms of education, ranking twenty-fourth in the region.

Women are severely under-represented in the top levels of business, at just 11 per cent of senior executives in Germany's 160 biggest-listed companies. In secondary management, their representation improves at 40 per cent, but it's still shy of their 44 per cent share in the total workforce.[27] Ingrained attitudes persist that separate professions into female categories like office administration and dental hygienist, diverting many young women away from technical-oriented jobs and exacerbating shortages of skilled workers.[28] The tax system also disincentivises married women from working more. Since their time is often spent caring for family, they subsequently earn less and rules that spread tax rates across a married couple mean wages of the secondary earner (generally the woman) are taxed disproportionately higher than those of the primary earner (generally the man). The greater the difference between primary and secondary earner, the greater the benefits, so working more doesn't necessarily pay off.[29] Consequently, nearly half of women have part-time jobs, the third-highest level in the EU.

Germany is still very much a man's world, despite Angela Merkel and in some ways because of her. As the country's leader, she avoided gender issues in the same way she sidestepped her East German past, taking on calculated impartiality to avoid attacks for being a crusader. From her trouser suits to her hairstyle, she exuded post-gender sensibilities. That made Germany appear like a bastion of progressiveness, but the realities were different. For years, Merkel resisted enforcing quotas on corporate boards before finally backing a law in 2015 for a limited number of top companies. And in 2017 there was legislation to improve wage transparency, but employees need to make a written request to receive the information, creating a relatively high hurdle. Mothers are also supposed to have an easier pathway into the workforce with the right to a daycare spot, but places are still rare because of a lack of funding. For the most part, Angela Merkel's main benefit was to serve as a guiding light for women, and that's still something. 'Today, no one laughs at a young girl anymore when she says that she wants to become a minister or even chancellor when she grows up,' Merkel said in November 2018 on the 100-year anniversary of women's right to vote in Germany.[30]

The chancellor didn't openly embrace feminism until the end of her tenure. Even then, it was in a characteristically awkward Merkel way. At an event shortly before the 2021 election, after nearly a generation in power, she said she hadn't previously identified with feminism because she linked it to committed activism and didn't feel comfortable giving herself that kind of credit. But Queen Maxima of the Netherlands, who married her way into royalty, was evidently Merkel's mentor by broadening her understanding of feminism to a view that men and women should have an equal role in society. 'In that sense, I can affirmatively say: yes, I am a feminist,' Merkel said.[31]

That was too late to help recast Germany's views on gender. And the government perpetuates traditional stereotypes. Not least through the fictitious character of Erika Mustermann, Germany's official average woman. The figure, who has been entirely made up by the government, has appeared on sample documents since the 1980s and is generally depicted as blonde with green eyes, and of course white. She's usually from Cologne, but sometimes Munich and occasionally Berlin. And one time, on the presentation of a refugee identification card in 2015, the same woman was surprisingly from Damascus. Her maiden name is Gabler, because she naturally took the name of her husband Max Mustermann, a white male with short-cropped hair and glasses.* She also has a son named Leon, rounding out the cast of the fake German family. Other countries don't have the same sort of stock characters. When other Western governments depict people in their communication, they're generally more generic and less normative. Britain has featured a white woman named 'Angela Zoe UK Specimen' to illustrate features of its passport, and the United States has used images of men and women named 'Happy Traveler'.

Erika Mustermann is just one example of how traditional roles are deeply anchored in the national psyche and shows that there's been less progress than Germany might want to believe. Similar depictions of dominant males and submissive females are prevalent in media and entertainment. Those views have a definite dark side. In a survey in March 2023 one in three men aged between eighteen and thirty-five said that violence against women was acceptable to instil respect.† The Federal Ministry for

---

* Angela Merkel was born Kasner and took the name of her first husband Ulrich Merkel, who she divorced in 1982. She did not take the name of her second husband Joachim Sauer, whom she married in 1998 after she was already a senior CDU official.
† About 1,000 men and women under thirty-five were asked about their views on masculinity in an online survey in March 2023. See the results at: https://www.plan.de/fileadmin/website/04._Aktuelles/Umfragen_und_Berichte/Spannungsfeld_Maennlichkeit/Plan-Umfrage_Maennlichkeit-A4-2023-NEU-online_2.pdf.

Family Affairs estimates that one in every three women in Germany will suffer physical or sexual assault at least once in their lives. In 2023, women in Germany suffered violence from a partner or ex-partner every four minutes, prompting the UN to complain that Germany lacks an overall plan to stop gender-related attacks.[32]

If left to the AfD, male and female roles would be even more clearly delineated. Björn Höcke, one of the party's thought leaders, has said that men stand for 'fortitude, wisdom and leadership' and women 'intuition, gentleness and devotion'. It's not an isolated opinion. The party's official programme complains about a dramatic decline in the 'ancestral population' because of childless and unmarried women, and the AfD echoes abortion opponents in the United States when it says even 'unborn children' have rights. 'Preserving the nation's own people is the primary task of politics and every government,' the party says.

The country's skewed social structures and lack of self-awareness about its shortcomings extends to the role of minorities. Despite more than one in every four Germans having a so-called migration background, they're under-represented in leadership roles. There have been exceptions like Agriculture Minister Cem Özdemir from the Greens, the son of Turkish guest workers, as well as Bijan Djir-Sarai, the FDP's former general secretary, and Omid Nouripour from the Greens (both were born in Tehran). But of course not all migrants are alike and the definition, which only came about in 2005, is broad and includes offspring of mixed parents. So the son of a German dad and an American mother is just as much a migrant as a woman from Afghanistan who fled the Taliban. The superficial nature of the statistics is deliberate. Given its experience under the Nazis, Germany didn't want to monitor ethnicity over concerns people could be tracked and persecuted. While well-meaning, that policy has outlived its purpose by creating blind spots and allowing structural issues to go largely undetected.

The Black German community consequently has undertaken its own effort to understand itself and raise awareness, initiating the Afrozensus in 2020 in an effort to be counted. In a very diverse group of more than 1 million individuals, one of the most unifying elements was the experience of 'otherness'. Over 90 per cent of Black Germans have had their hair touched without permission and over half have

been asked if they sell drugs or stopped by the police without cause.*
Germany certainly isn't alone in that sense, but because of the lack of awareness, racism often isn't seen as a problem. More than half of respondents in Afrozensus said they frequently aren't believed and then are accused of being angry when they discuss discrimination.

On the flipside, statistics showing a shrinking share of 'pure' Germans have been used to fuel anxiety that they're 'losing their country' to migrants. The risks of that were demonstrated at a school in Brandenburg in the touristic Spreewald region, a place for quiet boat rides through the marshy landscape and world-famous pickles. A threatening atmosphere evolved with students performing the Hitler salute, drawing swastikas on school property, and bullying others in an upswell of right-wing activity that's far from isolated to rural East Germany. Two teachers went public with the issues after feeling ignored by school officials, local leaders and parents. Both left the school and the community after feeling threatened, including open altercations and accusations of besmirching the town's reputation. Four more progressively minded teachers later departed.[33]

It's one of many incidents that show how Germany is not as mature and advanced as it wants to believe. Instead of more honest introspection, it clings to the self-image of the good nation that has learned the right lessons from history, looking past problems rather than addressing them. The consequence is that people pointing out issues can be dismissed and marginalised as attention-seekers. 'There is a feeling of powerlessness and forced silence,' Laura Nickel and Max Teske wrote in their public letter in April 2023. 'What should actually be self-evident becomes a gauntlet.'[34]

Myth of moral clarity

'Man wird alt wie eine Kuh
und lernt immer noch was dazu.'†

Every year on 27 January, the anniversary of the liberation of the Auschwitz death camp, public officials across Germany pay tribute

---

* Results available at Afrozensus.de.
† Literally, 'One can be as old as a cow and still learn how', or 'It's never too late to learn.'

to the victims of the Nazis. They hold solemn speeches calling for vigilance ('Never again is now') and post sombre videos on social media (#WeRemember). Rituals of remembrance are flanked by physical reminders, like the Holocaust monument in Berlin, the preserved concentration camps including Dachau in the northwest of Munich and Buchenwald near Weimar, and embedded in the pavement in front of buildings in more than 1,200 German communities are over 100,000 *Stolpersteine* (literally, 'stumbling stones', which are cobble-sized brass memorials to honour individual victims by name and at the location where they last chose to live). Few other countries in the world display their shame as regularly and publicly as post-war Germany does. It's a praiseworthy display of national guilt, and it deserves credit for that.

The effort has allowed Germany to act more like a 'normal' country and do things like wave the flag (on select occasions), cheer the national football team, and build bridges to the pre-Nazi past with the reconstruction of the Prussian-era city palace in Berlin. And yet two events occurred within a few months of each other that raised questions about Germany's process of coming to terms with its history.

One was in spring 2023 when authorities clamped down on a conference to discuss Palestine in the name of combating the threat (rather than the act) of antisemitism. The other was the soft touch towards Nazi allegations made against a Bavarian politician. On the one hand, a hardline was taken towards intolerance when it comes from outside, especially from dark-skinned migrants, but a more understanding approach is taken when allegations are directed at one of their own. The incidents raise questions over the extent to which Germany has learned from its past and how those lessons are being applied.

In the first incident, 2,500 Berlin police were deployed to the three-day Palestine Congress that was harshly vilified in advance. Mayor Kai Wegner (who incidentally took office after the re-run of the botched 2021 election) had bluntly labelled it a 'hate event', and in the run-up, one of the organisers, *Jüdische Stimme für einen gerechten Frieden in Nahost* (Jewish Voice for a Just Peace in the Middle East), had an account blocked by the public-sector Sparkasse bank, which demanded the names and addresses of its members.

Further efforts to disrupt the event were targeted at individual participants. Ghassan Abu-Sittah, a British-Palestinian reconstructive surgeon and the rector of the University of Glasgow, who has been called 'the doctor who fixes broken faces',[35] planned to speak at the event about his experiences over six weeks in Gaza during the Israeli bombardment in retaliation for the Hamas terror attack on 7 October 2023. He was detained for more than three hours at Berlin airport and then banned from Germany beyond the duration of the event. He was told that if he participated in the conference via a video link he would be in violation of German law. A similar fate befell Yanis Varoufakis, the former Greek finance minister, as well as Salman Abu Sitta, an author and activist who was expelled from Palestine as a child in 1948 during the Nakba ethnic cleansing.

Within hours of the Palestine Congress starting on 12 April 2024, police entered the venue, turned off the power, and disbanded the entire event. The official justification was that a speaker appeared on video who was banned from activity in Germany. The Berlin police said they saw a risk that 'antisemitic, violence-glorifying and Holocaust-denying speeches' could be made. In other words, nothing deemed disruptive had been said at that point – but could be. It was a preventative intervention that Interior Minister Nancy Faeser praised as 'correct and necessary'.[36] The aggressive approach transformed a relatively small event with a few hundred participants into an international incident.

To be sure, the conference was provocative. It called Israel's actions in Gaza a genocide and accused Germany of 'aiding and abetting' the crimes.[37] Salman Abu-Sitta had justified the 7 October terror attacks by Hamas and referred to Gaza as a 'concentration camp',[38] touching a nerve in Germany's view of Nazi crimes as unlike anything else in history. Ghassan Abu-Sittah has criticised Germany for making money off weapons sales and providing political support for Israel's actions. 'Germany is trying to silence the witnesses and that's what accomplices do,' the doctor said.[39]

Yanis Varoufakis has been a critic of German government policy ever since his role as the Greek finance minister when he fought against austerity policies imposed by Angela Merkel's administration during the debt crisis. But is he a threat to security? In the text of his speech at the conference, which he subsequently published, he said: 'a proud, decent people, the people of Germany, are led down a perilous road to a heartless society by being made to associate themselves with another genocide carried out in their name, with their complicity'. Clearly stating his opposition to antisemitism, he added that 'universal human rights are either universal or they mean nothing'. These sentiments should be shared by Germany, which has the defence of human dignity written into its constitution.

Outrage wasn't limited to the participants. The celebrated Slovenian philosopher Slavoj Žižek warned that cancelling Varoufakis showed Germany was crossing into authoritarianism. With public sympathy for the suffering of Palestinians diverging from steadfast state backing of Israel, the stage has been set for a backlash, according to Žižek, who had previously criticised the cancellation of a literature prize for a Palestinian author at the 2023 Frankfurt Book Fair as 'scandalous'. Treating criticism of Israel as a form of antisemitism risks redirecting the anger towards Jews and making preventative actions like the clampdown on the Palestine conference a self-fulfilling prophecy. 'The Varoufakis affair would then be a new, particularly twisted chapter in the history of antisemitism,' Žižek said.[40] The implication is that Germany's strident actions in the name of tolerance pose the risk of the country backsliding into intolerance.

But the approach was decidedly more understanding a few months earlier, when Germany chose to take an entirely different tack after echoes of Nazism involved a senior politician. Hubert Aiwanger, the deputy premier of Bavaria, was drawn into a scandal in the run-up to the 2023 state elections after muckraking German media uncovered a crude pamphlet that he had in his possession as a teenager. The one-page flyer celebrated the Nazi death machine. It proposed a casting contest for the 'biggest traitor to the fatherland'. Prizes included a 'free flight up the chimney at Auschwitz', 'a lifelong stay in a mass grave', and 'one year in Dachau, including board and lodging'. The typewritten document was found in his school bag as a sixteen-year-old student in the late 1980s, thirty-six years before it was reported. It might seem odd that something like this could still be relevant decades later, but this is Germany and sensitivity to glorifying the Nazis is a key part of post-war identity, especially in the 1980s when the country was still grappling with how to process its collective guilt.

Aiwanger had a natural political response: he went on the attack. He charged political rivals with orchestrating a campaign against him. He distanced himself from the text and claimed his brother was the author. But Aiwanger's defensive and evasive reaction raised questions over his involvement and kept it in the public eye.

Persistent doubts prompted Bavarian Premier Markus Söder to put together a catalogue of twenty-five questions for Aiwanger, with the aim of putting the firestorm to bed.[41] In terms of political background, Aiwanger is the leader of the right-leaning *Freie Wähler* (Free Voters), and this regional party is critical for the centre-right Christian Social Union (the sister party of the national Christian Democrats)* to maintain power. That means dismissing Aiwanger could have caused the alliance to collapse. In that context, the questionnaire was more of a thinly veiled attempt to defuse the criticism rather than an actual fact-finding effort. That was also evident in Aiwanger's answers, which were mainly variations of 'I don't remember.' He did show regret, calling the pamphlet's content 'disgusting and inhumane', and noted that it didn't represent his views then or now. After Söder and Aiwanger talked it over, the latter got to keep his job. Not only were there no direct repercussions, but he gained a national profile from the scandal (bad publicity, after all, is better than no publicity), which he used to shore up his personal ambitions by attacking the federal government in Berlin in the hopes of one day getting a job there.[42]

Clearly, the Palestine conference and a Bavarian political crisis are very different and isolated issues, but they both deal with the issue of Germany's self-image in regard to its Nazi past. The Palestine conference challenged the country's view of itself as good and rehabilitated and consequently provoked a harsh response. It was also irritating to the prevailing view of itself that Jews were part of the event, criticising Germany rather than appreciating its acts of contrition.

On the contrary, Aiwanger's situation was easier for most Germans to identify with. He admitted to making mistakes and apologised. Frustrated that it wasn't enough, he turned defiant about having to answer for events that happened so long ago. In his

---

* There's no good justification for why there are two conservative parties beyond Bavarian exceptionalism.

final response to the twenty-five questions, Aiwanger could have been speaking for all of Germany when he said: 'Mistakes made in one's youth shouldn't stick forever. Everyone needs to be given time to develop and mature.'

That kind of sentiment is exactly what the country wants to hear, but time alone doesn't heal wounds. There's an active role to be played, and sometimes the bandages need to be ripped off and the wounds exposed. And just because bad things happened in the past and haven't been repeated since doesn't mean lessons have been fully learned. Germany wants to believe that 'Never Again' is always and forever. But vigilance is a process that goes beyond self-affirming speeches and rituals. Humility is needed for Germany to accept that it doesn't always have the clearest view on tolerance and intolerance, and its own views of itself and its relations to its past create distortions that fuel bad behaviour even in its striving to be good.

Aside from spectres from its Nazi past, Germany's moral clarity has been tested in other ways and left wanting. Between 2001 and 2007, Siemens offered bribes totalling $1.4 billion to government officials around the world in return for business, triggering record fines in the United States and criminal penalties in Germany.[43] Deutsche Bank helped fuel the global financial crisis by selling billions in mortgage-related securities in America that a senior executive internally referred to as 'crap' and 'pigs'.[44] During the eurozone debt crisis, German media and politicians took to lecturing Greece on the perils of corruption, ignoring the issues that were coming from German firms.[45] In 2015, Volkswagen acknowledged that it systemically cheated on emissions tests, scoffing at public health in favour of profit, and yet was rewarded with government protection. These are just some of the most sensational examples to illustrate how the country strays from the prized values of its constitutional patriotism.

But there is even a bigger failing that also exemplifies the double standard applied to Germans with money and those without. One of the biggest recent breakdowns in Germany's moral compass has been Cum-Ex, a massive tax-evasion scandal that crossed the thin line between business and politics. It has involved damages to the state of at least €10 billion, a sum that more than doubles when related dividend-stripping deals (with the dreadfully unfortunate name of Cum-Cum . . . Latin for 'with-with') are added. And yet there has been relatively little outrage from the elite, which were naturally the main profiteers. Arranged by well-paid professionals, the scam worked by swapping stocks back and forth around dividend payouts and allowing multiple parties to claim refunds on taxes that were paid only once. Some 1,800 people have been under investigation.

Chancellor Scholz was pulled into the scandal over allegations he helped Christian Olearius, the former head of the private bank M. M. Warburg, dodge Cum-Ex-related payments. In 2016, while he was mayor of Hamburg, Scholz met twice with Olearius. At the time, the city's tax office was considering reclaiming nearly €50 million in refunds, but it called off the effort a few weeks after those meetings. Scholz has denied playing a role in the decision and said he doesn't recall the conversations with Olearius. But the impressions are unseemly and the murky links between the finance elite and politics go further.

Olearius's diary notes indicated that Scholz suggested the banking executive reach out to the city's top finance official Peter Tschentscher. The Social Democrat, who become Scholz's successor as mayor of Hamburg, also denied intervening on Warburg's behalf, of course. After a Cum-Ex-related search, more than €200,000 in cash was found in a safety deposit box that belonged to an SPD official.[46] And a former civil servant who switched sides to represent Germany's financial elite as an advisor and lawyer became known as 'Mr. Cum-Ex', fully aware that his efforts meant fewer funds would be available for services like kindergartens.[47]

Links between money and power are widespread, and Germany indeed performs well in international comparisons of corruption.* But the reality still isn't in line with the ambition that Germany strives for, and perceptions and trends matter, with a fresh blow coming in April 2024. Anne Brorhilker, the chief Cum-Ex prosecutor, decided to quit after eleven years investigating the financial crimes. Dealing a blow to Germany's credibility for law and order, she complained of insufficient political support that allowed wealthy perpetrators to pay their way out. 'The little ones are hung and the big ones are allowed to run,' she said, justifying her move to an advocacy group aimed at fighting Germany's powerful financial lobby. 'That's unjust and poses the risk that the general

---

* In Transparency International's Corruption Perceptions Index, Germany ranked ninth in the world in 2023, although its score slipped two years in a row.

public loses its faith in the rule of law.[48] That's a serious statement from a lifelong prosecutor, and it's a warning that Germany should take to heart.

In June 2021 after England beat Germany 2-0 in London and knocked its nemesis out of the European football championships, Gary Lineker posted on social media that 'it's time "the Germans always win" phrase was put to bed. Rest in peace.'[49] While it was a reaction to a specific game, it was also an acknowledgement that the image of the country isn't what it used to be. Germans aren't an army of efficient robots that always do the right thing. While there are a lot of failings associated with the death of these legends, every end is a new beginning, and there are opportunities for the House of Germany to weave new narratives about itself, ones that are less rigid and more textured – like the country itself.

The American philosopher Richard Rorty once wrote that 'a nation cannot reform itself unless it takes pride in itself – unless it has an identity, rejoices in it, reflects upon it and tries to live up to it'.[50] Germany needs these kinds of positive ideals to strive to become the nation it wants to be and to worry less about what it is or was. Pining for these lost myths or trying to be something that it's not will hold the country back, when it needs to look forward, especially as economic headwinds intensify and gnaw at the underpinnings of its solidarity.

4
Cracked Pipes

> Whoever acts like a worm can't complain later if
> they get stepped on
>
> Immanuel Kant

Flames leap as molten iron pours from giant ladles at ThyssenKrupp's Duisburg steel plant, home to one of Europe's largest blast furnaces. Near where the Rhine and Ruhr rivers meet, iron ore and other materials are combined with primeval force to form steel – the quintessential material of the modern age. Inside the colossal space, fire and darkness alternate as liquid metal begins its journey to become products like washing machines or car parts.

Within the furnace's seven-foot-thick walls, temperatures soar to 2,000 degrees Celsius and workers lumber around in suits made of reflective silver foil to protect them from the searing heat. The Schwelgern 1 furnace, dubbed the 'black giant', devours fiendish quantities of fuel. Along with its three siblings, the steel-making colossus consumes energy on a scale rivalling that of Hamburg, Germany's second-largest city, and accounts for about 3 per cent of the country's annual greenhouse-gas emissions. Running day and night, the 360-foot-high oven looms over its surroundings like an infernal temple, ceaselessly performing rituals of sacrifice.

The ultimate deity here and in the hissing chemical plants, the cavernous turbine halls and the casting foundries that make up Germany's industrial underworld, is energy. Without energy, no steel. Without steel, no screws, no pistons and no cars. Without energy to make steam, no chemicals that keep kitchens clean, supermarkets stocked, and homes warm and bright. For an industrial economy without abundant energy, there is no prosperity for some and much less for all. It's the lifeblood that keeps foundries smelting, chemical plants cracking, and press plants stamping. Germany's success is inextricably bound to it and by extension so is the country's identity as a manufacturing power. Whereas the United States has cowboys and pioneers as icons of its self-image, Germany has engineers and industrialists.

But even before decades of Germany's energy policy imploded in the aftermath of Russia's war in Ukraine, its manufacturing prowess was already under strain. Producing steel for automobiles, glass for lighting, or fertiliser for agriculture has become increasingly uncompetitive. Despite Germany's reputation for manufacturing resilience, the country has been steadily deindustrialising for decades, struggling to compete with Asian countries where energy and labour are cheaper. Until recently, factory closures in Germany were managed at a pace that avoided the depressions seen in places like the South Wales valleys or Youngstown, Ohio. But since Russia's invasion of Ukraine in February 2022 severed Germany's relationship with its main energy supplier, the future of the country's industrial base has accelerated a structural decline, dealing a double blow by undermining prosperity and the nation's self-image at the same time.

The nearly 1 million households directly reliant on energy-intensive industries have started to feel the aftershocks first hand, but the impact will ripple well beyond steel mills and chemical plants. Instead of diligence and foresight, the country chose expediency and dirty deals. After acting for decades like it could siphon fuel from an unsavoury neighbour without consequences, the reckoning has come for the House of Germany.

Deep trouble

In late September 2022 a Danish F-16 fighter jet roared eastwards over the Baltic Sea at around 700 knots, its pilot scouring the water's surface for disturbances among the calm autumn waves. In the dead of the previous night, Sweden's Seismology Agency in Uppsala had recorded four large explosions in the deep. Around the same time 800 miles away, in an unremarkable office block in the Swiss town of Zug, nightshifters at the control centre of the Nord Stream pipeline watched as pressure plunged in the subsea link connecting Germany to Russia. Someone, or something, had severed the main artery piping natural gas to the beating heart of Europe's biggest industrial economy.

Just off the Danish island of Bornholm the pilot from a squadron usually charged with warding Russian heavy bombers away from NATO airspace spied a circle of bubbles half a mile wide.[1] Cheap Siberian gas that was intended to fire the furnaces of German industry was bubbling to the surface and dispersing into the atmosphere.

The sabotage on both the functional Nord Stream 1 line as well as the completed, but not yet operational, Nord Stream 2 marked the ignominious end of decades of German energy policy. The impact of the attack was mainly symbolic as the Kremlin had already ceased deliveries through that route in retaliation for Germany supporting Ukraine, but the detonations showed once and for all that there was no going back. German officials raced to avoid winter blackouts, pleading with citizens to turn down thermostats, shut off lights, and skip hot showers.[2] The levels of gas reserves became front-page news after the country hadn't noticed that Moscow-controlled Gazprom, which owned the biggest storage facility, had almost completely drained it in the months before the invasion of Ukraine. In order to guard against the risk of freezing households, experts worked out detailed scenarios over what businesses would be shut off and when. The minister for economic affairs Robert Habeck, from the environmentalist Green Party, was forced to take uncomfortable steps, ordering mothballed coal power plants back on line, extending nuclear reactors, and sealing deals with autocratic leaders in Qatar to secure deliveries of liquefied natural gas. In the end, Germany got through the winter without much-feared rationing, demonstrating its resilience. The government's quick action was key, but so was a warm winter. And there were costs.

As gas prices surged to record levels, energy-intensive companies halted production. Manufacturers of products from fertiliser and glass to paper and chemicals scaled back their output and some of those cuts have become permanent. That further sapped Germany's industrial strength, which has been on a downward slide since 2017.[3] Households would also feel the pain as bills surged, stoking anger and frustration with the government. For some Germans, the price of Ukraine's independence was too high and the risks were too great. But there was no turning back the clock. The comfortable days of relying on cheap Russian energy imports to heat homes and power factories were over, and an uncertain new chapter was being forced upon Europe's largest economy.

Germany had lost the battle for energy long before the Nord Stream pipes were sundered at the bottom of the Baltic Sea. The careless approach to such a critical issue reflects the country's tendency to focus on its own needs and obscure those of the world around it. What mattered to Germany was cheap energy. Consequences had not been taken into account. It was in many ways like the actions of a pampered child used to getting its way.

Dating back to Chancellor Willy Brandt in the 1970s, German governments had been turning to Russia for energy. Besides being relatively cheap, the supplies gave Germany an additional source of gas and oil as North Sea production declined, and politically it opened up a chance for dialogue with East Germany's overlord. During the rule of Gerhard Schröder – who after his departure from office became a well-paid lobbyist for Russian state-owned companies – the dependency deepened, with the approval of Nord Stream I, a link that would pump gas directly from Russia to Germany, bypassing Ukraine's pipeline system. While governments in Kyiv and Warsaw as well as NATO officials in Brussels warned of security risks, German officials ignored them, insisting they understood Moscow better. Not even Russia's 2014 annexation of Crimea or the downing of Malaysia Airlines Flight 17 over eastern Ukraine by Moscow-backed militants (an incident that killed almost 300 civilians, including four Germans) could get Berlin to reconsider its approach. To be fair, boardrooms across the country were cheering the government. Russia had the cheapest energy on offer, and Germany needed vast quantities of it. As is often the case, political and commercial interests aligned and circumspection took a backseat.

Germany was fully committed to its energy policy and nothing was going to change that. When US President Donald Trump told the UN General Assembly in September 2018 that Germany was growing too reliant on Russian gas, Foreign Minister Heiko Maas smiled disparagingly and shook his head. The threat of sanctions by Joe Biden's administration didn't sway Germany either. For years, Angela Merkel dodged responsibility by labelling the Nord Stream 2 pipeline as a 'commercial project', a tactic that Olaf Scholz adopted in his bid to succeed her as chancellor. 'I want to say very clearly that in the US, there's a false understanding that we'll become very dependent on Russian gas, but that's not correct when you look at the overall energy mix in Germany,' he said in a campaign debate in May 2021.[4]

A few months later, he would learn how mistaken he was. Shortly after being appointed to lead Germany in December of that year, and with Russia massing troops menacingly on Ukraine's border, Scholz gathered his advisors in Berlin and asked whether there was a Plan B if Putin decided to weaponise energy – only to be told, there wasn't one. If a cold snap hit in early spring, Germany's depleted gas reserves might only last days.

In the end, it turned out, the only real alternative was to buy liquefied natural gas from Qatar and the United States, which is structurally more expensive than using pipelines because of the transport costs and the conversion to and from liquid form on both ends. That strategy involved setting up the country's first intake terminals, including around half-a-dozen ships leased and moored off the Baltic and North Sea coasts. It was a rapid turnaround and a testament to Germany's ability to act in a crisis, but the sudden move to secure infrastructure and supplies was costly. Robert Habeck lamented that Germany had to pay 'moon prices' to shore up its energy security.

For a country considered careful and diligent, it was an incredibly naive approach. Energy is the lifeblood of an industrial economy, but price rather than prudence was the guiding factor for German policy. Russia was a cheap and willing supplier, so the answer to the needs of the growing economy more often than not was another contract with Moscow. Entire industrial sectors were hooked up to Russian energy supplies. Dependence was especially deep in towns like BASF's home of Ludwigshafen on the Rhine and Schwedt in the former East Germany, where an ageing oil refinery processes Russian crude to supply Berlin with gasoline and jet fuel. Security risks were rationalised away under the self-serving policy of *Wandel durch Handel* (change through trade), which posited that authoritarian regimes could be brought to heel if there was enough money at stake and interests were intertwined. But that proved to be woefully misguided, as not all countries are as mercantilist as Germany.

Before Putin ordered tanks to roll towards Kyiv, Russia had supplied more than half of Germany's gas and the reliance was set to intensify with Nord Stream 2. The fossil fuel had taken on an outsized role in the country's energy mix because of decisions to exit two major sources of electricity at the same time: nuclear and coal. But it wasn't an inevitable choice. When Merkel set the clock ticking on the shutdown of atomic reactors following the Fukushima disaster in Japan in 2011, there were eleven years to prepare and develop more wind and solar sources, which are the main domestic alternatives available. But gas was a convenient choice and labelled a 'bridging fuel' to supply a clean, green Germany up to an indefinite point in the future.

Germany's bet on Russian energy could only have been saved by an improbably swift improvement in relations with Moscow. In some boardrooms, hopes flickered that Putin might be deposed after the Blitzkrieg-like invasion fell short, leading to sanctions getting lifted and for gas to flow again like 'normal'. Instead, Russia moved its economy to a war footing and sidestepped sanctions by reimporting necessary components via old Soviet channels in Central Asia.[5] Vladimir Putin's gas gambit didn't quite work as planned, but for Germany, there was no going back.

The crisis exposed a fundamental miscalculation in prioritising economic expediency over long-term resilience, another serious knock to the country's reputation as diligent. At the core of the strategic blunder is the naive assumption of its political and business elite that German fortitude is enduring and will win out in the end. *Wandel durch Handel* was asserted as a truism because it conveniently echoed the country's own mercantilist mindset. Since post-war Germany is mainly a commercial enterprise, its leaders struggle to fathom that other countries might pursue objectives that don't always maximise economic returns.

The bill for the country's missteps on energy is adding up. High prices and uncertainty increase the pressure on heavy industry, and the response has been to curtail investment and eliminate jobs. BASF plans to cut back in Ludwigshafen as the world's biggest chemical maker tilts production to locations with cheaper energy, like the United States and China.[6] Concerns about whether Germany will be in a position to supply sufficient power at competitive prices risks a mass exodus of industrial plants and jobs, warned Yasmin Fahimi, the head of the *Deutscher Gewerkschaftsbund* (German Trade Union Confederation).[7] So while Putin may not have managed to cow Germany into submission with a winter of fear, the Russian president's energy war has still been a blow to Europe's powerhouse economy.

Faustian pact

It was meant to be so different. About a decade before the Danish fighter pilot pinpointed the gas leak near the island of Bornholm, a grand marquee was filled with the clinking of champagne glasses and the genteel music of the Baltic Youth Philharmonic Orchestra. Angela Merkel and Dmitry Medvedev, who served as Russian president during a job swap with Putin, beamed as they turned a mocked-up pipeline tap to mark the opening of the $10 billion Nord Stream 1.

The project showed that 'we rely on secure and resilient cooperation with Russia in the future,' Merkel said at the 2011 event in a woodland clearing in the coastal town of Greifswald, home to the ghostly remains of an East German nuclear plant and where the 750-mile pipeline makes landfall. 'The purchasing countries and Russia will profit equally,'[8] said the chancellor at the prestige project, which comes ashore in her election district in the northeast corner of Germany. Medvedev agreed. 'We have a bright future ahead of us,' said the Russian, who after the invasion of Ukraine threatened Germany and Europe with nuclear destruction and freezing to death.[9] As the festivities in Greifswald continued, a grin spread across the face of Johannes Teyssen, the chief executive of German utility E.ON. His satisfaction was emblematic of the corporate elite's enthusiasm. Germany had secured a steady flow of cheap energy and that meant the money would start flowing even if that also meant fuelling Russia's imperial ambitions.

The German champion of the dirty deal was Schröder. The pipeline project wouldn't have seen the light of day if he hadn't hurriedly approved it in one of his last acts as chancellor. Putin rewarded the man derisively referred to as 'Gas Gerd' with a stream of cushy boardroom posts that paid for lavish holiday homes on the Aegean Sea and other luxuries that would have been unaffordable on a politician's pension. In return, Schröder has been a useful idiot for Putin, describing the Russian leader in the past as a 'flawless democrat' and legitimising him in the eyes of Germany and the West. Although Schröder has been shunned by Scholz, who rose to SPD general secretary under the former chancellor, he hasn't become a complete pariah for Germany's elite. Representatives of most major parties attended his eightieth birthday celebration in 2024, despite his unapologetic tone towards the invasion. The event was a minor media event and took place at Borchardt, a glitzy schnitzel eatery that Hollywood star Tom Cruise has called his favourite restaurant in Berlin (at least according to its website). While stepping out for a cigarette, one attendee made light of Schröder's obsequious loyalty to the Kremlin, joking to journalists that 'Putin has already left'.[10]

An industrial economy can't run without power, and Germany has few resources of its own but still has to compete with the United States and China, where energy is bountiful and affordable. So while there's a strategic rationale for seeking out the best deal, Germany didn't follow the old adage *'Lieber Vorsicht als Nachsicht'* (the German version of 'better safe than sorry') and is paying the price. Germany used to be energy rich, but that was a long time ago.

The early era of German industrialisation was fuelled by veins of black gold in the Ruhr Valley. Workers scrabbled deep underground at sites like the Zollverein colliery in Essen. Multiple deep-shaft coal mines opened in the 1820s, and around them sprouted steel mills and processing plants that established the country as an industrial and military power. The dirtiest fossil fuel also played a crucial role in Germany's reconstruction, with mining employment peaking at over 600,000 workers in the late 1950s.[11] Coal and lignite (a soft, wet and dirtier variant of the fuel) have continued to power factories and cities, and helped make the country one of the world's worst carbon polluters.[12] Germany has accepted the fact that it needs to quit coal to make good on commitments under the 2015 Paris climate agreements. But it's been a bumpy road and has become a game of political one-upmanship. Merkel's administration settled on a 2038 exit date, which Scholz's government accelerated to 2030 at the prodding of the Greens. None of these target dates bring the vision of clean industry any closer, but they do unsettle the workers and communities caught in the rhetorical crossfire.

The transition is difficult in part because the overhaul of the energy system is more than an abstract project but has implications for the country's identity and has even reshaped the landscape. That's evident when FC Schalke 04 and Borussia Dortmund play each other in one of the fiercest rivalries in German football. Both teams are based in the smokestack Ruhr region, and matches pit the region's premier mining team against its steel-making nemesis. The Ruhr region that envelops both cities is indelibly marked by industry and mining. While deep-shaft coal mining here ceased in 2018, engineers will continue to work underground to prevent effluence seeping into the water supply and to prevent hillsides from collapsing. Known as *Ewigskeitaufgaben* (eternity tasks), the engineering works will quite literally go on so long as humans live in the Ruhr region.[13] The cultural legacy of generations of miners also remains. As the teams prepare to walk out onto the pitch before kick-off, Schalke supporters rise to sing the *Steigerlied* (miner's song) that wishes fellow pitmen luck as they descend into the perilous black below.

Aside from cultural associations, the energy transition sucks up vast resources. The coal exit includes compensating companies and regions most impacted by the closure of plants and lignite mines, massive landscape-scarring, open-cast pits. The price tag for leaving coal behind: €40 billion. Alongside the challenge of replacing its only native energy commodity, Germany shut another door when it decided to phase out nuclear power at a cost of over €24 billion.[14]

Shutting down atomic reactors was a German decision and the result of a long tradition of opposition. Straddling the Iron Curtain, the country was positioned among the first to be annihilated in a nuclear war. In the 1980s, pop singer Nena gave voice to that fear with the global hit '99 Luftballons'. The Chernobyl disaster in 1986 further fuelled anti-nuclear sentiment, when swathes of Germany were covered in radioactive fallout. Fears of contamination led to crops being destroyed and sand replaced in playgrounds. The Greens rose to prominence as a political force from that episode. Phasing out nuclear power was top of the agenda when the party entered government for the first time in 1998 as the junior partner to Schröder's Social Democrats. The result was a landmark nuclear-exit deal in 2000, and the power source remains taboo for the Greens even if it is a low-carbon source of electricity.

Early in her second term, Merkel's administration softened the agreement and extended the lifespans of nuclear reactors by as long as fourteen years. Just months after the Bundestag approved the move, an underwater earthquake unleashed a tsunami that overwhelmed the Fukushima Daiichi nuclear power plant, knocking out the reactors' primary and back-up cooling systems. As Japanese engineers fought to avert a catastrophic meltdown, Merkel raced to avoid a political disaster at home.

In the days following the Fukushima Daiichi disaster, protesters were massing across the country and opinion polls showed 80 per cent of Germans opposed the nuclear extension.[15] Merkel wasn't in a great place when the disaster struck, with the economy flat-lining due to the global financial crisis. The European sovereign-debt crisis was also still unfolding, and voters were unhappy with her support for multi-billion-euro bailout packages for Greece and feared much larger tabs for Italy, Portugal and Spain. Her Christian Democrats lagged behind the Greens as elections loomed in the state of Baden-Württemberg, a key industrial stronghold that's home to Porsche and Mercedes-Benz. Merkel was caught between the calculus of power and ensuring Germany's long-term energy security. She chose politics. In her memoirs, Merkel denies accelerating the nuclear exit for political reasons, asserting that public safety was her primary concern. She doesn't, however, explain why she didn't follow Japan in pursuing a more rapid closure of nuclear reactors.

After just two days, she began to undo her decision. The new plan called for all reactors to be shut down by the end of 2022. It was a shock, and the share prices of energy companies plunged at the surprise announcement. Lawsuits followed against the government, leading to eventual compensation. The about-face cemented Merkel's control of the centre of politics in Germany, but meant the country would burn more coal and gas to make up the difference. That left Germany with the most carbon-intensive electricity system in Western Europe.[16]

While Russia's invasion of Ukraine led to a brief extension of Germany's nuclear-plant licences, the final three were taken offline in 2023. Although surveys suggest most Germans believe the exit was a mistake and triggered a revival of pro-nuclear rhetoric from some parties,[17] a return to the atomic age looks improbable. Private investors are unlikely to risk money on new reactors in Germany, given the country's past flip-flops. Also, recent experiences raise questions about whether new reactors would bring much relief. Pro-nuclear France has struggled with reliability in recent years, and the UK's Hinkley Point has suffered delays and cost overruns.

Germany's hasty exit from nuclear energy is yet another instance where its idealistic tendencies backfired, leaving the nation in a precarious situation. Much like the misguided faith in the idea that importing Russian gas would nudge Moscow towards democracy, this abrupt policy shift was driven by ideals rather than hard realities. In this case, the fear of nuclear risks overshadowed the pragmatic need for a stable and diversified energy mix. The decision, fuelled by environmental aspirations and public pressure, quickly became the lodestar for policy, ignoring the long-term ramifications. Now Germany finds itself grappling with energy insecurity and soaring costs, consequences of letting idealism steer policy without a clear-eyed assessment of the potential fallout.

The consequences leave Germany with few options. Committing to liquefied natural gas means baking in higher costs than rivals like the United States and China, along with environmental impacts. The other alternative is going all in on the *Energiewende*, but the transition to a clean energy system hasn't gone according to plan.

Green shoots

Germany's clean-energy shift hinges on places like Bergrheinfeld in tradition-rich Bavaria. High-voltage power lines carrying electricity from North Sea wind farms to manufacturing heartlands in the south are supposed to pass through the picturesque town in the lush Franconian wine country. Without them, Germany cannot hope to resolve the tension between its climate targets and keeping industry competitive. On the surface, the town of 5,300 on the banks of the Main River appears idyllic. There's a digital cafe for seniors, walking groups, summer wine tents and cinema festivals. But when it comes to the proposition of hosting electricity superhighways, they've revolted.

It's been over a decade since German officials decided the country needed electricity superhighways and they still haven't been built.[18] Originally slated to open in 2025, the SuedLink (South Link) transmission line should eventually carry electricity to Bavaria and Baden-Württemberg, home to advanced manufacturing companies like BMW, Bosch and Siemens. The project includes a four-metre-wide tunnel that will run for 5.2 kilometres under the Elbe River in northern Germany. For the total 700-kilometre length of the line, just over 90 kilometres had been built by the end of 2024. By contrast, China has already completed thirty-four such projects and is constructing others.

As well as Germany's perennially slow bureaucracy, the project is meeting resistance from citizens protest groups like Bürgerinitiative Bergrheinfeld e.V. Its members would rather Germany build a decentralised electricity grid made up of small-scale rooftop solar. But the country's grid-management authorities have ruled that out, saying there's no way such a system would cover demand from major cities and industrial sites.[19] The citizens' group is holding firm, insisting that the plans for the electricity superhighway are of 'no use'.[20] Unfortunately for grid planners, they're not alone. Across Germany, there are over fifty such groups promising to fight against the electricity superhighway plans. Yet when it comes to restoring Germany's energy competitiveness, time is precious and the country has dragged its feet too long, with grid expansion running at least a decade behind schedule.[21]

Despite the headaches, Germany's *Energiewende* has notched up remarkable achievements. The country has already committed in excess of €500 billion to the transition, a figure that's expected to double.[22] That would be roughly four times more in adjusted terms than the United States spent on the entire Apollo space programme, which included six manned landings on the moon.[23] High spending has yielded results. In 2023 renewable energy provided over half of the country's electricity generation, comfortably beating coal and gas.[24] Construction of wind and solar plants reduced Germany's emissions from electricity generation by over 40 per cent compared to 1990.[25] On blustery and clear days, renewable energy can provide most of Germany's electricity supply. As more wind and solar farms are built, the share prices of their manufacturing firms will rise.

But that's not the full picture. In summer months when demand is slow but solar and wind generation is strong, spot power prices can become negative. That means utilities are paying industrial consumers to use power in order to keep the network balanced. That's a result of an inefficient grid and insufficient investment in storage systems to keep cheap, green power for when it's needed. And getting more renewables into the electricity system is, relatively speaking, the easy part. When it comes to transporting people and goods, heating homes and offices, Germany still gets 70 per cent of its energy from fossil fuels.[26] Making those sectors emissions-free marks a greater technical and economic challenge, and the tasks ahead are daunting.

To cut oil use in line with its climate targets, Germany needs to get 15 million electric cars on its roads by 2030, and over 1 million charging points to keep the cars moving.[27] The country also needs to shift most of its home and office heating to electric heat pumps, a challenge made harder by a worsening shortage of skilled technicians (see more in chapter 6). Still, even those are relatively straightforward tasks. The country faces a more intractable challenge in turning renewable electricity into combustible, clean-burning industrial fuels (such as hydrogen). These steps will require massive amounts of renewable energy as the country electrifies processes currently based around fossil fuels. The government estimates capacity will need to increase by half by 2035 compared to the early 2020s, and it may need to almost double by 2040.[28] If Germany doesn't accelerate the rollout, electricity prices could more than double.[29] That's a gloomy outlook for households and spells uncertainty for the hundreds of thousands of families that rely on glass-making, chemicals and steel to pay their bills.

Launched with the noble goal of creating a carbon-free future, the *Energiewende* sought to shift Germany away from fossil fuels towards clean energy sources like wind and solar. The decision to abandon nuclear power, a reliable and low-carbon energy source, made that objective more difficult and investment didn't keep pace. It points to the struggle to follow up on aspirations with concrete policy measures. At the end of the day, Germany wants to be seen as an environmental leader but doesn't want to make the sacrifices and commitment that it will take to get there. That goes for the elite as well as wide swathes of the public. While Germans profess that they want to protect nature, powerful 'not in my backyard' movements fight tooth and nail against renewable-energy projects, proposals to set speed limits on the Autobahn are batted away as an affront to public freedoms, and it is argued that the combustion engine can still play a role in a green future. The dissonance stems from Germany's desperate need to feel good about itself. That feeling is more important than actually doing good.

But the fallout from its national insecurities is starting to catch up with Germany. Energy-intensive industries are relocating, frustrated by high costs and regulatory uncertainty. In the East German chemical triangle of Leuna, Buna and Bitterfeld, Dow Chemical has cut back and its fellow American industrial conglomerate 3M has decided to close a plant entirely.[30] Further social instability looms as a result. 'A dangerous underlying mood of fear of relegation and disillusionment with the state is spreading among the population, which only plays into the hands of the radicals and populists,' said Michael Vassiliadis, head of Germany's mining and chemical workers' union.[31] The steady pace of deindustrialisation has exposed the fragility of an approach that has often prioritised grandstanding over tangible action. Yet new dreams keep coming.

So-called green hydrogen is touted as the solution to resolving the tension between the competing visions of industrial superpower and environmental idyll. Hydrogen burns hot and clean, reacting with oxygen in the air to form water, rather than carbon dioxide. The gas can be extracted from water by using an electric current to split off the hydrogen and oxygen elements. If that electrolysis process is powered by renewable energy, then the fuel is considered emissions free. Germany's government and industry are putting serious money behind projects for green hydrogen to fire furnaces in the future. Nationally, the country has set up a €9 billion hydrogen fund that disperses grants to hydrogen projects. One proposal includes the H2 Mare plan, one of Germany's flagship hydrogen projects, a collection of initiatives to develop electrolysers that can turn wind power into combustible hydrogen gas.[32]

What looks like a perfect system on paper has a major flaw: a lack of wind and sun. Despite the fact that we all enjoy the same sun, its rays aren't evenly distributed. For Germany, that's especially an issue during winter months when demand is high for lighting and heating. The country also has a relatively small coastline, where winds are steady and reliable. The government is aware of this dilemma and has acknowledged that Germany won't be able to generate sufficient renewable power to produce hydrogen at competitive prices.

Instead, the plan is to import green hydrogen from countries with better conditions for renewable power, such as European neighbours Portugal and Spain or further afield like Canada and Saudi Arabia. But can German industry offset those increased transport and infrastructure costs? That's a big if and means the country needs to focus even more on productivity and technological innovation. Otherwise, the jobs and the prosperity will go elsewhere, closer to where the energy is. It would be a similar evolution to the one that saw industrial clusters form near Germany's coal belts in the nineteenth century.

Ashes to ashes

In many ways, the rise and fall of the Krupp steel-making dynasty underscores Germany's inseparable bond to energy. Like the Rockefeller family (emigrants, incidentally, from Germany's Rhineland), the Krupp empire was built on fossil fuels. For almost 200 years, the family, for good and ill, shaped Germany's particular take on capitalism. From expanded social-protection schemes for workers that were later adopted throughout Europe, to an intensifying belligerence that led to two calamitous world wars, the Krupp family played a facilitating role.

In the beginning, there was water. Having fled the Netherlands as refugees from the Spanish counter-reformation, the Krupps' first foray into steel-making came in 1811 at a water-powered mill on the outskirts of Essen in the Ruhr Valley. At that time, Germany was a patchwork of duchies, principalities and kingdoms, hemmed in by France to the west and Austria to the east. Friedrich Krupp too was constrained by the Berne stream that turned the foundry's forging hammer.[33] The flows proved fickle. The family's real breakthrough came under his son and heir, Alfred Krupp, and the emergence of coal.

Steadily building up the business, he finally had enough money by 1837 to purchase a coal-fired steam engine, allowing for a tremendous increase in output and profits. It was the start of the coal age, which combined with Germany's river systems would provide easy transport for materials and finished goods. The region would boom, fuelling outsized and destructive ambitions in the process.

Across the Ruhr, mine shafts were dug in places like Bottrop, Gelsenkirchen and Oberhausen, and metal and iron mills sprang up around them. After lagging behind the industrial advances of Britain and France for decades, the regions that would form modern Germany were catching up at breakneck speed. Political turmoil accompanied the shift. An emerging middle and working class sought to loosen aristocratic rule, which led to a failed national revolution in 1848. The resulting lack of orders prompted a relative setback for the Krupp family's growing influence, as Alfred melted down the family silver and sold it to the Düsseldorf mint.[34] But business was roaring again by the 1860s, and Alfred made a critical move to cement the family's position at the top of German industry by purchasing coal mines to feed his steel business with cheap energy. The wealth and power was manifested in the family's Villa Hügel residence in Essen, a sprawling neoclassical manor with a copper-green roof and Grecian pillars.

Growing rich and powerful on the back of coal, the unifying German state looked to break its territorial shackles. Alfred Krupp became the emergent nation's armourer, earning him the moniker *Kanonenkönig* (cannon king). When a confederation of German states prevailed against France in the war of 1870–1, many called it a victory of Krupp's forged steel guns over French bronze weapons. The company's association with German militarism didn't end there. Its prowess in artillery production led to an international arms race as Armstrong in England and Schneider-Creusot in France strained to keep up. As Europe plunged into war in 1914, the forces of Kaiser Wilhelm II fought with Krupp guns and aboard Krupp-built ships.[35]

When Adolf Hitler was elected chancellor in January 1933, the Krupp company was central to his rearmament plans. The firm built submarines, tanks, artillery, naval guns, armour plate, munitions and other armaments for the Nazi war machine. The Führer even exhorted Germany's youth to be 'nimble as greyhounds, tough as leather and hard as Krupp steel'.[36] Upon Germany's eventual defeat, Alfred Krupp von Bohlen und Halbach was tried and convicted of crimes against humanity for his use of slave labour, and sentenced to twelve years in prison. Wrecked by Allied bombers, his steelworks were steadily rebuilt.

While Krupp was imprisoned, European diplomats worked to make sure Germany's energy and metal industries could never combine to threaten peace again. In 1950, France, West Germany, Italy and the Benelux countries signed the European Coal and Steel Pact to pool resources, an agreement that eventually developed into the European Union. Upon the commutation of Krupp's sentence to three years in prison and his release in 1951, he returned to head the company and by 1958 it had again become Germany's biggest in terms of revenue. But it was also the beginning of the end.

Energy would prove the eventual undoing of Krupp. As global trade was liberalised in the second half of the twentieth century, it became clear that mining the Ruhr was more expensive than imports. After peaking in 1955, German coal production fell into rapid decline. Steel would soon follow. While Germany accounted for around a tenth of global crude-steel output in 1967, the share had almost halved by 1990. Krupp's once-swaggering steel business was forced into a merger with its rival Thyssen in 1997. China's inclusion in the World Trade Organisation in 2001, which cut tariffs on the country's goods, further exposed German steel-makers to lower-cost competition from mills powered by abundant coal. These cheaper steel imports flooded Europe, and by 2010, Germany's share of global production had almost halved again.[37] In an ill-fated bid to escape its German roots, the company expanded into the Americas with advanced steel facilities but faltered due to cost overruns, delays, and a steel market downturn, culminating in heavy losses and eventual divestment.

The consummate material of the modern age, going into everything from automobiles to wind turbines and household cutlery, was increasingly made elsewhere. What remained of Krupp's dynasty was struggling to break even and the break-up of the region's biggest industrial employer loomed large. The concern was so severe that the Catholic Church intervened in 2018. 'There are signs that the unity and continued existence of the company, which is so important for Essen and the Ruhr region, is at stake,' said Essen's Roman Catholic Bishop Franz-Josef Overbeck.[38]

But even the Holy See has little influence over industrial cycles, especially when geopolitical events are added to the mix. European Union efforts to trim pollution had further dented the business case for steel, and for some of ThyssenKrupp's peers in Germany, Russia's invasion of Ukraine was the last straw. ArcelorMittal (the world's second-largest steel-maker, trailing naturally behind a state-owned Chinese company) announced plans to close a blast furnace in Bremen and a factory that produces wire rods in Hamburg. Vallourec, a French manufacturer of steel pipes, closed a century-old plant in Düsseldorf and another in Mülheim an der Ruhr.

The former German icon has continued to retrench as well. It sold its elevator division in 2020 to offset mounting losses in steel, and in 2024 it started plans to shrink steel operations by a quarter. That's bad news for Duisburg, home of the company's main steel mill. 'The thousands of employees are the backbone of the steel industry in Duisburg, and Duisburg is the heart of the steel industry in Europe,' Mayor Sören Link said after the latest round of cuts. Underlining local fears about falling behind, he added, 'Preserving jobs in Duisburg must be top priority.'[39]

The city at the confluence of the Rhine and the Ruhe isn't the only municipality counting the cost of Germany's energy tribulations. Industrial decline risks intensifying into something resembling the collapse of British heavy industry and the decline of Detroit in the 1980s. Almost 7 million people live in areas of Germany blighted by industrial decline such as the Ruhr region, Saarland, and the Lusatia mining region in the east of the country. They face jarring disruptions, even though it was long clear that Germany would struggle to compete with the scale and costs that India and China could offer. But instead of managing the transition more smoothly and shaping the change, Germany tried to preserve the status quo.

Just as Krupp's rise hinged on energy, the same goes for the survival of what's left of the industrial empire. That hangs on a successful switch to green hydrogen. Can Germany produce or buy enough at a competitive-cost level? Will an infrastructure of pipelines and tankers be ready in time? Will industrial users be ready in time?

There are a lot of doubts, but there have been some glimmers of hope. After years of slow progress under Merkel, Olaf Scholz's administration has tried to accelerate the transition. In early 2023 the government unveiled measures aimed at tripling the speed of Germany's harnessing of renewable energy. It called for every federal state to ensure that 2 per cent of Germany's surface area (equivalent to the size of the Pearl River Delta in China) is made available for onshore wind farms, double the previously allocated space. When it comes to grid planning, permit procedures will be simplified and hurdles lowered, including giving the construction of renewables precedence over the protection of species until climate neutrality is achieved. The plan has shown early results, with an acceleration in the construction of solar and wind farms.

But the political volatility that comes with sudden change has raised questions about maintaining that momentum. Fragmentation poses the risk that establishment parties veer towards populist positions to win over unsettled voters. With the outlook for energy-intensive industry uncertain, much will depend on the country's performance in advanced manufacturing where know-how is a more important factor than energy prices.

Overall, higher-value manufacturing directly and indirectly employs around 15 million people, and making complex machinery has been part of the economy that's strengthened in recent decades. But headwinds are growing here too, especially in the automotive sector. Here too, preserving the status quo was more important than pushing for progress. That means the gloom over Duisburg and the Ruhr Valley Rust Belt could spread to cities like Wolfsburg, Munich and Stuttgart, as a century of automotive leadership starts getting unplugged.

5
Busted Boiler

'Everything in the world ends by chance and fatigue.'
Heinrich Heine

Before dawn on 5 August 1888, Bertha Benz quietly woke her teenage sons and took them on the first joyride in history, creating a milestone for the auto industry and Germany in the process. Two years previously, her husband Carl Benz invented the world's first functional automobile. Although he held the patent, Bertha was the driving force, literally and figuratively. She used her dowry to fund Carl's work and played an active role in refining the vehicle, which her fellow Germans dismissed or feared. Even the Catholic Church condemned it as the 'devil's carriage'.

Rather than working to shift perceptions, Carl was tinkering in his workshop and so Bertha decided to take matters into her own hands. Leaving a brief note, Bertha set off on the world's first road trip, driving over 60 miles from Mannheim to her parents' home in Pforzheim. Along the way she bought rudimentary fuel from a chemist, cleared a clogged fuel line with a hat pin, insulated a frayed spark-plug wire with her garter belt, and invented brake pads by convincing a shoemaker to add leather to the worn wooden blocks. The jaunt was also, strictly speaking, illegal as the vehicle's permit was only valid for Mannheim. 'She was more daring than I,' Carl Benz later remarked.

Bertha's bold journey* was a moment of commercial validation and visionary courage – qualities Germany would channel to achieve automotive pre-eminence. It's a trailblazing ethos that the country would do well to embrace once again, as the value of its traditional strengths fades.

Even before that historic driving test, Germany had been good at making things, especially shaping and assembling bits of metal into desirable objects like wrought ironwork, tableware and printing presses. That prowess has been the foundation of the promise of *Wohlstand für Alle* (prosperity for all). Throughout the post-war era, the country has maintained a manufacturing sector that is proportionally larger than in almost all other advanced economies, and skilled manual labour for decades offered a path to material comforts like annual holidays in the snow or sun and a new car now and then.

It's about more than just money. Manufacturing infuses towns and regions with purpose and meaning. Across Germany, streets and squares are named after engineering greats like Werner von Siemens, inventor of the electric tram, and Rudolf Diesel, creator of the eponymous combustion engine. Bertha Benz too has several schools named in her honour. When asked what makes her think of Germany, Angela Merkel summed up the centrality of manufacturing with the reply, 'I think of well-sealed windows. No other country can make such well-sealed and nice windows.'

Yet this pre-eminence is increasingly under threat. Brought low by arrogance and strategic missteps, Germany's automotive workforce is feeling the sting of a lost competitive edge. The travails facing German manufacturing extend beyond the big automotive marques. And just as Germany's economy requires a historic reset, there are signs the country's famed *Erfindergeist* (spirit of invention) has faded. Germany is sliding down patent rankings, overtaken by nimbler and hungrier rivals. Its mighty research base, still a source of hope for renewal, is not giving life to the companies of tomorrow due to suffocating regulations and a cultural aversion to risk, unlike Bertha Benz. Storied companies including chemicals giant BASF

---

* Bertha Benz would likely be more celebrated internationally had it not been for her enthusiastic support of the Nazi Party later in life. Dying before Hitler became leader of Germany, her husband Carl Benz avoided having his reputation besmirched by association with fascism.

and engineering behemoth Siemens are shifting resources outside their homeland to regions with better prospects, leading to a net outflow of capital of more than €650 billion since 2010, according to figures from the Bundesbank.[1]

For populists attacking the country's establishment, Germany's manufacturing decline plays into their hands. In towns and regions where the economic outlook is darkening, parties on the political extremes are gathering strength, and not only in the former east.

Decades after emerging from the ashes of reconstruction, the House of Germany's engine room is sputtering and spewing, raising concerns about how the residents will stay comfortable as rough weather approaches. It also gnaws at the self-assured spirit of invention and industriousness that was once core to Germany's image at home and abroad.

Sunset in Autoland

In the Delta Airlines lounge at Miami Airport in January 2017, Oliver Schmidt and his wife were about to fly back to Germany after their annual vacation in Fort Lauderdale, Florida. For over a decade, the couple had come every Christmas to escape the long, grey winter back home. This trip had seemed like any other, save for a jaunt across to Cuba. After washing his hands following a toilet break, the Volkswagen executive headed out the door to rejoin his wife. Emerging into the light, he spied five agents from the Federal Bureau of Investigation approaching him, changing his life forever.

In hindsight, it was foolhardy for the bald, blue-eyed German to have travelled to Florida. In 2015 he was head of Volkswagen's emissions and environmental office in the United States when the company was caught cheating on regulations. To comply with clean-air rules, Volkswagen equipped diesel-powered vehicles with software that could adjust the engine to run below normal power and performance during a test. Under normal driving conditions, they would spew out as much as forty times the legal limits of nitrogen oxides, compounds that cause smog and damage respiratory health. The number of cars with the so-called cheat device totalled some

11 million worldwide, mostly in Europe. In America, where half a million cars were affected, the company's actions caused around sixty premature deaths from air pollution, according to one study.[2] Others pointed to a substantially higher number of fatalities in Europe.[3] Admitting guilt, Volkswagen eventually spent $35 billion on fines and recalls, but that wasn't the full damage.

The scandal that started on 18 September 2015 with a notice of violation from the US Environmental Protection Agency was the moment that Germany's reputation as an automobile innovator cracked. Diesel wasn't just any technology. It was the 'Made in Germany' answer to the hybrid power-train pushed by Toyota, Volkswagen's long-standing rival for the title of the world's biggest car manufacturer. It was advertised as 'clean diesel', offering the perfect combination of driving performance and efficiency, and without the expense and complexity of combining combustion and electric-power systems. The crisis would also embroil Mercedes-Benz, which would pay a $1.5 billion fine related to its own efforts to dupe regulators.

The German government played a supporting role. With a critical cog of the economy on the line, Chancellor Angela Merkel's administration rallied to protect Volkswagen and the rest of the auto industry. Unlike in the United States, where the vehicles were ruled as unfit for the road, German regulators determined they were fixable. That meant costly recalls of about a year's worth of production, but avoiding what would have been debilitating buy-backs. And then there was a concerted effort at damage control. Clean-air activists were vilified as anti-diesel campaigners,[4] while the transport minister, Alexander Dobrindt, intervened to kill legislation that would have made a class-action-like lawsuit against Volkswagen possible, reacting with hand-written notes: 'We reject it!!! Cancel completely!'[5] It was a clear example of how Germany's political class sees its role as protecting economic actors rather than holding them to account.

Despite having deliberately misled investigators, Schmidt didn't think he could be held personally responsible. After all, he was just following orders (an attitude not unfamiliar in German history). Faced with suspicions from air-pollution researchers, he did his job and dodged any acknowledgement that Volkswagen had installed an illegal device. So with the clean conscience of a good soldier, he had returned to the United

States for holidays and was arrested on conspiracy to defraud the country. Put on trial later in 2017, Schmidt was sentenced to seven years in jail after a plea deal that avoided a potential 169-year sentence. Rather than express contrition for his role in the deadly swindle, Schmidt in interviews bemoaned the conditions in US prisons, such as communal cells and form-filling when it came to family visits.[6]

For Chief Executive Martin Winterkorn, the convictions of Schmidt and four other engineers meant the blame for the fraud could be laid on the actions of rogue employees. Appearing before a Bundestag committee in 2017, the heavy-set Swabian expressed shock upon hearing of the device, claiming he was surprised that something like that was even technically feasible. He joined the outcry and called for a swift and thorough clarification. 'Complete information was and is the order of the day,' he said.

His account was highly questionable. Winterkorn was known as detail-obsessed. At car shows, he would walk around with a tape measure and a magnet to help evaluate the bodywork of rival models. On a visit to an important new plant in Tennessee, he demanded staff attach all chrome components side by side to make sure that they glistened uniformly. After a lengthy internal investigation (which Volkswagen boasted was the biggest in German corporate history), the supervisory board accused Winterkorn of being instrumental in the cover-up. Despite maintaining his innocence, Winterkorn agreed to pay €11.2 million in compensation, triggering Bundestag members to press charges for lying to parliament.

Its reputation in tatters, Volkswagen's management were forced into reinvention to regain the trust of consumers, regulators and investors. The challenge though was massive, and Germany's protection meant Volkswagen didn't fully learn the lessons from the risks of its imperious top-down structure. Instead, it stuck to its traditional approach. In doing so, the Wolfsburg-based company showed how complex a turnaround really was and how ill-suited its methods were for a new automotive era.

The technological changes sweeping the auto industry were unlike anything Volkswagen had faced since Ferdinand Porsche drew up plans for what became the Beetle. Throughout the company's entire history, the fundamental underpinnings of auto-making had remained relatively stable, but everything was changing, and VW attempted the transition with the procedures of an old era. The first race was to turn cars into rolling computers, with software and sensors promising everything from back seat karaoke sessions to automated driving. The second was the shift to electric propulsion. Volkswagen's struggles with both dramatic adjustments epitomise Germany's awkward embrace of new technologies.

Volkswagen is robust but complex and slow-moving. It worked in seven-year product cycles that suited the complexity of the combustion-engine era. Over the course of its empire-building, the company had acquired the mass-market Škoda and SEAT brands in the Czech Republic and Spain, respectively. It also owned luxury brands such as Audi, Porsche, Lamborghini and Bentley. Each of its divisions has its own headquarters, management team and corporate identity. Getting units to collaborate was cumbersome.

Adding to the complexity is Volkswagen's ownership structure. The most powerful group are the descendants of Ferdinand Porsche, which are broadly split into the Porsche and Piëch clans. The group, which holds the majority of the voting rights, comprises dozens of individuals who are several generations removed from the original patriarch. They seek to find a consensus in a process that's typically slow and arduous. Volkswagen's home state of Lower Saxony has a blocking minority. Its interests often, but not always, overlap with the company's powerful works council, which can veto factory closures and has a strong say in management appointments and strategic decisions through its control of half the seats on the supervisory board.

Rounding out the power players is Qatar, which acquired voting shares in the messy aftermath of a takeover battle that involved competing factions of the Porsche-Piëch clan. Public shareholders own mainly non-voting shares, meaning there are few checks on the vanities at the top. With most of the power in the hands of dividend-seeking heirs and job-focused politicians and unions, Volkswagen is structurally predisposed to expansion.

Turning Volkswagen into a software and electric-car leader was never going to be easy, but the stumbles surprised even sceptics. In fairness, it wasn't just Volkswagen that struggled to pivot from combustion engines to a new automotive era. As recently as 2010, the average car contained around 100 processors. That has since risen fifteen-fold, with the onboard computers monitoring everything from tyre pressure and braking to road markings and creature comforts like diffusing the scent of bergamot and blackcurrant, in the case of Mercedes.[7] In-car entertainment has also undergone a radical shift. Instead of fumbling with cassettes or CDs, customers expect seamless, on-demand streaming. The software underpinning that is epic in scale. A modern car contains around 100 million lines of code, which is expected to triple by 2030.[8] It adds up to an unsettling new world for a behemoth like Volkswagen.

Fearing obsolescence, Volkswagen executives in 2019 settled on an ambitious new software project. Although few had programming experience, they decided Volkswagen needed its own operating system, like Microsoft Windows but for cars. The concern was that if they let Silicon Valley take control of the vehicle's brain, Volkswagen might suffer the fate of Nokia, the Finnish firm that dominated mobile phones before they got smart. The vision looked good on a PowerPoint slide: be Apple or Google, but on wheels.

When it came to carrying out the strategy, Volkswagen's management tried to apply development processes that had worked for decades for piston-powered cars. Traditionally automakers build several models on the same underpinnings to spread costs for development and manufacturing. Outwardly, an Audi Q2 SUV looks different to a Skoda Octavia family saloon, but for years they've been built on the same platform. In 2019, Volkswagen decided it would tackle software in a similar way. But while the company understands how to develop a vehicle that can perform at high speeds and stop-and-go traffic, and under both desert heat and arctic cold, software is an entirely different undertaking.

Volkswagen did what it usually does and established a separate division, which became known as Cariad (a mash-up of 'Car, I am digital'). Headquartered in Wolfsburg, a remote industrial town that was built up by the Nazis around the sprawling factory, the unit set to work with around 1,500 software engineers while seeking to recruit more. The division was headed by a former BMW manager who had spent much of his working life building cars, not software. As part of Volkswagen's technology pivot, it also set up a software school that would train the Cariad staff of the future. It quickly found a former food-storage plant, and named it 42 Wolfsburg, the number a reference to the meaning of life offered by the computer in Douglas Adams's novel *The Hitchhiker's Guide to the Galaxy*. Staff taking breaks from coding training could relax by playing table tennis or computer games.

Despite the techie trappings, Cariad's workload was old-school VW. The unit was quickly overloaded with projects and tasked with building three separate operating systems from the ground up: one for pending mass-market cars, a second for more upmarket models like Audis and Porsches, and a third for future electric vehicles. Because of organisational silos, coders and vehicle developers were often physically separated, going against what's considered best practice in the tech industry. It wasn't the only unwritten rule that Volkswagen broke. Software companies also typically have flat management structures, giving developers close access to counterparts on the hardware and operations side. That enables quick-fire troubleshooting and decision-making. Instead, Cariad's task of building software for multiple brands meant going through a hierarchy to reach consensus among fiercely territorial power players. The brands in turn made uncoordinated demands on overstretched software teams. Tiring of turf wars, talented staff like Björn Goerke, former chief technology officer at SAP, left.

When Cariad's first products reached customers, it was clear that something was amiss. Software for the ID.3 electric car, billed as the Beetle of the electric-car era, wasn't actually finished when it went on sale in the autumn of 2020. Despite its almost €40,000 price tag, customers had to go to dealerships for updates in order for certain functions to work. It also took almost a minute for the computer system to load and the car to be ready to drive. Several users reported the loudness of the radio would occasionally increase when the vehicle accelerated. Others noted failures with the navigation system and feedback from parking sensors. In a world where consumers were accustomed to the easy functionality of Apple and Samsung devices, the ID.3 stood out in an unflattering way. Germany's influential *Auto Motor und Sport* magazine gave it a negative review,[9] and the roll-out made a mockery of the brand's advertising slogan: 'If only everything in life was as reliable as a Volkswagen.'

Yet even buggy launch software issues would pale in comparison with the delays in building an operating system for all the group's vehicles. After mounting setbacks, Volkswagen in 2022 announced it would restart the software project. Amid a flood of new competition, the German automotive icon's product pipeline was blocked. Crucial models like a Porsche SUV designed to take on Tesla were pushed back. CEO Herbert Diess, a former BMW executive who joined just before the diesel crisis, resigned as his strategy faltered and opposition from VW power-players mounted.

Oliver Blume, head of the Porsche brand and close to the family, was named as the new CEO and charged with fixing the Cariad mess. His makeshift solution underscored how far Volkswagen had drifted away from the role of innovator. In China the namesake VW brand would use technology from Xpeng, a start-up founded in 2014. Audi would get software from SAIC, a state-owned Chinese automaker headquartered in Shanghai, undermining its claim to *Vorsprung durch Technik* (progress through technology).

Volkswagen's software woes were an extension of the German auto industry's halting technology shift, symptomatic of the nation's struggle to embrace change. Former Volkswagen patriarch Ferdinand Piëch said there wasn't any space in his garage for electric cars, and Winterkorn was slow to develop plug-in vehicles. In 2017, when Tesla introduced the Model 3, which would become the world's top-selling electric car for three straight years, Mercedes complained about the negative impact its first electric SUV would have on its profitability.[10] While BMW was an early mover with the innovative and quirky i3, its electric-car momentum faded after a tepid reception.

The hesitation could be attributed to traditional German perfectionism. Rather than experimenting with new ideas that might fail, Germany tends to stick to what is tried and tested. That was certainly true in the auto industry. The companies were good at the mechanical engineering and thermodynamics of combustion engines. Built up over more than a century, the country has expertise that extends to a deep ecosystem of suppliers. But bits and bytes were foreign terrain.

There was also hubris in play. German auto executives dismissed the threat posed by Tesla and the Chinese, believing they had an unassailable advantage. The attitude was summed up by a remark

Winterkorn made after Volkswagen introduced its first hybrid over a decade after Toyota's Prius, saying when the German auto giant makes a move, it does it 'for real'. But the imperious former boss and the rest of the industry miscalculated badly. Lured by the bravado of CEO Elon Musk, investors have poured money into Tesla instead, giving it vast resources to expand with new factories in Texas, China and outside Berlin. The message has been that Tesla is the future and Volkswagen, Mercedes and BMW are the past, to the extent that the American company was valued in 2024 at more than double the level of the three German automakers combined. BYD, a Chinese version of Tesla, was also worth twice as much as VW.

In China the auto industry had learned production techniques thanks in part to joint ventures with Volkswagen and its peers. Chinese rivals may not have mastered the intricacies of the combustion engine, but they didn't have to. As early as 2001, China designated EV technology as a strategic objective, channelling financial and intellectual resources to the sector. In 2007 the country's nascent industry got another shot in the arm when Wan Gang, an engineer who had worked for Audi in Germany for a decade, became minister of science and technology. Since then, EV development was prioritised in national economic planning.

Starting in 2009, government bodies paid subsidies to EV companies for making vehicles ranging from buses to electric cars. Other measures like restrictions on registrations for combustion-engine vehicles bolstered the shift away from Western technology. Chinese companies also built battery factories and established the largest refining capacity in the world for the chemicals and materials needed to store electricity, giving them a cost advantage. The strategy has paid off for China, which has since become the world's largest market for electric vehicles.

As the transition progresses, Germany's automakers are losing their footing in their most important and lucrative market. With VW, BMW and Mercedes struggling to keep pace in electric-vehicle technology, home-grown manufacturers like BYD, Geely and GAIC have topped the charts in the segment. As China moves to phase out combustion-engine models, German brands are threatened with declining relevance and putting some €35 billion of investment at risk in a country that no longer needs or wants them there. Turn-around efforts face an uphill battle as the playing field tilts towards local players.

The competitive risk isn't isolated. Chinese automakers have used their domestic success to challenge German automakers globally. Helped by their cost advantage when it comes to batteries (the most expensive component in an electric vehicle), 'Made in China' cars have climbed to account for 60 per cent of global EV sales, compared to around 15 per cent for German cars.[11] Even in Europe, Chinese models have accounted for around a quarter of EV sales.[12]

Germany bears a significant part of the blame for China's emergence as a nation of automakers. In a quest to boost bottom lines, China accepted conditions that extracted German engineering know-how in exchange for market access. For decades, China's government insisted that companies partner with local manufacturers to build cars locally to avoid punitive tariffs. But it's looking like Germany traded short-term gain for long-term pain. BYD, a company that learnt how to build cars partly through a partnership with Mercedes, overtook VW as China's overall best-selling car brand in 2023, deposing the German giant from a position it had held since records began in 2008.[13]

This is an insurgency that German automakers will struggle to contain. Since reunification, the industry has leaned into globalisation, developing new sites in the former East Germany and further behind the Iron Curtain. They've also expanded in the United States, but the biggest area for investment has clearly been in China. Volkswagen alone has thirty-three factories in the country, including a plant in the far west that has been dogged by allegations of forced labour. Increasingly, the country has become a production hub for exporting German-engineered products, including sending cars back to Europe.

That physical footprint has affected their approach even as Beijing becomes more adversarial on the global stage. Rather than pull back or hedge, German automakers have opposed measures that might stall China's advance, concerned more with getting squeezed in any trade war. Although a flood of Chinese imports threaten to overwhelm Europe's car market and put jobs and plants at risk, BMW CEO Oliver Zipse has called anti-dumping efforts against China equivalent to 'shooting oneself in the knee'.[14]

And yet, the threat posed is getting closer to home. At Germany's premier auto exhibition in Munich in 2023, there were glitzy presentations from the likes of Geely and Nio. BYD displayed the Seal, which has the looks and power of Porsche's flagship Taycan, but costs less than half the price. While Chinese brands sought to trailblaze, German companies seemed to pine for simpler times. Both BMW and Mercedes displayed concept cars that deliberately evoked models from the late 1960s, a period in which the grip over their home market was supreme and they established their reputations for excellence. It was an era in which German soft power was on the rise, leading the American singer Janis Joplin to appeal ironically to the Almighty for a Mercedes-Benz. That sort of aspiration seems long gone.

Remnants of German auto-making prestige are still on the road in the Moroccan city of Marrakech, but there too it's fading. For decades, taxi drivers in North Africa and elsewhere bought imported Mercedes vehicles, treasuring them for their superior build, quality and comfort. One such model is a diesel-powered sedan driven by Ihissou Brahim, a vehicle the taxi driver claimed has covered over 1.5 million miles.* After almost forty years of fifteen-hour shifts, its interior is a wreck. The steering wheel is held together by gaffer tape and there's a hole where the Mercedes three-point star once was. Strips of leather hang loose from the roof. Yet despite the toll of the years, the vehicle's soul still sings. As Brahim heads off, its engine purrs with a smoothness that most contemporary cars can't match. Its suspension too still delivers the magic carpet ride intended by its long-retired engineers. Still turning heads as it glides over the potholed lanes of the city's Kasbah, the ivory-coloured automobile remains an emissary for German engineering prowess.

Yet even in developing countries like Morocco, public officials have taken aim at the pollution from ageing German diesels. In 2014 the Moroccan Ministry for Transport offered taxi drivers 80,000 diram (around €7,400) to scrap their old Mercedes diesels, citing air pollution from their engines. Tens of thousands have been replaced under the scheme, filling Morocco's taxi ranks with cleaner cars from French automaker Renault's budget Dacia brand. As the kingdom

---

* The odometer on the vehicle had reached its limit, precluding verification of the actual distance covered.

shifts to electric vehicles, Chinese influence also looks set to grow and potentially crowd out pricey German models. BYD, the world's leading seller of EVs, is expanding its foothold in Morocco and Chinese battery companies are building production plants.[15]

The competitive challenges are showing signs of taking a toll. Automotive production in Germany has been trending lower for around a decade.[16] And offshoring is a major reason. Since 2018, German car companies have built more cars in China than they have at home.[17] That's had an impact on the sector's employment, which has shed about 11,000 jobs on average each year between 2018 and 2023.[18]

To counter the risk of declining sales, German automakers are seeking to move even more upmarket to pad profits and see off challengers on quality and desirability. That means elitist models like the €111,000 Mercedes AMG-GT and the €107,000 BMW 8 Series Coupe. That's a departure from the days when Germany's upscale brands sought to expand their appeal to a wider audience by offering a range of vehicles, including more affordable models like the Mercedes A-Class and the BMW 1 Series.

Focusing on the lucrative top-end of the car market might still prove successful in helping finance the investment needed for the technology transition. There have been some promising signs, with the Porsche Taycan winning 'Car of the Year' awards in China, Germany and the United Kingdom. And while Elon Musk frequently boasts that Tesla is a world leader in hands-free driving, Mercedes has satisfied US regulators that its technology can function safely, whereas the American firm hasn't. But there have been struggles as well. BMW has resorted to steep discounts to sell EVs, and the Mercedes EQS (the electric version of the flagship S-Class saloon) proved a flop.

That leads to questions about what role Germany will play in the future auto market. Will it have a defining role or gear down and become a niche player? And what does that mean for Germany? Brands like Porsche, Mercedes and BMW will still have allure in one way, shape or form. But that same level of certainty can't be given for the vast network of companies that feed off these giants and have become global players in their own right. The backbone of German manufacturing known as the *Mittelstand* faces a very uncertain path ahead.

End of the line

In July 2013, Angela Merkel got a closed-door briefing on secret plans from a champion of German industry and innovation. Far from Berlin and screened from the public eye, the chancellor received an exclusive sneak preview of new developments before the rest of the world. The topic that lured Merkel out to Gütersloh, a small city in Westphalia with half-timber buildings and a rich history, was ... household appliances from Miele.

In the public part of the tour, she was warmly greeted by assembly line workers, whom she praised as a 'major strength' for the company and by extension the German economy. She discussed the importance of keeping energy prices affordable to help tradition-rich companies like Miele stay competitive on the global stage. And she let slip some personal links to the company. She admitted that she grew up with a Miele vacuum cleaner in communist East Germany (what would have been known as a *Westprodukt*) and shared the fact that her father worked at a Miele plant to earn money for wedding rings when he was a theology student. Above all, she praised the company as a shining example of the commitment of Germany's *Mittelstand* to the local community. 'This company is deeply rooted in the region,' Merkel said, before being whisked away by helicopter.[19]

A decade later, things have changed. Miele is still in Gütersloh, but the mood is far less jubilant. Confronted with soaring energy costs and mounting regulation, the company is moving washing-machine production to Poland from the site that's been the company's home base since 1907.

Miele's exit reflects a broader trend that's indicative of the pressure on Germany's industrial backbone. Hellma Materials, a manufacturer of crystals used in microchip production, has put investment on hold. Wefa Inotec, a maker of aluminium tools, will build its next factory in Switzerland. Stihl, a world leader in chainsaws, has cancelled plans to expand production at home, threatening hundreds of jobs. And the Frankfurt-based Viessman family took the opportunity of booming demand to sell its namesake heat-pump business to the American firm Carrier Global in 2023.[20] While these companies often slip under the radar because they're relatively small and privately owned, they are the heart and soul of the German economy, and Miele is a prime example.

The company was founded in 1899 in the midst of the *Gründerzeit* by two entrepreneurs. Its beginnings were modest. Taking over an old saw and grain mill, the company started making dairy centrifuges with eleven employees, four lathes and a drill in Herzebrock, a small village near Gütersloh. With the motto *Immer Besser* (always better), they had ambition. After adding production of butter-makers and washing machines, the company even tried its hand at automobiles, building 143 cars between 1912 and 1914. But Miele exited the auto business because of capital demands and uncertainty as World War I started.

Instead, that hardship and turmoil created demand for the simple transport of hand carts, which became part of Miele's output from 1915 until the *Wirtschaftswunder* started to take hold in the 1950s. As Germany pushed ahead with reconstruction of its shattered towns and cities, demand for Miele's household goods boomed. Newly affluent West Germans turned to the company for washing machines, vacuum cleaners and tumble dryers. Its advertising posters reflected attitudes of the day, featuring beaming German housewives accompanied with the slogan *'Mutti macht's mit Miele'* (Mummy does it with Miele). For decades, Miele's success and resilience was built around flexibility. The post-war period would bring greater focus and global expansion.

Like many other *Mittelstand* firms, Miele went out into the world. During the 1960s it opened its first sales office in the United States and a production plant in Austria. After the Cold War ended, that expansion accelerated and Miele opened factories in the Czech Republic, Poland and Romania. China too offered a new route to export riches, and in 1996 the company and a partner established a vacuum-cleaner plant in Dongguan, a city in China's Pearl River Delta that's now the largest urban area in the world. New markets in turn secured jobs in Miele's home town of Gütersloh.

Maligned before World War II and by the Nazis, which preferred big powerful enterprises like Krupp and I. G. Farben, the *Mittelstand* was recognised as a growth engine by politicians during the *Wirtschaftswunder* and the segment flourished. Their local roots, often in smaller cities, has shaped the way Germany is today, with prosperity widely spread and anchored by these local stalwarts. Three-quarters of *Mittelstand* companies are rooted in peripheral areas and towns with fewer than 100,000 residents. By contrast, countries like France and the United Kingdom are heavily reliant on Paris and London respectively for wealth. The private German companies don't have to answer to shareholders and their owners tend to think in generations rather than financial quarters. Aware of their roles in maintaining local stability, *Mittelstand* owners often keep staff during downturns that would have pushed listed firms into layoffs, and most people in Germany's vaunted vocational-training system undertake apprenticeships at these kinds of firms. The companies are also regular donors to local charities and sports clubs, making them pillars of small-town civic life.

But these companies are far from provincial, they're often leaders in niche areas like tunnel-boring machines, industrial adhesives and ball bearings. Based in the quaint countryside town of Beckum, Beumer Group makes the luggage conveyor system in use at San Francisco Airport and the sorting system at sportswear brand Nike's logistics centre for all of mainland China. With a view of the Alps from the Bavarian town of Wolfratshausen, EagleBurgmann is a world-leading manufacturer of industrial sealants used in nuclear power plants as far afield as Canada. Overall, Germany's family owned businesses had foreign turnover of more than €600 billion, equivalent to around three-quarters of the UK's total exports of goods and services in 2023.[21]

So in an ideal world, everything would stay just like it has been and nothing would change, but we live in the real world and signs of trouble have accumulated. Some are homemade problems, like soaring energy costs from an over-reliance on Russia, a proliferation of red tape, and underinvestment in infrastructure. Others are external, like mounting competition and geopolitical volatility. There are also just normal human cycles like age.

As founders from the *Wirtschaftswunder* era get older, many don't have heirs prepared to take charge. Hundreds of thousands of *Mittelstand* companies are facing ownership changes in the coming years, and the numbers that can't find a successor has been rising.[22] The risk for Germany is that these companies just shut down or slowly wither as the owners lack the energy and skills needed to fight through the intensifying headwinds.

And then there are signs of a growing distrust between politics and the country's economic actors. In 2023 the German government introduced legislation that requires even small companies with a few dozen employees to set up anonymous whistleblower systems. 'That feeling that we are building Germany together is no longer there,' says Tom Rüsen, director of the Witten Institute for Family Business.[23]

Italy offers a warning about what can happen when the segment stumbles. Like Germany, the country experienced a boom after World War II, and family-owned firms in sectors like car components and construction helped spread wealth around. In the 1980s, the success even sparked the interest of Bill Clinton, who was governor of Arkansas at the time. The future American president travelled to the cities of Reggio Emilia and Modena to visit local companies and see the flourishing communities around them, examining whether a similar system could work in the United States.[24]

Yet by the 1990s, Italy's family-owned businesses had entered decline as they struggled to adapt to new technology and lacked support from the government. When the euro was introduced in 1999, Italy's manufacturing firms had to go head-to-head with German rivals and many started to fold. Since 2001, manufacturing output has declined by around a quarter, devastating once-thriving towns. The breakdown in Italy's family-led business model has since helped fuel inequality and political fragmentation. As scandal-hit mainstream parties grappled with chronic economic trouble, fringe parties emerged and the once-niche populist Brothers of Italy, which has been described as 'Mussolini's grandchildren', rose to power in 2022, giving Italy its first far-right-led government since 1945. One coalition member especially, the right-wing Northern League led by Matteo Salvini, has positioned itself as the champion of family-owned businesses.

Despite all the differences between German and Italian society, the parallels are clear. Like Italian populists, the AfD portrays the establishment parties as betraying national interests in pursuit of a globalist agenda. 'This policy makes citizens poor, strangles the *Mittelstand*, drives away productive industry and destroys public finances,' the AfD co-leader Alice Weidel said during a parliament debate over the government's budget crunch in December 2023.

In communities dependent on a single employer, it doesn't take much for uncertainty to spread. It's a siren call that Reinhold Würth, one of the elder statesmen of the *Mittelstand*, wants to head off. Born in 1935, he took over his father's screw-manufacturing business in 1954 at the age of nineteen, building the company into a global player from the quaint village of Künzelsau in Baden-Württemberg. One of Germany's richest people, Würth stands for *Mittelstand* success and local responsibility. The company's cultural ties to its home town and beyond run deep, supporting initiatives in culture, science, education and integration through a charitable foundation. Contributions to local life include the Würth Open Air music festival in Künzelsau, a two-day event that attracts international pop, rock and R&B stars. The local patriarch also sponsors the Würth Philharmoniker, giving the town of 15,000 its own professional orchestra.

Disturbed by the AfD's rise and the growing divisions in Germany, Würth wrote a five-page letter imploring his employees not to vote for the party. He warned against getting caught up in the AfD's fear-mongering and anti-foreigner rhetoric. Extolling widespread prosperity in Germany and the political freedoms guaranteed by the country's constitution, he said there's little actual reason for the country's depressive mood. In the region around Künzelsau, 'we describe a person who is well-placed and yet stands out for being particularly discontented as someone "who needs to have their tongue scraped". Perhaps that would be appropriate for one or another voter,' Würth said in the letter he sent to 25,000 of his workers.[25]

In the appeal, which the AfD dismissed as ignoring the 'existential worries' of German citizens,[26] the billionaire criticised Olaf Scholz's government as at times acting like 'a bunch of chickens', but he downplayed parallels with the Weimar Republic as going too far. Still in a subsequent interview, he noted he was greatly worried about the country, even likening conditions to 'a pre-war period' and accusing the government of 'lacking a common line and, above all, an idea for the future'.[27]

Alongside the auto industry, the *Mittelstand* has been a critical source of German post-war prosperity and so warnings should be taken seriously. But adjustments in one or the other segment of the economy don't have to be disruptive on their own. Change is part of the nature of things, and economic power could be transferred to new industries or sectors. But as we look into that prospect a little later in this chapter, new champions aren't emerging. Meanwhile, there's a more immediate threat in ageing workers, sapping skilled labour from the economy, and adding stress to the social system.

Clocking out

For residents at St Josefs-Heim, an elderly care home in the Haidhausen neighbourhood of Munich, the run-up to Christmas 2023 proved bewildering. Unable to resolve a chronic staff shortage, the institution was to close that winter. Residents would have to go elsewhere, but that was difficult too with a shortage of beds across the city. The lives of nearly sixty people, most fragile and in poor health, were plunged into uncertainty. 'Why does this exact home have to fall apart? I feel really bad. I'm scared,' said a ninety-year-old resident, who was alone after the death of her husband and two sons.[28]

The crisis at the Munich care home is indicative of the demographic issues facing Germany. Like many other countries that fought in World War II, part of the peace dividend was a baby boom and that generation is getting older, but there aren't enough young people to care for them. New births in Germany peaked in 1964 at nearly 1.4 million. Rates dropped by a third by 1975 and have been setting new record lows almost every year since 2020, at fewer than 800,000 annually. The government expects birth rates to continue to trend lower. Unions estimate Germany is short of around 100,000 care workers and will need an additional 300,000 by 2030.[29] Some advocates warn the system could collapse unless action is taken.[30] But it's not just a matter of shifting resources from schools to care homes. It's a broader economic and social problem.

It hits Germany in two main ways. The shrinking workforce affects the government's ability to fulfil its constitutional duties of taking care of the German people. At the same time, it saps economic power. Both aspects undermine the image of Germany as a strong, fair nation.

Businesses of all sizes, as well as schools, hospitals and government agencies, can feel the pinch from too few workers. The manufacturer of commercial aircraft, Airbus, was forced to slow production of its best-selling jet because it was short of around 1,000 staff at its plant in Hamburg.[31] Hotels and shops can't find workers for reception desks and tills. In the public sector, shortages are weakening the state's ability to tackle everything from childcare to the housing crisis by slowing approvals. Even the once-secretive chief of Germany's BND intelligence service has come out of the shadows to front a recruitment campaign.* Across the economy, nearly 2 million unfilled jobs have cost the economy more than €90 billion in lost output.[32]

Germany's demographic decline casts a particularly long shadow over its manufacturing sector, intensifying existing struggles in the automotive industry and revealing its shortcomings in digital transformation. An ageing population and a dwindling pool of young, skilled workers have created a talent drought, striking a harsh blow to multiple sectors. The problem deepens as Germany's lag in digital adoption comes to the fore; a workforce lacking in sufficient digital skills stifles efforts to modernise production lines to keep pace with global competitors. Without a strong pipeline of innovative minds and tech-savvy workers, German companies risk losing their edge, threatening the nation's status as a manufacturing leader, which has consequences for the country's economic well-being as well as its self-image.

Tackling Germany's demographic decline is more daunting than other economic challenges because you obviously can't just manufacture people. Encouraging higher birth rates, for instance, means overhauling housing, childcare and work–life balance – no mean feat. Attracting a skilled immigrant workforce faces a knot of cultural, political, and integration challenges with which Germany has struggled. Adding to the complexity is the urgent need to retrain the current workforce to fill the gap in digital skills, a time-consuming and resource-heavy undertaking. These entrenched demographic problems pose a far more enduring and intricate threat to Germany's economy and by extension its health as a nation.

The shortage of workers is already slowing Germany's shift to a green economy. Hitting climate goals requires the widespread

---

* Germany's BND launched the 'Komm Dahinter' recruitment programme in March 2024.

electrification of systems that currently run on fossil fuels, like replacing gas boilers with electric heat pumps and installing hundreds of thousands of EV charging points. Germany's electricity grid also needs an overhaul, and tens of thousands of wind turbines and millions of solar panels need to be set up. Yet the country is short of well over 200,000 electrical engineers.[33]

Germany's digital transition is also under threat. In the *Mittelstand*, three-quarters of firms can't find enough IT staff,[34] and government agencies point to a similar challenge. Backed by generous state subsidies, TSMC and Infineon plan to build semiconductor factories in the east of the country, but a shortage of engineers risks hampering the multi-billion-euro plans.[35] Setting out a vision for a new economy is one thing, finding the workers to realise it is another.

Migration needs to be part of the solution, but that's a divisive issue. Since 2015, Germany has seen a surge in arrivals, but mainly driven by refugees. In 2022 alone around 1.5 million people arrived in Germany. Of that number there were around 960,000 people fleeing the war in Ukraine and 360,000 who claimed asylum from elsewhere. Integrating these people into the labour market is difficult. Because of their situations, they start from scratch and need to begin the arduous task of learning German. Language courses are helpful, but often oversubscribed (due in large part to a shortage of teachers). German bureaucracy also gets in the way. Qualified migrants often complain of Kafkaesque processes. Even if a Syrian engineer has a copy of their engineering degree, bureaucrats can refuse granting work permits if applicants can't produce high-school certificates. Social media is regularly filled with horror stories about migrants trying to navigate German bureaucracy, even when their skills and energy are desperately needed.

Openly easing migration, though, is politically explosive. For instance, recruiting tech staff from countries like India for a new fab in the Silicon Saxony tech cluster risks alienating locals as they see themselves shut out from opportunities, and to be fair, they have been because Germany has done a poor job at promoting IT skills. Despite its alleged *Willkommenskultur* (welcoming culture), German society doesn't extend a hand to migrants. Aside from the AfD's openly anti-immigration stance, the CDU has become suspicious of foreigners. 'We want to give immigrants the opportunity to find a home here. This can only succeed if they are prepared to adapt to our way of life,' Germany's leading conservative party says in its platform. There's also scepticism on the left. Sahra Wagenkecht, founder of the left-wing populist BSW party, has said Germany is 'overwhelmed' and 'has no more space'.

Voters appear to be split on immigration, which largely depends on how the issue is framed. Asked whether Germany should take in a high number of workers in areas of the economy where there are labour shortages, around three-quarters have voiced support. Asked whether Germany should accept more economic migrants, a similar-sized majority have been opposed.[36] This ambivalence risks complicating efforts to attract qualified people to Germany and getting them to stay, and that's a significant problem. The country needs 1.5 million migrants every year to maintain the size of its workforce, according to Germany's Council of Economic Experts.[37]

Enabling more women to work more could also alleviate some pressure on the labour market. But traditional views on family roles have made that a hurdle. Due to persistent expectations that childcare is for women, many female workers drop out of full-time work following childbirth and never return.[38] German women also do more work caring for elderly relatives than their counterparts in Italy and Portugal. Overall, women work eight fewer hours per week than men, one of the biggest gaps in Europe. Opinion polls suggest this isn't a path women have chosen for themselves, and a greater share of women would like to increase their working hours if they could, according to the Bertelsmann Foundation.[39]

The demographic issue is about more than economic capacity. Without enough workers paying into the system, Germany will struggle to maintain its welfare state, the essential connective tissue holding the country together in the absence of a strong civic identity that's open to newcomers and natives alike. From pensions to unemployment benefits, Germany's social cohesion comes in the form of government cash, and a reckoning is coming by 2030, if not before. Already the system is barely sustainable. Germany spends €1.2 trillion each year on social protection, equivalent to a third of annual output.* Around a third of that spending goes towards

---

* That's about €14,000 per person, more than double the £5,000 per capita spent in the UK.

state pensions, which for many Germans is the basis for retirement, especially in the east of the country. Public pensions are largely funded by the social-security contributions from the current labour force, with a gap plugged by the federal government. As more and more people retire, the government will have to cut back elsewhere to fill the hole. A government study published in 2021 warned that the pension system in its current form won't function beyond 2030. A separate study warned that Germany's entire welfare state will become unsustainable by that time.[40]

Politicians have largely kicked the can down the road for years, or offered minor patches. In 2024, Scholz's cabinet approved a plan that aims to keep the system stable until 2039, including the introduction of a programme to invest money. The so-called *Generationenkapital* (generations capital) is supposed to yield €10 billion a year for the pension system by 2036, which is a drop in the bucket but at least the start of a shift. The main financing method remains social-security contributions, which will rise from 18.6 per cent of wages to 22.3 per cent in 2028. The plan has been criticised as a short-term fix to ease the anxiety of current retirees at the expense of young people, who have few prospects of getting anything back for paying into the generational contract. Other options to spread the burden like delaying the retirement age, capping benefits, or raising taxes weren't addressed.

It's not an easy dilemma, but half-baked reforms do little to increase confidence that the state can resolve major problems. The burden therefore falls on the young to support the elderly while dealing with fading economic potential and the risks of the climate crisis. Making the future even more uncertain is Germany's struggles to adapt to the digital shift in the global economy. Despite years of talk, there's still no viable answer.

Barren frontiers

When American presidents visit Berlin, history is often made, and so expectations were high when Air Force One roared over the capital on 18 June 2013 with Barack Obama and his family on board. At the very least, it promised to be a feel-good moment. The

Wall was long gone, and the first woman chancellor of Germany would host the first Black president of the United States.

Obama was set to speak on the east side of the Brandenburg Gate, showing the progress made since Ronald Reagan famously reprimanded the Soviet Union from the west side. But instead of any historic words from Obama, Merkel inadvertently grabbed the limelight with a phrase that revealed an uncomfortable reality about Germany. 'Das Internet ist für uns alle Neuland' (The internet is for all of us a new frontier), she said during her press conference with the American president.

It was the political equivalent of a face-palm emoji. At the time she made the observation, Amazon had been around for almost two decades, Google was fifteen years old, Twitter (or X) was seven, and even Bitcoin was four. Her guest had won two US presidential elections in part by leveraging social media. Even in Europe, three-quarters of the population regularly used the web at the time.[41] It was an indication that despite her background in quantum chemistry, Merkel wasn't up to speed on the modern world.

Ahead of her final term, it had become glaringly clear that Germany was trailing in its efforts to catch up with digital technology. There was talk of creating a new ministry to focus on efforts from infrastructure rollout to e-government initiatives. Instead, she named Dorothee Bär, a functionary from the Bavarian CSU party with no evident technical expertise, as digital czar. She vowed to think big . . . like flying taxis big. Meanwhile, Germany was falling behind on the basics.

Germany hasn't just been overtaken by rivals, it's been lapped. The Digital Riser Report, comparing the competitiveness of countries on all things digital, ranks Germany towards the bottom of the G20 group of major economies. Another league table shows Germany at fifty-second in the world for technological skills and fortieth for the application of digital technologies.[42] In terms of public services, Germans still can't legally change their official residence without filling out a paper form and submitting it in person to a local civil-service office. Public administration is typically conducted by letter and post, helping to make Germany the world's second-biggest consumer of paper per person at about a quarter tonne each year.[43] The public is sluggish as well, with about half of Germans lacking basic online skills like the ability to find things on the internet or stay safe online.[44] On the corporate level, more than four in five German companies still use fax machines.[45] And in terms of commerce, bank cards aren't universal, and many restaurants still only take cash.

That plays out on the country's industry-heavy economy. SAP is the only software company on Germany's blue-chip DAX Index. But it's hardly a newcomer. It was founded in 1972 by a group of former IBM engineers. It's the old-economy version of software, managing inventory and accounting for big multinationals. One of its key advantages is that SAP installations are so complex that once they are installed, customers don't dare switch. One of the founders is Hasso Plattner, a gruff Berliner who started his own tech school in 1999 to try to fill the gap in Germany's higher-education system. The Potsdam-based Hasso Plattner Institute cheekily has a podcast where it discusses digital trends and developments called 'Neuland' – an obvious dig at Angela Merkel's 2013 quip. The entrepreneur often expresses his frustration over Germany and its struggles to face the future with more confidence. 'In Germany, we have developed self-doubt to the point of self-destruction,' he said. 'That is a special German characteristic.'[46]

That's more of a post-war development. In the swashbuckling days of industrialisation, Germany was rife with innovators like Gottlieb Daimler, Nicolaus Otto and Wilhelm Maybach.* Ferdinand Porsche created an electric car as far back as 1898. But since World War II, Germans have developed a zero-sum mentality, with change becoming synonymous with loss. That's led to an unwillingness to experiment and invest in new technology for fear of having to give up something else. This has cast a long shadow as the country's leaders cling to a model built around industrial and automotive prowess. Investing in new technologies or alternative strategies was kicked down the road as long as the old model was working, but economic value has shifted ever more away from traditional strengths and the country is in catch-up mode. In other words, the House of Germany failed to repair the roof when the sun was shining – and now it's raining.

---

* Nicolaus Otto developed a motor in the 1860s which ran on petroleum gas and was a forerunner of the modern internal combustion engine; Wilhelm Maybach was an early engine designer.

The country and its people need to throw those misgivings aside more than ever. With the auto industry sputtering, much of the *Mittelstand* running out of steam and the *Wirtschaftswunder* labour force clocking out, long-standing risks are being exposed. The country lacks raw materials to feed its industrial machine, energy prices are among the highest in the world, and labour costs are expensive – all disadvantages compared to the United States and China. To keep ahead, Germany needs innovation, but the trends have not looked promising for a country that once brought forth world-changing inventions like the printing press, the automobile and rockets (not to mention geniuses in music, art and literature). At the turn of the millennium, Germany was among the top three for patents in forty-three of fifty-eight key technology areas, but by 2019 it held that rank in barely half of them.[47]

Part of the problem is that much of the country's innovation power is tied to long-established firms devoting resources to incremental advancements like improving efficiency of a fuel pump or a new compound to reduce tyre wear. In 2022, Germany's top patent applicants included three companies that were more than 100 years old: Robert Bosch, an automotive parts supplier, its peer ZF Friedrichshafen and BMW.[48] The rest of the top ten were also all automakers or parts suppliers. The largest share of patents were for automotive at around a quarter, while computer technology accounted for less than a tenth.[49] While this might help defend Germany's position in auto-making at a time when the sector is facing massive technology shifts, new frontiers aren't opening elsewhere.

That's clear from the slow pace of new businesses. Rather than ramping up to potentially replace fading champions, the number of start-ups fell in 2023 to the lowest level in four years, bucking the trend seen elsewhere in the developed world.[50] In a global perspective, Germany languishes in seventh place behind Indonesia, Australia and Canada, while the density of new companies is five times higher in the United States.[51]

Even if Germans do take the plunge, it's hard to break through to the next level because there's significantly less growth capital available than in the United States.[52] Of that German funding, almost half comes from American investors. A lot of that has to do with the country's infamous *Risikophobie* (fear of risk), which prods some Germans to insure themselves against even minor eventualities like getting sick and not being able to use a movie ticket. The mindset affects would-be entrepreneurs as well, with a fear of financial failure more pronounced than in other countries.[53] That shows up in 'rich lists'. Almost all of the top-ten wealthiest Americans had at least co-founded companies, whereas in Germany they're mostly heirs.[54]

A wall of bureaucracy also serves as a deterrent for would-be innovators, creating roadblocks before any momentum can even get started. In 2015 a rule was introduced stipulating that for every new regulation foisted on companies, one must be removed, but it hasn't helped much. Nevertheless, an independent study by the ESMT Management School in Berlin shows that the number of regulations affecting German companies has risen sharply. It grew from around 34,000 pages in 2015 to nearly 50,000 in 2024, indicating a steady increase since the introduction of the Bureaucracy Reduction Act.[55] Germany has been put at the bottom of the Group of Seven most advanced economies for regulation, below France and Italy, which are hardly known for laissez-faire policies.[56] In one business survey after another, bureaucracy and regulation in Germany is highlighted as a hindrance to investment.[57]

It's not all completely bleak though. The number of German unicorns (start-ups worth more than $1 billion) has quadrupled to thirty-three since 2020. These include internet bank N26 (founded the same year as Merkel's 'Neuland' remark); wefox, an online insurance platform; and Celonis, a so-called decacorn (meaning worth more than $10 billion), which provides software to improve business processes. The UK, in contrast, has nine decacorns, such as food delivery company Just Eat and online grocery retail company Ocado.

Also, Germany does have significant research muscles to flex. With over 450,000 people employed in full-time research, it has one of the highest R&D bases in the world, behind only China, Japan, the United States and South Korea.[58] Around a third of patents filed in Europe originate from Germany. The country is also home to world-leading research organisations like the Max Planck Society and the Fraunhofer Institutes. The problem is that many of their ideas end up untapped due to breakdowns in the transmission between lab and boardroom. The government is trying to change that. It introduced a package of measures aimed at making it easier for start-ups to emerge from these well-funded research groups.[59] As part of the effort, it started the German Agency for Transfer and Innovation in 2023 to accelerate the process of turning research results into businesses. But awkwardly, it's based in Erfurt, far away from the start-up hubs in Berlin and Munich.

Germany's struggle to develop new businesses is underscored by a recent success story. BioNTech was founded in Mainz in 2008 and toiled away obscurely for years on developing therapies for cancer and other serious diseases. Even at its outset, BioNTech was different from most German companies. Its husband-and-wife founders, Uğur Şahin and Özlem Türeci, are German citizens from Turkish immigrant backgrounds, a group that's under-represented in business circles. The company's rise to global prominence came with the onset of the Covid-19 pandemic. After reading a paper on the new virus, Şahin realised that the company's mRNA technology could be used to create a vaccine and started a task force called 'Project Lightspeed'. Working nights and weekends, the forty-person team had a plan in place by the end of January 2020.

BioNTech's leaders knew it would need to partner with a bigger firm to get through the approvals process, and there weren't many options in Germany. Biotechnology is high risk. Development of new therapies often involves unexpected delays and costs, and success is never guaranteed. In short, there's limited appetite from German investors and the sector has been starved of capital. So BioNTech turned to the American pharma giant Pfizer. In April 2020, while Germany was still in its first full lockdown, the Pfizer-BioNTech shot entered clinical trials. Just eight months later, regulators in the United Kingdom granted an emergency approval and public vaccination campaigns began. Along with similar vaccines from AstraZeneca and others, the Pfizer-BioNTech inoculation would save millions of lives and defuse the global threat. In 2023, BioNTech researcher Katalin Karikó won the Nobel Prize for medicine in a testament to the firm's role in ending the acute phase of the pandemic.

Although BioNTech was a big win and shows Germany's potential, in many ways it was the exception that proves the rule.

There are still too many roadblocks in the way of desperately needed new endeavours, from regulation to the German mentality. The company's founders have used their hard-earned profile to point out that the country needs to improve and reform its often hostile approach to start-ups and entrepreneurs. 'In this country, we have a certain reluctance towards innovation and risk,' Türeci said. 'The Germans focus more on perfection, the finale.'[60]

With economic turmoil intensifying and posing risks to social and political stability, Germany can ill afford to make the perfect the enemy of the good. If Germany could become more open to trial and error, it could make significant strides, but it needs to act faster than it traditionally feels comfortable with. Globalisation has been a tailwind for Germany's economic model, but as the war in Ukraine shows, the security order on which it grew rich and prosperous has fragmented. And as geopolitical fronts harden, Germany is caught in the middle, but without the comfortable position of being a favourite for any major power.

6
Neighbourhood Decay

'Madness is rare in individuals —
but in groups, parties, nations and ages, it is the rule.'
Friedrich Nietzsche

Mounted atop a former warehouse in Hamburg's industrial-era docklands, the billowing form of the Elbphilharmonie concert hall points towards the open seas, rising above Germany's second-largest city like an ocean wave. The glass-panelled building crowns a new, forward-looking section of the city, a modern and elegant counterpoint to the seedy Reeperbahn nearby. Around 10,000 drywall plates were individually shaped with painstaking precision to disperse sound waves and create world-class acoustics. Built with the help of taxes raised from round-the-clock trade from the sprawling port it overlooks, it's a testament to the country's remarkable success as a trading nation, as globalisation opened new markets for 'Made in Germany' goods.

The building's scope and ambition echoes the Victorian grandeur that can be found in Liverpool and London, and the epic public buildings of Paris, Antwerp and Amsterdam. It's a building that marks a golden age. Its foundation stone was laid in 2007, when Germany was still *Exportweltmeister* (world's top exporter) and before the convulsions of Brexit, Donald Trump's trade wars, and Vladimir Putin's efforts to carve up and control Ukraine. Running into delays and cost overruns like so many other major projects in Germany, the opulent venue was finished in 2017, the same year Angela Merkel secured her final term as chancellor and the far-right

AfD showed signs of its political potential. Less than a decade later, it's already starting to look like a totem to a bygone era.

Few countries profited from the post-war order as much as Germany. It was well protected from the tumult of power politics thanks to the protective shield of the United States, allowing the country's leaders to pursue a mercantilist agenda that put trade at the forefront of foreign policy. But at least since Russia's invasion of Ukraine, it's become clear that the world has turned more volatile. The re-election of Donald Trump, a self-declared fan of protectionist tariffs, effectively killed off the post-Cold War vision of ever greater global integration. That's a particularly acute problem for the world's most trade-dependent major economy and creates a dilemma about where and how Germany will sell its goods to uphold living standards and its sense of self.

To lean on our metaphor, the House of Germany is waking up to the realities of a neighbourhood that's mired in a series of nasty spats. The brawny policeman is no longer interested in keeping the peace like he used to, and a new bully who once needed to borrow power tools is now churning out much of what the House used to and is flexing his muscles in a menacing way. The residents, meanwhile, are unsettled by how relations have changed. They might want things to return to how they were, but the good old days aren't coming back.

Cracks in the pavement

Just how unprepared Germany is for the crumbling world order emerged in April 2022, when a diplomatic scandal unfolded. It involved Frank-Walter Steinmeier, the president of Germany – a ceremonial role that was created in some European countries to replace the monarch. The position is often filled by a former politician, but the role is supposed to be apolitical, outside the fray of government, and to provide guidance where and when needed. So it's unusual for a German president to get embroiled in an international spat. But that's what happened.

A few weeks after the war in Ukraine broke out, in March 2022, Steinmeier was getting ready for a journey from the stately Bellevue

Palace on the edge of Berlin's historic Tiergarten park to Warsaw and then onward to Kyiv. Joining fellow heads of state from Poland and the Baltic countries in a show of support was a tantalising opportunity for the silver-haired former foreign minister, but the ensuing fiasco served as a prime example of why Europe's largest economy struggles to take a leading role in global affairs.

It was less than two months after Russia's full-scale invasion of Ukraine, and the neighbour's neighbour* was valiantly holding back the Kremlin's forces but paying a heavy price, with hundreds of civilian deaths under brutal circumstances.[1] Just days before Steinmeier's planned departure, a train station in Kramatorsk in the hard-fought Donetsk Oblast was hit by a Russian rocket armed with cluster munitions, killing dozens of people who were trying to flee to safer areas.[2] In the midst of that carnage, Steinmeier was hoping to make an appearance, but Ukraine baulked. It was a shock given Germany's critical role in the country's support network and because of its proximity and power. Despite a desperate need for aid, there were plenty of reasons why Steinmeier wasn't the emissary Ukraine was eager to host.

Shortly before his departure, a brief note arrived via diplomatic channels stating that his visit would be 'more substantial and more acceptable' if he travelled independently. That's diplomatic language for 'stay away'.[3] It was a clear affront, and Steinmeier's ego was bruised. For weeks he stewed. Chancellor Olaf Scholz rallied to his party comrade's side, vowing not to travel to Kyiv until the issue was sorted out. So while Ukraine was fighting for its survival and clamouring for artillery, air-defence systems and ammunition, it had to deal with the vanities of a man who played a key role in emboldening Russia's aggression. Germany's policy of appeasement with Russia dates back at least to Willy Brandt's *Ostpolitik* in the 1970s. At that time, the fate of the East Germans was at stake and reaching out to the Kremlin opened up the prospect of creating holes in the Iron Curtain. After reunification, Germany didn't have the same noble aims. Instead, the focus was on money.

---

* Dresden in eastern Germany is about 525 miles from the Ukrainian city of Lviv, which is roughly the equivalent of driving from New York to Columbus, Ohio, or a little longer than from Brighton to Edinburgh in the UK.

Heavy-set and thin-lipped, Steinmeier has spent his entire professional life in public service, generally as an aide. He is a prime example of Germany's political class and embodies the kind of unreflective, self-assured groupthink that dominates Berlin. Germany's political parties are dominated by tight networks of careerists. Those who advance do so by toeing the party line and then there are regular moves from government posts to senior corporate jobs, underlining the tight relations between commerce and politics. Combined with latent notions of German superiority after decades of economic success and resilience, the result is an echo chamber of mutual affirmation. Although the country gives lip service to liberal ideas, it regularly pursues deals that prop up autocrats, while concerns from the outside are dismissed with disdain as lacking the far-reaching insight bestowed upon Germans.

Before being appointed as president in 2017, Steinmeier helped deepen Germany's dependence on the Kremlin. He was foreign minister under Angela Merkel and before that the chief of staff for Gerhard Schröder. After leaving power, the former chancellor was quickly and controversially hired as a well-paid advisor to Russian firms.[4]

Under Steinmeier's watch, Germany started mainlining Russian gas via the first Nord Stream pipeline following a deal between Schröder and Putin in 2005, just before the chancellor's switch from politics to millionaire Russian advisor. Steinmeier extended those ties while serving as Germany's top diplomat twice. In his first stint (2005–9)[*] he refused to let the murders of opposition figures Anna Politkovskaya and Alexander Litvinenko or the invasion of Georgia get in the way of good vibes between the countries. During his second term as foreign minister (2013–17), Russia illegally annexed Crimea, which Steinmeier and many other leading German figures quickly normalised.

Shortly before the land grab in early 2014, Steinmeier was in Moscow and set an accommodating tone. Alongside polite chat with his counterpart Sergey Lavrov about Germany's medal haul in

---

[*] In between his terms as foreign minister, Steinmeier led the Social Democratic opposition after his loss as the party's chancellor candidate in the 2009 election.

the Olympics in Sochi, Steinmeier urged a new 'positive agenda' in relations with Russia.[5] He underscored that message, which was the mainstream view in Berlin, in an interview with the *Kommersant* newspaper during the visit, saying: 'It is important to me to offer a trusting and constructive cooperation with Moscow.'[6] He even suggested that the Kremlin had a role to play in resolving political tensions in Ukraine – a dangerous signal for pro-democracy demonstrators. At the time, the deadly Maidan uprising was in full swing after Russia clamped down on a planned cooperation pact with the European Union. The message from Berlin was that Germany's relations with Russia were a higher priority than whatever else was going on in the region.

That approach didn't change following Crimea's annexation or after Russia-backed forces took control of parts of the Donetsk and Luhansk regions of Ukraine. Instead, Steinmeier sought to continue negotiations with Moscow and lobbied for reining in sanctions, citing concerns that Russia could be destabilised.[7] He then went a step further and proposed a formula as part of the Minsk talks to freeze the conflict in eastern Ukraine.* In 2016 he criticised a NATO military exercise in Poland and the Baltics as 'sabre-rattling' that risked opening old wounds with Russia.[8]

It was clear what the priority was: Germany needed its fix of cheap Russian energy. And like any addict, it wanted more. The Nord Stream 2 pipeline was supposed to be another direct injection from Russian gas fields to Germany's industrial infrastructure. The project was given the green light in 2015, just one year after the annexation of Crimea – so much for punishing the aggressor and standing strong for liberal values.

For years, Steinmeier and the rest of the German establishment continued to back Nord Stream despite warnings by the United States and other European allies that it posed a security risk for Germany and in turn NATO. Merkel defended Nord Stream, as did Olaf Scholz, as did the entire political mainstream in Berlin, collectively dodging political culpability by disingenuously labelling the pipeline as a mere commercial project. The attitudes towards

---

* The Steinmeier Formula was presented in 2015 as part of the Minsk agreements. https://www.auswaertiges-amt.de/en/aussenpolitik/steinmeier-formula/2254244.

Nord Stream and Russian gas stand out, but aren't unique. German politics is largely an extension of the country's business interests. Commerce regularly outweighs broader concerns of politics, security, or much less moral values, because of the central role that economics and affluence plays in the identity of post-war Germany. So when Germany's elite saw how much money could be made in tapping Russia's vast resources, the political establishment fell into line by not poking the bear in Moscow, regardless of its actions. It didn't end there.

A veritable conga line of executives gave their seal of approval to the Kremlin's aggression. Joe Kaeser, the head of Siemens, went to meet with Putin less than two weeks after Crimea's annexation and the industrial giant facilitated Moscow's plans to decouple the peninsula from Ukraine's power grid.[9] Siemens also got deeply involved with the Russian rail network. BASF had joint ventures with Gazprom. Uniper became the biggest German importer of Russian gas and a key player in the country's utility landscape. Volkswagen and Daimler were active as well. So while the post-war order was under attack in Germany's own backyard, the country was actively profiteering.

Ahead of the planned trip to Kyiv, Steinmeier did offer a *mea culpa* after being accused of having a 'spider's web' of contacts in Russia.[10] 'We held on to bridges that Russia no longer believed in and that our partners warned us about,' he told journalists in the Bellevue Palace, connecting his stance with a long-running and broad-based shift towards detente starting with the 1975 Helsinki Accords.[11] But given his efforts to engage with the Kremlin (even inviting Russian musicians to a post-invasion benefit concert for Ukraine), it's hardly surprising that Kyiv wasn't thrilled about serving as a backdrop for his rehabilitation.*

As clumsy as the snub might have been, a skilled diplomat could have avoided escalating the dispute and damaging both sides. The spat lasted for weeks, taking up precious time as authorities in Berlin and Kyiv sought to smooth things over. To be clear, Steinmeier has no role in government decision-making. The German president's main role is to stay above the political fray, give speeches and

---

* Ukraine's official explanation was that a formal request was never made by Berlin.

hold receptions. He's not supposed to become the centre of an international incident. A thaw started with a telephone call between Steinmeier and Ukrainian President Volodymyr Zelenskiy in May 2022. Finally in October (more than seven months after the war started), the German president had his tour of battle zones and was even ushered into a bunker when air-raid sirens blared. 'My message to the people in Ukraine is: You can rely on Germany!' he said during the visit. The boast rang hollow then and the emptiness echoed long after.

Ahead of the invasion, with 100,000 Russian troops massed on Ukraine's border and the United States warning of an imminent attack, Germany offered to send Kyiv 5,000 helmets.[12] The widely lampooned move shows just how badly Berlin misjudged public perception and bungled communications. It wasn't isolated. Germany regularly missed the moment to show leadership and project strength, highlighting its limitations more often than showing it was ready to stand up and offer Ukraine real support.

To be fair, there are historical reasons why Germany has a soft spot for Russia. Berlin is dotted with a dozen Soviet monuments, including an imposing memorial and a cemetery with the remains of more than 13,000 Red Army soldiers. Unlike in former Eastern European countries, no cranes or bulldozers have come to topple them.[13] That's part of Germany's post-Nazi memory culture. Soviet troops were the first to enter Berlin, and their scribblings remain enshrined on the walls of the Reichstag as a testament to the country's sacrifices to liberate Europe from the Nazis. In addition to that historical debt, the people in former communist East Germany have a certain affinity towards Moscow that was nurtured during years of hardship following reunification. Having said that, standing up to Russia doesn't come as naturally to Germany as it does to America and Great Britain. And it's especially hard to do when cheap Russian energy is fuelling the economy.

On top of the Russia question, Germany struggled to get its mind around a military conflict. For Berlin's mercantilist mindset, the economic risks of an invasion of Ukraine were too high even for Putin. That stems from a post-military perspective. After spending decades under America's shield, the country's leadership had embraced the 'end of history' idea after the Berlin Wall fell.[14] As posited by

Francis Fukuyama following the end of the Cold War, the great ideological battles were over and liberal democracy had won. Rather than brinkmanship and bloodshed, conflicts could be resolved through diplomacy and international institutions. That made a robust military unnecessary. It was an appealing (and indeed self-serving) approach for Germany in its reconstituted form, straddling the former Iron Curtain and striving for affluence above all else.

There was also solid public support for leaving militarism behind. A strong tradition of pacifism followed World War II, and the connection with national defence became even more tenuous after obligatory military service was dropped in 2011. For most Germans, military spending was a waste of money and an uncomfortable reminder of the country's Nazi past. Every mission was hotly contested by the public, and hardly any politician was going to stick their neck out and demand more money for weapons and soldiers. Before the invasion of Ukraine, German news coverage underscored doubts about the military, focusing on the Bundeswehr's scandals, mishaps and dysfunction – from neo-Nazi plots[15] to the costly spectacle of the *Gorch Fock*, a three-masted sailing vessel used for naval training that cost thirteen times as much as was originally planned to refurbish it.[16] The outcome was feeble spending, with Germany regularly missing NATO's guidelines to spend at least 2 per cent of GDP on defence. You would have to go back to 1991 to find that level of investment, and it was just 1.2 per cent in 2017, when German–US relations hit a fresh low with the election of Donald Trump.[17]

In that context, Scholz's *Zeitenwende* speech a few days after Russia's invasion of Ukraine was indeed historic.[18] He took advantage of the moment by announcing a special €100 billion fund to upgrade the military and broke with post-war tradition by promising to deliver lethal weapons to a conflict zone. Germany did become one of Kyiv's chief suppliers of military equipment, behind only the United States. But the momentum was choppy and every new step was accompanied by hand-wringing over fears of escalation, which signalled loud and clear to the Kremlin that Germany was not a serious adversary.

That was certainly the case with modern battle tanks. Rather than take the initiative in a field in which Germany has an edge, Scholz hemmed and hawed to the frustration of Ukraine and other allies. He eventually agreed to supply a few dozen Leopard tanks, but only after reaching a deal with President Joe Biden that he would send American Abrams tanks as well.[19] Similar drawn-out debates accompanied other weapons systems, like Gepard air-defence tanks and Marder infantry-fighting vehicles, and spawned the word *Scholzing* – the equivalent of dithering. In the case of long-range Taurus missiles, Scholz rejected deliveries after months of deliberation under the pretence that German soldiers would be needed to programme them and that could make the country an active participant in the war, sparking new waves of criticism.[20]

The slow walk of support gave the impression that Germany doubted that a Ukraine victory was possible and preferred normalisation sooner rather than later. Some officials said the quiet part out loud. In June 2022, Chancellor Scholz's security advisor Jens Plötner – who previously ran Steinmeier's office during his second stint as foreign minister – said that while weapons deliveries were filling up newspaper copy, there wasn't enough discussion about future relations with Russia, indicating he was eager to turn the page.[21] Erich Vad, Merkel's top military aide, predicted the war would last just a few days and became an anti-war activist, lobbying for negotiations with Moscow and warning against efforts to defeat Russia militarily.[22] Public figures like the feminist Alice Schwarzer have also added pressure, with half a million people signing an open letter to Scholz warning of the risk of World War III.[23] And the Russia-friendly BSW scored key electoral victories in eastern German states by opposing weapons deliveries and calling for talks with Russia.

At the end of the day, Germany's motivations are rather straightforward. Although the country moralises about freedom, democracy and human rights, its chief aim is protecting German affluence. Even after the invasion, the country continued filling up Russian coffers. In 2022 it transferred €97 million every single day for energy and other imports, a 6.5 per cent increase. The following year, trade with Russia still totalled nearly €12.6 billion despite sanctions and the end of most energy purchases, making the country more important to the German economy than EU partners Greece, Bulgaria and Lithuania – and of course more important than Ukraine. Also, exports suddenly shot up to Central Asian countries like Kyrgyzstan, indicating former Soviet republics were serving as a way station for goods heading to Russia.*

Aside from the blow to Germany's credibility, *Scholzing* hampered progress towards a military capable of deterring or containing conflicts in the future. 'Decades of counting pennies' left the country's defence forces with a stockpile of ammunition that would only last days in the event of an attack.[24] Radio equipment, armoured vehicles, ships and planes were all dated. The total price tag for modernising the German military has been pegged at some €300 billion, or three times the *Zeitenwende* budget,[25] and that's looking optimistic given the proliferation of crises.

Germany's military impotence isn't just about money and hardware. There are also severe structural issues that are very common across the economy. Navigating the labyrinth of approvals and procedures means upgrading the Bundeswehr's infrastructure alone would take half a century and getting approval for a commercially available flight helmet took ten years – a negative highlight of German inefficiency.[26] And on top of hard-power failings, Germany's intelligence network has displayed alarming gaps throughout the years, downplaying threats and being unable to keep Russian and Chinese espionage in check.[27]

Immediately after Russia's invasion of Ukraine, General Alfons Mais, head of the German Army, lamented that the Bundeswehr was 'more or less bare'. It was a collective failing. The political establishment had turned a blind eye to dangers, even if they were clear and present. That points to an issue of mentality, a more vexing problem than money or structure. Does Germany really want to lead? There are legitimate doubts about that. 'We all saw it coming' after the annexation of Crimea but failed to act, General Mais said. 'That doesn't feel good! I am angry!'[28]

Germany has a natural tendency to drift back to a reassuring status quo and avoid change. The uncomfortable reality is that it doesn't have that luxury anymore. Business is no longer just business, and security is no longer a spectator sport, especially after the first Trump administration raised doubts about American commitment

---

* Made in Germany, CNC machines – equipment that can cut, shape, drill and mill metals – are particularly sought after by arms manufacturers that supply Russia's war machine.

to its pampered European allies. The German Council on Foreign Relations warned that it's a question of when and not if the country has to fight in a war, predicting a window of less than a decade. Eva Högl, parliamentary commissioner for the Armed Forces, took a swipe at the country's leadership qualities. 'Readiness means the courage and responsibility to make decisions and implement them. At all civilian and military levels,' she said.[29] Defence Minister Boris Pistorious echoed those concerns when he countered critics' doubts over stationing a German brigade on NATO's eastern flank by 2027 as 'typical German faintheartedness'.[30]

Despite the shock over its missteps, the country has struggled to shift gears. It took two years following Russia's full-scale invasion of Ukraine for Rheinmetall (the maker of Leopard tanks) to break ground on a new munitions factory. Scholz attended the ceremony, grabbing a shovel and tossing some dirt to honour the moment. Despite all of its lauded manufacturing prowess, Germany hasn't come close to gearing up for the security challenges it faces, raising questions over the political will.

The war in Ukraine has exposed the country's naïveté, even to Germans. Tanks rolling towards Kyiv showed clearly how foolhardy it was to tie Germany's energy system to a former KGB agent nostalgic for the dark days of the Soviet Union. The war also ended Germany's soothing illusion that hard power is passé. The impact of the conflict could be seen on the streets through an influx of more than 1 million war refugees – the equivalent to the city of Cologne showing up in need of food and shelter.* Although Germans answered that call admirably, the situation has contributed to a new wave of anti-migrant backlash.

There's at least one positive thing to come out of Germany's foreign-policy reality check: the country's diplomats will almost certainly never justify deals with autocrats with the smug *Wandel durch Handel* policy. That means deals with autocrats will be justified differently, like post-Ukraine pacts with Qatar and Saudi Arabia sealed in the name of energy security. But at least that requires a

---

* According to the United Nations High Commissioner for Refugees, Germany took in about 1.1 million refugees, while Poland took in 1.6 million. https://data.unhcr.org/en/situations/ukraine.

more active, case-by-case justification. The risk is that the interest in a fundamental reorientation of defence and foreign policy fades as soon as pressure eases. That's often been the case in Germany, which is good at mobilising in a crisis, but equally adept at reverting to regular routines as soon as the heat is off. Security, though, is a long-term game and failing to find its voice and back that up with a big stick would make Germany less safe and the global order even more unstable. Germany's leaders need to accept that challenge and communicate the strategy to gain public support. Simply repeating the word 'Zeitenwende' isn't enough.

Undersized compared to the United States, Russia and China, Germany of course can't go it alone. Carrying out this historic shift requires working with and through the EU. A bloc of 450 million people clearly has more resonance than a country of 84 million. Despite all the praise for Merkel and her alleged efforts to hold the EU together, she never had a grand vision for the bloc. Scholz hasn't shown that either. The chancellor describes himself as a 'European' and has called for the EU to be reformed to play more of a geopolitical role. 'Fantasies' of national power are stuck in the past, he said.* But there has been little follow-through. Instead of bolstering the EU, Scholz's government has toyed with it. Scraps in his fractious coalition have spilled over to Brussels, which can't be a global player without Germany's support. That was highlighted by the embarrassing theatre around the FDP's initiative to hold up a ban on combustion-engine cars and box through a loophole for costly and impractical e-fuels in a political feud with the Greens. It's difficult to reconcile those actions with the comments of the previous FDP leader Hans-Dietrich Genscher, who said: 'Europe is our future, we have no other.'

Instead of shoring up Europe, a 'Germany First' attitude has crept in. During the Covid pandemic and the energy crisis, the country leapt to the aid of its companies with more than €158 billion of financial support, over 50 per cent higher than in France and tilting the table in its favour.[31] Germany has also been a drag on a range of integration issues like banking union, as it's keen

---

* Olaf Scholz address as part of the European Parliament's series of plenary debates 'This is Europe', Strasbourg, France, 9 May 2023.

to protect domestic champions like Commerzbank and provincial publicly owned savings banks, or Sparkassen.

The biggest losers from a gummed-up and ineffective EU will ultimately be Germany's exporters, which could set off a vicious circle by further stoking resentment towards Brussels. Ever since the sovereign-debt crisis, the narrative within Germany has been that the country gets taken advantage of by its spendthrift neighbours. Heavy-handed Covid policies and a ballooning bureaucracy have stirred further controversy and muddied public attitudes towards Brussels, which range from exuberant enthusiasm to open animosity.[32] What gets less attention is how Germans have been the biggest winners from EU integration, benefiting from the euro to the tune of almost €1.9 trillion, or around €23,000 per person.[33] A powerful EU should be an extension of German power rather than a threat to it, but it's not often seen that way.

Amid Germany's inner confusion over whether to push or rein in the EU, there has been a cacophony of smaller countries vying for influence. The Baltics want a more aggressive stance on Russia and faster enlargement to the east. Hungary has been disturbingly in step with Moscow and others like Slovakia and Austria have drifted in that direction. Overall, the rise of nationalist populism from Italy to Sweden remains a direct challenge to the supranational ethos of the EU. A strong and focused Germany could cut through that noise and bolster the bloc to help it vie for influence with the United States and China, but a weak and confused Germany would leave Europe at the mercy of forces all too eager to pick the region apart. And as the biggest exporter in Europe, that's a direct threat to the prosperity that Germany is so keen to protect.

Wobbly bridge

Pressure on Germany to step up has been intensifying since at least 2017. When Donald Trump became the 45th president of the United States, it was quickly clear that things had changed in the transatlantic relationship. Fresh off Trump's first G-7 meeting in the Sicilian resort town of Taormina in May of that year, Angela Merkel made a campaign stop in Munich and reset reality. 'The times when we could fully rely on others are to some extent over,' she told supporters in a Bavarian beer tent. 'We Europeans must really take our destiny into our own hands.'[34]

Interestingly, Merkel put maintaining good ties with Russia on a par with traditional transatlantic allies, a sign that she felt the need to cast a broader net for support. 'Of course we need to have friendly relations with the US and with the UK and with other neighbours, including Russia,' the chancellor said. It was unusual for the normally reserved Merkel to make foreign-policy statements in the midst of a feel-good rally of beer and pretzels, and the comment shows how shaken she was about her new American counterpart. But the strains in German–US relations didn't start or end there. The fissures just became impossible to ignore.

Germany was one of Trump's favourite punch bags during that four-year term. He complained about how many BMW and Mercedes cars were on the streets of Manhattan, how little Germany paid for NATO protection, and how intolerable Germany's trade surplus with the United States was. When he pointed out that Germany was 'totally controlled' by Russian energy,[35] he elicited condescending smirks or shrugs from German officials. He peevishly ignored Merkel's handshake during a visit to the White House in March 2017 and consistently lambasted one of America's closest allies for years. What didn't happen was an uproar in Washington or among the American public about defending Germany. In fact, Trump's anti-German antics hardly registered in the United States at all. During his presidency, roughly three-quarters of Americans saw relations between the two countries as good, whereas about two-thirds of Germans thought they were bad.[36] The vast discrepancy in perception underlines the differing expectations about the alliance. Germany needs it a lot more than the United States does, and that kind of imbalance is never a recipe for stability.

It wasn't always that way. For generations of American leaders, Germany was critical for projecting US power and influence. For Harry Truman, the 'Candy Bombers' like Gail Halvorsen who kept West Berlin fed and fuelled during Stalin's blockade from 1948 to 1949 were essential to his doctrine of standing up to totalitarianism. After the Wall divided the city and ideological divisions took on physical form, John F. Kennedy sent an enduring signal of solidarity in 1963 by declaring '*Ich bin ein Berliner*' (I am a Berliner). With the Soviet Union sputtering, Ronald Reagan stood across from the Brandenburg Gate in 1987 and challenged Mikhail Gorbachev to 'tear down this wall'. Alongside these iconic moments, physical signs of that special status are everywhere in Germany.

At the height of the Cold War, there were more than 250 American military facilities scattered across the country. In Berlin, there was of course Checkpoint Charlie, where a tense standoff took place in 1961 when Soviet and American tanks aimed their guns at each other from less than 100 metres apart. There's the Teufelsberg listening station built atop a hill created out of rubble from the bombed city to spy on communists. Glienicke Bridge, which connects Berlin and Potsdam, was the site of spy exchanges and was memorialised in a 2015 film by Steven Spielberg. More prosaic locations show how the relationship had been integrated into everyday life. Alongside schools, movie theatres and dance clubs, there were developments like Dreipfuhl, an array of thirty bungalows built for American officers and their families in leafy southwest Berlin. Today, the flat-roofed, one-storey homes with carports and open front lawns represent a time capsule of 1950s Americana and serve as a silent testimonial to how self-evident the Allied presence was in West Berlin.

The end of the Cold War brought about a decided shift in relations. Germany was no longer on the frontlines and so lost its special status. During the 1990s, over 200 American military facilities in Germany were closed as the threat level receded. American attention turned to Asia and the Middle East, especially after the terror attacks of 11 September 2001. As George W. Bush's administration sought retribution, Germany joined in the US-led campaign in Afghanistan to clamp down on the Al-Qaeda terror group. But when Washington set its sights on Iraq, claiming Saddam Hussein's regime possessed weapons of mass destruction, Germany refused – along with France (a fellow beneficiary of American post-war generosity). Staring down a stone-faced Donald Rumsfeld, America's hawkish defence secretary, Foreign Minister Joschka Fischer famously questioned the grounds for the 2003 invasion with the comment: 'I am not convinced.'

Although Fischer's doubts may have been justified, the resistance was tantamount to betrayal for Washington. Germany was a country lifted out of the ashes by American support and therefore was not in a position to refuse when called. The days of the Truman Doctrine of fighting autocracies around the world had given way to a strong-armed, unilateral approach. To put it bluntly: we paid, you play, and might makes right. This clashes with post-war European sensibilities that see power as a process embedded in laws and structure – a stance based on its relative weakness.[37]

With its defiance over Iraq, Germany became relegated to 'Old Europe', a country stuck in its ways and unwilling or unable to adapt to the New World Order. To be sure, there are still a lot of shared values and links between the United States and Germany, including the Landstuhl military hospital, where injured soldiers from Afghanistan and Iraq were treated. And there was the Barack Obama era, when he was enthusiastically welcomed in Berlin – first as a candidate in front of the *Siegessäule* (Victory Column) and then again as president in front of the Brandenburg Gate. Merkel and Obama had a personal affinity, highlighted by a viral photo of the two leaders relaxing together in the Alps at the G-7 summit in 2015. Despite such warm moments, the character of the relations between Germany and America has become decidedly cooler. That was highlighted not least by US intelligence services surveilling Merkel's mobile phone during Obama's term. It was a sign that suspicion was more than fleeting.

With Biden, the tone became more civil than under Trump, but the direction didn't change much. It was still 'America First', but between the lines instead of in neon lights. Trump-era tariffs continued, and then came the landmark Inflation Reduction Act (IRA) in 2022. The legislation was aimed at reversing decades of deindustrialisation in the United States through $485 billion in spending and tax breaks, and showed that Washington was playing hard ball in the historic shift to green manufacturing.[38] While the main target was China, the EU has braced for significant collateral damage, reflecting the new dynamic in transatlantic relations. Europe has become more of an afterthought when formulating American policy rather than a partner to coordinate with. Brussels complained about protectionist Buy American incentives in the IRA, and the bloc fretted that European companies would be lured to relocate production facilities to avoid being disadvantaged in the world's largest economy.[39] A series of senior officials from Germany, France and the European Commission cycled through Washington in an effort to get concessions, but to no avail, and showed that the United States is fine about geoeconomic competition with Europe, which had reason for concern.

By targeting operating costs and offering tax breaks, the American subsidies were more direct and simpler than what Europe planned, focusing mainly on grants for capital expenditures and taxes on carbon to encourage cleaner products. In other words, Europe would help set up green technology, but the United States would help companies make money. The American approach paves the way for battery prices dropping 30 per cent and solar panels by two-thirds by 2030, and the cost of producing clean hydrogen could even fall to zero, according to a study by the Hertie School in Berlin.[40] The EU cobbled together a response (largely composed of previous measures with the addition of some streamlined regulations), labelling it the Green Deal Industrial Plan. The tit-for-tat policy initiatives don't say much about the strengths of transatlantic ties and that's a worrying situation for Germany.

In 2020 there was a clear warning on just how tenuous those links had become. Trump lashed out with a plan to withdraw a third of the American troops left in Germany, framed as a punitive move over money 'owed' for NATO protection. The decision was taken without any consultation with Berlin, which should have been better prepared. Trump's stance had been flagged well in advance. Back in 1990, when he was just a flashy real-estate developer seeking attention, Trump included Germany in a list of partners he deemed were taking advantage of the United States. 'I think our country needs more ego,' he said in an interview with *Playboy* magazine, where he first hinted at his political ambitions. 'It is being ripped off so badly by our so-called allies; i.e., Japan, West Germany, Saudi Arabia, South Korea, etc.'[41]

The troop-withdrawal announcement triggered a stream of disgust from German politicians. The comments focused on emotional aspects like the break with tradition and accused the United States of abandoning its leadership role to the benefit of Russia and China.[42] Politicians near the massive Ramstein air-force base (the largest American military facility in Europe) bemoaned the loss of jobs and tax receipts and worried about the impact on the community.[43] But there was little reaction to the substance of Trump's criticism, namely that Germany was doing too little to safeguard itself and the rest of Europe. After the Biden administration froze the withdrawal a few months later, Germany returned to its blissful indolence. Military spending went from 1.4 per cent of GDP in 2020 to 1.3 per cent the following year. From there, it's a pretty direct line to 24 February 2022, when Russia invaded Ukraine and burst Germany's bubble for good.

While the United States and Germany are still on the same side ostensibly, the transatlantic bridge isn't very secure. In his campaign for his second term, Trump continued his attacks on Germany. 'I want German car companies to become American car companies,' he said in a speech in Savannah, Georgia. That means Berlin needs to chart a new course, likely with more bridges but also more self-reliance and a more careful assessment of who its friends are. The world isn't waiting. As painful as the loss of Russian energy was, the bigger risk in the long term for Germany's status is China.

End of the road

Just what China's threat for the German economy looks like can be seen in Arnstadt, a historic town at the edge of the Thuringian forest in former East Germany. Johann Sebastian Bach started his career there as an organist at a local cathedral, which has been elegantly restored after reunification along with the town's cobbled streets and central square. Like much of the former communist region, there are relatively few young people, and weed-strewn industrial sites are testimony to the painful disruption of reunification. But there are also signs of revival. Just north of the town centre is a sprawling industrial park known as Erfurter Kreuz, which offers rail and highway access near Germany's geographic centre. It's home to a mustard manufacturer and a jet-engine maintenance company, but one particular tenant stands out: CATL. The Chinese giant makes batteries for electric vehicles for the likes of BMW, Mercedes-Benz and Volkswagen in a sleek grey-clad hall. The building was vacated as a result of Chinese competition and represents the vicious circle of Beijing industrial policy.

In 2008, the German manufacturing giant Bosch – which makes everything from car components to power tools and heat pumps – entered the fast-developing market for solar cells with the acquisition of Ersol Solar Energy. A year later, it broke ground on a factory in Arnstadt. Chancellor Merkel attended the ceremony and called it 'a real ray of hope' for the region. But around five years later, the push collapsed as Bosch struggled to compete with the low rates offered by rivals from China. As Beijing funnelled money into the industry, prices for solar cells tumbled by half in 2011 and then again by nearly a quarter the following year.[44] The prospects were too bleak and Bosch pulled the plug, taking a $2.6 billion hit in the process.

Hundreds of people lost their jobs in a fresh blow to the region and leaving the site in Erfurter Kreuz vacant. And then, lo and behold, CATL came along in 2018 to buy Bosch's former building for its first production facility outside of China. Underlining the importance of the battery maker's expansion to Germany, the contract was signed during a state visit by Chinese Premier Li Keqiang. With eastern Germany still desperate for investment and Trump sowing doubts about the transatlantic partnership, Chinese money was welcome and Merkel praised the move as 'an important day for Thuringia'. But it was also an indication of how China was turning the tables on Germany and dominating a key technology of the future. With more than a tinge of remorse, she added: 'If we could do it ourselves, I wouldn't be sad either.'[45]

China's encroachment has been deliberate, and Germany walked right into the trap with its eyes wide open but refused to believe what it was seeing. Berlin should have been well aware of the risks, but steadfast conviction in the immutable prowess of German engineering allowed it to look past the jeopardy to which it was exposing the country. In 2015 (just three years before CATL bought the former Bosch site in Arnstadt), Beijing unveiled its 'Made in China 2025' strategy for all the world to see. The stated goal was to transform the country's industrial sector from a source of cheap labour into a leader in advanced manufacturing. In short, China wanted to knock Germany from its pedestal.

To a large extent, Berlin's Industrie 4.0 concept was a template. The roadmap for the so-called fourth industrial revolution aims to chart a path towards 'smart manufacturing' in which components and factory equipment communicate to create a more sustainable, flexible and efficient process. But there was a decisive difference between the two countries' approaches. Whereas Germany sought to encourage innovation by promoting research with a couple of hundred million euros, China wanted to steer the transformation from the top. The Chinese strategy set 'self-sufficiency' goals for its manufacturers: supplying 70 per cent of core components and critical materials, 40 per cent of mobile-phone chips, 80 per cent of the domestic electric-vehicle market, and 80 per cent of renewable-energy equipment.[46] It was a throwback to classic central planning but backed with hundreds of billions of dollars in financial support and mobilisation from all levels of the state apparatus, including military hackers.

China's industrial strategy was a nationalistic development plan and a clear challenge to globalisation. Despite massive investment in manufacturing joint ventures by Volkswagen and others, liberal values were not flowing back towards the Asian autocracy. Germany's *Wandel durch Handel* had failed again. The growth in trade had not bound China more tightly with the international community nor paved the way for democratic processes. On the contrary, intercontinental commerce gave the country a fast track for development by trading know-how for market access, and the 'Made in China 2025' initiative was pushing that further. The European Chamber of Commerce in China warned that the strategy amounted to an 'import substitution plan'.[47] But it was more than that. It signalled that the days of relying on China for easy growth were over.

At the time the strategy was released, Germany's trade deficit with China had already climbed to €20.6 billion. That had nearly tripled by 2023, and Germany was regularly doing more business with the Asian superpower than the United States despite growing concerns about China's aggressive practices. While slapping sanctions on Russia undermined Germany's energy stability, links with China run deeper. In some ways, the country is building a replica of itself there. Volkswagen has more car factories in China than Germany. BASF unveiled a €10 billion project to build a sprawling chemical facility in Zhanjiang, mirroring its home plant in Ludwigshafen.

Thousands of smaller manufacturers, the so-called *Mittelstand*, are also active in the country. Overall, about 1.1 million families in Germany depend on China for their livelihoods.[48] If all those people lived in one place, it would be the second-largest German city by a clear margin.

In pursuit of the 'Made in China 2025' plan, Chinese companies acquired technology and skills from abroad, and Germany was a favourite target. A year after the strategy was official, the home-appliance maker Midea swooped in to acquire KUKA, whose industrial robots line the assembly halls of German automakers. There were concerns about jobs and the risk of China accessing sensitive customer data, but the transaction went through. And just like that, the Augsburg-based national champion had become Chinese property.

The semiconductor-equipment maker Aixtron was also a target in 2016 and while the deal was foiled, it indicated the lengths to which China was willing to go. Fujian Grand Chip Investment Fund made a bid shortly after a company owned by the same Chinese fund cancelled a critical order. That hit Aixtron's shares and made the planned purchase cheaper, but it raised concerns about collusion. After its economy minister was hauled into the American Embassy in Berlin for a briefing by CIA officers, Germany withdrew its approval and the bid failed.[49] But the writing was on the wall – the Chinese were coming. That set off alarm bells in Berlin. Sigmar Gabriel, the economy minister during Merkel's third term, complained about German companies being 'sacrificed on the altar of free markets', while China restricted access to its economy.[50] But beyond words of concern, there was little concrete action. After all, China was the golden goose, especially for German automakers.

It's long been clear that Beijing plays by its own rules, and that also impacted Arnstadt. After Bosch pulled the plug, the facility was first acquired by its German rival SolarWorld. The deal helped maintain some of the jobs, but in 2012 the Bonn-based company was sent reeling by a series of hacks from Chinese military operatives, according to a 2014 indictment from the US Department of Justice.[51] At the time of the data breaches, SolarWorld was investing in a new type of technology and expected to have a competitive edge for years. Instead, Chinese rivals got a jump-start, and SolarWorld suffered damages from the theft totalling more than $120 million, according to testimony to the US Trade Representative.[52] Struggling to keep pace on price after its intellectual property was stolen, SolarWorld filed for insolvency in 2017. That ultimately cleared the path for CATL to acquire the Arnstadt facility. 'Many other companies face the same issues of cyberhacking and technology theft . . . but are unwilling to come forward publicly due to fear of lost sales or retaliation by China,' SolarWorld representatives testified.

By encouraging companies to ride roughshod over open markets, the 'Made in China 2025' policy played the role of 'central villain' in efforts to undermine the West's technology leadership,[53] but Germany has been an unwitting accomplice. It's not just corporate investment. German research institutes have played a supporting role. The Fraunhofer Society has a smart manufacturing centre in Shanghai and an industrial cooperation project in Foshan, the Max Planck Society has a biomedicine research lab in Guangzhou, and the Helmholtz Association cooperates with about ten Chinese partners. Such links at the highest levels of German research risk leaking knowledge that Germany needs for its own industries.[54]

What that looks like is evident in the auto industry. Following the financial crisis, the country recovered faster than most other industrial economies in part because Volkswagen and its peers massively expanded in China's fast-growing car market. To bolster its bottom line, Mercedes was thrilled to sell more S-Class luxury saloons there than anywhere else in the world, and BMW and Volkswagen enjoyed similar success. But there was a catch of course. To produce locally and avoid hefty tariffs, Germany's automakers needed joint ventures with Chinese companies, generally state-owned entities. They gladly fell in line and did things the Chinese way – including VW brushing aside concerns of forced labour at one of its plants.[55] But in the process, they helped teach China how to build cars, and that expertise has helped fuel the country's expansion in electric vehicles. BYD (China's version of Tesla) overtook VW as the biggest car brand in China in 2023. As 2024 drew to a close, the market share of BMW, Mercedes and Volkswagen in China was in steep decline as officials and consumers shun their models for those of Chinese rivals. BYD and other home-grown brands have used their power base in China to export low-cost EVs to Europe and other foreign markets, threatening German automakers globally. That's how the trap closes.

China's strategy isn't just about manufacturing. Beijing is also seeking to redraw trade routes through the Belt and Road Initiative. Vast new networks of highways, railways and pipelines are planned to run through Central Asia and on to Europe to tie dozens of countries closer together. With maritime spurs running from Southeast Asia to India and Africa, the scope is an expression of Beijing's ambitions and represents 'a new phase in China's rise'.[56] That puts the country on a collision course with the United States. The trade spats stoked under Trump haven't gone away, and America is not going to allow Beijing to expand its influence without a challenge.

Germany is extremely exposed to that crossfire. The physical signs of that are in Duisburg, the westernmost terminus of the so-called New Silk Road. The municipality at the confluence of the Rhine and the Ruhr is home to the world's largest inland port and is Germany's self-proclaimed 'China City' — a testament to reliance on the Asia superpower in the same way that the Elbphilharmonie epitomises Germany's bygone status as the world's largest exporter. For the downtrodden industrial town — where a shuttered steel plant became the centrepiece of a public park — the chance to participate in the New Silk Road was too good to pass up. In 2021 some fifty trains arrived every week from China with cargo to be reloaded for other European destinations, but in a sign of the trade imbalance, they embarked on the three-week return journey only about half full.[57]

Berlin is trying to respond, but the implementation is choppy. In 2022 the government blocked the sale of a chip factory to a Chinese company on the grounds that the deal would compromise national security. 'Germany naturally is and will continue to be an open destination for investment, but we aren't naive,' said Robert Habeck, the economy minister and vice-chancellor under Olaf Scholz.[58] The country's firmer line isn't universal though. Scholz then allowed a Chinese shipping company to buy nearly a quarter of a Hamburg container terminal. Although that was lower than the initial plan for a 35 per cent holding, the facility was determined to be 'critical infrastructure', which should have made it off limits for overseas investment, especially from an antagonistic power.

The tensions between wanting to stand up to Beijing and protecting commercial interests were evident in Berlin's strategy on China. The paper was unveiled in 2023 after the war in Ukraine sparked widespread concerns in Germany about a sudden break with its biggest trading partner.[59] Following months of talks, it was a long-overdue assessment, and the vibe that came through is that breaking up is hard to do. Business considerations clearly tempered tough language on politics and human rights. 'Our aim is not to decouple from China, but to reduce risks as far as possible,' Foreign Minister Annalena Baerbock said at the presentation.[60] 'We are showing that we are realistic, but not naive' (repeating the word used by Habeck as if repetition was powerful enough to undo the mistakes of the past).

While Germany acknowledged concerns about its exposure, reducing that will be a slow and delicate process, if it happens at all. The strategy mainly depends on setting up a network of partners that can help offset China. That's no small task, especially given the Asian country's dominance in minerals needed for batteries and climate-friendly technologies. While much of the initiative makes for good political rhetoric, there's little incentive for businesses to turn their backs on China. If a break comes because of an attack on Taiwan or some other major breach, corporate bosses would be forced to react to sanctions or whatever transpires, and Germany has shown a propensity to bail out companies in need. So why would German boardrooms pull back pre-emptively and give up on profits as long as they're still available? And in reality, there's not much Germany can offer to counter the firepower behind China's development plans. So unsurprisingly, there are few signs that a 'de-risking' process has started, with German direct investment in China rising to a record of nearly €12 billion in 2023.[61] Automakers especially are doubling-down, deepening their ties in China despite mounting warnings – an approach that's been dubbed 'automotive foreign policy' because the manufacturers are following their own objectives rather than those of the government.

Henry Kissinger famously quipped that Germany is 'too big for Europe, but too small for the world'. That was in the 1970s, when the post-war order was very much intact. Now, nothing is certain. Globalisation is under threat, the American security umbrella has flown away, China is seeking to bend the world to its will, Europe has again faced the spectre of war, and the climate crisis threatens even further instability. Germany's true stature is about to be measured like never before. Many of the country's politicians lean towards a middle way: between allegiance with the West and keeping options with Russia and China open. That's driven by economic interests, but it's unlikely to work for long. At best, tiptoeing between the fronts might slow the loss of power and influence, but eventually Germany risks becoming sidelined and having its prosperity eroded further.

The situation puts Germany in a conundrum. It needs a clear and assertive presence on the international stage to defend the trading position that underpins its economy, but unsteady prospects make the job of forging a public consensus over Germany's global role even more problematic. That task of determining when, where and how Germany should engage in geopolitics then gets tougher as society splinters. In other words, the more Germany needs a clear profile, the harder it is for the country to define one. And those domestic hurdles are getting bigger as society polarises and as the promise of prosperity (the central element of Germany's social contract) crumbles.

7
Broken Ladder

'If people knew how to make do with as little materially as they do spiritually, the world would be a much better place.'
Peter Sirius

Concerns about the cleft between rich and poor have a long tradition in Germany, not least through the writings of Karl Marx. In *Metropolis* – a classic silent film from the Weimar era – director Fritz Lang depicted the city's elite perched high in a New Tower of Babel. Known as the Club of the Sons, it represented the natural expectation that privilege and status would be passed down family lines. Toiling in subterranean conditions, the harried and downtrodden workers are disconnected from the luxurious world above. Made during the end of the boom-and-bust 1920s, the futuristic film was meant to depict life a century later: in other words, now. While Germany hasn't evolved into Lang's dystopian vision, there are familiar echoes. The divides are vast between the growing ranks of the poor and the country's 130 billionaires and almost 3 million millionaires (many of whom are heirs), making the century-old film a sharper commentary on inequality than many might like to admit.

Vaunted as a model of stability, Germany's social cohesion is being stretched by glaring disparities. Social strata have become ossified, with little opportunity to move up. At the top, there are protections in place to guard against a decline, making the generational decay of Thomas Mann's well-to-do Buddenbrooks appear unlikely today. Mobility is possible in the squeezed working class, but more likely tumbling downward into precarity. The lower rungs have almost no chance of climbing up at all. In other words, the stairs in the House of Germany are out of order.

Despite its considerable national wealth, prosperity is unevenly distributed. Beyond the well-known East–West divide, there are other significant gaps, such as between the minority fortunate enough to own homes and the majority who do not. The gulf between rich and poor has widened, exacerbated by inflation and soaring energy costs following Russia's invasion of Ukraine. While some German industries remain world leaders (like biomedicine), steel-making, automotive components and basic manufacturing are struggling, leading to wage stagnation for workers in less competitive sectors. Wealth is increasingly concentrated at the top. Among Europe's Big Four (Germany, France, Italy, and the UK), Germany has the highest wealth inequality, with the largest share of assets held by the top 1 per cent. At the lower end, a fifth of the population, almost 18 million people, are threatened with poverty and social exclusion. The post-war dream of *Wohlstand für Alle* (prosperity for all) is fading, replaced by a reality that's much more like *Wohlstand für Wenige* (prosperity for a few). As the idea of shared prosperity fades, the door opens for ethnic and anti-establishment alternatives.

Inequality, of course, isn't just a German problem. In Great Britain, more children go to school hungry and return to poorly heated homes compared to those in Germany. In the United States, inequality is starkly visible in the contrast between affluent suburbs and violent inner cities and neglected rural areas. Yet in Germany, hope for upward mobility is particularly bleak. On several measures, the federal republic has the worst social mobility in Europe. More importantly, for many Germans, the growing divide between rich and poor feels like a betrayal of the post-war social contract.

There is always hope that Germany can turn things around. In *Metropolis*, the final scene offers a symbolic reconciliation between the city's elite and its oppressed workers. After a violent struggle, the hero Freder joins the hands of the capitalist leader (his father) and the workers' foreman Grot. A title card declares: 'The mediator between head and hands must be the heart!' With political rhetoric often caught up in a cycle of poor-shaming, Germany is still looking for that heart.

Heir apparent

To understand widening divisions, a trip to the genteel town of Bad Homburg just north of Frankfurt is in order. The community at the foot of the low-lying Taunus mountains boasts fourteen mineral springs. The waters are supposed to be able to treat rheumatism, digestive distress and cardiovascular disorders, and can be drunk or bathed in. A centrepiece of the spa business is an elegant nineteenth-century bath house named in honour of Wilhelm I of Prussia, the first Kaiser of the united German Empire. Bad Homburg boasts an elegant pedestrian zone and a market square with cafés. The city park has an ornate Thai temple erected as a gift by the king of Siam following his stay in 1907. Bad Homburg also suffered its share of German-style tragedy. During the Nazi period, its Jewish community was wiped out, and in 1989 leftist radicals from the Red Army Faction claimed credit for murdering Deutsche Bank Chairman Alfred Herrhausen by blowing up his car. The assassination took place just two days after Helmut Kohl presented his ten-point plan for German reunification.

Bad Homburg's connection to Germany's woes is its attachment to money. That was established in 1841, when a casino opened that became known as the 'mother of Monte Carlo' because it was founded by the same twin brothers who created the famed gaming palace on the French Riviera. Then in 1888, Bad Homburg's exclusive cachet was cemented when it became the summer residence of Wilhelm II, the third and last Kaiser of imperial Germany. Town officials celebrate the association with the elite through its official marketing slogan *Champagnerluft und Inspiration* (champagne air and inspiration). The privileged position of German wealth is personified in the form of the local Quandt family, who, like members of a new aristocracy, are well-isolated from the common folk.

The heirs to the BMW fortune have called Bad Homburg home since 1950, moving from Brandenburg which had become part of the Soviet zone and therefore not a good place for capitalists. The process of settling in their new home town included clearing the view by physically moving a 450-ton building 62 metres, because they weren't allowed to tear it down due to a post-war housing shortage.[1] Rather than suffering from the effects of World War II, the family emerged wealthier, thanks to deep and opportunistic ties to the Nazis. The Quandts and the elite of the Third Reich moved in the same circles. That was true to the extent that Magda, the second wife of family patriarch Günther Quandt, later married Joseph Goebbels, Adolf Hitler's propaganda chief, after their divorce. As Nazi Germany was collapsing, she and Goebbels killed their six children and themselves in Hitler's bunker in Berlin on 1 May 1945. Before the murder-suicide, Magda wrote to her eldest son Harald Quandt, the half-sibling of the victims, saying: 'Our glorious idea is coming to an end, and with it everything I have known in my life that is beautiful, admirable, noble and good.'

During the Nazi era, the businesses in the Quandts' complex network of holdings manufactured munitions and weapons, provided raw materials and made batteries for submarines. Günther Quandt's business dealings included acquiring assets seized from Jews.[2] Companies in the portfolio employed tens of thousands of forced labourers, and there was a concentration camp adjacent to a battery factory in Hannover, where a lack of safety measures exposed many prisoners to lead poisoning.[3] Günther joined the Nazi Party in 1933, and in 1937 he was honoured as a *Wehrwirtschaftsführer* in recognition for his service supplying the military. Unlike some other business leaders such as Friedrich Flick (who would become Germany's richest man in the post-war era) and Alfried Krupp von Bohlen und Halbach (the last industrialist of the Krupp steel-making dynasty), the Quandt patriarch was not convicted of war crimes. His oldest son Herbert, who helped organise forced labourers during the war, is credited with the move that established the family as one of the biggest winners of the *Wirtschaftswunder*.

In the late 1950s, BMW was in trouble. Its first post-war car was the so-called Baroque Angel, a huge sedan that could seat six and was too expensive for the times. The automaker tried to tap the low end of the market with the Isetta mini-car, but that wasn't enough. In 1959 the Munich-based manufacturer was about to be swallowed up by rival Daimler-Benz. But after the workforce and minority shareholders rejected the deal, Herbert Quandt bankrolled a restructuring plan and saved BMW, helping it on its way to becoming an icon of post-war affluence and success. It also established the family as one of the silent powers of German business. Herbert's children, Susanne Klatten and Stefan Quandt, hold just shy of half of BMW and since the late 1990s have served on the supervisory board, which hires and fires top executives and signs off on key strategic decisions.

The two heirs have diversified their holdings to become even wealthier. Susanne owns the chemical company Altana as well as a stake in graphite and composite materials manufacturer SGL Carbon. Stefan has holdings in a logistics firm, a credit-card company, and a maker of homoeopathic products. In early 2024 they ranked as the third and fourth richest people in Germany, respectively, and together they control some $55 billion in assets.[4] In June 2024, Susanne announced plans to transfer holdings to her three children, keeping wealth secured within the clan.[5]

None of their holdings bear the family name, and that makes it easier to fly under the radar. It was a strategy followed by Günther Quandt, a classic corporate raider. He didn't invent anything, but he inherited a textile plant and used those resources to accumulate more wealth. The fortune and the family's foundation* are run out of quaint Bad Homburg, which is well insulated from the problems facing much of the rest of Germany.

Despite their enormous wealth and the power that comes with it, the siblings rarely appear in public. It's unclear what their access to political decision-makers are or what agenda they pursue. But they raised eyebrows in 2013 when Susanne, Stefan and their mother Johanna Quandt donated a combined €690,000 to the Christian Democratic Union and €210,000 to the Free Democrats at a time when a decision loomed on tighter auto emissions.[6] The generosity resumed in 2016 (a year after Johanna passed away). Between then and 2023 the siblings quietly contributed €1.2 million to the Christian Democrats, generally in annual donations just above the reporting threshold of €50,000 and sometimes more.[7] It's the kind of money that's easily parted with for the family, which received over €2 billion in 2023, just in dividends from BMW.

To be sure, the Quandts have had bad things happen. Harald died in a plane accident in 1967. Susanne was the target of a foiled kidnapping along with her mother in 1978, and in 2007 she was

---

* The Herbert Quandt Stiftung says it's involved in supporting arts, science and civic engagement, but doesn't list any of its projects and doesn't accept funding requests.

blackmailed by a former lover. But without a doubt, the family is a key beneficiary of a system that protects wealth, making them complicit in the growing cleft between Germany's rich and poor. Stefan did express 'deep regret'[8] for his father's role in the exploitation and deaths of forced labourers, but also excused it as the way things were done in the day. That might be true, but the transparency only came in 2011 after the family opened its archives following a damaging documentary that included a comment from Herbert Quandt's son Sven wishing Germany would stop talking about the Holocaust and move on.[9]

Like many wealthy Germans, the Quandts don't like the attention and want to be treated as if they're just like other private individuals. But they have benefited extraordinarily from the German system, and that makes them public figures whether they like it or not. Instead, they want sympathy. In a rare joint interview in 2019, Susanne and Stefan said that dealing with the responsibility and jealousy from inheriting a vast fortune is a misunderstood burden. 'The role as a guardian of wealth also has personal sides that aren't so nice,' said Susanne, dismissing wealth redistribution in favour of a society that allows equal opportunities.[10] But in reality, the playing field is tilted in the Quandts' favour and the slope is getting steeper.

Germany's billionaire class extends beyond just the Quandts. And it's expanding. Among Europe's major economies, Germany now has the highest share of billionaires. While wages for the lower rung of society have stagnated, the share of wealth owned by the top 1 per cent has surged. Since 1990, the wealth of billionaires has grown from being 50 times greater than that of the bottom half of the population to 100 times greater.

Although the trends that have widened the gaps between ordinary workers and the mega-wealthy have been common across advanced economies, Germany's case is particularly stark. Its Gini coefficient (a measure of wealth or income inequality, with the higher the number the greater the gap between rich and poor) is the highest among Europe's major economies. A score of 100 means one person owns or earns all the money, while zero means perfect equality. Although Germany does well on income, its wealth score is 77.2, seven points higher than Britain, where the aristocracy own more than a third of the country's land. Meanwhile, the wealth share of the bottom 50 per cent in Germany has halved since 1990. This marks a significant departure from the equal opportunity envisioned by Ludwig Erhard, the former chancellor and a key architect of post-war German identity. Instead, the country's socioeconomic conditions are slipping towards the explosive disparities reminiscent of the *Gründerzeit* in the late 1800s, just before the bloody nightmares of Germany's twentieth century started.

Despite the tensions, families like the Quandts have been adept at staying out of the public eye. Some even go to great lengths to ensure they have a low profile. The Boehringer family has taken advantage of Germany's generous media protection laws to sue *Manager Magazin*[11] to keep its name out of the publication's annual list of the richest Germans,[12] even though the owners of the pharma company Boehringer Ingelheim may have challenged the Quandt heirs for the top spots. Other silent billionaires include Dieter Schwarz, owner of the retail giants Lidl and Kaufland. In a striking example of wealth inequality, one researcher calculated that a Kaufland cashier would need to work for over a million years to match Schwarz's fortune. Despite his immense power and potential influence, little is known about Schwarz's political or personal beliefs. He avoids interviews and there are only three known photos – fewer than those of 'Mad' King Ludwig II of Bavaria, a notorious recluse (and Richard Wagner's patron) who died in the nineteenth century before the rise of photography.

Although reclusive and out of the public eye, the influence of the super-rich appears evident in German tax policy. The state collects revenue mainly from wages, whereas there are gaping loopholes for capital and financial gains. Tax rates rise quickly on the lower end of the scale and then plateau at an annual income of €67,000 before bumping up a bit at €278,000. The focus of tax collectors is on active income (money earned through work) rather than passive income (money earned by kicking back and collecting from other people's work, i.e., dividends and interest). Unlike the UK where dividends are taxed progressively in relation to income, in Germany they are subject to a flat tax rate, hitting lower-income individuals harder in relative terms (in the unusual scenario that they own stocks in the first place). According to the *Netzwerk Steuergerechtigkeit* (tax justice network), the structure of the tax system means an average working couple will pay almost double the rate of a multimillionaire: 43 per cent versus 24 per cent.[13]

The breaks for the rich were broadened in 1997, when a levy of a mere 1 per cent on wealth was suspended following a court decision that questioned the basis for assessing the value of holdings. In the decades since it's never been reinstituted, because of theoretical concerns that the wealthy would flee to tax havens. Over that time – with authority trading hands between the conservative CDU and the worker-friendly Social Democrats – the German government has lost over €380 billion in revenue that could have helped pay for improving schools, upgrading technology, and repairing roads to strengthen the economic foundation. Meanwhile, the wealth of the wealthiest increased during that time by some €460 billion, according to a study by Oxfam Deutschland.[14] That's good for them, but bad for Germany's social cohesion.

The benefits of the wealthy aren't just limited to their annual taxes. Other rules ensure that wealth is protected for generations. Every year in Germany an estimated €300 billion is inherited or passed along as gifts. Very little is skimmed off by the state and ploughed back into the broader economy. The first €500,000 to a spouse is tax-free, €400,000 to a child, and €200,000 to a grandchild. There are similar levels in the UK, another country where parental wealth often determines the financial well-being of children. The same tax-free amounts apply to gifts. So a lot can be divided up before tax even becomes an issue. And then there are tax-avoidance methods like creating companies that manage the family's homes and other assets. The kid-glove treatment allows wealth to remain concentrated in a select set of families (almost exclusively from West Germany since there was little wealth in the post-communist East to pass along).

The rationale is that a lot of money is tied up in family-owned companies and taxing inheritance could force families to take on debt and weaken the competitiveness of the firms in the process. There would be ways around that though – like allowing payments to take place over years or offsetting human capital from asset values – but the political will isn't there. In 2022 receipts from passing along wealth totalled a mere €9.2 billion, or a tax rate of less than 3 per cent.[15] The Finance Ministry has even ranked concessions for passing along businesses to friends and families as the top tax gift.[16]

It wasn't always this way. In 1952, Germany implemented a wealth tax to help share the burden of reconstruction. It was levied on the value of assets as of 1948. In other words, it was retroactive, so the wealthy couldn't rejig their holdings to dodge payment. Reconstruction was a historic effort and the tax was structured that way. Households were allowed to spread out payments over twenty-five years. The measure raised a total of €75 billion to help compensate for damage from the war.[17] It reduced the wealth share of the richest of Germany's rich by 3 percentage points, doubling the impact from the war but hardly debilitating.[18] It also brings us back to Bad Homburg, where those funds were managed and administered by the *Bundesausgleichsamt* (Federal Equalisation Office) located just a few kilometres from the family home of the Quandts.

These protections for the wealthy aren't accidental. They are part of a system that keeps social strata rigid at least at the top end, while failing to help those at the bottom climb up – despite the professed social contract of prosperity for all. To be blunt, let's call it what it is: Germany has erected institutions of inequality.

Hard ceiling

Germany's post-war identity is rooted in principles of equality, fairness and shared prosperity. The welfare state has been the instrument of implementation of those national ideals. Where the United States has flag-waving patriotism, Great Britain fealty to the king, and France pride in the republic, Germany has transfer payments. Its constitution describes the country as a 'social state',[*] and yet the dissonance between the nation's lofty goals and the realities of many citizens has become deafening.

While Germany prides itself on its *Soziale Marktwirtschaft* (social market economy) – a system meant to balance economic freedom with collective well-being – cracks are deepening. Working Germans struggle to hold on to their living standards as the country's rich

---

[*] Article 20 of the Basic Law.

get richer (even more so than in other Western countries). Since the early 1990s, average wealth more than doubled for Germany's top 10 per cent, while stagnating for the bottom half.[19]

These conditions stem to a large extent from institutions created with the aim of securing social cohesion, but they haven't been working as intended. The result is that inequality in Germany is among the worst in Europe, and nowhere in the developed world does a parent's socioeconomic status so heavily dictate a child's future – not even compared with more notoriously stratified societies like Great Britain, Italy and the United States. An OECD study found that it would take descendants of a low-income family in Germany six generations just to claw their way to average.[20] To be fair, the United States and Great Britain aren't much better at five generations, but that's still a generation faster.

To understand how Germany traps citizens in the class they were born in, we'll look at three areas where the system stifles mobility: housing, healthcare and education. After the devastation of two world wars, provision of the three were among the pillars of the democracy established in the Federal Republic. For Konrad Adenauer, post-war Germany's first chancellor, housing was one of the most urgent tasks of reconstruction, a preoccupation that drove forward the building of millions of affordable homes. On healthcare too, his government sought to broaden medical coverage, recognising fair access to care as essential for social cohesion. While education remained stratified, efforts were made for schooling to forge a path to economic security – whether it be by going to university or by learning one of the trades fuelling the country's *Wirtschaftswunder* (economic miracle).

More than just an aspiration, social security was effectively engraved in the social contract. As Ludwig Erhard, Adenauer's finance minister and later chancellor, said, the government would set the framework so that 'people can live free from worries and hardship, that they gain the opportunity to acquire property and thus become independent, that they can develop more human dignity because they are then no longer dependent on the mercy of others, not even on the mercy of the state'.[21] Fast forward seventy years and the promise looks like a cruel joke. The institutions that Germany created to underpin its social system have erected formidable barriers to advancement. Security has instead become ossification.

That's especially true of housing. Contrary to Erhard's vision, citizens are at the mercy of landlords because of the state's failure to ensure sufficient supply of affordable homes. Fewer than half of German citizens own their living space, one of the lowest rates in the developed world and below the two-third share of home owners in France and the United Kingdom, or three-quarters in Italy, the Netherlands and Spain.[22] That means the majority of Germans have little opportunity to build wealth and are exposed to the anxiety of rising rents eating up more and more of their pay cheques.

That imbalance is created by a system that charges steep entry fees for getting into the property club. Up-front taxes and fees jack up the cost of purchasing a home by 10 per cent or more and are paid out of pocket at the time of purchase when money is tight. An example: A couple with a small child are looking for a flat in the greater Munich area, where a compact three-room flat could easily cost over €650,000. In addition to financing the mortgage, they have to pay €22,750 in property purchase tax, €23,200 in estate-agent fees, and €9,750 for the notarisation of the contract. That adds up to just under €56,000 in cash, which is roughly equivalent to the average annual income in the region. While conditions vary by state, the outcome is similar, creating an almost insurmountable hurdle for people living from payslip to payslip. As a result, the median net wealth of Germany's home-owning minority is over €300,000, whereas it's little more than €16,000 for those stuck in the rental system.[23]

To be fair, Germany's approach kept home prices relatively steady and prevented the kind of widespread speculation that inflated the American real-estate bubble before the global financial crisis. But that relative stability has come at the cost of upward mobility and social stability. It leaves millions of Germans exposed to being a layoff away from slipping into a precarious living situation. If rental housing is plentiful and affordable, the lack of home ownership doesn't have to be a problem. But that's not the case and much of it is a self-inflicted problem. And waiving taxes on profits from property sales after ten years is another gift to the wealthy that skews the system in favour of old money and against those struggling to claw their way up.

Desperation over the growing gaps in German civil society has added to the chaos. Berlin's rapid transformation from 'poor but sexy' to 'expensive and chaotic' led to a referendum in 2021 that sought to prod the city to shift the balance of power away from profit-hungry landlords, who have incentives to squeeze out tenants on cheap contracts. That move followed the city's effort to freeze rents for five years, which was struck down in court but had the fallout of reducing supply of long-term rentals as landlords sold or rented on short-term contracts at higher prices. A collapse in new construction across Germany has sent foreboding signals for the years ahead.

Shelter is a basic need and Germany used to do it well. The Fuggerei in Augsburg dates from the sixteenth century and is the oldest social-housing development still in use. About 150 Catholic families live in the quaint car-free district for the cost of three daily prayers and 88 cents a year, plus heating and utilities. From the early 1900s, there were standard-setting developments for working-class families like Hellerau in Dresden, the Zickzack housing in Frankfurt, and the Horseshoe Estate in Berlin. There were building booms in the post-war reconstruction period and following reunification, but since the start of the Angela Merkel era in the early 2000s, building rates have stagnated. Onerous zoning laws mean it's hard to find new land with permission to build on. Social-housing supply has also been slowed by well-meaning, but strict energy-efficiency standards, which skews projects towards the luxury segment.

As Germany increasingly handed control over housing to private investors, supply of affordable homes has dwindled from year to year, especially in cities where demand is greatest. In the late 1980s there were about 4 million public-housing units in West Germany. That had declined to a little over 1 million by the end of 2022.[24] That year fewer than 300,000 homes were completed, short of the 400,000 target set out by Chancellor Olaf Scholz's government. Demographic trends towards smaller households intensify the demand as people move into cities where there are better prospects for jobs and more dynamic lifestyles than in rural areas. In Germany's seventy-seven biggest towns or cities, there is a shortage of 2 million affordable homes, with the largest shortages in Berlin, Hamburg and Cologne.[25]

For most people, the mainstream's policy responses have seemed woefully ineffectual, further undermining faith in the state. Introduced in 2015, during Merkel's third term, the *Mietpreisbremse* (literally 'rental price brake') is a legal measure introduced to curb excessive rent increases in cities and regions with a tight housing market. It hasn't worked. Since its launch, rental prices in thirty-seven of the country's biggest cities have risen by double-digit amounts, outstripping gains in most people's wages.[26] Across Germany, homelessness rose steadily during the Merkel years even as outsiders marvelled at the overall economy's resilience. 'For the social cohesion of our society, it is essential that rents and apartments remain affordable for the majority of people,' said Lukas Siebenkotten, president of the German Renters Federation. 'This principle has been shaken.'[27]

Healthcare is another area where the German system thwarts social mobility. Structural impediments start at birth, or even before. Like housing, Germany's medical system is very much a story of riches for the haves and closed doors for the have-nots. There are public and private insurance plans, and the level of provision varies markedly, not least when it comes to prenatal and postnatal care. Low-income women often miss out on essential preventive services, with nearly one in three having no contact with a midwife before childbirth — an alarming contrast to just one in ten among women from well-off households.[28]

There's also widely varying access to other support. Private care plans pay for biweekly check-ups after the thirty-second week of pregnancy (complete with 3D ultrasounds that give a detailed view of the baby's facial features). Some plans even include hypnobirthing, a technique promoting a serene birth through self-hypnosis. In stark contrast, state insurance covers only three ultrasounds for routine pregnancies, and in poorer or out-of-town areas where services have been cut back, even those can be hard to access. While most women can happily skip hypnobirthing, more equal access to care might reduce stress or spot treatable conditions faster.

Healthcare disparities continue through paediatric care and into adult life, limiting poorer citizens' ability to get ahead. Data show Germans with low socioeconomic status are in poorer medical condition and have increased risks for various physical and mental illnesses. Whereas 90 per cent of affluent men aged thirty to sixty-four say they feel good about their health, that drops to 60 per cent for those in lower social groups.[29]

Germany isn't unique in facing healthcare inequalities, but few countries have made the welfare state such a core part of their identity. Unlike Great Britain or the United States, where economic freedom takes centre stage, Germans expect their state to balance individual freedoms with the collective good. This balance has long been the cornerstone of Germany's economic model, fostering both prosperity and social cohesion. However, widening differences in healthcare and the erosion of welfare provisions undermine faith in the system. If you're born into a wealthy family, you get quality healthcare; if you're born into poverty, you don't. What was once a model of equitable access has become increasingly stratified, holding a mirror up to broader economic divides. As Marcel Fratzscher, an economist who heads the German Institute for Economic Research in Berlin, has remarked, 'the social market economy is dead'.[30]

That leaves education. Schooling should be a sturdy rung to help those climb up. But instead of levelling the playing field, it often misses the mark – a worrying trend for an advanced economy. Rather than empowering disadvantaged students with the tools to overcome their challenges, the system frequently serves to deepen existing divides. The early-tracking process, which funnels children into academic or vocational streams at a young age, disproportionately impacts those from lower-income backgrounds. These students are often deprived of the same resources, support and opportunities available to their more affluent peers, leaving them struggling to compete on an uneven playing field. What should be a clear path to a middle-class lifestyle becomes an arduous journey filled with roadblocks and detours, where each step forward is hard-won. This structural inequality leaves the promise of education as a great equaliser unfulfilled, trapping many in the very circumstances they might hope to escape.

Disparities start in daycare. Although there's a right to childcare (and it's relatively affordable), ranging from being free in Berlin to around €400 per month at its most expensive, there's not enough capacity, with about 430,000 missing spots.[31] While places are theoretically assigned on a first-come, first-served basis, over-subscription often leads to informal favouritism, benefiting children from affluent families. A well-placed word, a friendly visit to staff, or even a thoughtfully timed cake can influence acceptance decisions. Blogs and message boards are filled with tips on how to secure a place, often emphasising the need to be assertive and persistent – a challenge for parents who lack the language skills, the time or the connections. Major publications offer tips for securing a place, with one suggesting that parents brush up on their musical skills so they can provide entertainment at daycare festive events.[32] In Berlin, where it's estimated that around 20,000 nursery spots are lacking, some have resorted to more drastic measures. Frustrated at the prospect of a forty-minute commute to daycare, one father in a rapidly gentrifying part of the capital offered a €5,000 reward via an advertisement on eBay for a better spot.[33]

While well-off Germans openly play the system, others get bypassed. Low-income families don't have the resources to invest in a search, and foreigners have had the idea drummed into them that this is a country of order and rules need to be followed. Consequently, children from families where German isn't the primary language or where parents lack academic credentials start off at a disadvantage. They are far less likely to attend daycare, especially between the ages of one and three – and often beyond.[34] If they do get a place, the quality of care in socially disadvantaged postcodes compared to rich ones is much lower.

And even when children get a place, standards vary widely. High-quality Kitas are staffed by well-trained educators and maintain a low child-to-staff ratio, ensuring children get enough attention. Daycare centres serving children from socioeconomically disadvantaged families face an especially severe staff shortage, leaving the most vulnerable with the least support. In 2023 almost 300 early childcare experts and professionals from across the Federal Republic wrote a letter to the government, stating that 'the system of early childhood education, care and upbringing in Germany is overburdened and on the verge of collapse'.[35]

If pre-school seems unfair, junior school is even worse. Instead of lifting children up, it holds a mirror to the country's social disparities. After World War I, Germany introduced primary schools called *Grundschule* with an ambitious goal: to provide free, compulsory education for all children, regardless of class. It was a bold step away from a system that was more clearly separated into rich and poor. The vision was simple but powerful: level the playing field by assigning children to local schools, stripping parents of the ability to perpetuate social divides.

Yet, as cities became more segregated, so did their schools. Facilities in wealthy neighbourhoods thrived with abundant resources, whereas schools in poorer areas struggled. The gap becomes painfully clear when students transition to secondary school. Those from affluent backgrounds are far more likely to move on to Gymnasium, gaining a smooth path to higher education. Their disadvantaged peers, however, are often funnelled into lower-tier schools, where future opportunities are more limited.

The polarisation is deepened by the emergence of more and more private schools, which have quadrupled in number since 1992. In the 2018/2019 academic year, about 1 million kids went to private schools, or one out of every eleven students.[36] The level of education isn't necessarily better, but it creates a closed club and keeps well-off kids segregated from the problems and experiences of those less fortunate, undermining social understanding.

It's not hard to see why some parents want to opt out of the state system. The quality in Germany's publicly administered schools lags way behind international peers. There was supposed to be a wake-up call in 2000 when Germany scored below average in reading, maths and science on international assessments. Despite the public shock, it's still struggling and in some cases getting worse in terms of school quality, integrating kids from migrant and disadvantaged backgrounds and avoiding 'education poverty' (a lack of at least upper-secondary or vocational qualifications).[37]

Rigid, complex structures are a big part of the problem. Education is organised on the state level, all but ruling out nationwide adjustments on curricula and teaching methods. Educators are also generally job-for-life civil servants, a protected status that's supposed to guarantee independence from political influence. In practice, it means the system has become inflexible, making a career in education unattractive for many young people. Across the country, there's a shortage of more than 35,000 teachers and projections are that the gap could double in a decade.[38]

Germany's educational inequalities would be far worse if not for the country's vaunted vocational training schemes, known as the *Duale Ausbildung* (literally, dual-education system). This programme offers a valuable alternative to university, combining classroom learning with hands-on work experience. It's celebrated not only for equipping students with practical skills but also for offering job security in fields like engineering, manufacturing and healthcare. For students who may struggle with traditional academic routes, it opens doors to well-paying, skilled jobs, giving them a real shot at stability and success. By partnering with companies to provide apprenticeships, the dual system bridges the often daunting gap between education and employment, especially for those from disadvantaged backgrounds.

While vocational training helps close the gap, jobs for life are no longer a guarantee in Germany, and blue-collar heroes are disappearing as stable industrial jobs come under threat. The prospects of a comfortable working-class existence then is undermined by access to housing and unequal healthcare. That kind of uncertainty has in turn reduced the appeal of trades. The number of people entering apprenticeships has dropped by nearly half a million since 2000, as young people are increasingly drawn to service sector jobs and the academic qualifications that unlock them.[39] Those who do pursue apprenticeships often feel regret; nearly one in five report that their training allowance barely covers living expenses, and an additional third also face financial difficulties. While apprenticeships at major companies like Mercedes-Benz or Siemens offer better pay, about a third of those working for *Mittelstand* businesses have to get by on €935 per month or less, leaving little after factoring in living costs and transportation to Germany's often remote factories.[40] For companies already grappling with digitalisation and a flood of complex regulations, taking on apprentices can be a costly investment in both time and money. As a result, apprentices bemoan distracted managers and an inadequate learning experience.

With the rich well protected and opportunities hard to come by due to Germany's misfiring institutions, the middle class is shrinking. Although social-welfare reforms under Chancellor Gerhard Schröder in the early 2000s sparked a 'job wonder', record employment levels didn't lead to prosperity trickling down. New positions have often consisted of low-paid service jobs and temporary work. The changing nature of German employment is evident in declining union membership, which has halved since reunification. Growing polarisation has meant that the middle class has shrunk from 70 per cent of the population in the mid-1990s to 63 per cent in 2019.[41] In terms of its relative size, Germany's middle class has fallen behind Belgium, Finland, France, Poland and even Greece, dropping to fourteenth place in Europe in 2019.[42] Anxiety is stoked by social mobility being skewed downward for most Germans. For blue-collar families especially, the metaphorical ceilings are low and hard, but the floors are slippery and full of holes.[43] That's a particular problem for a country like Germany, which is founded on egalitarian ideals.

If the middle class shrinks further and others slip into poverty, it's likely more voters will abandon centrist parties in favour of more radical alternatives that promise to reverse their economic decline and protect their livelihoods. 'Roughly simplified, you can divide the history of the Federal Republic into two stages,' said the German social scientist Oliver Nachtwey. 'In the first, the pieces of the cake grew. Since then, the downward trend has dominated.'[44]

The fear of slipping into poverty – significantly, it gets its own word *Abstiegsangst* (literally 'fear of decline') – stems from the harsh reality of life on the lowest rung of society. While the welfare system still provides a safety net, it's increasingly stretched thin and the divide between the poorest and the middle class has grown wider. Today, poverty in Germany is not just a matter of economic hardship but also of deep social isolation. The opportunities to climb out are few, as welfare benefits barely cover the basics and come with layers of bureaucracy and social stigma. It's another area where Germany's post-war promise of *Wohlstand für Alle* (prosperity for all) is coming up short.

Empty promises

Germany's *Grundgesetz* begins with the declaration that 'human dignity is inviolable. Respecting and protecting it is the duty of all state authorities.' It's one of the most often-cited statements in the founding document of post-war Germany. Intended as a clear break with Nazi race ideology, it set out admirable aspirations for the country, which includes securing the welfare of its citizens as a 'social state'. But the system has been increasingly failing to meet those lofty goals.

In chic Charlottenburg, not far from the Baroque Prussian-era palace that gave the Berlin district its name, a homeless camp has developed under the broad expanse of a railway bridge (one of many in the city as shelters struggle to keep pace). Some of the people have tents or mattresses, and others just a bundle of possessions, protected at least from the rain as trains trundle overhead. During the day, many of the city's homeless hobble through the U-Bahn trains. Some are clearly ill and need medical or psychiatric attention, and more than a few are in such a bad state that passengers cover their noses because of the stench. Others keep to themselves, seemingly resigned to the situation – like a quiet gangly man who for years has lived near the entrance of a supermarket, graciously accepting handouts when offered, but never asking.

It's not just Berlin. Similar conditions can be found throughout Germany. At least 607,000 people (about as many people as Düsseldorf) didn't have a fixed residence in 2022, including around 50,000 living on the streets, and average numbers for the year climbed by about 17 per cent.[45] Homeless rates in the country are more than double those in Great Britain, although the latter has more people housed in emergency accommodation.[46] Old schools, unused offices and conference centres have been repurposed as shelters. Even in Berlin's reconstructed Stadtschloss, an *Ort der Wärme* (place of warmth) has been set up by a charity to give people a refuge in cold winter months.

Demand at food banks has surged since 2022 in the fallout from inflation. The so-called *Tafeln* (literally, 'tablets') are volunteer-run organisations that rescue food from being thrown away and have become a lifeline for many families. At more than two-thirds of the ninety-seven outlets, the need has climbed by at least half, and at one in six, the need has more than doubled.[47] Overall, as many as 2 million people in Germany rely on the organisation for sustenance.

Social instability has become part of the fabric of daily life. From notices taped to lamp posts pleading for help finding a place to live to darker signals. In Frankfurt, between the main train station and the financial centre's glistening towers, drug use is rampant and barely concealed in a seedy red-light district where violent conditions are reflected by signs declaring that firearms, knuckledusters and knives are prohibited between 8 p.m. and 5 a.m. (raising questions about what happens outside those hours). And every year tens of thousands of people are locked up in Germany because of unpaid fines. It's the most common form of incarceration in the country, and punishments can be for as long as a year. The crime is effectively in being poor. Because welfare support isn't as generous as reputed, people who don't buy a train ticket usually don't have the money and so fines tip them into a downward spiral.*

In Munich, train cleaners leave bags of recyclables open for scavengers to scour for bottles and cans to turn in for a few cents. The country's world-class recycling system has become an informal system of redistribution, a few cents and bottles at a time. It speaks to the social conscience of average Germans that the etiquette has developed to leave *Leergut* (deposit packaging) next to garbage bins to save the *Flaschensammler* (bottle collectors) the indignity of rummaging through. But at a maximum of 25 cents a bottle, it's hardly enough to close the gaps that have opened in Germany's welfare system.

Despite the country's objective affluence, nearly one in five Germans live in poverty, and about a quarter of those are working poor, meaning their wages aren't enough to cover basic needs. On a demographic basis, poverty disproportionately hits the young and the elderly. One in five kids grow up in poor households and more than 40 per cent of single parents are below the poverty line.[48] The number of pensioners at risk of poverty is above the EU average.[49] The result is that inequality in Germany is among the worst in Europe.

The faltering of the welfare system that was supposed to secure the 'dignity' of German citizens hasn't been an accident. It's been gradually hollowed out with the intention of getting more people into work. In some cases it went too far. Following a complaint over Chancellor Gerhard Schröder's welfare reforms, known as Hartz IV, the Federal Constitutional Court in 2010 forced the government to reconfigure the programme, ruling that the government's obligations as a social state require it to secure not just physical needs like food and shelter but also provide enough support to allow for the participation in social, cultural and political

---

* Civil society is leaping into the breach where it can. The organisation Freiheitsfonds has paid for the release of about 1,000 people since December 2021, accessed 23 May 2024, https://www.freiheitsfonds.de.

life. It sounds generous in theory, but in practice it's calculated to amount to less than €19 a day.*

Despite the growing need, callousness has entered the political debate. At the time of the 2010 decision by Germany's highest court, the global financial crisis was fresh and the country had enforced austerity on itself by enshrining parsimony into the constitution with the debt brake to limit borrowing. It was the start of an era that openly set the angst-ridden working class against those even worse off: namely, welfare recipients (migrants and asylum seekers were added after the refugee crisis in 2015). Guido Westerwelle, head of the Free Democrats and vice-chancellor during Chancellor Angela Merkel's second term, helped frame the poor-shaming debate in 2010, claiming generous social welfare undermines the value of work and leads to 'late Roman decadence'.[50] Bashing the underprivileged has continued with the Christian Democratic leader Friedrich Merz, popularising the term 'social tourism' in connection with Ukrainian war refugees.

The hard-line narrative is that indolent welfare recipients are living the easy life at the expense of hard-working taxpayers. Sanctions have been unleashed to cut benefits with the proposed aim of getting more people working. Facts don't bear that out though. While there are indeed people that play the system, the number who collect support but refuse to work is only about 15,000 people out of a total of 5.5 million who collect *Bürgergeld* (citizen's money) – the rebranded Hartz IV welfare programme.† Rough estimates of welfare fraud run to as high as €20.5 billion.[51] That's indeed a large sum of money, but it's still less than 2 per cent of overall social spending and a fifth of the €100 billion lost annually to state coffers from tax evasion.

Costs for supporting the poor are climbing, but haven't necessarily surged. Between 2002 and 2022 social spending rose 26 per cent in Germany. That was the third-lowest rise in the OECD, and the share of GDP was similar to the United States when accounting for health-insurance costs.[52] Those facts haven't blunted the culture wars against

---

* The standard *Bürgergeld* rate for a single adult for 2024 is €563 a month. Additional household members, including kids, get less.
† That includes 1.5 million children. Of the adults, 1.6 million are available to work, 1.6 million are not available to work or only have limited capacity because they're in training or are caring for family members, and 800,000 earn some money, which reduces benefits if it exceeds €100 a month.

the poor. With Chancellor Olaf Scholz's government in austerity mode, the focus of the political debate is on cutting support for the most needy using the theory that the pressure will force them into the labour force. It's an approach that sows division and deepening fault lines in Germany. It's also not that easy to implement.

The case of Thomas Wasilewski shows just how cruel the system can be. The native of Mönchengladbach, a struggling industrial city near the Rhine, had gone through two apprenticeships – one in IT and the other in foreign and wholesale trade – and worked for the coal-mining powerhouse Ruhrkohle AG, helping young people with learning difficulties into training programmes. In other words, he was a productive and engaged member of society until tragedy struck in 2007, when he suddenly fainted. Later he was diagnosed with heart problems. During an operation, his heart muscle was injured and he had to be reanimated. By 2013, it was clear that Wasilewski, who was still in his forties at the time, would no longer be able to work. He received a pension, but it wasn't close to enough for a family of five. His wife could only work part-time because of back problems. So the family was provided welfare support to help them with the basics.

What that means in reality is that he rides his bike from one discount shop to the next looking for deals on food that's about to expire, picking up what's on offer and noting when and where deals might be available in the coming days. When the money runs out before the end of the month, it means a trip to food banks for handouts. He's noted year after year how the lines have got longer. There have been legal disputes with the authorities to get money for schoolbooks. When a son went on a school trip, friends helped out with extra clothes for the trip, but they kept it quiet for fear the authorities would deduct money for the clothing 'gifts'. When politicians talk about wanting to lift up kids out of social welfare, 'that's a blatant lie. We are being pushed up against the wall and ruined,' he said.[53]

The crunch time for Wasilewski came in 2022, when inflation made life on social welfare even more bitter. He went public with his story to become an advocate for people on welfare and give voice to the silent suffering of millions of Germans. He gave an interview to the *Süddeutsche Zeitung*[54] and sent the article to some

500 politicians: few answered. The representative from his district claimed he wasn't responsible for the issue, but the committee for social issues in the Bundestag demurred as well. 'What am I to make of a democracy that has distanced itself so far from its weakest members?' asked Wasilewski, who's continued to raise awareness on social media and in talk shows.[55]

Indeed, political freedom has limited value if people feel hemmed in economically. What good is it to have the right to vote and speak your mind if you can't afford food for your family. In China, capitalism functions without the people having a political voice, but the opposite can hardly be true. A lack of economic choice can barely sustain a democratic system. That's true for any liberal democracy, but the link between democracy and economic well-being is especially strong in the German system. In the 1930s, the Nazis exploited the anxiety of the Great Depression to sweep away the Weimar Republic. And now, as the promise of prosperity collapses, the lure of populism threatens to grow stronger.

While post-war Germany never pretended to be a meritocracy, it is supposed to be a nation that cares for its people. The price of relative limited mobility is a social safety net that's supposed to ensure a life of 'dignity'. It's a key part of Germany's post-war identity and the foundation of its social cohesion, and so the failure of the promise of prosperity raises unsettling questions about the country's stability.

Mainstream parties have provided little response, but German civil society is not indifferent to the widening wealth gap. Citizens are pushing to expose the reality that Germany is no longer providing for everyone, shattering a myth and opening the door to constructive change. From anti-poverty campaigners highlighting deprivation on social media to Frankfurt activists spray-painting *Stadt für Alle* (city for all) on unoccupied investment properties, signs of discontent are widespread. And organisations are springing in to the breach where government policy is failing, helping welfare recipients pay energy bills, cover pandemic costs, and fight legal battles against benefit cuts.[56] In an effort to level the playing field with Germany's lucky heirs, activists have proposed a 'universal inheritance', which would provide young adults with a set sum of money as start-up capital to rebalance opportunities.* There's no indication mainstream parties will adopt any such plan, especially at a time of austerity. Overall, the stage is set for more inequality and greater social strife.

In *Metropolis*, unity was forged with a simple gesture, but in Germany's reality the path to bridging the bottom and top rungs of society will require more than just symbolism. Repairing the House of Germany will demand action, empathy, and collective will, but that seems a struggle with the economy wobbling and political leadership in short supply. Rather than the head and hand of Germany reconciling, the country looks set to descend into an intensifying fight over resources, as if society wasn't divided enough already.

---

* *Stiftung Ein Erbe für Jeden* proposes €20,000 for every thirty-year-old.

8
House Divided

'Oh friends, not in these tones!
Rather let's strike up more agreeable ones.'

Ludwig van Beethoven*

On 6 November 2024, Europeans woke to find Donald Trump had won a second term as president of the United States of America, and it wasn't even close – winning not only the electoral college but also the popular vote. That placed an isolationist with authoritarian tendencies back in the White House amid war within Europe's borders. After Trump's first election, an anxious world looked to Germany and Angela Merkel to be the standard-bearer of liberal democracy. But eight years later, there were no such delusions.

As night settled over Berlin, leading members of Olaf Scholz's ruling coalition gathered to hash out a budget, knowing that with Trump returning to the White House the stakes were even higher. There was already a financing gap of some €15 billion, and the spending plan had to revive the sluggish economy as trade conflicts loomed with the United States and China. Germany also faced greater pressure to sustain support for Ukraine's defence effort, with the transatlantic alliance under more strain than at any point since the end of World War II. After months of public squabbles, tensions flared. Instead of a sober compromise, an emotionally charged Scholz fired Finance Minister Christian Lindner (who was also the

---

* Ludwig van Beethoven, Symphony No. 9 in D minor, Op. 125. Whereas the text of 'Ode to Joy' was largely written by Friedrich Schiller, this passage was penned by the composer himself.

head of the fiscally hawkish Free Democrats) and brought down his own government. Instead of grace under pressure, Germany's leaders squabbled like overtired children. Instead of rallying to the moment, the parties that promised 'progress' when they took power in 2021 splintered. Instead of serving as an anchor for Europe, Germany caved. After a fierce exchange, Scholz issued an ultimatum and Lindner baulked. After a long moment of stunned silence as the implications of the outburst became clear, Scholz said: 'Well, that went badly.'

While the collapse of the unloved 'traffic light' coalition – named for the party colours of red for the Social Democrats, yellow for the free-market FDP, and green for the Greens – might be seen as an isolated incident, it really isn't. For almost the entire post-war period, Germany could get by with tidy two-party alliances. The future looks set to be different as the political mainstream has fractured permanently. All of the parties, including the centre-right Christian Democratic Union (which incidentally has the colour black), have played a role in Germany's gradual drift into fragmentation. Even though the return to power of the party of Angela Merkel and formerly Helmut Kohl might seem like a revival of stability, the underlying trends are still there.

Society has shifted, and the old political parties have struggled to adapt, losing legitimacy as more and more Germans struggle with a system stacked against them. The numbers grasping for answers have grown and the political class hasn't delivered. Voters in other countries might take that as par for the course, but Germans aren't apathetic. They expect their elected representatives to deliver on the social contract, especially providing for basic needs and security. But rather than sketch out visions of where Germany should go, mainstream parties have resorted to sniping at one another, scrapping for the eroding political centre. It's a consequence of the rising tide of economic fear and social division, facilitated by an undeveloped national identity that has left room for the siren songs of fringe politicians promising easy answers.

The collapse of Scholz's coalition is consequently a symptom of decaying stability. That drift to the extremes was evident at elections in Thuringia a few weeks before the showdown in Berlin. The state bordering Bavaria to the north is where Germany's first democracy was founded, but it was also where the Nazis secured an early stronghold. A century later, the forest-filled region was again at the forefront of national politics for the wrong reasons. *Alternative für Deutschland* ('Alternative for Germany', known as the AfD and by the colour blue) became the largest party in the state parliament, a first for a far-right movement in the post-war era. The successful campaign in the region known as Germany's green heart was led by the nationalist provocateur Björn Höcke, who has been fined for using Nazi-era slogans and can legally be called a 'fascist', a label Germany doesn't use lightly. The AfD's Thuringia chapter began its election programme with a text from Franz Langheinrich, a lyricist who was known as an enthusiastic supporter of the Nazis. One of its platforms calls for the end of 'state-sponsored' illegal immigration, saying it risks the 'nation's inner solidarity, creates parallel societies and threatens our children's and grandchildren's right to a homeland'. In other words, the party reached the historic milestone not despite its appeal to 'blood and soil' German nationalism, but because of it.

If that was the only problem that came out of the Thuringia election, it would be bad enough, but there was more. A fledgling pro-Russia party (founded in January 2024 by an opportunistic left-wing politician with links to East German communists) mustered enough support to beat all three parties in Scholz's coalition combined. So in normally staid German politics, it took *Bündnis Sahra Wagenknecht* ('Alliance Sahra Wagenknecht', named after its founder, and known as BSW for short) just nine months to eclipse the oldest party in Germany and its allies. All it needed was a well-known candidate (Sahra Wagenknecht has been in the public eye for decades) and a fear-soothing platform, including seeking appeasement with Russia and taxing the rich. The only mainstream party to crack the top three was the Christian Democrats. Along with the demise of Scholz's government, it was the clearest sign yet that Germany's long-cherished stability was in jeopardy.

In short, the House of Germany is divided and getting more so as the strains and anxiety over its clanking pipes and draughty rooms unsettle the residents.

False friends

In the weeks before Germany's election in 2021, several dozen people (from children to pensioners) gathered in a former shop front in a tidy village on the edge of the Thuringian forest. With a customary array of cakes and rolls topped with slices of sausage and cheese, it looked like any other community event in Germany. That this gathering was different became evident as soon as the presentation started: the topic was to decry the state's Covid-19 policies.

Sonneberg was home to a flourishing toy industry a century ago and still boasts one of the world's largest teddy bears, but the mood here was dark like much of Germany, and especially in the east of the country. Economic struggles had made it fertile ground for anti-establishment rhetoric, which helps explain why people were ready to spend a pleasant late-summer evening listening to a man with glasses, a goatee and salt-and-pepper hair vilify the government in Berlin. In many ways, it was like the anti-Covid rhetoric anywhere, but in the former communist region opponents quickly drew parallels with the East German police state. Masks were an effort to take away people's identity, while stricter social-distancing rules for the unvaccinated was a plot to divide society and implement 'immunisation Apartheid'. A back room was filled with protest signs against Angela Merkel and the federal government. The group's marches regularly took place on Mondays, deliberately echoing the tactics used in the demonstrations that helped bring down the Berlin Wall. Anti-establishment forces in the East see themselves as part of the same movement that cast off the communist regime, viewing the Federal Republic as similarly repressive.

No one enjoyed Covid restrictions and the incursions on everyday life, but the frustration and fear already present in German society — from rising levels of social precarity and an undeveloped sense of national identity — made the pandemic more of an entry point for fringe sentiment, chipping away at the centrist consensus that had dominated Germany for decades. Two years later, in 2023, the town of 23,000 turned into a milestone for the AfD, when Robert Sesselmann was elected district administrator. It was the first time since the Federal Republic was founded in 1949 that a far-right party had won an election outright. While the protest group, called *Sonneberg zeigt Gesicht* (Sonneberg shows face), was non-partisan, many of its ideas overlapped with the AfD, making it an effective feeder organisation like many others in the country.

The AfD is German nationalist, anti-Islam, anti-Europe and anti-immigrant. It's more extremist than many other populist movements in Europe. Ahead of the European Parliament elections in 2024, Marine Le Pen's *Rassemblement National* refused to cooperate with the party, which was also shut out of the right-wing caucus Identity and Democracy. The AfD is linked to an ecosystem that recruits supporters and pushes the boundaries of public debate towards the nationalist right.

There are also other even more outright extremist parties in Germany like *Die Heimat* (The Homeland), *Die Rechte* (The Right) and *Der III. Weg* (The Third Way, a not-so-subtle nod to the Third Reich), making the AfD look relatively moderate by comparison. Its presence in the Bundestag and its momentum has dragged national debate far beyond what was once thought possible, normalising discussions around forced deportations and tempting mainstream politicians to adopt their talking points. The party would remake Germany if it ever got the chance. And its leaders are preparing the ground to do so.

Surveillance of multiple parts of the AfD by Germany's domestic intelligence services has done little to dent its momentum. Instead, it's all fired up. The party casts itself as the disruptor of a broken power system, so efforts to silence it are seen as proof of systemic corruption rather than a threat. Other parties have vowed not to work with the AfD, creating dysfunctional coalitions to keep the movement out of power, but that also risks backlash by playing into the narrative that the system is protecting itself and subverting the will of the people (the implication here is the *Volk*, in the sense of ancestral Germans).

Victory in Sonneberg marked a waypoint on a political journey that exposed Germany's dark underside and raised questions over just how resistant the country is to the lures of nationalist populism. Founded in February 2013, the AfD started out as a eurosceptic movement opposed to Germany-backed bailouts during the eurozone debt crisis. Its name references Angela Merkel's insistence that there was 'no alternative' to multi-billion-euro aid packages for insolvent Greece.

From the outset, the AfD included far-right extremists in its ranks, but it was dominated by conservative critics of Europe's common currency such as Bernd Lucke, a University of Hamburg economics professor and devout evangelical Christian. Its marquee policy was to dismantle the eurozone and revive the Deutsche Mark, a much-missed symbol of German financial rectitude. That message reaped the AfD 2 million votes at the 2013 federal election, just below the hurdle required to get seats in the national parliament.* But party leaders wouldn't have to wait long for a breakthrough. In May 2014 the party won seven seats in elections for the European Parliament (traditionally an outlet for grumpy protest voting).¹ In little over a year, the AfD had gone from non-existence to representation in a major assembly.

Its next campaign would bring even greater success and kick-start a shift to political positions that most Germans thought were consigned to the past. In late summer 2014 the AfD contested regional elections in Brandenburg, Saxony and Thuringia. While the party's academic leadership lectured on debt ratios and sovereign credit ratings, its leaders in those former East German states pointed to family and flag.

In Saxony, Frauke Petry primarily campaigned on upholding Germany's Christian identity, arguing that mosques with minarets should only be built if they're approved by residents in a referendum.² The Dresden-born businesswoman (and mother) added that the AfD would champion the traditional family and was opposed to widening marriage and adoption rights to same-sex couples.†

In neighbouring Brandenburg, Alexander Gauland, a former CDU functionary who left the party in protest over Merkel's policies, focused on law and order and the delayed construction of Berlin's new airport. The Chemnitz-born lawyer, who typically

---

* Under Germany's proportional representation system, a party must win at least 5 per cent of the vote to qualify as a parliamentary party. The AfD won 4.7 per cent at the 2013 federal election.
† Frauke Petry had four kids at the time and then had two more children with her second husband, who she married in December 2016.

wears British tweed suits and a dog-motif tie (an accessory he reportedly purchased while road tripping through Sussex),[3] also advocated closer ties to Russia. Asked in an interview whether voters cared about the bailout issue pushed by the national leader Lucke, Gauland replied 'no, not at all'.[4]

In Thuringia, Björn Höcke took a more populist tack, railing against the shortcomings of globalisation and the liberal democratic order.[5] The former sports and history teacher, whose grandparents were expelled from lands Germany lost after World War II, would later play a crucial role in the party's radical drift.

The combined emotive messaging cut through, and the AfD outperformed opinion polls in all three states and entered regional parliaments for the first time. Addressing her supporters on election night, an excited Petry proclaimed: 'The AfD has arrived!'

So too had internecine warfare. Shortly after the AfD's nationalist wing stunned everyone with its performance in eastern Germany, the eurosceptics flopped in an equivalent vote in Hamburg. The disparate results turbocharged a fight over the party's direction. In early 2015 a group around Höcke signed a document called the *Erfurter Resolution* (Erfurt Resolution), formalising a shift to the far-right. The declaration called for partnering with the ethno-nationalist protest group *Pegida* (an abbreviation for Patriotic Europeans Against the Islamisation of the West). It also called the AfD 'a resistance movement against the further erosion of Germany's sovereignty and identity'.[6]

As well as Höcke, signatories included Andreas Kalbitz, a presence at neo-Nazi rallies who would later hospitalise a parliamentary colleague by punching him in the side.[7] While the AfD's national leadership tried to resist the shift, they were rapidly losing control. Far-right views that had for decades been confined to a disorganised fringe in Germany were suddenly espoused by figures commanding millions of votes. A beast slumbering in Germany's political subconscious was reawakening.

A showdown between the warring factions came on 5 July 2015, at the party's annual convention in Essen, a city in Germany's smokestack Ruhr region. In a bid to reassert control, Lucke called a leadership election and defied the emerging right-wing group to propose a challenger, which they did, and the eurosceptic academic was roundly beaten by Petry, who won almost two-thirds of the votes. Just days later, Lucke announced his departure, saying the party was moving to the xenophobic right and had 'fallen into the wrong hands'.[8] That sparked an exodus of relative moderates, including co-founder Hans-Olaf Henkel. The former president of Germany's powerful BDI business lobby would later confess that he helped create 'a real monster'.

To outsiders, the AfD looked hopelessly consumed by turf wars. And Merkel's CDU welcomed the infighting as 'excellent news' that would help them win back lost votes.[9] Opinion polls appeared to confirm the optimism, as support for the AfD dropped to just 3 per cent, significantly below the double-digit results achieved in the previous year's state elections. Germany breathed a sigh of relief. It appeared that the lessons from history were still strong enough to repel extremism. But the AfD was written off too soon.[10]

In reality, the party was just getting going. An intensifying refugee crisis would soon pour fuel on embers of populism that had subsided along with the euro crisis. The Syrian civil war underwent a major escalation, driving millions of people from their homes and across the border into Turkey. From there, refugees would make perilous sea crossings to Greek islands and then continue through the Balkans towards central Europe. Already in 2014 the number of refugees arriving in Germany was at its highest level since during the Yugoslav wars in the 1990s.[11] By 2015, it was clear that things were out of control. Hundreds of migrants were drowning in the Aegean Sea, while others were left in squalid refugee camps in Serbia, Hungary and Croatia. On 27 August 2015 the lifeless bodies of seventy-one migrants on their way to seek refuge in Europe's most powerful economy were discovered in a lorry on an Austrian Autobahn near the border with Hungary, an event that shook Germany to its core.

Back in Berlin, Angela Merkel had initially been cautious. Despite the suffering of refugees and mounting tensions in Balkan countries over the flows, she insisted on sticking to European protocols. During a school visit in July 2015, a girl from Lebanon asked the chancellor when her family's asylum application might get approved so that she could continue her studies. The chancellor coldly replied that not everyone would be allowed to stay, prompting the fourteen-year-old to burst into tears and bringing home the human element of the suffering for Merkel, the daughter of a Lutheran pastor.

Sticking to procedure wasn't possible for long. By August 2015, Germany's refugee agency was overwhelmed and could no longer process asylum cases.[12] Rather than turn away migrants at Germany's borders (an action that would likely have required the use of force), Merkel decided to open the country to an unlimited number of arrivals. At the time there was a genuine outpouring of concern in Germany. The sight of thousands of Munich residents welcoming refugees at the city's central station made headlines around the world, but worries were also emerging about hordes of foreign men sleeping in makeshift shelters in gym halls where kids used to play, or wandering the streets looking for work and in some cases trouble. Moved by the scale of the humanitarian needs, Merkel underestimated the impact and disruption of integrating a sudden influx of more than 1 million people. Speaking at a press conference at the end of August, she appeared to dismiss these doubts with the quip: '*Wir schaffen das*' (we can do it).

Seemingly down and out, the AfD's fortunes revived. The Brandenburg leader Alexander Gauland would later say that the refugee crisis proved to be a gift.[13] Although almost all new arrivals quietly got on with their lives and sought ways to contribute, dramatic security incidents rocked the public's faith in Merkel's open-door policy. On 13 November nine Islamic State operatives launched a brutal attack on Paris, killing 131 people and injuring an additional 400. The French Prime Minister, Manuel Valls, said the extremists had been smuggled into Europe in refugee flows.[14]

In Germany, hundreds of mainly Arabic men from North Africa harassed and sexually assaulted women passing through Cologne's central train station on New Year's Eve, prompting over 1,000 criminal complaints.[15] That incident marked the moment when Germany's attitude shifted.[16] The mood soured in the coming months as incidents piled up. In June 2016 in Würzburg, a seventeen-year-old refugee from Afghanistan stabbed and injured five people on a train.[17] On 19 December, the Tunisian migrant Anis Amri would use a truck to attack a Berlin Christmas market, killing eleven people.[18] By the end of 2016, over four in five Germans wanted Merkel to change her approach to the crisis. It was a sentiment that the AfD weaponised. Around that time, the party instigated protests outside the chancellor's office in Berlin under the slogan *Merkel muss weg* (Merkel must go).

By the time the 2017 election campaign started, the AfD swung behind a stridently anti-immigrant message. Election posters fixated on Merkel's handling of the refugee crisis, evoking the Great Replacement conspiracy theory with non-white foreigners taking the place of Germans and stoking fears of sexual violence against German women. Surveys showed the messages gained traction, and for voters who resented Merkel's refugee stance the AfD became the party of choice.

As exit polls flashed across TV screens on the night of 24 September, AfD supporters who had gathered near Alexanderplatz in Berlin punched the air in triumph. The party had surged into the Bundestag for the first time, winning over 12 per cent. The results placed it in an astounding third place, behind only Merkel's CDU and the Social Democrats, which slumped to its worst postwar result. In the eastern state of Saxony, the AfD even came first.

The former Bavarian politician Franz-Josef Strauss had once said Germany could not permit a legitimate party to the right of the Conservatives and that was taken as a truism until 2017, when almost 6 million voters disagreed. It showed that the political centre in Germany, once the stalwart and stuffy guarantor of stability, was collapsing. A new era of uncertainty was emerging and it was a warning that the mainstream has struggled to heed. After yet another unloved Grand Coalition between the two traditionally biggest parties, the AfD ended up as the largest opposition force in the Bundestag and had revealed the vulnerabilities within the political establishment. Addressing a jubilant throng of supporters, Gauland said: 'We will hunt them. We will hunt Frau Merkel . . . and we will reclaim our country and our people.'

Just a few hours later, Petry delivered a shock by quitting the AfD. The woman who wrested control from eurosceptics was disturbed by how radical it had become. What started off as a conservative party with an extremist minority was becoming a radical party with a fading conservative minority. It's a transformation that is still underway. But what could have been seen as a red flag was instead seen as evidence that Germany was self-correcting and had indeed learned from its past. Petry's surprising departure made it easy for the establishment to dismiss the AfD as an undisciplined bunch of rabble-rousers that would ultimately implode. That grossly underestimated the risks.

The AfD is the political spearhead of a broader far-right movement focused on controlling and remaking Germany, with a time horizon that stretches beyond election cycles. Flanked by even more extreme groups, the party brings right-wing ideas into the mainstream. Its parliamentary status secures a share of political power and provides the state funding and legitimacy that come with that.

While the AfD calls itself a party of 'free citizens' and 'committed democrats', beneath the packaging is an ethno-nationalist definition of Germany. The party openly rejects multiculturalism and non-traditional families. It proclaims Islam as non-German and maintains that the German language should form the centre of the country's identity. But it's also full of contradictions.

Co-leader Alice Weidel is well-educated, cosmopolitan, and married to another woman. She is fluent in Mandarin and English and lives in Switzerland with her Sri Lankan wife. She serves as a contrarian public face, sowing doubts about the party's nationalistic underpinnings. Three state chapters in eastern Germany and the *Junge Alternative* (or JA) youth organisation have been classified as 'confirmed extremist' by Germany's domestic intelligence agency, giving it wide-ranging powers of surveillance.[19] The entire AfD could receive such a classification at some point, but it hardly matters. While there are numerous legal battles over the issue, the party embraces its outsider status and casts the moves as persecution by a corrupt system seeking to silence the voice of the people. That's a message that has resonated with millions of voters who also feel let down by the government and the so-called *Altparteien* (literally, old parties). There have been calls to ban the party, but such processes are long and complicated, and they risk solidifying support even further.* That anti-establishment sentiment is present

---

* An effort to disband the right-wing National Democratic Party, or NPD, as anti-constitutional failed in the early 2000s because of issues with the investigation. Another attempt collapsed in 2017 after the constitutional court ruled the group had little hope of carrying out its anti-democratic goals.

at rallies, where supporters regularly wear vests in the party's blue colour with the word 'dissident' on the back.

For Germans feeling alienated from their homeland, the AfD seems like an authentic defender of their identity. And the JA actively recruits young people seeking direction via online-gaming evenings, walking tours and paintball events (which are viewed critically in Germany for being militaristic). While relatively small compared to other political youth organisations,* the group has an unabashed commitment to far-right ideology, proclaiming itself a 'resistance' for defence of the German nation. Alongside T-shirts and hoodies with the JA's flame logo, its online shop offers stickers with motifs reminiscent of Nazi iconography, such as blond-haired, blue-eyed men and women or families in pastoral settings like a wheatfield. On social media, the JA leader Anna Leisten has made white-power gestures and shows herself in military-style training as well as sitting in seminars alongside Martin Sellner, leader of Austria's extremist Identitarian Movement.

The AfD's success at the ballot box launched various studies exploring its supporters and their motivations. The simplistic notion that it's backed by a German version of the 'basket of deplorables' that originally swept Donald Trump to power doesn't hold up. Increasingly, its adherents defy the notion that support is mainly based on disaffected people in the east of the country. While the party gets proportionally more votes in the less populated and economically precarious region, the phenomenon is broader. Around three-quarters of AfD voters in the 2021 federal election were from states in western Germany.

In the 2023 elections in Hesse (home to Germany's financial capital Frankfurt), the party came second to the CDU and was clearly ahead of Scholz's SPD. In Bavaria the AfD beat all three parties that make up the ruling federal coalition. The appeal also isn't limited to middle-aged cranks. The AfD performed well in Hesse and Bavaria among voters under twenty-five, helped by an active presence on social-media platforms like TikTok and Instagram.

Some polls have suggested that the AfD is among the most popular parties among Germans aged under thirty.[20] As Germany

---

* *Junge Alternative* has 2,000 members compared to 100,000 in the CDU's *Junge Union*.

enters rougher economic waters, AfD strategists expect to increase their share of the youth vote further as those facing a bleaker future than their parents spurn mainstream parties. The only age-related drop-off in support comes from people over seventy, who have more vivid links to the horrors of World War II.[21]

Socioeconomic status appears to be a greater factor for AfD support. People at the lower rungs of society with little education and low incomes tend to support the party more than those better off.[22] These are Germans who have lost faith in the promise of prosperity that was the foundation of social cohesion for decades. As the economy sputters and pathways to advancement are blocked, their ranks risk increasing.

So far the AfD has been drawing support mainly from two pools. The largest one is from the mainstream, with the party luring over 1 million voters from the CDU/CSU and paradoxically around 830,000 from the Left party, showing how the traditional left–right spectrum is breaking down.[23] The other pool is from people who were previously non-voters or voted for fringe parties, highlighting how the AfD is adept at mobilising and uniting disaffected Germans. That stems in part from its grassroots outreach. The party is a regular presence at weekly open-air markets and public gatherings across the country, showing local commitment in contrast to its rivals, which tend to show up just before elections when votes are on the line. That effort helps build familiarity and rapport. The message that we're part of the community and care about what happens is especially important in rural areas and during periods of economic insecurity. The party's victory in Sonneberg was a case in point, coming in the wake of the inflation wave unleashed by Russia's invasion of Ukraine. Since then, the uncertainty has intensified rather than ebbed.

Disputes over costly climate policies, fears of deindustrialisation, and worries over military action are repressing historical lessons over the risks of ultra-nationalism. Germany's extreme right is preparing the ground to broaden its support, and central to that is an assault on Germany's *Erinnerungskultur* (literally, 'memory culture', which refers to the way National Socialism is commemorated). Showcasing Nazi horrors has played a central role in defining how contemporary Germany views itself. As Joachim Gauck, a former federal president, said: 'There is no German identity without Auschwitz.'[24]

Instead of solemnly revering the Holocaust, the AfD's leaders have sought to brush it aside to restore German pride and make nationalism less taboo. Gauland, who was co-leader of the party between 2017 and 2019, has described the Nazi era as merely 'bird shit on more than 1,000 years of successful German history'. Weidel too has decried the German 'cult of guilt'. The influential firebrand Höcke has gone further, calling the Holocaust memorial in Berlin a 'monument of shame' and has used Nazi-era slogans including *Alles für Deutschland* (everything for Germany). The AfD has sought to put that into practice by reducing funding for remembrance activities wherever it has entered regional parliaments.[25]

The command centre of the fight was in Schnellroda, a pastoral hamlet of fewer than 200 people in the thinly populated countryside west of Leipzig. It was home to the innocuously named *Institut für Staatspolitik* (IfS; Institute for State Policy), a think tank that's part of the *Neue Rechte* (New Right). Headed by Götz Kubitschek, IfS nominally disbanded in May 2024, but its work is widely expected to continue. The former teacher a few days after the announcement appeared at a Pegida event, saying that the movement's 'opponents' have been busy 'transforming society on all levels'.[26]

Kubitschek has been active in spreading far-right ideas deeper into German intellectual life and preparing the ground for an eventual nationalist shift of society. His group pushed anti-liberal positions to undermine democracy and the separation of powers. The network includes alternative media to counter what they call system-supporting propaganda from Germany's public broadcasters. The IfS itself had operated the journal *Sezession* and the publishing house Antaios. Links between Kubitschek and the AfD have been very close. At an IfS event in 2015, Höcke gave a speech that perpetuated replacement-theory concepts, bemoaning African population expansion at the expense of 'self-negating' Europeans.* Erik Lehnert is another crossover. He was IfS's managing director, while also on the payroll of the AfD Bundestag member Harald

---

* Höcke's speech stated that 'In the 21st century, the life-affirming African expansion type meets the self-negating European placeholder type.'

Weyel. Gauland has given a lecture at the institute and Weidel was a guest there. As Hans-Thomas Tillschneider, an AfD state lawmaker from Saxony-Anhalt, says: 'What we're proposing in the AfD was likely discussed three years earlier in Schnellroda.'[27]

The German public got a peek into the secretive world of the far-right in January 2024 when the investigative media outlet *Correctiv* published a story detailing a closed-door meeting in Potsdam to discuss plans to 'remigrate' (euphemism for 'deportation') millions of German residents.[28] At the meeting were a mix of participants including high-ranking AfD officials, the Austrian extremist Sellner, two members of the new far-right *WerteUnion* (Values Union) party, and sympathetic business people, raising concerns about a broad-based plot. The shock rallied the public into action, and protests broke out across the country against the AfD and in favour of democracy.

It was a feel-good moment, but not much more. Other scandals ahead of the European elections in June 2024 followed, including claims that a AfD lawmaker accepted money from Russia and allegations of links to Chinese espionage by the party's lead candidate. Although the AfD suffered a dent in the polls, it remained above all three governing parties and second only to the centre-right CDU/CSU. Under Friedrich Merz, the conservative alliance has been drifting more to the right, raising doubts about whether the so-called *Brandmauer* (firewall), which rules out cooperation with the AfD, will hold. And within months, 'remigration' went from shock to an open topic of political debate, with Scholz's SPD also backing more rigorous deportation procedures.

The AfD has exploited a void left in the country's political life: Germany's unresolved post-war identity. There was no real nation-building after World War II, not only because it was an impossible task but also because Germany was oblivious to it. A common language, a rich tradition of folklore, and hundreds of years of history gave the country all the trappings of a nation, but that is by default an ethno-nationalist concept. Although modern Germany wanted to move on, it never really did and 'blood and soil' visions retained their power. That's hard to respond to when the mainstream parties continue to push the broken promise of *Wohlstand für Alle* without a realistic plan for the future.

Instead of rallying together, the governing alliance of the SPD, the Greens and the FDP continued to bicker and snipe at one another, undermining their credibility in the process. Political futility and the darkening mood has prodded many to evoke echoes of the 1930s, a decade in which Germany's progressive forces were outflanked by the National Socialists' offer of strong and decisive government. The edgy mood has fuelled polarisation and fragmentation, but there's one political opponent that's become a favoured target of animosity and frustration from the AfD as well as its establishment peers: the Greens.

Public enemy

The captain of the MS *Hillegenlei* churned the waters as he steered the ferry away from Schlüttsiel, a harbour that looks out to the Halligen islands off Germany's North Sea coast. When the wind is still and the Wadden Sea calm, it's among the most tranquil places in the country. Halligen islanders are known for their laid-back manner, with Brent Geese digging for seagrass in the mudflats being the only signs of busyness.

Heading out to sea that morning, Robert Habeck, Germany's economy minister from the Green Party, saw Hooge island as a welcome getaway from political squalls on the mainland. As 2024 got underway, the vice-chancellor hoped for a better year ahead. The previous twelve months had seen anger with his government mount, culminating in a bad-tempered farmers' protest in Berlin over cutting subsidies in response to a homemade budget crisis. Once the most popular politician in Germany, Habeck's approval ratings had plunged to make him one of its least popular.[29]

Under gin-clear skies, Habeck could stroll along the shoreline and visit souvenir shops at the island's terp, a settlement raised for protection from wrathful seas. Unfortunately for the novelist turned politician, he wasn't alone on the boat. A local artist and accordionist who had stood for the AfD in recent municipal elections was also a passenger and spotted Habeck aboard, so she relayed the information to her partner, a fellow right-wing activist. Some farmer-protest and political groups were notified and rallied for an impromptu 'citizens dialogue' with Habeck that afternoon. 'Let's do him a favour and come with anything that has wheels!' one of the organisers posted in a WhatsApp group, according to a report in *Die Zeit* newspaper.[30]

As Habeck's ferry attempted to return after dark, a group of around 300 waited on the shoreline. The throng prevented passengers from disembarking, while shouts and insults filled the air, punctuated by the fizz and bang of fireworks. Around 100 trucks and tractors blocked the road to the ferry terminal. Habeck, who often travels around Germany trying to convince industrial workers that a governmental push to cut emissions won't cost them their livelihoods, offered to hold talks with three protesters. The agitators declined, demanding that Habeck address the entire crowd. His bodyguards judged that doing so would put the minister at risk of attack. As protesters attempted to storm the boat, police deployed pepper spray to drive them back. With little other alternative, the captain steered the ferry back out to sea.

Habeck eventually returned quietly to shore after midnight, flanked by four bodyguards. His hopes of forgetting the burdens of office on Hooge hadn't worked out. It was the latest setback for one of the key architects of the Greens' electoral success in 2021. It also wasn't the end of the threats. Just a week later, a banner at a protest in Bavaria suggested Habeck and his colleague Cem Özdemir, Germany's agriculture minister, should be shot.[31] Those incidents came after a scare the previous month, when Habeck's office in Flensburg was evacuated after a letter arrived containing a suspicious substance.[32] Addressing attempts to storm the ferry, the father of four said that he was thankful for his bodyguards. 'What really makes me think, what worries me in fact, is that the atmosphere in the country is getting so heated,' he said. 'Many, many others must deal with such attacks on their own.'[33]

Habeck isn't the only prominent Green facing open hostility. During the Bavarian regional election campaign in late summer 2023, a protester hurled a rock at the party's lead candidates.[34] In February 2024 the Greens' national co-leader Ricarda Lang abandoned an indoor rally after potentially violent protesters confronted police.[35] Party offices in Bremen, Gütersloh, Leipzig and elsewhere have been attacked, leaving doors broken and windows smashed. In Lower Saxony in December 2023, people from a farmer-protest group gathered outside the private home of the state's agriculture minister, scaring her teenage children who were home alone at the time.[36]

The threats and attacks evoke darker times. Through the 1970s and 1980s, the Red Army Faction, a left-wing militant group, conducted assassinations of prominent politicians and business figures, a period known as *Blejerne Jahre* (the Years of Lead). But at the time, the political centre remained intact, a situation that has become far less certain. The most extreme recent attack on a politician was in 2019 when a neo-Nazi shot and killed the CDU lawmaker Walter Lübcke because of his welcoming stance towards refugees. Other incidents have included vandalism and arson attempts on offices and homes of SPD lawmakers, including Karamba Diaby, the first African-born Black Bundestag member. In Dresden a fellow Social Democrat was beaten while hanging campaign posters for the European election in 2024. AfD members have also been targets, including Frank Magnitz who was hospitalised for head and eye injuries following an assault by three assailants in Bremen. Yet it's the Greens who get the worst of it. Of around 2,800 attacks on politicians in 2023, 1,200 were against the Greens, followed by around 480 against AfD officials.[37] In a country often praised for its grown-up political culture, the line between passionate debate and outright violence is thinning.

Vilification of the Greens has become a vibrant part of political rhetoric, even among mainstream officials. Addressing a crowd in a beer tent during campaigning for the 2023 Bavarian state election, Premier Markus Söder, an influential conservative who was angling to be chancellor candidate in 2021, said that the Greens don't fit with the state and that he couldn't accept a conservative and Green coalition at the federal level.[38] The Bavarian cabinet member Hubert Aiwanger (following the scandal over a Nazi-glorifying text) equated the Greens with extremists. Even the FDP, the Green's partners in Olaf Scholz's ruling coalition, have attacked their colleagues. Bijan Djir-Sarai, the former general secretary, has called the Greens a threat to national security.[39] Sahra Wagenknecht, the founder of the new leftist BSW party, has called the Greens the most dangerous party in the Bundestag.[40] Hans-Georg Maaßen, the controversial former head of Germany's domestic intelligence agency who leads the new right-wing *WerteUnion* (Values Union) party, has also singled out the Greens as a threat to German society.[41]

It's not just hard-ball between politicians. The tabloid *Bild* undertakes frequent campaigns against the Greens, including labelling a plan to switch to electric home furnaces '*Habecks Heiz-Hammer*' (Habeck's heat hammer). The agitated public rhetoric is naturally only intensified on social media. An analysis by *Der Spiegel* magazine found that online political abuse was aimed mainly at the Greens.[42] Luisa Neubauer, a climate activist dubbed Germany's Greta Thunberg and a Green member, is a regular target of opprobrium. 'This constant threat situation, the death threats, the stalking, the rape fantasies in mailboxes, I don't want to accept that as normality in my life,' she said.[43]

The Greens' path to political enemy started on the fringes in 1980 as a rallying point for environmentalists, feminists, and other progressive protest groups. Its defence of nature found a niche in a country with a particularly intense tradition of Romanticism, which spawned the *Lebensreform* (life reform) movement that rejected industrialisation and materialism. With support further driven by issues like concern about acid rain and the stationing of nuclear-tipped missiles in West Germany, the Greens entered the Bundestag in 1983.

It faced an existential crisis in 1990, when the party got the mood completely wrong, with the campaign slogan: '*Alle reden von Deutschland. Wir reden vom Wetter*' (Everyone's talking about Germany. We're talking about the weather). Instead of quick-trigger reunification, the party promoted coexistence between the two Germanies in a type of confederation, but it lost badly.[44] To maintain a voice in parliament, it merged in 1993 with Alliance 90, a loose collection of former East German pro-democracy movements. That experience was a hard lesson in the realities of power, but it cemented the party's place in German politics. Following the SPD's victory in 1998, the Greens got their first chance at helping run the country in a coalition under Gerhard Schröder. Entering government for the first time, the party's leader Joschka Fischer – a former left-wing radical who had assaulted a policeman and took part in violent street protests in the 1970s – became vice-chancellor and foreign minister. The days of staunch idealism gave way to a Green version of *Realpolitik*. Fischer became a proponent for German participation in NATO airstrikes against Serbian forces during the 1999 Kosovo war, the first time the country's military had seen active combat since 1945.

During the 2021 campaign, the Greens looked close to realising their dream of becoming a *Volkspartei* (people's party), a movement that cuts across age groups and social class. Its globalist agenda was antithetical to the nationalist, anti-immigration AfD, but also has grated with the increasingly 'Germany First' tones of the conservative bloc. With Annalena Baerbock as chancellor candidate, the Greens were ahead in the polls for a time before she stumbled over plagiarism allegations and padding her credentials, a sign of the party's naivete. Still, the widespread appeal was a warning to rivals, who are struggling to articulate visions for the future that convince voters. Adding to the pushback, the Green Party's call for a more ethical and strategic approach to trade and foreign policy threatens the interests of German businesses that have grown rich on deals with autocratic countries, especially China. Moral flexibility in the service of commerce is ultimately at the heart of Germany's political class.

For the CDU/CSU, the internationalism of the Merkel era looks confined to the past. Where Merkel sought to lead Europe through the refugee crisis, her successor Friedrich Merz stokes fear with talk of failed integration, runaway crime by migrants, and the risk of imported antisemitism.[45] Although Germany's commitment to its Paris 2015 climate goals once seemed sacrosanct, the Conservatives want to overturn the EU's end-date on fossil-fuel-powered cars. The SPD's leadership is also turning inward, seeking to position itself as a protector of German security and stepping back from a more assertive stance on Russia and China. The FDP has become fixated with the country's debt ratio (still one of the healthiest in the Western world) and casts itself as the voice of reason amid the climate and migration zeal of the Greens, along with the social-spending excess of the SPD.

The Greens have unwittingly aided its opponents with clumsy missteps. In the wake of Russia's invasion of Ukraine and as Germans were battered by the biggest cost-of-living squeeze since reunification, Habeck's team brought forward legislation that would have effectively banned all new oil and gas boilers in favour of electric heat pumps. The reform might make sense in the long run, but it was poorly handled and ill timed, creating the threat of costly and unpredictable investments for home owners squeezed by inflation and higher interest rates.[46] Making matters worse was the fact that the party's own attempt to install a heat pump at its national headquarters (a pre-war building in central Berlin) suffered planning delays and technical setbacks, attracting ridicule for appearing as ideologues with little real-world experience.[47] It's an allegation that's not entirely unjustified. Ricarda Lang and Omid Nouripour, co-leaders throughout most of Scholz's government,* studied various subjects but never earned a university degree before working their way up the party's hierarchy.

At the same time as reaching inside people's homes, the Greens threatened a fundamental German right: the need for speed. Proposing limits on Autobahns touches a nerve in the homeland of Porsche and BMW. While that position might not affect the Greens' base in the affluent, urban elite, it hits home for rural voters who will defend the privilege of racing down highways with the fervour of Americans protesting their rights to own assault rifles. The Greens also have darker baggage, including their free-love past when in the 1980s they sought to open the door to sex with minors. The party has paid compensation to victims of child abuse where its culpability was suspected.[48]

And yet, despite the incessant attacks and its awkward role in Scholz's widely unpopular government, support for the Greens has proven resilient and held up better than the other two governing parties. That's another cause for concern among Germany's embattled mainstream. At the end of the day, it's easier to attack a well-known and familiar adversary like the Greens than risk articulating a vision that might get rejected. But that tactic alienates voters who are unsettled and want answers, stoking apathy or driving them towards new parties on the fringe rather than winning them over.

For much of Germany's post-war history, two dominant political forces vied for power in Berlin: the centre-right Christian Democratic Union (CDU) and its centre-left counterpart, the Social Democratic Party (SPD). The conservative bloc is

---

* The leadership duo resigned after election debacles in eastern German states in the autumn of 2024.

complicated in that it's an alliance between the national CDU and its Bavarian sister party, the Christian Social Union (CSU). This split is one of the realities in German politics for which no one can really explain the rationale. It's just the way it is, and means the CSU plays second fiddle to its bigger partner, which almost always nominates the chancellor candidate.

Because of Germany's conservative leanings, the chancellor has been a CDU member for more than fifty years of the post-war era, championing the economy and promoting more of a pro-business agenda. Meanwhile, the SPD – the country's oldest political movement with its roots in the social and economic upheavals of the nineteenth century – is the only other party to win the chancellery, pushing more for social justice and workers' rights. Often, the balance of power hinged on the Free Democratic Party (FDP). As the perennial kingmaker, the FDP – with its focus on free markets, civil liberties, and minimal state intervention – would strategically ally with either the CDU/CSU or the SPD to form governing coalitions.

For decades, the dynamics encouraged consensus and compromise, creating an aura of political stability around the *Bundesrepublik*. The Greens were the first sustained challenge, but political fragmentation accelerated after reunification and then got turbocharged under Angela Merkel. It's now reaching a frenetic pace. Aside from the AfD, the new leftist BSW under Sahra Wagenknecht, the far-right *WerteUnion* and the right-leaning *Freie Wähler* are seeking to lure voters. That leaves the former guarantors of German stability with shrinking shares of the ballot and fighting with one another, denting their credibility in the process. As things stand, the FDP is fighting for its survival.

Straightforward two-party majorities are increasingly difficult to form. Even a so-called Grand Coalition of the CDU/CSU and the SPD, which backed three of Merkel's four terms, is a struggle and a sign of systemic stress. Not to mention that there's not much 'grand' about it these days. Support for the Social Democrats has regularly lagged behind the AfD, while the CDU's rightward shift has made alliances with the centre-left SPD even more fraught. The failure of Scholz's coalition was ultimately about a lack of shared vision. It worked as long as money was there, but as soon as the money dried up the solidarity vanished. The threat with centrist options is that it offers a veneer of stability without the ambition that Germany needs. A renewed period of stasis as in the Merkel era could be catastrophic.

With all the new entrants and centrifugal forces pulling apart the political centre, Germany had more parties polling above its electoral threshold in 2024 than Italy. In short, the days of predictable German politics are over and with establishment actors squabbling with one another, anti-democratic forces are plotting in the shadows to keep it that way, seeking to take advantage of declining faith in a system that's struggling on so many levels.

Day X

Police commandos moved into Frankfurt's affluent Westend quarter before dawn on 7 December 2022. Taking up position near the city's Palmengarten botanical gardens, officers prepared to start the largest counter-terrorism operation in post-war Germany. They had come for one man – a silver-haired property developer with the improbably grandiose name of Heinrich XIII. Prinz Reuss. By day a sparkling wine merchant and property developer, the seventy-one-year-old Reuss had developed a sideline in fomenting insurrection.

At 6 a.m. officers rang the doorbell at Reuss's apartment, demanding to see the septuagenarian. At addresses across Germany and abroad, around 3,000 security officials were swooping on co-conspirators in the *Patriotische Union* (Patriotic Union), an offshoot of the *Reichsbürger* movement whose believers long for a return of the German Empire. Weapons and ammunition stores were seized and planning documents taken for examination.[49] Without resistance, a stony-faced Reuss was led away for questioning. As Germans switched on the news, events unfolding before them appeared surreal. An elderly man in garish trousers and a mustard-coloured jacket had been planning nothing less than a coup. Long dismissed as a collection of fringe crackpots, the Reichsbürger threat was suddenly real.

With Reuss at its head, the *Patriotische Union* had been plotting for months. Meeting at the *Jagdschloss Waidmannsheil* (a hunting lodge in the Thuringian forest), Reuss and other Reichsbürger listened to presentations by Matthes Haug, a former physics teacher and amateur historian who has argued that the German Empire was never truly dissolved.* To restore order, the group planned to storm the Reichstag in Berlin on an undetermined 'Day X' and execute Chancellor Olaf Scholz along with other leading figures. To conduct the daring operation, the group had recruited former elite soldiers. Two in their fifties and sixties had been members of Germany's KSK special forces unit, equivalent to the British Army's SAS.[50] Another ex-soldier had served in the Bundeswehr as a lieutenant-colonel.[51] Together, they sought to enlist other military personnel and police officers.

To execute their plan, they had collected maps of the Reichstag building and photographed potential entry and exit points. They'd also stockpiled 380 firearms, 148,000 rounds of ammunition, and 350 bladed weapons.[52] In their logic, the group would act as a vanguard of the *Volk*, and the initial assault would lead to a wave of defections from Germany's armed and security forces. The Federal Republic would collapse and Reuss would seize control of an interim government and seek restoration of the Reich. Birgit Malsack-Winkemann, a judge and former member of parliament for the AfD, would be installed as justice minister.[53] Planning had been thorough, to the extent that a former TV chef had purchased groceries and stockpiled cooking utensils. He had also used his credit card to purchase a camper van.[54]

Unbeknownst to the plotters, Germany's security forces were onto them. Following a tip, the *Bundeskriminalamt* (Federal Criminal Police Office, analogous to the FBI or Britain's National Crime Agency) hacked Reuss's phone and installed eavesdropping software, allowing them to read his messages. Undercover officers were sent to monitor members, including one of the former elite soldiers who offered survival courses for right-wing extremists. Investigators used this to get close to him, with one BKA official joining the suspect on a six-hour walk in the Fichtelgebirge, a mountain range that straddles the German–Czech border.[55] A catalyst for action

---

* While Haug admitted to speaking at the Jagdschloss Waidmannsheil, he has denied that he took part in the coup plot. Investigations into what role he may or may not have played are ongoing. A report by broadcaster ARD said Haug would have been made minister of legal affairs in a Reuss cabinet.

was the death of Queen Elizabeth II on 8 September 2022. The conspirators surmised that shadowy actors were signalling a broader international plot was under way and urged that Day X be brought forward. That effort met with resistance from Reuss and caused a fallout. But the continued plotting unnerved German security forces.

On 7 December the security forces launched the raid. Reuss's hunting lodge in Thuringia was stormed by an elite unit of armed police, with teams of sniffer dogs searching the grounds for stashed weapons and explosives. Nationwide, and at addresses in Austria and Italy, around twenty-five members of the group were arrested. Due to the links with Germany's military, the barracks of the Bundeswehr's special forces unit in Calw, Baden-Württemberg, were searched.[56] The group has been dismissed as 'wheelchair revolutionaries', and a relative of Reuss branded its chief as nothing more than a 'confused old man'. But Thomas Haldenwang, chief of Germany's domestic intelligence agency, wasn't laughing, saying the group represented a clear and present danger to democracy. While the successful investigation showed Germany's security services had the matter under control, 'the danger was quite real,' he said.[57] It also showed unusual insight into just how unstable and radical elements of German society have become.

Officials estimate there are around 23,000 Reichsbürger and related activists in Germany, a number that's risen steadily in recent years.[58] One study suggests that the official figures may be a gross underestimation.[59] While varying subgroups hold different views, they almost universally reject the legitimacy of the Federal Republic as well as its liberal democratic constitution. Adherents instead believe the German Empire remains the legitimate sovereign of the German people. Many Reichsbürger believe that the Federal Republic isn't a state, but rather a limited-liability company established by the Allied powers after World War II, and Germans are employees of BRD GmbH rather than citizens – effectively taking the country's obsession with commerce to a conspiratorial extreme.

For Reichsbürger, the appeal of returning to a German empire is vague. Matthes Haug, who provided historical context for the coup plotters, has suggested that a restored empire could repudiate the Federal Republic's immense debts to enable a 'reset', although he didn't elaborate on what that would mean.[60] Others are drawn to the strict discipline, hierarchy and power of the empire, rejecting the modern Federal Republic as weakened, globalised and effete. For some, the vision is more ethnically driven, longing for an idealised vision of a culturally homogeneous Germany. This vision is selective. On the one hand, Reichsbürger glorify nationalism, monocultural identity, and authoritarian structures, while on the other, ignoring the empire's social inequality and political repression. Ultimately, the movement stems from a deep discomfort with modern Germany's pluralism, which is disconnected from traditional concepts of German identity. The adherents instead want to resolve that by reinstalling the certainty of authoritarianism and nationalism.

Age-wise, Reichsbürger are almost unique among extremists. While left- and right-wing militants are typically young, its members often become radicalised in mid-life. Experts believe that's because the movement's anti-systemic stance appeals to older people who face insurmountable financial problems, such as high debt or bankruptcy.[61] They also display a strong mistrust of public institutions, particularly the government and the media. Around one in twenty Germans are sympathetic to a Reichsbürger worldview, suggesting potential for further membership growth.[62] Geographically, the movement is more of a rural phenomenon, with many members in non-urban areas of Bavaria and Baden-Württemberg where communities feel threatened by modernisation. Declining rural populations and the closing of shops and medical facilities increasingly make such areas feel forgotten. And mainstream parties have little to offer.

As social cohesion frays, police and security officials warn of the risk of a rising tide of attacks from extremists. Reichsbürger are considered particularly dangerous, with Germany's domestic intelligence office estimating that around one in ten adherents are potentially violent, and there have been numerous cases that underscore those concerns. In 2016 one Bavarian Reichsbürger shot and killed a policeman who was trying to seize his weapons. In 2021, during the Covid pandemic, a fifty-year-old Reichsbürger shot and killed a petrol-station attendant for asking him to put on a mask. In April 2022 security forces approached the home of a Reichsbürger to force him to comply with a court order to surrender a pistol he owned. As officials approached the building, he opened fire with a machine gun, injuring two officers. After a two-hour standoff that ended in his surrender, police found three automatic machine guns, two automatic pistols, and 5,000 rounds of ammunition.

As with Reuss's co-conspirators, the members often have links to the military, where there are other sympathisers. Hundreds of officers in Germany's security services have been investigated for connections to Reichsbürger and other right-wing extremist groups. In 2020 an entire troop of Germany's KSK special forces (around 300 soldiers) was disbanded due to its links to right-wing extremists. 'Large parts of this scene are prepared for active violence or express their violent fantasies against state representation more freely than before,' Federal Prosecutor General Peter Frank told the newspaper *Welt am Sonntag*. 'This makes these people dangerous from the point of view of state security.'

Reichsbürger often align with other conspiracy movements, such as QAnon which believes that a cabal of satanic child molesters influences world events, and many believe in classic antisemitic theories. While there are proportionally more Reichsbürger in the areas that make up former East Germany, the highest total number operate in the wealthy western states of Baden-Württemberg and Bavaria.

One Reichsbürger in the eastern state of Saxony-Anhalt has gone to extraordinary lengths to make the group's folklore real. Established in 2012, the *Königreich Deutschland* (Kingdom of Germany) lies in Wittenberg, a village on the Elbe River with ties to Martin Luther.[63] Founded by Peter Fitzek, a ponytailed former martial-arts instructor with convictions for assault and driving without a licence, Königreich Deutschland has its own flag, currency and online video channel, KRD Tube.[64] Claiming around 6,000 members, some 800 of which are deemed actual citizens, the kingdom seeks to attract new members with open days on its territory, a former meat-canning centre. Paying €340 gives members access to Fitzek's self-help videos with titles like 'Be Your Own King' and 'The Power of Thought: Parts 1–5'. Crowned Peter the First at a 2012 ceremony that included candles, swords, sceptres and robes, Fitzek claims his state offers a more humane alternative to the capitalist Federal Republic. His kingdom has a seventy-page constitution as well as shops, a technology centre and a bank. Its founding document describes the microstate as an electoral monarchy – Fitzek has been elected for life.[65]

Unsurprisingly, the so-called kingdom has connections to right-wing extremists, such as a Holocaust denier who appeared at open days and in videos on its website.[66] Fitzek has purchased several properties for his kingdom, including paying over €2 million for a former hotel in Wolfsgrün near the Zwickauer Mulde River, much of that figure covered by five-figure donations from individual investors.[67] The building has been used as an alternative health centre and seminar space. The domestic intelligence agency bluntly warns against transferring money to Fitzek, saying 'you won't get anything back from these savings. The money is gone.'[68]

While it's easy to dismiss such groups as fraudsters or a deluded fringe, they are successfully tapping into a breakdown in Germany's social contract. Feeding off widening inequality, those railing against an uncaring and ineffective system are increasingly getting a hearing. While Germany gained international praise for its approach to the coronavirus pandemic, at home it led to a substantial loss of faith in the governing class and the wounds haven't healed, because age-old German myths have been allowed to persist. Restrictions on freedoms, as well as the most severe economic downturn in the post-war period, stoked perceptions that the governing class was simultaneously totalitarian and incompetent.

Those sentiments have also found expression through groups known as *Querdenker*, who think the pandemic was part of a grand conspiracy. Although many of the pandemic protests were peaceful and legitimate, others strayed into outright violence, including the attempt to storm the Reichstag in August 2020. While the movement stalled as the pandemic faded, it was able to use the inflation wave that was intensified by Russia's invasion of Ukraine as a new cause to rally people against out-of-touch elites. Security officials fear that potential measures needed to achieve Germany's ambitious decarbonisation targets, such as restrictions on flying and other freedoms, could further stoke conspiratorial sentiment and drive support for anti-democratic groups. Online activists have already referred to looming 'environmental lockdowns'.

The country's violent fringe extends beyond German nationalists. The right-wing Turkish Grey Wolves movement is made up of ethno-supremacists in Germany's Turkish population and espouses homophobic, antisemitic and authoritarian views. The group has attacked Kurdish businesses and threatened German Bundestag members who voted to declare the ethnic cleansing of Armenians from Anatolia between 1915 and 1917 as a genocide. There are around 30,000 Islamists in Germany, some of whom are potentially violent, according to the country's domestic intelligence service.[69]

Considering the various brands of extremism and the potential for divisions to deepen and widen, it's fair to say that Germany's democratic order is facing its greatest test in the post-war era. Already in 2022 a survey by the Friedrich Ebert Stiftung showed that a majority of Germans aren't happy with the functioning of democracy.[70] That figure is greater for people who perceive themselves as economically disadvantaged. For the second half of the twentieth century, Germany's system of proportional representation resulted in stable two-party coalitions that ruled from the centre, allowing for consensus-based politics. Those days appear to be over.

Feeding off voter frustration at the squabbling, ineffectual and out-of-touch political class, anti-democratic forces stand to profit from arduous economic and social change in the years ahead. While Germany's history was supposed to make it resistant to extremism, complacency from those well-off and frustration from the growing numbers of those left behind are creating a volatile mix. The state's reaction has often been to clamp down on undesirable opinions like people who question the government's unwavering support of Israel or brutally breaking up climate protests. That in turn hardens fronts and creates a vicious cycle, with no evident exit plan. As mainstream leaders struggle to articulate solutions, people on the extremes are motivated but those in the middle turn away in frustration and disgust. The combination poses a significant danger, according to the head of domestic intelligence, Thomas Haldenwang. 'People have become very comfortable in their private lives and are not sufficiently aware of how serious the threats to our democracy have become,' he said.[71]

9
Angst and Isolation

One could dismiss the discomfort of expressing pride in one's country as typical German self-hatred and yet one would have overlooked the very reason why the Federal Republic has become liveable and lovable

Navid Kermani

Germany's political fragmentation reflects the intensifying undercurrents of anxiety coursing through society. As the dream of *Wohlstand für Alle* (prosperity for all) fades, Germans are struggling for orientation. Creating a sense of community, though, is not something with which Germany is familiar. From the outset, the ebb and flow of German territory consisted of a hodgepodge of peoples. The connective tissue was mainly a common language, and then the fledgling nation started waging war on everyone around it in a grotesque form of identity-building.

In the post-war period, the Nazi experience was showcased but in a way as something outside and separate from its current incarnation, and thereby becoming the 'other' through which the nation defined itself. But that's not solidarity and it doesn't counter the root causes that led to the destructive rise of ethnic nationalism. Instead, the country did what it often does when confronting problems: it evaded it. Adolf Hitler's *Mein Kampf*, slogans like 'Deutschland Erwache' (Germany awake) and 'Alles für Deutschland' (everything for Germany) were banned.

What the country didn't do was actively incorporate lessons from the Nazi past to build a robust civic identity that offered an alternative to 'blood and soil' nationalism. And so the ideas and symbols of the past were allowed to retain their power to provoke and serve as an outlet for Germans alienated by the status quo. On the flipside, there's fear in the mainstream over a renewed descent into darkness, which has contributed to a desperate clampdown to defend its image as the 'good' Germany. That's created a disconnect between the state and the populace that has widened on both ends of the political spectrum, and there's no clear way to bridge it.

The result is something akin to national paralysis. Anxiety about the past and how that manifests in the present is preventing a constructive pivot toward the future. That's splintering German society, which doesn't have much of a positive reservoir to draw upon to keep it together when times get tough.

While the outside world wants to view the House of Germany as a bastion of stability and a symbol of human redemption, the residents are anxious and at odds with one another. As a way to cope, some are reviving old rituals that were merely repressed and never replaced, while others are lashing out or withdrawing.

Creating a stronger sense of community, with a new, more inclusive narrative, is the most complex part of the nation's recovery, and probably the one Germany is least equipped to handle.

Trouble with 'you'

To understand the risks Germany faces and why the country is so fragile, it's important to get in the heads of Germans, and that starts with the language. It's one of the few things that really is common nationwide. And Germans cherish their mother tongue in a way that Americans can't understand. Some Brits do, but most are generally grateful they don't have to learn other languages (something the vast majority of Americans don't even think about). In any case, no one owns English the way Germany owns German – although there is some input from Austria, Switzerland, and a few scattered territories.

True to form, there is a structure managing what's seen as a cultural asset that needs to be preserved and protected, rather than a mere means of communication that evolves as people and society do. The *Rat für deutsche Rechtschreibung* (Council for German Orthography) has forty-one seats, with Germany holding double the representation of Austria and Switzerland. The chairman, who started a new term in 2024, studied Catholic theology, is a former functionary in Lower Saxony and a member of the Bavarian Conservative Party – in other words, about as old-school as you can get in Germany. Liechtenstein, Italy's Südtirol, and a German-speaking community in Belgium each have single members, while Luxembourg has a non-voting representative. The council makes weighty orthographic decisions, such as a controversial reform in 1996 that, for instance, changed the spelling of 'ship voyage' from '*Schiffahrt*' to '*Schifffahrt*'.*

And where there's an authority, there are lobby groups. The *Verein Deutsche Sprache* (German Language Association) is the most notorious. The organisation, which boasts more than 36,000 members, advocates for a puritanical form of the language, claiming there's an 'unwritten generational contract' that's been broken by English terms and gender-neutral usage.[1] To put it polemically, it wants to freeze the language in time somewhere in the 1930s, or at the latest the 1950s. Unsurprisingly, it's been criticised for nationalistic leanings.†

The point is that a fundamental aspect of Germany's sense of self is controlled by a structure. It's not left to the people to decide the best way to communicate. Language doesn't filter up but is dictated from above in obscure meetings. Individual Germans are dissociated from the process, while the rule-making underscores a sense of powerlessness as well as rigidity that's endemic in German identity.

And yet there have been attempts to drag the German language into the modern era, but they are divisive. Since German has masculine and feminine forms of plurals (like Italian, for example), there's a patriarchal tone when colleagues are referred to as *Kollegen* (the masculine plural), but the feminine form *Kolleginnen* would be equally awkward. And both exclude non-binary people. So gender-neutral alternatives have been cobbled together. In this case, it could be: *Kolleg*innen* (yes, the asterisk is intentional but adding to the confusion, there could also be a colon, an underline, a slash or a capital I, as in *KollegInnen*).

---

* The *Rat für deutsche Rechtschreibung* is analogous to the *Académie Française* for the French.
† A *Verein Deutsche Sprache* board member attended a closed-door meeting about a proposal to deport foreigners in the autumn of 2023 and subsequently resigned.

Two-thirds to three-quarters of Germans are against *gendern*, depending on the survey. Some administrations, institutions and media use it, whereas others reject it. Bavaria has had one of the most extreme positions, with the state government banning *gendern* for administrative use as well as in schools. The state's premier, Markus Söder, has even encouraged citizens to blow the whistle on usage of gender-neutral terms. Positions on *gendern* very much reflect political leanings and show where the fault lines are. Supporters of the Greens are most in favour of the practice, whereas AfD backers are the most against it. On one side, it's seen as a necessary reaction to the in-built patriarchal structure of the German language. On the other side, it's seen as part of a woke conspiracy to undermine national cultural characteristics for the globalist agenda. But aside from stoking anger, it has little real impact. People can *gendern*, or not, without much consequence either way.

The *Rat für deutsche Rechtschreibung* sidestepped the dicey question at a meeting in December 2023 by determining that gender-equitable language is a societal task and not a topic for orthographic rules. *Duden*, the benchmark German dictionary, had previously stirred up trouble by giving *gendern* its seal of approval.[2] And it stirred the pot when it introduced feminine versions of guest and villain (*Gästin* and *Bösewichtin*) alongside the masculine versions, which were previously considered generic catch-alls. That sparked a backlash from the conservative advocacy group *Verein Deutsche Sprache*. It called on 'friends of the German language' to oppose *Duden*'s initiative, substantiating its position with a 2018 decision by Germany's top court which ruled that the term '*der Kunde*' (the customer) can refer to people of any gender. In other words, process and structure should supersede usage, and it is a particularly German trait to refer to institutions and structures in order to determine something as elementary and personal as communication.

On top of the struggle to adapt the language, its fundamental structure contributes to an us-versus-them divide. German speakers love the complexity of *der*, *die*, *das* and the different versions of 'the' in accusative, dative and genitive cases. It gives them ample opportunity to correct learners in a tone that can range from paternalistic to condescending. They are proud of a sentence structure that throws verbs at the end to keep listeners in suspense, and relish the word-engineering involved in compound nouns like *Geschwindigkeitsüberschreitung* (speeding) and *Rechtsschutzversicherungsgesellschaften* (legal-insurance companies). But some of the most powerful German words are short ones like *doch*, which means 'on the contrary' but can also express a range of subtleties. The CDU – the party of Angela Merkel, Helmut Kohl and most recently Friedrich Merz – calls the language 'the key' to German society, and the state of Bavaria defines that in law by requiring foreigners to communicate adequately in German after three years of residency.[3]

As fascinating as the language of Johann Wolfgang von Goethe and Friedrich Schiller is, it's complicated to learn. Locals often undermine good intentions by automatically switching to English (which usually isn't as good as they think it is) if they hear an accent. It's a not so subtle form of 'othering' that sends the signal you are not one of us, even for Western 'expats'. The emphasis on language also establishes a pecking order that gives native Germans an edge and creates leverage over newcomers even in areas where language skills play little to no role. A thirty-year-old Venezuelan, for instance, was threatened with deportation from rural Brandenburg, where young people are in short supply, in part because his German skills were deemed insufficient to continue his work cutting up dead pigs into cutlets and smoking sausage. The butcher, named Heberth, ultimately received an extension after a public campaign by his employer, which included a social-media hashtag (#heberthsollbleiben . . . Heberth should stay).*

Understanding Friedrich Nietzsche in his native tongue, though, is hardly a gateway for commonality, even among Germans. The language's capacity for division is evident in *gendern*, but a more fundamental issue is *du* versus *Sie*. The two forms of 'you' have significant differences that don't exist in English. In Australia or Great Britain a complete stranger might call you 'mate', and in the American South you might be referred to as 'honey'. The tradition has developed that aims at bolstering a sense of familiarity. That's not the case in German, where distinctions and distance are intentional. *Du* is for friends and family. *Sie* is impersonal and can refer to one

---

* *Fleischerei Kadach* in Spremberg documented the efforts to keep their employee, reflecting how hard it is to find German workers for something as fundamental to community life as a butcher, at https://fleischerei-kadach.de/heberth-abschiebung.

or many 'others'. Addressing someone with *Sie* is like looking at the floor during an audience with the queen (and maybe also her court). But *Sie* doesn't express hierarchy but rather formality, and is used for a bus driver, a store clerk or a work colleague.

People in your *du* circle are addressed by their first names, whereas the rest are typically on a last-name basis, if they're addressed directly at all. That means gender-specific *Frau* or *Herr*, in addition to an elitist obsession with academic titles, which can accumulate to *Prof. Dr. Dr.* and beyond. The point is that *Sie* people are a universe of abstract entities rather than individuals. They are the 'other' among us, and it's hard to feel affinity for people that aren't addressed as equals. Other European languages have similar formal and informal words for 'you', but they're more readily overcome. In places like Italy, that structure is happily dropped or subverted with a warm gesture, and it frequently happens that a face-to-face conversation with a stranger starts formally, quickly turns convivial, and finishes with an invitation to dinner. Spontaneous acts of camaraderie are far rarer in Germany. The nation starts out splintered because of mental categorisation, but without the tools or pathways to bring people together.

People in the United States and Great Britain use small talk to establish basic rapport, and to be fair, Americans tend to feign cloying intimacy with just about everyone. Germans, by contrast, are very selective and deliberate about who they're familiar with. As an adult, *du* has to be offered. It's a little ceremony that includes first-name introductions. Once in that circle, it's always and forever – and they are truly loyal and earnest about it. They're the group you decide to care about, and then there's the rest. In Germany there are no illusions that the country is a big social club. That might be honest, but categorising the world into discrete groups leads to us/them attitudes and raises the threshold on interaction. The supermarket line consists of objects delaying your transaction, people in a crowd can be jostled aside without a word, and there's little need to hold doors open for 'others' coming through.

Queuing is a particular struggle. Unless there are clear demarcations, an amorphous blob rather than a straightforward line tends to form. Nervous shuffling ensues over concerns about getting overlooked. Almost inevitably some 'body' presses ahead, and if called out for the transgression to common decency, they'll often feign shock at the sudden appearance of a small mob gathered for the chance at getting a coffee, a *Döner*, or a loaf of bread. It creates a degree of separation between individuals and their peers in society. If someone has paid to reserve a train seat, don't expect them to surrender their place for an elderly person or so a child can sit with a parent. Jerks are clearly everywhere, but compartmentalising the universe into us and them intensifies apathy. Random acts of community do occur, but they are more of an exception than the rule.

Clearly not all of Germany's ungainly social behaviour can be attributed to the *du/Sie* disconnect. Such differences in second-person pronouns exist in other languages. But an underdeveloped sense of national solidarity means there are relatively few ways to bridge these divides and see one another as part of the same community. So linguistic divisions translate a little more directly into public behaviour.

The consequences can be polarising. On the one hand, a relatively homogenous *du* bubble can become a self-affirming echo chamber. Subjective views become magnified to appear as universal truths. That bursts out in what Germans call *Obrigkeit* (imperiousness), which includes confronting others for perceived indiscretions (something most foreigners have painfully experienced).[*]

The opposite end of the spectrum is a feeling of isolation. In a world of cold, unapproachable others, it's hard to feel at ease. In Germany, trust in strangers is lower than most other developed economies,[4] about half of Germans worry society is falling apart,[5] and one in four feels lonely.[6] The country's youth has become particularly pessimistic in recent years, with more than half of fourteen- to twenty-nine-year-olds complaining of high stress levels and more than a third feeling exhausted.[7] The trends towards social withdrawal are recognised as enough of an issue that the government released a strategy paper with the goal of countering the feeling of isolation, mainly by talking about it rather than

---

[*] A haughty sense of superiority played a key role in German nationalisation. Emanuel Geibel's 1861 poem *Deutschlands Beruf* (Germany's Calling) gave birth to the nationalistic slogan 'Am deutschen Wesen soll die Welt genesen' (The German character shall heal the world).

actually finding ways to encourage more interaction.[8] But more than a 'loneliness barometer' is needed. Action can be taken to create a greater sense of community and promote empathy and interaction (we'll discuss some ideas in the final chapter).

Social distrust in turn manifests itself in widespread state supervision. It's deemed acceptable for the government to regulate bad behaviour, from when to throw out rubbish to where to skateboard. That includes what's allowed to appear on a birth certificate. Names deemed harmful to the child or not culturally appropriate can be rejected – as if a conventional name would fix whatever parenting issues might be wrapped up with a person wanting to name their child 'Bierstübl' (beer bar).*

These are levels of interference that wouldn't be tolerated in many other countries, but are accepted as normal in Germany, where structure is a crutch that avoids messy interpersonal disputes. It extends to when and how people are allowed to spend their time. Every week, Germans get Sunday as a day of rest, which effectively means the shops are closed (so if shopping was part of your relaxation routine, best to get used to fighting through the crowds on Saturdays). That's because it's a Christian country, right? Yes, but increasingly less so. In 2022 a record 1.3 million people left the Catholic and Evangelical Churches, bringing the total number of registered Christians to less than half of the population, down from two-thirds in the late 1990s.[9] The trends are unlikely to change unless Germany starts actively recruiting and converting new faithful. But that would mean convincing people to pay *Kirchensteuer* (church tax), which the poor can't afford and the rich are unlikely to volunteer for. And yet it remains a national custom. From parenting to weekend planning, the message is that the power and wisdom of the state is needed to maintain a functioning society over wayward and unpredictable individuals.

The national aversion to investing in stocks is usually attributed to traditional cautiousness stemming from the country's tumultuous twentieth century. Those are certainly significant factors, but there are also undercurrents that go back further in time and reflect deep-seated distrust of the contemporary system. While the country itself

---

* That's an actual name that was rejected by the German authorities.

is strongly mercantilist, there is an anti-modernist streak rooted in the nation's philosophy and culture. Germany's Romantic movement was particularly strong and tilted towards rejecting Enlightenment values. Goethe's *Faust* sold his soul for deeper worldly knowledge before being saved by angels, and Caspar David Friedrich's painting *Wanderer above the Sea of Fog* celebrates the mystery and wonder of nature. In practical terms, Romanticism gave rise to *Lebensreform* (life reform) initiatives, which emerged in the mid-nineteenth century as a counter-culture reaction to industrialisation and materialism. The movement endures in the *Reformhaus* chain of organic shops, *freikörperkultur* (literally, 'free body culture' but in reality it means nudism), and a zeal for hiking. It also comes out in an innate scepticism towards technological advances among other changes, which has certainly held the country back in adapting to the digital age.

The message we're trying to send is that there's an internal complexity in Germany that creates uncomfortable tension, even at the best of times.

Culture clash

Indeed, it's not easy being one of 84 million Germans. There's no consensus as to what that means. Is it just Bach, *bratwurst* and beer? Or is it also techno, *Döner* and Club-Mate carbonated iced tea? Germany is still the birthplace of the Reformation, the creator of the automobile, and the fatherland of the printed word, but how much does that matter now? And if that legacy holds over, how about Nazism? Where does the idea of Germany start where and does it end? If so, why? Probably nowhere in the world devotes as much time and effort trying to define who and what it is, and with as little success. The United States was a state that created a nation. But in Germany there's a sense that it was a nation before it was ever a state, so there's an identity that's pure and stretches back into history and exists beyond political structures. There's a border between what belongs and what doesn't, even if reality has blurred the lines.

In 2010, Christian Wulff, who at the time served as president of the Federal Republic, tried to push that boundary. The Christian Democrat said Germany needed to rethink itself, not just due to the strains of merging its East and West but because the country had evolved. It was no longer exclusively the home of Müllers and Schmidts, and at the time had about 15 million people with a migration background (as Germany likes to call it). 'We need a clear stance,' said Wulff on the occasion of the twentieth anniversary of reunification. 'An understanding of Germany that does not limit belonging to a passport, a family history or a faith, but is more broadly based.'[10] He then declared Islam to be a part of Germany alongside Christianity and Judaism (a devotional reference to Nazi guilt).

From an outsider's perspective, that seemed obvious. For decades the country had been recruiting people from Turkey, Tunisia and Morocco to help fuel its economy. About 5.5 million Muslims live in Germany and their ranks have included political leaders, entrepreneurs and FIFA World Cup winners. They have built homes, businesses and of course mosques: over 2,500, from small facilities tucked away discreetly in courtyards to the impressive DITIB-Central Mosque in Cologne. There's hardly a town in the country that doesn't have a shop serving Döner Kebab, Germany's street food of choice introduced by Turkish immigrants.

And yet, Wulff's statement ignited a firestorm. While Chancellor Merkel backed the stance, fellow conservative politicians reacted brusquely and rejected it. Two years later, Wulff's successor Joachim Gauck – a former Lutheran pastor and activist in East Germany – rowed back, saying that 'Muslims that live here belong to Germany' – but not the religion.[11] So effectively Muslim Germans reside in the country as a legal and administrative fact but are not 'real' Germans since Islam is a foreign belief system.

For a country that aims to draw a line under its Nazi past and protect individual rights and freedom of expression, that's a slippery slope. It not only accepts systemic and structural discrimination but closes the idea of Germany. Identity is something that's lived and not monochrome. So of course Germany includes Islam, just as much as it includes *Mettwurst*, Riesling and Birkenstock sandals. Cultural inclusion can't be dictated from above, but Germany still keeps trying.

Ahead of the Christmas holidays in 2023, Friedrich Merz – Merkel's long-time antagonist and her eventual successor as head of the CDU – included buying and decorating a tree as one of the elements of being German. That is indeed *urdeutsch* (originally

German). Goethe wrote about a tree decked with candles, candies and apples in 1774,* when parts of America were still British colonies. But of course, connecting German identity to a Christian holiday tradition is problematically narrow and excludes Jews, Muslims, Buddhists, atheists, and people who'd rather have trees living in the woods than dead in their living rooms. Merz's hot take was part of an ongoing battle to define and defend German *Leitkultur*, a contrived debate that suggests *urdeutsch* ways of life are under attack. It conveys a sense of superiority through the prefix '*Leit-*' (in terms of guiding or leading). Coupled with the innocuous idea of culture, it lightly skips past ethno-nationalist taboos. But the effect is similar.

It's deemed safe ground, though, since the German-Arab sociologist Bassam Tibi originally coined the term with the aim of shifting Germany towards universal Enlightenment ideals. But Merz appropriated it and gave the term a nationalist tinge.[12] In 2000 he argued for a 'German *Leitkultur*' based on freedom and democracy, deeming the country's Basic Law as 'the most important expression' of these values and thus part of German cultural identity.[13] The term popped up again in 2017, a few months after the Tunisian Anis Amri rammed a truck into a Christmas market in central Berlin, killing thirteen and injuring sixty-seven people. Merz's CDU colleague Thomas de Maizière, who was interior minister at the time, published ten theses on German *Leitkultur*, which he called 'guidelines for living together'. The tenets included hard work, enlightened patriotism, and the populist phrase 'We are not Burka', drawing a clear distinction between Islam and German identity.[14]

By effectively ghettoising Islam, the country lost the opportunity to shape a German version. Instead of providing a safe space for moderate Muslims, the isolation created fertile ground for radicalisation. The Egyptian Mohammed Atta studied in Hamburg, where he drifted into extremism before crashing a plane into the World Trade Center in New York on 11 September 2001. Munich-born Fritz Gelowicz converted to Islam as a teenager and later joined a cell of the Islamic Jihad Union in Sauerland. He was found guilty in 2010 of planning attacks on the Ramstein airbase and other

---

* In his novel *The Sorrows of Young Werther*, Goethe refers to the joys of a Christmas tree in 'die Erscheinung eines aufgeputzten Baumes mit Wachslichtern, Zuckerwerk und äpfeln'.

American facilities along with three other members, including fellow German Daniel Schneider.[15] In 2016 the Syrian asylum seeker Mohammad Daleel, who had links to Islamic State, injured about a dozen people in a suicide bombing attack in Ansbach after dodging deportation. Such events have fuelled negative representations of the religion in the media* and intensified the vicious circle of anti-Muslim sentiment, with deadly consequences. In Hanau, a forty-three-year-old German went on a racially motivated rampage in 2020, killing nine people before shooting his mother and himself. Before that, the National Socialist Underground (a neo-Nazi group) killed nine migrants and a policewoman between 2000 and 2007. The killings, which took place across Germany, were initially linked to Turkish gangs and trivialised as 'Döner murders'.

Around the time of de Maizière's ten theses on German identity, Seyran Ateş, a lawyer and the target of an attempted assassination, established the Ibn Rushd-Goethe mosque in Berlin, providing services that allowed men, women and non-binary people to pray together and explore their beliefs. It was an effort to establish a tolerant and inclusive form of Islam in Germany and break with the religion's patriarchal system. But in 2023, after years of hate from conservative Muslims in Germany and abroad, Islamic State targeted the mosque as a 'place of devil worship' and threatened an attack. Due to safety concerns, it decided to close. 'We feel let down by politicians who have failed to include us in Islam policy in order to give progressive Muslims a voice,' leaders of the mosque wrote to its congregation.[16]

The CDU says its *Leitkultur* concept is about freedom and tolerance and not *Leberwurst* and Richard Wagner. But if that's the case, why use a term that comes across as a softly whispered 'Make Germany Great Again', with all the eerie historical echoes. To put it polemically, it's because sowing divisions is *urdeutsch*. It's also politically expedient rabble-rousing for Merz, who has derisively called boys from migrant families 'little pashas' and alleged that asylum seekers are coming to Germany to get their teeth fixed

---

* According to a 2023 report on anti-Muslim sentiment from the German interior ministry, Islam had negative representations in 57 per cent of print media and 89 per cent of TV reports between 2014 and 2019, which was consistent with long-term trends. https://www.deutsche-islam-konferenz.de/SharedDocs/Anlagen/DE/Publikationen/Studien/richter-paasch-colberg-analyse-islam-berichterstattung-in-deutschen-medien.pdf.

and taking capacity away from locals. He's not an isolated voice though. The Christian Democrats have enshrined the concept in the party's platform: 'All those who want to live here must recognise our *Leitkultur* without reservations.' The AfD clearly embraces the concept and goes further by declaring multiculturalism a 'serious threat' to the nation as a 'cultural entity'.

Implicitly linking anti-democratic sentiment to migrants helps shift the blame for social unrest onto 'other' Germans, especially dark-skinned ones. The problem becomes people who are resistant to integration, deflecting attention from political failings like a structural lack of educational and social mobility. Focusing on the 'other among us' also sidesteps home-grown outsiders like the *Reichsbürger*. Such authoritarian sentiments have been gradually on the rise, and not just in the former communist East Germany.

The *Leitkultur* movement in turn fuels anxiety by creating a sense that something is under threat and needs to be defended. It's supported by the related concept of *Willkommenskultur*. The 'culture of welcoming' is promoted by the government with the aim of encouraging the migration of skilled foreigners. The concept still embodies control. Germany opens the door and therefore holds the power. But in a liberal society, there can't be distinctions between members who really belong and those who don't. And after decades of immigration, Germany is evolving regardless of what *Leitkultur* guardians might want.

Many of the things that might be seen as *urdeutsch* are indeed losing ground, yet it's not because of a globalist conspiracy but because tastes are evolving naturally. This indicates that the notion of Germany needs to change more to embrace new ideas, rather than look backward and try to preserve an artificial concept of purity.

In the homeland of *Schweinshaxe* (roast pork knuckle), eating meat has hit record lows. Beer drinking has been on a downward slide since reunification, despite or because of the country's renowned 1516 *Reinheitsgebot* (beer purity law), which makes Germany's 'liquid bread' boring and samey compared with the quirky variety of American microbrews and the vast array of British ales, lagers and bitters. Struggles to adapt to changing tastes also explains why Germany has among the lowest share of domestic cuisine in the world. *Sauerbraten* (marinated roast meat), *Spätzle* (thick egg noodles) and *Maultaschen*

(German-style ravioli) in turn barely register on other countries' menus.[17] Its food and drink are also deemed less unique. Germany has 188 local delicacies registered and protected in the EU after *Dithmarsch* goose was added in 2024, joining six different varieties of asparagus. That compares with 789 for France and 906 for Italy. That might not be entirely surprising, given their renowned cuisines, but Germany also trails Greece, Spain and Portugal, countries with vastly smaller populations.[18] That's not because there's an anti-bread and anti-sausage conspiracy, but because tastes have changed and German cooking hasn't evolved enough to keep pace.

In other cultural endeavours, Germany is also struggling. Although the country has world-class classical ensembles like the Bavarian Radio Symphony Orchestra and a thriving opera and theatre scene,[19] it scarcely plays a role in international pop culture. Apart from cars, footballers and sneakers, its biggest contribution might be Heidi Klum, a bubbly former Victoria's Secret model who's posed in lingerie ads with her daughter. In the Eurovision song contest, Germany finished dead last in 2023 and 2022 and second to last in 2021. A twelfth-place finish in 2024 was a surprising success. To be sure, the world's most popular song contest is hardly the arbiter of musical refinement, but it does reflect a certain amount of soft power and how a country can tap into the zeitgeist.

Techno is an exception for Germany, but it doesn't enjoy the same type of recognition from public authorities. Although Berlin's techno scene was recognised by UNESCO as part of Germany's cultural heritage, clubs are struggling to recover from Covid restrictions. And a number of establishments in Berlin, including Watergate and Wilde Renate, have succumbed to rising costs as part of a trend known as *Clubsterben* (club death). The Loveparade, once an annual mecca for ravers, collapsed in 2004 under commercial pressures; attempts to keep it going in other cities ended in tragedy with a deadly stampede in Duisburg in 2010. Techno provides space for alternative conceptions of German identity, which are otherwise hard to find.

And unlike in Great Britain, where the BBC tries to maintain broad appeal, Germany's taxpayer-financed public-broadcasting system sticks to narrow formats, offering a steady stream of *Volksmusik* galas, flourishes of classical music, and swooning dramas about romance or intrigue in rural villages or vacation hot spots.

That's alongside supporting twelve orchestras, eight choirs and four big bands. Although there are avant-garde theatres and performance groups, there's little effort to evolve and experiment for a broader public despite funding being available.

The most enduring pop-culture phenomenon is *Tatort*, a crime drama that rotates between different cities and occasionally hops the border to Austria and Switzerland. It's emblematic of cultural ossification. Broadcast on Sunday evenings to close out the weekend, it's been airing since 1970 with an unchanged intro. It's been described as 'the last big campfire' in Germany, where the country gathers to hear stories. An underlying theme is often the German concept of family, and detectives (generally white men) are mostly on-edge loners with broken personal lives. The episodes range from preachy and arty to slapstick and gritty, representing a sense of diversity. But the federalist approach also reflects how difficult it is to build commonality and national archetypes. Since the episodes skip, relationships with the characters are broken and isolated. There are also elements of how awkward interpersonal relations are. In a 2024 episode set in Munich, a young detective was abducted and almost killed. After the ordeal, his more senior colleagues initially scolded him for carelessness. Then they softened and allowed him to use *du* (the informal form of 'you'), prompting obligatory and superfluous first-name introductions ('I'm Franz. I'm Ivo.').

As verbal communication struggles to unite and food and culture have remained bland, football is one of the few bastions left to connect Germans. But that's also been a struggle in recent years. Winning the FIFA World Cup for the first time in 1954 was a formative event for the war-ravaged nation. Its third win came in 1990 just after the Berlin Wall fell, giving something for the reunited country to rally around. Germany hosted the tournament in 2006, when it was recovering from a period of high unemployment as the 'sick man of Europe'. While it only placed third, the event finally made waving the flag and donning the national colours of black, red and gold acceptable and fun (even if the event was later tainted by corruption).[*] So a few

---

[*] Wolfgang Niersbach resigned as head of the German football association over questionable payments to FIFA, the sport's governing body. The scandal also involved allegations against football icon Franz Beckenbauer.

bad tournaments can weigh on the national psyche, especially when there's not much relief elsewhere.

Germany's most recent FIFA World Cup victory in Brazil in 2014 was a missed opportunity to turn football into a pillar of shared identity. The squad that stormed to victory in South America – trouncing hosts Brazil 7-1 in Belo Horizonte before overcoming Lionel Messi's Argentina in the final – was a showcase for Germany's particular version of multiculturalism. Captained by Philip Lahm, a Bavarian from Munich, the squad contained star players with various migration backgrounds. Miroslav Klose, the tournament's top goalscorer, came from a Polish-German family expelled from Silesia at the end of World War II. His partner in attack, Lukas Podolski, was also born in Poland. Mesut Özil, a mercurial midfielder who had starred at Arsenal, was born to Turkish *Gastarbeiter* in Gelsenkirchen, in the heart of the Ruhr Valley. The Berlin native Jérôme Boateng has a Ghanaian father. Toni Kroos represented eastern Germany from the Baltic seaport of Greifswald and would win numerous 'Man of the Match' awards. Their victory over Brazil was described by the *Guardian* as 'the night Germany removed the crown from football royalty'.

But rather than become a validation for the potential of a diverse Germany, football has become a petri dish for ethno-nationalist takes on identity. Several non-white members of the 2014 team would go on to suffer discrimination. The AfD co-leader Alexander Gauland said that while Boateng was appreciated as a footballer, he wouldn't be welcomed as a neighbour. When Germany's national team fell on harder times, Özil said he was a victim of abuse from the country's fans: 'I am a German when we win, but I am an immigrant when we lose.'

While Germany's DFB football association claimed it was successfully clamping down on racism, independent studies differ.[20] In the run-up to the Euro 2024 championships, the public broadcaster ARD asked Germans in a poll whether they'd like to see more white members of the national team. Around a fifth of those surveyed said they would. Addressing abuse directed at minority players on Germany's successful Under-17 football team, Boateng wrote on social media: 'Young German national players who are racially insulted after winning in the World Cup for Germany? In 2023? Are you serious? When will this ever stop . . .!?'[21]

Since the FIFA World Cup win in 2014, the men's national team has spurred waves of *schadenfreude* by crashing out of consecutive World Cups, and the once-solid women's team followed suit in 2023. National pride took another blow when the American giant Nike beat out home-grown Adidas to outfit the teams, leading to accusations of betrayal from across the country. That followed shock over a pink jersey for the men's team for the European championships, which was 'too woke' for people like the influential far-right firebrand Björn Höcke, who called it emblematic of Germany's spiritual decay.

It's not just football. The Olympics has become a sore spot too. Once a critical expression of national prowess (even after Jesse Owens humiliated the Nazis in 1936 by winning four gold medals), Germany has struggled. The country hasn't dared host the games since an attack on Israeli athletes by Palestinian terrorists in Munich in 1972, thus avoiding trauma rather than facing it – a recurring German tendency. Hamburg toyed with the idea, but residents rejected it in a referendum in 2015. In a sign of a broader malaise and fading focus on grassroots organisation and investment, its medal haul in the 2020 summer Olympics in Tokyo was the lowest since reunification and less than half of what the first combined team managed in 1992.

The poor performance is linked to fading amateur sports. More than one in four athletic associations have reported significant declines in membership.[22] For a country once considered fit, more than half of adults are overweight. Obesity rates have almost doubled between 1990 and 2015,[23] driving up health costs and adding over €400 to Germans' annual tax burdens.[24]

Germany is even losing out in motor racing. In a country where the Nuremberg racing track is open to the public, Nico Hülkenberg was the only German driver in Formula 1 in 2024. Mercedes' team for the glitzy racing series that was once dominated by Michael Schumacher (an international icon left incapacitated after a 2013 skiing accident) is based in England and hasn't had a German driver since Nico Rosberg in 2016.

Even steadfast German traditions have had their issues. As Merz was defending tree trimming, some Christmas markets faced an existential crisis brought on by the country's music-rights monopoly

GEMA. The entity has its roots in the Nazi organisation STAGMA, which was established in 1933 to control German music and weed out Jewish and 'degenerate' artists. The original director was known to have handed out copies of Hitler's *Mein Kampf* as a reward to staff. GEMA is known for its hard-line, including a long dispute with YouTube that blocked music videos. It enjoys sweeping authority under the so-called 'GEMA presumption', which means an organiser has to prove beyond doubt that only royalty-free music was played at an event to avoid payments.[25] GEMA had flexed its powers ahead of Christmas 2023 by informing several dozen cities that they would be charged more for playing holiday carols, claiming the areas were bigger than registered to the watchdog. In some cases the fees increased tenfold, threatening the pleasant tradition of listening to '*Stille Nacht*' (Silent Night) while drinking *Glühwein* (hot mulled wine, which is one of the best things about winter in Germany).

And if all that wasn't hard enough to bear for Germany's self-image, then there's Richard David Precht. The talk-show philosopher — an unlikely addition to a long line of thinkers from Immanuel Kant to Hannah Arendt — ruminates on any number of topics from orthodox Judaism to fuel-cell vehicles, with all the nuance of reality TV. His incisive take on Germany's post-war identity: 'The Mercedes star has replaced the swastika.'[26] That's hardly an image that many Germans would want to rally around, but alternatives are indeed sparse and underscore that something needs to change in Germany's approach to creating a sense of community.

But there are few opportunities for active engagement with a more inclusive idea of Germany. Traditions that bring people together in a positive way are scarce. National holidays are dominated by sombre political speeches and closed stores, which typically trigger a shopping scramble on the day before. New Year's Eve is celebrated in a big way, but that's not German. Instead, the holiday has underscored division, and clashes with authorities are often quickly pinned on 'poorly assimilated' migrants. The point is that there are few shared experiences to build a sense of national belonging and help people, including *biodeutsche* (a somewhat ironic term for ethnic Germans), live the idea of being German.

The response to the nation's shaky sense of self is the defensive and hollow *Leitkultur* debate that stirs up fears more than it builds bonds and perpetuates the alienation of Germany's structure-driven society. The country needs to let go and embrace the people that it has, all of them. Identity is not an either/or issue. A person can feel German and Polish, and be gay and Muslim. A sense of self is layered like *Schwarzwälder Kirschtorte* (Black Forest cake), with limitless varieties and combinations. Cultural values and concepts are worth upholding, but the best will endure. The problem is when reality becomes disconnected from rhetoric. That kind of dissonance, rather than a dilution of German culture, is the country's real threat. Professing integration while erecting hurdles, demanding assimilation while thwarting inclusion, and preaching tolerance while acting intolerant.

Closing the gates

To defend its self-image as one of post-Nazi 'good' Germans, the country has become zealous in recent years. In May 2019 a broad coalition of parties in the Bundestag condemned a Palestinian-led movement that aims to isolate Israel economically. In the kind of cross-party collaboration that only comes about when fundamental issues are at stake, the centre-right CDU/CSU, the Social Democrats, the Greens and the Free Democrats joined forces on a resolution to outflank a similar initiative by the far-right AfD to reject the so-called BDS movement, which stands for boycott, divestment and sanctions and is an effort to put pressure on Israel over its treatment of Palestinians.

The nationalist party has questionable interest in protecting Israel,[*] but doing so helps wave away Nazi allegations while also pushing the notion that Jewish life is at risk from imported antisemitism – a narrative that's much easier for mainstream Germans to accept than the domestic variety. The assertion, which isn't backed up by official statistics,[†]

---

[*] Israel isn't mentioned once in the AfD's platform, but 'Islam' and 'Muslim' are mentioned fifty times. While the party rejects Islam as a part of Germany, it acknowledges that some Muslims have integrated into society.
https://www.afd.de/wp-content/uploads/2023/05/Programm_AfD_Online_.pdf.
[†] About 84 per cent of antisemitic crimes in 2022 were attributed to the political right, according to Germany's annual report on political crime. https://www.bmi.bund.de/SharedDocs/downlo ads/DE/veroeffentlichungen/nachrichten/2023/05/pmk2022-straf-gewalttaten.pdf.

helps promote an agenda that seeks to clamp down on migration from Muslim countries.

But even if the AfD's aims were insincere, Germany's entire political centre could hardly sit idly by and look lax on protecting Jews, which has been part of post-war Germany's image and has gained in intensity after reunification went awry. The rationale is that as it became clear that East and West Germany weren't really united, the country needed even more to underline its credentials as the reformed baddies. And so the mainstream parties took out a broad brush and painted the diffuse BDS movement as anti-Israel, and by extension anti-Jewish. 'Our unending historical responsibility requires us to refrain from and prevent everything that is antisemitic or even raises the impression that it could become antisemitic,' the Christian Democrat lawmaker Axel Müller said during the debate in the Reichstag in Berlin. The resolution likened BDS's 'Don't Buy' stickers slapped on Israeli goods to the Nazi boycott action *Kauft nicht bei Juden* (Don't buy from Jews). None of the resolution's supporters, though, noted the significant difference between action by a totalitarian state and protests by a loose collection of private activists.

A Nazi comparison that went the other way (i.e., against Israel) got the Jewish writer Masha Gessen in hot water and highlights the disturbing trend towards thought-policing in the supposedly enlightened reboot of the German nation. On 13 December 2023 the Heinrich Böll Stiftung, a foundation connected to the co-ruling Green Party and dedicated to promoting democracy and fighting discrimination, withdrew from a ceremony to award Gessen the Hannah Arendt Prize for Political Thought. The honour was recognition for the Russian-American writer's work on 'totalitarian tendencies as well as civil disobedience and the love of freedom'. But when Gessen (who uses the pronoun 'they') directed their powers of observation in a way that challenged German orthodoxy about its past, they became a target.

The catalyst for the controversy was an essay in the *New Yorker*, in which Gessen had drawn links between 'ghettoized Jews' of the Nazi era and 'besieged Gazans' facing the risk of liquidation.[27] That breached taboos in Germany for criticising Israel, which is equated with antisemitism, and worse yet compared actions of the Israeli government to those of the Nazis. In a sign of the status of the award ceremony, Bremen was scheduled to host the event at the ornate Upper Hall in the historic Rathaus (a UNESCO World Heritage site), referred to as the city's 'most beautiful and prestigious room'. But the administration called the comparison 'unspeakable' and pulled the venue. The Heinrich Böll Foundation said Gessen's 'unacceptable' comments shut down dialogue and pulled out of a planned panel discussion (evidently without seeing the irony).[28]

The uproar touched a nerve by raising questions over Germany's absolute authority over Nazi memory. But Gessen is entangled in the experience of totalitarianism, and more so than most Germans. The Moscow-born writer grew up in a Jewish family that was impacted by the Nazi death machine as well as by Soviet antisemitic purges and faced censorship in Russia. Gessen and post-Holocaust Germany should be on the same side in the effort to prevent further genocidal atrocities. And yet, German functionaries appeared more focused on preserving the country's view of the Holocaust as an episode unlike anything else.

Germany embraces its role in highlighting Nazi atrocities and has put them on display for all the world to see, but the main audience for its memory culture is itself. Alongside the numerous monuments and acts of remembrance, the government has called defending Israel's existence part of modern Germany's *Staatsräson* (the state's reason for being). It sees it as an enduring responsibility, and after the Hamas terror attack in Israel on 7 October 2023, the government made individual payments of €220 to over 110,000 Holocaust survivors living in Israel to help them cope with the incident. To what extent that money really helped those people is debatable, but the displays did help maintain Germany's feeling of being a cleansed nation 'liberated' from the Nazis, separated from that trauma by regular acts of contrition. In this 'theatre of memory',* Jews are supposed to fall in line and play a supporting role in 'this German notion of "becoming good again",' in the words of Max Czollek, a Berlin-born poet, playwright and political scientist.[29]

But guilt is backward-looking. Its focus is atonement. It's not the same as responsibility, which requires action and vigilance. To

---

* The term was coined by Y. Michal Bodemann in his 1996 book *Gedächtnistheater: Die jüdische Gemeinschaft und ihre deutsche Erfindung*.

be truly rehabilitated, Germany would need to be attentive to its own actions and those of others to prevent similar crimes against humanity. The consequence of Germany's memory culture is that 'Never Again' becomes an empty tautology, because something unique and outside history cannot by definition be repeated. 'The Germans have created a strange dilemma for themselves, which consists of trying to be constantly very aware of the Holocaust on the one hand, but on the other hand to be wary of levelling or relativising this memory by universalising it,' Gessen said. They added that the main difference between now and before World War II is that people are aware that a killing machine like the Auschwitz death camp did exist, which gives a frame of reference to try to head off other genocides.[30]

Concerns over Germany's restrictions on expression haven't been isolated to Masha Gessen. The BDS resolution proposed cancelling funding for artists linked to the pro-Palestine movement, and there has been real fallout. In September 2019, Dortmund reneged on awarding the British-Pakistani author Kamila Shamsie the Nelly Sachs Prize for Literature, and Aachen withdrew from an award for the Lebanese-American artist Walid Raad a couple weeks later. In 2020 the Cameroonian philosopher Achille Mbembe, a leading figure in postcolonial theory, was effectively blacklisted in Germany over claims he relativised the Holocaust. In 2022 the German federal government put the funding of the *Documenta* art exhibition in Kassel under review and demanded greater control following controversy over a mural that included a Jewish caricature. In late 2023, Berlin cancelled funding for the Oyoun cultural centre for alleged 'hidden' antisemitism. In February 2024 the Max Planck Institute for Social Anthropology ended its working relationship with the Lebanese-Australian scholar Ghassan Hage over a series of social-media posts, and in April the University of Cologne cancelled a professorship for the American philosopher Nancy Fraser because she signed a letter in support of Palestine. In September 2024 the Heinrich Böll Foundation followed up the Gessen affair by not publishing a text it commissioned from the Israel-born writer Tomer Dotan-Dreyfus, who wrote about how Germany is suppressing Jewish freedom of opinion. 'Cultural institutions are increasingly driven by fear and paranoia, prone to acts of self-censorship and to pre-emptively de-platforming and excluding critical positions,' says an open letter to the German government signed by more than 1,500 artists, academics and cultural workers who live in or work for institutions in the country.[31] The Bosnian writer Lana Bastašić echoed those concerns, saying that her own views of Germany were naive. 'My big, free, loud Berlin was only free and loud as long as its freedom and loudness didn't contradict the system,' she said.[32]

The association between support for Palestine and antisemitism has intensified since the brutal Hamas attacks on 7 October 2023. The city of Berlin put that into action in January 2024 by tying cultural funding to a clause that precludes any form of antisemitism as defined by the International Holocaust Remembrance Alliance, which includes criticism of Israel.* Effectively, that means expressions of concern for civilian lives in Gaza could be interpreted as antisemitic. German police cracked down on pro-Palestine protesters, at times aggressively. The Jewish activist Iris Hefets was arrested in central Berlin for holding a sign in a one-woman protest that read: 'As a Jew and Israeli, stop the genocide in Gaza.' In October 2024 the CDU proposed banning the Swedish environmental activist Greta Thunberg from Germany after she appeared in Berlin at a pro-Palestine rally – participants in such events are routinely labelled 'Israel haters' by mainstream German media.

Internationally, there has been a backlash. A group called Strike Germany has called on international creative workers to refrain from working with the country's institutions because of policies that 'suppress freedom of expression, specifically expressions of solidarity with Palestine'.[33] The Instagram account – archive of silence – purports to document cases in which free expression in Germany has been shut down. The American philosopher Judith Butler, of Jewish descent, has decided to avoid the country voluntarily. 'Many Germans believe that unconditional support for Israel is full and final proof that they themselves are not antisemitic,' said the scholar, who has voiced controversial support for Hamas. Because of Butler's positions on Israel and Palestinian militants,

---

* The IHRA definition of antisemitism includes denying the Jewish people the right to self-determination by claiming the state of Israel is a racist endeavour, and comparing contemporary Israeli policy to that of the Nazis.

'they are excited to have permission to attack a Jew. In other words, this Jew is one that Germans feel free to hate.'[34]

If there was a starting point for the hard-line shift, it was 18 January 2018. That was when Germany passed legislation creating a federal commissioner to fight antisemitism. The move was in part prompted by a rise in vandalism and hate speech against Jews, including a video of a man accosting the owner of an Israeli restaurant in Berlin's upscale and cosmopolitan Schöneberg district and telling him he belonged in a gas chamber. But it was also a reaction to the far-right AfD becoming the strongest opposition party in the Bundestag in 2017, which challenged Germany's notion that it had put its ethnic nationalist past behind it. The antisemitism vote was backed by the same broad coalition of mainstream parties as the BDS resolution a year later. It was presented as the final piece of Germany's rehabilitation from the Nazis. 'We have succeeded in anchoring western ties, democracy and human rights and making them irrevocable. We have succeeded in coming to terms with our past. What we have not succeeded in doing is banishing the phenomenon of antisemitism from German society,' said Stefan Ruppert, a lawmaker for the FDP, during the Bundestag debate.

Since then, nearly every state in Germany has appointed its own official to combat discrimination against Jews, creating a vast network of bureaucrats focused on nothing other than scanning for comments, views and actions that could be inferred as antisemitic. That has included posting the Palestine independence slogan 'from the river to the sea'* on social media or supporting BDS petitions.

Felix Klein, a lawyer and diplomat from a Lutheran family, became the top dog in this apparatus by assuming the role of federal anti-antisemitism commissioner in May 2018, after previously serving as special liaison for Jewish organisations for the Foreign Ministry. He has been active in publicly calling out suspicions among intellectuals like Mbembe and has criticised the organisers of the Berlinale film festival in 2024 for comments from participants describing the war in Gaza as a 'genocide'. Klein has also denounced the entire field

---

* There have even been cases where satirical versions like 'from RISA to the Spree' have led to arrests. RISA is a chain of fast-food chicken restaurants in Berlin and the Spree is the river that runs through the city.

of postcolonial theory as antisemitic, claiming it seeks to demonise Israel. While he has insisted that criticism of Israel is allowed in Germany, his red lines include common areas of critique including casting the country as a colonial power for its settlements in the West Bank and likening the conditions of Palestinians to Blacks under South African Apartheid.[35] The heightened sensitivity has translated into demands for people seeking funding in Germany to undergo litmus tests over their views on Israel. The equivalent in Great Britain might be forcing artists or academics to submit an affidavit on their views on Brexit or the royal family.

Germany's efforts to impose its moral authority has hardly calmed things down on the streets. On 9 October 2019 an armed right-wing extremist tried to force his way into a synagogue in the East German city of Halle on the Yom Kippur holiday. He was thwarted, but then went on a random shooting spree, killing two people. In the weeks after the Hamas attack in October 2023, antisemitic incidents surged by nearly thirty a day. In Berlin there was an arson attempt at a Jewish cultural centre, while an Israeli restaurant shut down and switched locations because of vandalism.

On 7 November 2024 the Bundestag reacted, adopting yet another resolution called 'Never again is now: Protecting, preserving and strengthening Jewish life in Germany.' It urged widespread reviews of funding from local communities to the federal government and called for utilising 'repressive options' in German law, especially with regard to asylum and residency for those who engage in antisemitism under a controversially broad definition, which also protects Israel. The initiative openly backed the notion that antisemitism is an imported problem and widened the powers of the state to clamp down, including on Jewish critics of Israel. The resolution was backed by all mainstream parties as well as the far-right AfD. Amnesty International joined with other groups to warn about the initiative. 'Freedom of speech is at stake in Germany,' said Petra De Sutter, Belgium's deputy prime minister. 'Criticism of the Israeli government is not antisemitism.' But in Germany, there was little public debate on the issue and the country quietly narrowed civil rights.

Germany clearly has a special responsibility to protect Jewish life, but also more than that. The Nazis' crimes were against all of humanity, against ideals now enshrined in the country's *Grundgesetz* that aspires to counter discrimination in all its forms and respect human dignity. But Germany needs to have the humility to accept limitations that have been created from its own history. It does not have the moral authority to act as the thought-police on anything, much less ethnic and religious issues. It needs to understand that its efforts to recover from its ugly history have created blind spots of their own. Efforts to combat antisemitism have become subsumed in the country's efforts to show itself as rehabilitated. That's become so important, because there are few other constructive outlets for the country's sense of self.

Germany's focus on being a post-Nazi nation is not high ground. It's no man's land. It's a refusal to engage with the conditions that created the Holocaust and other genocides. The new threat will go by another name and take a different shape, so if defences are geared towards identifying a specific kind of enemy, they will ultimately fall short. History doesn't repeat itself exactly, but patterns repeat unless something is undertaken to break them. Germany's dogmatic approach to its past doesn't do that, but it makes fault lines deeper. 'It is precisely this prescribed attitude that is leading to a backlash, and not only from Muslim citizens but also from white ethnic Germans, whose old antisemitic clichés are now coming to the fore again,' said Susan Neiman, an American philosopher and director of the Einstein Forum in Potsdam.[36]

So what's the answer? For starters, Germany should get out of the way. It could offer a platform for discussion. It could moderate and mediate in ways that also provide an outlet for official perspectives, but also show it's trying to learn from others. Attempting to control the debate is a lost cause and stokes intolerance. Germany can ill afford to drive wedges in society and with the outside world at a time when the empty promise of prosperity leads more people in Germany (migrants and *biodeutsche*) to seek outlets for their frustration. Overcoming these risks is a complex task that entails facing up to the country's missteps and recognising its vulnerabilities.

The good news is that the House of Germany has shown it is capable of renewal when its residents are given the opportunity and its elites get out of the way.

10
Patchwork

'The mind is like an umbrella,
it functions best when open.'

Walter Gropius

The House of Germany is indeed in bad shape. The pipes are leaky, the furnace is sputtering, and the neighbourhood has become hostile. The staircases need repair to allow those at the bottom the chance to climb up. Worst of all, the residents are bickering with each other and losing sight of the solidarity that all communities need to thrive. The good news is that the foundation is solid, and the house still has energetic inhabitants and fascinating details that are worth keeping. Dispensing with self-delusions is also a chance to start afresh. The challenges are an opportunity for Germany to abandon anxiety over what it is or was and decide what it wants to be.

Germans are ready for change, and we've met many eager to contribute in the course of living in the country and working on this book. There are people like Onur, a software developer and third-generation Turkish-German who wants to show that Muslims can contribute to the local community, even though he struggles to identify as German because of his faith and skin colour. There is Peter, who's helping those falling through the cracks by running a shelter that provides warm meals and a place to sleep after his own experience of becoming homeless. And of course, there are Ernst and Yvonne Müller, who teach immigrant and German kids life lessons alongside boxing skills in Düren. There's good will in Germany if it can be given a positive outlet.

But we've also seen how Germany's tensions are playing out. Andreas in Hamburg is sending his wife and daughter to self-defence classes over concerns for their safety because of their Ukrainian Jewish heritage. For years, Sebastian in Dresden has organised demonstrations to counter the far-right, but as their power and influence grows he's considered leaving his home town. Nila, who arrived as a toddler from India, dropped her plans to study law in Heidelberg, because of growing feelings of being an outsider in the only country she's ever really known. After being spat on for looking foreign and having her talents dismissed for not being a 'real' German, she opted to study in England instead and her family has made preparations to go back to India if Germany's xenophobic politics intensifies. These are the people who don't show up in the polarising headlines but are ready to embrace change.

Germany's traditional approach to crises is to spring into action, implement a targeted fix, and then revert to business as usual. But that's not going to work anymore. The issues that the country faces are so fundamental and so deeply rooted in past failures that it needs a deeper overhaul in the very idea of Germany. That doesn't mean a new definition, but accepting that there is no definition. Germany is a complex *Mischkultur* (mixed culture) that needs to evolve to thrive. This isn't a new 'woke' idea. It isn't a plan to impose multiculturalism. Diversity of a certain kind is in fact *urdeutsch*.

The origin story of Germany involves a bunch of warring tribes with little in common besides a language. They banded together to defeat the mighty Roman army at the Battle of the Teutoburg Forest over 2,000 years ago. The unity was forged by a common enemy and that didn't really change. It was the threat of the French that led to a collection of kingdoms, duchies and principalities banding together under the Prussians a little more than 150 years ago. But even then, the Saxons, Hessians and Franconians weren't exactly one *Volk*. Whereas Prussians were once the hegemon of Germanic Europe, Bavarians generally see themselves as the cream of the crop these days.

Complexities have grown since the post-war *Wirtschaftswunder* (economic miracle) when guest workers laid down roots, and they intensified following reunification. Difference is part of Germany, but the nation has traditionally struggled with diversity rather than embraced it. The response can't be to demarcate what's in and what's out. That would be a recipe for defeat. Instead, Germany needs to drop the ethnic notions for good. The future of Germany is a civic identity that provides positive ways to channel a sense of belonging and opens up broader opportunities for commonality. It's not about giving up bratwurst and Bach but adding more options. It's like breakdancing in lederhosen or adding *sriracha* to your frankfurter. It's overcoming the fear of change and seeing it as opportunity instead of loss. It's also more of a process than an endgame. There are incremental steps that the country can take to change the mood and bring some good vibes back into the idea of being German.

Repair and reset

Germany has the potential to alter its course and set a new path forward. The country has been the wellspring of world-changing movements, for better and worse. From the Reformation and the Enlightenment to Marxism and Nazism, Germany has been a motor of history. And there is a powerful example of how the country has dared to attempt a constructive overhaul from its not-too-distant past.

The *Staatliches Bauhaus* school of art and design started in 1919 on the heels of World War I and the collapse of the German Empire. In a period of disharmony and upheaval, Walter Gropius, the founder and first director, laid out grand ambitions to shape the society of the *Neuer Mensch* (new man). With the tools of the industrial age and human-centred values, art and design was to become inclusive and not just the purview of the wealthy. Focused on simplicity and function, it was an effort to rebuild Germany and break with the backward-looking elitism of imperialism and the *Gründerzeit*. 'Let us build a new future for artisans without the class-dividing presumption that sought to build a haughty wall between tradespeople and artists,' Gropius wrote in the original Bauhaus manifesto.[1] The call was heard and about 150 students signed up, nearly half of them women.[2] Although the Bauhaus lasted a mere fourteen years before being closed by the Nazis, it showed what Germany can be capable of.

The Bauhaus itself was the descendant of the *Deutscher Werkbund*, a movement of artists, architects and industrialists that started in 1907. The goal was to elevate German products, which were at the time deemed inferior. The 'Made in Germany' label originally wasn't a mark of quality. It was introduced by England in the midst of the rapid expansion of production during the *Gründerzeit* as a warning for cheap, poor-quality goods. The Werkbund aimed to change that. The members devoted themselves to a high-quality design of the human environment in all its complexity under the motto 'from sofas to cities'.

The Berlin-born Gropius was active in the Werkbund and had already made a name for himself by designing a shoe factory with the radical idea of creating conditions that were pleasant for workers, including innovations like large windows to let in natural light. The Bauhaus was also the successor of an art school in Weimar founded by the Belgian architect Henry van de Velde. He was forced to leave Germany after World War I as the country's politics rejected undesirable foreigners, a precursor to what would follow later under the Nazis.

As home to Goethe and Schiller and the site where Germany's first democratic constitution was signed, Weimar was a location that bridged tradition and progress. The Bauhaus strove to build the 'cathedral of the future', but its vision was people-based and included everyday items such as door handles, lamps and chairs. The thinking was that society needed to change, and that starts at home with products embodying a new mindset. Many of those elements came together in Haus am Horn, a model home erected as a public showcase in 1923. It was built despite the harrowing difficulties posed by hyperinflation – making Germany's current fiscal issues seem trivial by comparison. Although Haus am Horn was a proposal for a new concept of living, it was still based around the traditional family. The layout was radically simple and inclusive, offering private space for each member of the family. The children's room was the biggest bedroom, incorporating space to play – a critical element of the Bauhaus ethos. But at the centre was a large, open living room, putting community at the centre of life. And naturally there were no servants' quarters as in bourgeois *Gründerzeit* homes.

A year later, German politics intervened when the nationalist right took power in Weimar, an early stronghold for the Nazis. The free-thinking approach of Bauhaus was unwelcome and so the school was pushed out of the city – the Buchenwald concentration camp was later built nearby. Strong ideas endure though, and Gropius had offers from Frankfurt, Mannheim and Munich to continue the school's work. He chose Dessau, an industrial city that was home to Junkers-Werke, an aviation and machinery manufacturer.

The Bauhaus was more than just a collection of workshops and studios. It was a creative engine that went beyond woodworking, ceramics and textiles. The school included a theatre programme that developed touring productions and hosted elaborate costume parties with fantastical and colourful figures, showing that fun and interaction were part of its concept of an active expression of community. It was denounced as 'degenerate' and 'un-German' by the Nazis and the school was closed soon after Hitler came to power in January 1933.

The Bauhaus was supposed to represent an approach to design and its role in society rather than a style. The aim was to put the function and the user in focus, an ethos that would require forms to evolve and shift based on what applications developed over time. Its reductive simplicity endures in the likes of IKEA bookshelves and Apple computers, but its students also experimented with forms and materials, created decorative patterns, and made playful use of bright primary colours.

Germany lost that talent after the school closed, with many of the Bauhaus teachers and students fleeing. Gropius and Ludwig Mies van der Rohe, the third and last director of the school, ended up in the United States, while the second director Hannes Meyer emigrated to the Soviet Union. Design then became a tool of Nazi power.

The Bauhaus was part of a broader flowering of creativity in the free-wheeling Weimar Republic. During the period there were nine Nobel prize winners from Germany (including five Jews). Along with the Frankfurt School of critical social theory, there were ground-breaking filmmakers like Fritz Lang, the agitprop theatre of Bertolt Brecht, Berlin's cabarets, and daring feats of speed on the city's AVUS racetrack. Even the Pilates exercise method had its origins in 1920s Germany.* The burst of energy shows how the country is capable of reinventing itself from within, if people are given the opportunity.

Despite Article 2 of the *Grundgesetz* laying out the concept of individual freedom in the right to '*die freie Entfaltung seiner Persönlichkeit*' (the free development of personality), post-war Germany hems in individual choice. There are rules on what trees can be climbed, where to ride a unicycle, and when barbecuing is allowed – even in your own garden. There's a sense that decent behaviour needs to be regulated because individuals can't be trusted, which in turn fuels expectations for the state to intervene rather than encouraging people to find common ground. The more control the political class exerts, the more it's in the firing line. The end result is societal paralysis.

As it is, the political system is reaching its limits. Mainstream parties are slow in developing policies that large swathes of the public can rally behind and are reluctant to acknowledge the scale of the challenges for fear of spooking voters, which in turn undermines the parties' credibility. Lacking answers, politicians stoke divisions or pander to voters with empty platitudes. The CDU's revamped programme, for instance, has twenty-two key messages that all end with an exclamation mark, including uncontroversial concepts like '*Wir wählen die Freiheit!*' (we choose freedom) and '*Wachstum statt Stillstand!*' (growth instead of stagnation). And the Conservative Party is still standing by *Wohlstand für alle*, nearly seven decades since Ludwig Erhard coined the phrase and despite years of worsening prospects for the lower rungs of society. To be fair, the other parties aren't much more inventive, but the ongoing challenges call for more substantive solutions.

That's why *Wir Sind die Brandmauer* ('we're the firewall', the slogan for anti-AfD protests) and other pro-democracy efforts fall short. The focus is negative. They're against far-right extremists, but there's little consensus beyond that. What's the answer for those seeking an alternative to an ethnic nationalist vision of Germany?

---

* Joseph Pilates was a German physical trainer in Germany, who collaborated with the dancer Rudolf Laban after World War I before emigrating to the United States in 1925. He called his technique Contrology.

Mainstream policies have been a bad deal for a lot of Germans, so why support one of those parties just to thwart the AfD? Fear isn't going to motivate people in the midst of existential anxieties. When establishment policies are generating roadblocks and creating hardship, evoking the evils of fascism falls flat.

Democracy isn't a service business. It's not just about what you get out of it. It requires participation for legitimacy, and to that end the political class needs to show it's responsive and capable of providing solutions. That's not just a German problem. It's endemic across the West and a major weakness of modern-day democracies. The difference with Germany is that there's a haunting pattern from history that's never truly been washed away.

To break through the gloom, there need to be tangible solutions that give people reason to identify with the system. More solidarity, better opportunities and a sense of shared purpose would already help counter the allure of populism. Moralising about democracy and political freedom might sway some voters for an election cycle or two, but the underlying trends stoking angst and division aren't going away on their own. There needs to be an active effort to build social bonds. That's not about money. Transfer payments and tax breaks will never be enough on their own. Germany needs to go beyond economic well-being if its political and social shortcomings are to be addressed. It needs a new sense of community, so that the forces holding people together are stronger than those pulling them apart.

We're well aware that calling for something like a revival of German nationalism might sound alarming, but not confronting the issue leaves it to others. And what we're suggesting is not nationalism in the 'blood and soil' sense, but civic solidarity. The focus should be on creating conditions to make it easier to identify with Germany positively, to forge a broader base of support for the tough transitions ahead. It's about changing the conversation about the German nation and shaping what that concept could be rather than tripping over what it was.

A refresh is overdue. An ethnic definition of German identity had been the post-war default until a reckoning started to take place in the early 2000s with the belated recognition that the country had become a mix of migrants and natives (just like most postcolonial powers). In the late 1800s, Germany held colonies that included territories in what's now Tanzania, Rwanda, Namibia and Ghana. As part of that occupation, some people naturally came to Germany, establishing a Black minority. That included people like Theodor Wonja Michael, who was born in Berlin in 1925. After his white mother died, he was forced to become a performer in *Völkerschauen* (human zoos) and survived the Nazi era as a child actor. Identifying as a German caused confusion and irritation. 'Being Black is still foreign to Germany today and we still have to fight,' he told *Deutsche Welle* before his death in 2019. That sort of ethnic complexity preceded the Nazi era. The diversity was accelerated by the guest workers of the *Wirtschaftswunder*, but only recognised belatedly by German officials, an observation that raised questions but didn't provide answers.

But there are ways to broaden the pathways to solidarity and provide more low-threshold touchpoints for shared experiences without threatening the country's existing sense of self. Here's a somewhat serious example of what we mean: *Spargelzeit* (asparagus season). The springtime fascination with asparagus (generally the woody white variety) is one of the few national German traditions that's secular and crosses socioeconomic boundaries. Everyone can partake in some way (even by wondering what all the fuss is about).

The seasonal tradition, though, is mainly about private consumption rather than shared community and takes place mainly at roadside stands, in restaurants and via grocery-store specials. Or it's localised with annual *Spargelköniginnen* (asparagus queens) in villages like Beelitz, Lampertheim and Schwetzingen, among others. It wouldn't be hard to change that, though, and make it more of an intentional effort to bring people together on a national level – a sort of German Thanksgiving for the coming of spring and the end of the long, grey winter. *Spargelzeit* easily links into a celebration of nature's cycles, which is very much in line with traditions of Romanticism. It also celebrates German cuisine beyond meat and potatoes (though they are very much in play in traditional asparagus dishes).[*] The season would also be an opportunity for a display of social consciousness by recognising farmers and *Spargelstecher* (asparagus harvesters), who are often itinerant

---

[*] The traditional *Spargelzeit* meal is boiled white asparagus with boiled potatoes and ham or schnitzel, accompanied by hollandaise sauce.

labourers from countries such as Romania and Bulgaria – linking farm-to-table production with the benefits of European integration.

A key point is that no one has to wait for the government to pass a *Spargelzeit* decree, but can go for it on their own with a little more intent and a little more creativity. It might sound frivolous, and to an extent that's the point. Germany is generally a serious place, so a little light-hearted fun wouldn't hurt.

There are pathways to stronger German solidarity that emphasise civic values over a revival of 'blood and soil' fanaticism. But a little flag-waving would not be so bad and could take the wind out of the sails of the ethno-nationalists. Certain symbols of national identity can be taken back by civic society. Celebrating the nation's black, red and gold colours, more openly and often, could certainly be part of that and would provide a visible counterpoint to the black, white and red colours of hard-core nationalists.

Our suggestions sketch out some ideas that address issues like inequality, climate transition and above all community. It's certainly not an exhaustive list, but it's well-intentioned food for thought and the principles aren't necessarily limited to Germany, but could be adapted elsewhere. The approach might sound idealistic, but surely that's better than the cynical alternative of watching things fall apart.

Habitat for Heimat

As Dorothy in *The Wizard of Oz* so aptly puts it, 'There's no place like home.' But for the majority of Germans, living space means forking over a large chunk of their wages to an anonymous investor or property company. Germans are house proud, but most rent and so don't participate in growing residential property values, much less have the opportunity to build a sense of wealth and well-being from home ownership. Instead, housing means just throwing money away month after month, with the risk someday of being evicted. After letting the free market take more and more control of residential housing markets, Germany needs a paradigm shift. The scarcity of affordable living space is one of the key sources of anxiety that wraps together economic insecurity, wealth inequality and feelings of alienation.

In a country of tenants, rising home prices due to a shortage of houses benefit a select few, while rising rents have a direct impact on millions. When the economy stumbles, jobs are on the line and tight housing markets make living conditions precarious. Even if many households are protected from increases by rent-control laws, a change of ownership in their flat or building can still lead to eviction, which would entail an almost certain loss in quality of life. Also, tight housing markets have a knock-on effect on the economy by limiting mobility because there's so much risk involved in moving to a new city even if a better job beckons. Meanwhile, home ownership is out of reach for most working families because of high prices and barriers to entry in the form of up-front costs and fees. The result is that many families are stuck, wringing their hands in the hopes that nothing bad happens.

We call our proposal Habitat for Heimat. The name deliberately links the emotional German word for 'homeland' with the programme Habitat for Humanity. The low-income house-building organisation started in the United States in the 1970s and has since established offices and activities around the world, including in Germany. The programme involves future home owners contributing 'sweat equity' by helping to build their home. Our idea isn't to entirely copy this, but instead find Germany-specific ways to create new affordable homes that would be available to purchase by people who otherwise would never make it on Germany's property ladder, because the lower rungs are missing.

Nothing's more basic than shelter. It's a fundamental need that the German government is supposed to provide as part of its constitutional role as a social state. With a lack of 800,000 to 1 million homes, a building offensive is overdue. That would mean changes to zoning to open up more land for home construction and streamlining approvals to make it easier and quicker to create new homes by repurposing or tearing down existing structures. It could be a kick-start programme to spur a rethink in how Germany develops housing, with a focus on rebalancing supply and demand. Clearly branded as government-developed would send a strong signal that the state is capable of concrete action.

By opening an avenue for wealth creation, the programme could help address inequality. Those who don't participate directly would also benefit as additional housing supply would ease the pressure on rental markets. Also, it would brighten the mood by showing that progress is indeed possible in tradition-bound Germany, where there's often a fixation on problems over solutions and the answer to glaring inefficiencies is *'aber wir haben es schon immer so gemacht'* (but we've always done it this way).

Here's how the housing programme could work. For new homes built under the plan, the state waives taxes on property purchases for first-time buyers as long as they live in those homes for at least ten years. If they move out before then, taxes would need to be paid accordingly after the sale. That would help ensure people aren't flipping government-subsidised homes. Mortgage interest would be deductible from income taxes, which it currently isn't. Purchase contracts could also be standardised and indemnified by the state to the extent that lawyers don't need to collect 1.5 per cent of the purchase price. Also, since these are new homes there are no broker fees. The idea is to open the door for home ownership to thousands of families who would otherwise be shut out, gaining a sense of stability and a stake in the system in the process. Since it's focused on new homes, it would be decidedly different from the disastrous 'right to buy' plan of Great Britain in the 1980s. Selling council flats without building new ones was mainly about privatising social housing and led to higher prices across the country.

To encourage construction of new homes at affordable costs, there could be a collection of pre-approved, standardised building plans. A century ago, Walter Gropius at the Bauhaus outlined ideas for a toolkit that would allow planners to combine units with different layouts to accommodate a range of needs from single occupants to families under one roof. That kind of concept could be revived to encourage liveable density and promote efficient multi-use and multi-family dwellings, including common space in the form of party rooms and shared outdoor space to encourage community building in the years following completion. There were housing projects like this in the 1920s and 1930s, but Germany let the concept lapse.

'Made in Germany' mass timber – which combines wood layers to create durable lightweight building components – could be a central element of the plans to improve sustainability, encourage local business, and lower costs. Government guarantees would backstop projects and facilitate implementation. Approvals should be a formality, rather than a bottleneck. As long as basic guidelines are met, authorities would need to justify a rejection of a project within set time limits. So if deadlines lapse, it would be a green light by default.

The programme would need to be set up digitally from the get-go (which might seem obvious, but that's not necessarily the case in Germany). Algorithms could match construction firms with interested families and help locate available building lots (a key issue in crowded urban areas). Future neighbours could connect as well (with all the data-privacy caveats that go along with life in Germany).

For the state, encouraging construction clearly has benefits by promoting economic activity and domestic consumption. There's also a halo effect. People who have the government to thank for their homes should be more positively disposed towards the state than those struggling to get by from month to month. Down the line, there would be chances to relieve strain on the strapped pension system by treating home ownership as a component of retirement planning, like Switzerland does.

There will of course be questions over how to pay for it. But that's solvable as shown by studies into the *Grunderbe* ('universal inheritance', a kind of start-up capital for young people, which has been proposed by activists to help reduce inequality). The DIW research institute in Berlin ran the numbers and determined that the programme could work. Estimated at costing €22.6 billion a year, including incentives for home ownership, the money could be financed with reforms to wealth and inheritance taxes.[3]

What's clear is that things can't continue as they are. With housing left mainly in the hands of the private sector, the government has consistently missed targets for new homes. That increases pressure on average Germans from year to year. Meanwhile, people see new asylum centres and refugee shelters get set up despite intensifying housing shortages. That makes it easy for populists to stoke anti-foreigner sentiment. Migrants (especially easily identifiable dark-skinned ones) have become a frequent target for frustration-stoked xenophobia, which makes little distinction between legal and illegal migrants. These tensions have already been on display and they are self-destructive. The country needs new workers to maintain its level of affluence as the *Wirtschaftswunder* generation retires, and those people need a place to live just as much as locals do.

But aside from economic and reputational concerns, it boils down to what kind of country Germany wants to be. Does it intend to live up to its constitutional goals of respecting human dignity as a social state, or not? This requires measures that break the mould. It's about Germany choosing the nation it wants to be. And that certainly could include embracing technological progress, rather than accepting its status as a digital no man's land.

Digital leapfrog

For train riders zipping through the lower Rhineland between Germany and the Netherlands, there's a traveller's joke about how passengers can recognise when they've left the Federal Republic for the Koninkrijk der Nederlanden. What's the clue? The internet suddenly works.

It's a quip that speaks to Germany's backwardness with all things digital. Patchy infrastructure is just the beginning, and fixable with the right motivation and investment. But the stickier issue is a lack of skills, which runs from politics through to the private sector. Turning this around starts with schools. Teaching information-technology skills is rudimentary at best. In Hesse, home to the finance capital Frankfurt, there's no obligation for state schools to hold IT lessons at all.[4] The tradition-bound education system means there's little effort to invest in new programmes or technology, leading to computer-per-pupil ratios among the worst in the developed world and closer to poor countries like Mongolia and Uzbekistan than leaders like Austria and the United States.[5] Asked to evaluate the country's digitalisation efforts, 180 economics professors gave Germany failing grades.

What's needed to overhaul Germany's fearful attitude towards technology is a cultural change, and the best way to start is with children. While education is a state responsibility (making any national reform cumbersome), there is a long-running and well-loved initiative that could chart the way: the *Bundesjugendspiele* (federal youth games). It's an annual athletics day in which all

German schoolchildren participate. The games have taken place since 1951, with the aim of 'communicating the joy of movement and sporting competition'. Activities include sprint races, long jump and throwing. Certificates are handed out both for placing well and simply taking part. Kids generally love it because it's a day in the open air and out of the classroom, and since the programme has been running for so long, they can even compare results with parents and grandparents. The *Bundesdigitalspiele* (federal digital games) could be implemented to kick-start interest in new technology on a national level.

Like the physical fitness counterpart, the main purpose of the digital programme would be to promote interest through action and interaction. It could take a myriad of forms like single-day or week-long events, depending on age and ability. A single-day event could be structured to promote EU guidelines for digital competency, which involves five areas: information literacy, collaboration, content creation, safety and problem-solving. Each grade could have age-appropriate tasks to test abilities. A week-long event could be a more advanced coding crash course, or hackathon. Using tools like Scratch, a simplified programming tool built by Massachusetts Institute of Technology developers for eight- to sixteen-year-olds, schoolchildren could work together in friendly competition with their peers.

Rather than a traditional teacher–pupil approach to learning, children should be shown the basics of the platform (which naturally needs to be digital and online) and then be encouraged to explore and experiment to solve problems. There's no one right answer. It could also be open for children to use even after the event as a safe space on the internet, also with opportunities for kids from Brandenburg to Bremen to connect. Digital artwork and animation tools could add creative elements, so it goes beyond tech nerds. Overall, it's a teaching method closer to the Bauhaus, halfway between learning and production, a cross between work and play. But at the end of the day, any engagement with digital technology is better than the current system. As it is, school digital policy is often confined to controlling mobile-phone use.

But for any of this to work, schools need proper equipment, from computers to WiFi routers. There's been progress, but it hasn't been wildly ambitious. While the federal government made grants available to purchase computer equipment in 2019, three-quarters of school directors said the funds weren't sufficient to truly enable digital learning.[6] Making such assistance open-ended until German schools have caught up with the leaders in the developed world could help bring the country up to speed.

To promote broader acceptance, the investment should be seen as part of community building, with school computer labs made available to others, bridging the digital divide. In one of the world's richest countries, around a fifth of poorer households can't afford their own internet connection, because of high prices.[7] One gigabyte of cellular data in Germany costs twice as much as in Italy and almost four times as much as in Poland.[8]

Having children staff computer labs for a couple hours after school could also help span the generational divide and build self-confidence as they show grannies how to google and avoid phishing scams. Many German seniors remain strangers to the web, and almost a third of those over seventy-five have never even been online.[9] Around half of Germans (often elderly people living alone) say they'd like to have someone to show them how to use digital technology. The same proportion wish they were able to participate more in online life. Birdwatchers, mushroom foragers or choirs could meet physically and/or virtually at school technology centres, creating connections to more people. Especially in small towns, they could become pillars of social life by opening up the digital world. Increasing the touchpoints here could also help Germany shape its community and promote much-needed skills.

Power to the people

For visitors to Weimar, the homes of Goethe and Schiller and the Bauhaus Museum are typically on the agenda, but they're likely to skip the nearby village of Großschwabhausen. By the high bar set by many German municipalities, the community of a little over 1,000 people is unspectacular. No great composer or philosopher was born here and architecturally it's much like thousands of villages across Germany. It has an old church, a few pretty old buildings, and a lot of newer uglier ones. Its biggest claim to fame might be that it's the site of an observatory that helped discover WASP-3c, a planet in the far-off Lyra constellation.

But Großschwabhausen could be a trendsetter when it comes to charting a path to a cleaner, greener Germany. The citizens' cooperative *Energiegenossenschaft Ilmtal* wants to build a wind farm in the village at the edge of the Jena forest, where a nature reserve for brown long-eared bats occupies the site of a former base for Soviet rocket artillery. According to the group's plans, local residents would put up the money to set up the park, which would be built and run with the help of an established wind-power company.[10] Once operational, proceeds would flow into local projects, bringing much-needed income to an area that faces decline (like much of Germany's east and growing swathes of the industrial west). The proposal recalls the early stages of Germany's wind and solar roll-out when civic groups would band together to help the local community go green. That was before the roll-out was co-opted by big business and became an abstract, top-down *Energiewende*.

During the Merkel era, the community-led vision lost allure. Changes to Germany's renewable-energy laws were introduced to boost competition, increasing financial risks for cooperatives, and leaving large developers and financial investors to dominate the sector, particularly the utility giant RWE. Just 3 per cent of Germany's renewable electricity supply comes from civic organisations.[11] While the financial muscle of big companies helps get renewable parks built, Germany shouldn't overlook the benefits from nurturing the grassroots. Played smartly, the push to net zero could be used to build community support and puncture populist arguments that combating climate change only matters to well-off metropolitan elites.

To change the narrative, Germany could support the creation of a *Bürgernetz* (citizens' grid), bolstering local empowerment and tapping into *Heimat* (homeland) pride, a particularly strong German yearning for harmony with nature and place. With vastly more solar and wind farms needed over the next two decades, there's plenty of room and need for greater citizen participation.

There are thousands of new projects in which cooperatives could take part, spreading ownership of the *Energiewende* well beyond a privileged few. As part of Germany's shift to low-emission heating sources, communities will need to find solutions such as collective geothermal pumps that extract heat from the ground. Providing loan guarantees that make it easier for citizens to band together would reduce financial hurdles for community ownership. Similarly, as Germany's hydrogen economy develops, ways could be found to fast-track cooperative participation, like setting up local electrolysis sites. These kinds of initiatives would help counter the idea that a green power shift is being imposed from the top and local communities get nothing in return except the eyesore of towering wind masts and fields of solar cells, while the money and energy flows elsewhere. That's been a sore point in eastern Germany, which has a high density of wind farms, while the power and the proceeds do more for the west of the country.

Local connections could be further strengthened with a little imagination. The artist Horst Gläsker has proposed painting wind turbines in fantastical colours to liven up the ho-hum monotony of their appearance. Taking that idea just a step further, local schoolchildren could create designs at least for the lower parts of the masts, which are more easily accessible.

Promoting community participation in the *Energiewende* could also provide an opportunity for rural towns to stem declines, especially places like Großschwabhausen in the east. Exempting such places from usual planning regulations for energy projects would give them new levers to revitalise. When it comes to erecting new wind or solar farms, planning laws could be streamlined so that former industrial sites are automatically approved for renewable projects, save for the most basic environmental impact and safety checks.

For individual households, German frugality could be tapped in a positive way. Instead of spending ever more on utility bills (already among the highest in the developed world), the government could provide an opportunity to slash expenses. A programme of zero-rate loans could be offered to finance emission-saving home improvements to overcome the issue of up-front costs. They could enable less well-off households to buy rooftop solar panels and heat pumps. Such systems can reduce household electricity consumption by 70 per cent on average, but coming up with the money to tap into this potential is often a barrier.[12] In most cases the savings on utility bills would cover loan repayments. For instance, a large rooftop system of solar panels with a battery costs around €20,000.

Repaying that sum with a fifteen-year, zero-interest loan amounts to less than the power bill for an average three-person household.* Studies have shown that over the long run German families benefit substantially from owning heat pumps or solar panels, but they're just prohibitively expensive for most people.

A *Bürgernetz* offensive wouldn't just help save money, but it could change the conversation around Germany's climate push. Debates around net zero are increasingly framed as an assault by elites on ordinary people's freedoms and finances. That was evident in the bitter debate over the country's heating reform and is part of the rhetoric resisting speed limits on the Autobahn. The left-wing populist leader Sahra Wagenknecht has said the renewable shift will impoverish Germans and has called for a return of Russian gas. The Christian Democrat leader Friedrich Merz has hinted that he thinks reductions in emissions are proceeding unnecessarily fast.[13] Going further, the AfD has called on the government to revoke all its international climate agreements,[14] and its co-leader Alice Weidel has said that German climate policy is 'always at the expense of the little people'.[15]

But a little financial engineering and a healthy dose of local empowerment could defuse opposition to climate initiatives and accelerate Germany's roll-out, while building a sense of national solidarity in the process. The emphasis is on giving people a stake in the developments rather than forcing them on people from above.

Zusammenfeiern!†

In 1997 on Germany's national holiday marking reunification (which falls on 3 October in the midst of the wet, cold autumn), Helmut Kohl wistfully remarked that he 'always envied' the French for Bastille Day on 14 July, when the country could celebrate their nation in the middle of summer and have a good time. 'People are simply happy together. They dance and sing in the streets, in the

---

* Calculation made using comparison website Verixox.de, assuming a three-person household uses 3,500 kWh per year.
† German for 'celebrating together'.

towns and villages,' he said. 'I like that very much.' Alas, there's little of that in Germany.

In more ways than one, 3 October is a grim day for a national commemoration. First of all, it's autumn and often gloomy. Also, the day itself recognises the signing of the treaty of union between East and West Germany, a cold bureaucratic act disconnected from any sense of emotion. The fall of the Berlin Wall in 1989 might have been that kind of event, but this occurred on 9 November, the same date as the Nazis' *Kristallnacht* pogrom against Jews in 1938. Besides that extremely unfortunate coincidence, the memory of reunification has become muddied, and German leaders have struggled to acknowledge the complicated experience of people from the East. In his Unity Day speech in 2024, Olaf Scholz called reunification 'a success story' in part because growth rates were higher in the former Communist region and mass unemployment was in the past – a rather narrow definition.

A better day of remembrance would be reinstating 17 June as a national holiday. That day marks the brutal repression of a popular uprising in East Germany in 1953. After widespread protests over a hard-line course mandated by Moscow, workers demonstrated in East Berlin and dissatisfaction quickly spread across the country. Authorities then cracked down, arresting thousands and causing 125 deaths. The response from the Allied powers was silence, sending the signal that East Germans were isolated and the Soviet Union could do as it pleased in its sphere of influence. Commemorating that sacrifice and the subsequent decades of isolation might not be fun, but it would do more to recognise the bravery of the people in the former East Germany and their active efforts to gain political and economic freedom, which was handed without struggle to West Germany by the Allies. It could also be a better occasion for Germany's leaders to atone for the missteps of reunification. Ironically, 17 June was a national holiday in West Germany, but it was dropped in 1990 as if the memory of the struggle of East Germans had become a moot point.

The Christian Democrats also see the need for a new national holiday, but they have proposed 23 May as Constitution Day. According to the proposal, the focal point would be a 'state of the nation' speech. While the idea of the German president or chancellor addressing the country may be rousing for some, it might not be quite the community-building event that the party imagines. What Germany needs is some fun and engagement and not more top-down political rhetoric.

The 1 May Labour Day holiday is promising and offers a number of avenues for participation. It starts on 30 April with *Walpurgisnacht* (Walpurgis Night), a celebration with pagan origins linked to legends of witches flying around the Brocken peak in the Harz mountains. By marking the coming of spring, it's connected to seasonality and fertility and lends itself to becoming the frenzied climax of *Spargelzeit*. The various festivities include bonfires and dancing into the night. The revelry continues on Labour Day on 1 May in what's become a day of protest. It's not exclusively German, but that hardly matters.

To throw a new idea into the mix, we humbly propose 4 June as the national celebration of *Eiserner Gustav* (Iron Gustav). That was the birthday of Gustav Hartmann, a folk hero from the late 1920s just before the dark descent into fascism. The coach driver became a public figure for riding from Berlin to Paris and back on a wagon pulled by his horse Grasmus. The stunt in 1928 was to protest the advance of the automobile, which was supplanting services like his. And to be fair, resisting change is a very German thing to do. But it's also a tale of civic action and personal conviction. Iron Gustav Day would be a good reminder, for a country where people often fear failure, that success is relative. Hartmann obviously didn't stop the automobile's progress to global domination, but his effort gave hope to a country suffering economic and social hardship. He also played a small role in European integration, when he was graciously received by peers in Paris upon arriving with his wagon decked out in German and French flags. And because of his story, there's plenty of opportunity for low-threshold activities like simply taking a ride somewhere to cross a boundary such as between east and west, rural and urban, or reaching a friendly hand across the *Gartenzaun* (garden fence).

The point here is to show that there are ways to create touchpoints to make it easy to 'be German' and feel good about it. Given its economic, political and social challenges, the country needs that sense of community. It needs to become a real nation and finally move beyond its ethnic past and internal divisions. The people who contribute to the German experience are the *Volk*, and they deserve a feeling of *Heimat* regardless of whether they were born in Ulm, Erfurt or Izmir. It doesn't have to be exactly the same feeling, but enough commonality that they all can put on the black, red and gold on 17 June and swap *Spargel* tips in spring, even if they later go to a rave, a mosque or a *Schützenfest* (a traditional festival for shooting clubs and considered very conservative).

Yuval Noah Harari, an adept chronicler of the human experience, described patriotism as a feeling towards a group of people you would be willing to 'go the extra mile' for. That doesn't mean 'blood and soil' fanaticism, but at least a degree of camaraderie, and that's within Germany's grasp. 'This is how we behave with our family, our friends, this is also how we should behave with our nation,' Harari said.[16]

Closing Remarks: Ein Haus für Alle[*]

'And suddenly you know:
It's time to start something new and trust the magic of beginnings.'

Meister Eckhart[†]

Germany isn't alone, of course, in facing a cluster of crises that tear at its social fabric. Across Europe and beyond, countries large and small face bewildering change. From childhoods upturned by social media through to insecurity and loneliness in old age, once-dependable certainties are breaking down. In the world of work, jobs for life are a bygone dream and technological shifts – from automation to artificial intelligence – will shake what stability remains. In Germany and elsewhere, welfare models are being pushed to breaking point by rising spending on pensions and elderly care. Migration is not going away and will continue to challenge traditional concepts of national identity, demanding new answers to counter the destructive escapism of ethnic division.

Just as domestic certainties crumble, international ones are in tumult too. In Europe, resurgent nationalism threatens the EU's drive towards greater integration, complicating efforts to stand up to autocratic powers. China and Russia are challenging the global security order, while the United States is seduced by Donald Trump's inward-looking MAGA ('Make America Great Again')

---

[*] 'A House for All' in an effort to update Germany's main slogan on identity.
[†] The source of the comment from the German theologian, also known as Eckhart von Hochheim, is unknown.

movement that would end the Pax Americana umbrella under which a reconstructed Germany grew rich and free. After forty years of relative peace, the number of armed conflicts around the globe has risen, including state-on-state aggression not far from Germany's borders. Far from the fall of the Berlin Wall marking the end of history (as theorised by Francis Fukuyama), humanity has continued to write bloody new chapters.

The natural world is also in crisis. Global warming is gathering pace, causing upheavals at home and abroad. In Germany, heat records regularly tumble and flash floods have claimed hundreds of lives. Hurricanes and typhoons are battering the United States and Asia with more ferocity and increasing frequency. Swathes of Africa and the Middle East are becoming uninhabitable. Permafrost is thawing and wildfires blight even northern countries like Canada and Russia. Since 2008, around 400 million people around the world have been displaced by natural disasters (most but not all linked to human-caused climate change),[1] and there are estimates that the number could triple to 1.2 billion people by 2050.[2] At a time when the global community should be coming together for the common good and to avoid the threat of extinction, it's devolving into ruinous national tribalism.

For Germany, like elsewhere, it's a disturbing time. But the country's upheaval presents opportunities too. For humanity to stem the deadly pace of the climate crisis, it will need major breakthroughs in science and technology as well as new low-emission products from transport to heating systems. Europe's engineering and research powerhouse is well positioned to help solve these problems. For ordinary people, there are chances to take their place in the manufacturing workforce of the future, especially if Germany can find a way to finally promulgate digital skills. The ageing trend, which is a reality across the developed world, offers the potential of global demand for 'Made in Germany' treatment solutions that allow citizens to age in dignity and health. Although the country's primitive civic identity may have allowed *Völkisch* nationalism to rekindle, there's enough blank space on the German canvas to draw in details and make the picture richer and more inclusive.

But before it can shape the future, Germany needs to deal with its unhappy present. Showing its age in the eighty years since reconstruction, our *Gründerzeit* House needs a top-to-bottom renovation. Cracks need to be mended, not least between its eastern and western halves, and the plumbing and boiler need a thorough modernisation. The economic model that brought jobs and affluence is in decline, yet vested interests cling to it, seeking to extract wealth for themselves while they still can. Building a bridge to a new economy won't be easy, but delay and distraction won't forge a 'new prosperity for all' either. In a country that knows the destructive powers of nationalism better than most, the electoral insurgency of the far-right marks an unambiguous point of shame. Yet lecturing and hectoring or just pretending things are fine don't address the anxieties driving support for the AfD. Germany needs to make a new offering to its people, based on shared opportunities, inclusiveness and a spirit of community.

Building a new Germany while fighting social, economic and environmental crises won't be easy, but what's the alternative? Leaving these issues unaddressed opens a wide flank to ethnic nationalists. Although their polling will go up and down, the forces steering the AfD are playing a long game and supporters of liberal ideals need to do the same. A lurch towards right-wing populism would plunge Germany into political crisis and intensify its economic and societal malaise. The two would feed off each other: fractious and weak governments won't have the energy or power to drive through much-needed reforms, leading to a further drop in competitiveness, an erosion of living standards, and swelling the ranks of disgruntled voters. Germany would increasingly turn inward at a time when Europe and other democratic nations need its voice to keep climate action on track and help maintain some sense of global order.

If Germans can come together, a major prize is there: a modern House that's welcoming to everyone and in which residents are proud to live. Like the Bauhaus's Haus am Horn, it should be built around communal space, its foundations firmly anchored in humanistic values and its interior open to enrichment by outsiders. Where there's discord, there are also chances to create harmony.

For all Germany's widening fault lines, there are abundant signs of hope. While siren calls from the far-right find disturbing echoes in the mainstream, other voices have called for unity and inclusion. Founded by the journalist Düzen Tekkal, the GermanDream initiative goes into schools to teach children about social cohesion, democratic values, as well as the power of equal opportunities and participation. It gives awards to people from civil society who've made a special contribution to the cause of integration. And while Gerhard Schröder unapologetically holds on to the fortune he's made selling out Germany's energy security, union leaders toil away to secure a socially just transition and cushion the impact on workers. Volunteers answer the call to hold back floodwaters, and activists like Helena Steinhaus seek to plug holes in the social safety net. Germany's future path will be defined by the struggle between efforts to build community and those that seek to tear it apart.

Having lived in the country for a total of about three decades combined, we've seen Germany's cycles of crisis and recovery, but there is something different about the current moment. The country has always been a little prickly and a little awkward, but an edginess has emerged that wasn't there before. There's a shrill tone and a desperation in the public arena. There are emotional touchstones instead of the traditional *Sachlichkeit* (objectivity). The scope for compromise and sober debate has narrowed. It feels very much like the pre-Trump United States or pre-Brexit Britain. But in contrast to Germany, our home countries have concepts of national belonging that transcend political discourse. That kind of solidarity might not counter everything, but it provides a tether in tough times. That's missing in Germany. The fallback consists of cultural myths that are divisive, and because of that, we worry that Germany can fall deeper and faster than our homelands.

The political class seems ill-equipped to provide answers. Mainstream parties are so steeped in their clientele and so worried about protecting their status that they show little capacity to come up with real solutions. Change is risky so they try to preserve as much as possible to ward off bad news. But Germans aren't stupid. They understand the problems and many feel them every month. That undermines the credibility of the establishment and gnaws at the system's legitimacy. At best, the result is apathy. At worst, it means turning to easy answers from populists, stoking destructive division. Despite all its problems and frustrating self-delusions, we believe Germany means well. There's plenty of evidence of good will in the people ready to hit the streets for a cause, or lug sand sacks to protect a neighbour's home from flooding, or provide meals and shelter for war refugees. But as a nation, Germany is desperately confused. It wants to be good so badly that it could stumble into dark places and struggle to get out again. That would be dire for our families and the liberal system in general, because if post-Nazi Germany strays, then so can anyone.

From the vantage point of exile, Thomas Mann understood the country unlike anyone else. Before his flight to Switzerland and then on to the United States and California, the novelist tried to appeal to the country's better conscience and reject the Nazis' barbaric ideology. Shortly after World War II, when the horrors of the Holocaust were still being digested, Mann wasn't vengeful against a society that had been complicit in driving him away through its indifference to savagery. Instead, he found words of sympathy and understanding for his homeland. 'In the end, the German misfortune is only the paradigm of the tragedy of human life,' he said. 'And the grace that Germany so sorely needs, my friends, all of us need it.'[3]

Acknowledgements

When we started this project, it was awe-inspiring. As journalists, we've written thousands of articles about the ups and downs of German business, the contortions of the country's politics and the challenges in society, but even our most ambitious features were bite-sized snippets by comparison. Wrapping our experience together in a book that tries to say something new and compelling about a big and complex country like Germany was humbling, but also one of the most rewarding experiences we've ever had. While we take full responsibility for any flaws in the manuscript, this project would not have been possible without the insights, encouragement, and generosity of so many people. But for starters, we'd like to thank each other. Neither one of us could have managed the scale of this undertaking on our own, and the collaboration was crucial and made us both better as journalists, writers and people.

But we wouldn't have had the opportunity to sweat over anecdotes or grit our teeth over the weighty undertaking of picking apart our adopted homeland without our agent Andrew Gordon from David Higham Associates. He improbably saw something in our clunky first pitch and challenged us to keep pushing. We wouldn't have made it here without his support and guidance, and will be eternally grateful. We're also very appreciative for the assistance from the rest of the team at DHA, including Alice Howe, David Evans and Anna Watkins.

We're incredibly honored to be part of such a renowned publishing house like Bloomsbury. We owe that to Ian Marshall, who championed the book from the beginning. Juliet Brooke was invaluable in shaping the manuscript and generously offered her

ACKNOWLEDGEMENTS

expertise and insight, reining us in and prodding us in all the right places. We also thank the Bloomsbury staff, including Brittani Davies, Francisco Vilhena and Amy Whitaker, who leapt to the challenge of accelerating publication after the collapse of Olaf Scholz's government made Germany's crisis impossible to ignore.

We wouldn't have had the knowledge, experience and connections to write this account without our day jobs as Bloomberg News journalists. We are deeply grateful for the support throughout this endeavor and for providing us with the resources to cover one of the most fascinating stories in Europe. While all our colleagues in Germany and beyond have provided valuable contributions, we'd particularly like to thank Chad Thomas, Christoph Rauwald, Edward Evans and Elisabeth Behrmann.

Aside from the professional aspects, we'd also like to thank countless friends, neighbours and random acquaintances from our years living in Germany. Alongside our jobs speaking with executives and politicians, union leaders and activists, we've been part of the country just like every other German. That includes mundane interactions in trains, buses, bakeries, doctor's offices and civil service agencies, and during sporting events, parent evenings and flea markets. We've felt the anxiety in the crush of shopping ahead of a holiday, seen the suffering of homelessness and the joy of World Cup success. We've seen Germany in good times and bad times, and those experiences have directly and indirectly shaped our understanding of Germany and enriched this book. For that, we'd like to thank the people we've encountered in our time in Germany, even the people that scolded us for some perceived transgression.

But our motivation and inspiration for undertaking this book is our families. Our parents – Horst and Susan, and David and Penelope – gave us the self-belief to venture away from our birth countries, and our partners and former partners – including Sandra and Daniela, who helped provide an anchor in Germany, and Vanessa, the best companion on a delayed train – joined us on this journey and supported our decisions to make a home here. For that, we thank them. But this book is also forward-looking, and that means it's largely for our children – Clea, Hannah, Eliot, Stella, and Nathan, and Emilia and Alba. They are part of the German experience now as well, and more so because they were born here. So in the process of being part of the country's future, we've got something at stake. That means for them and because of them, we remain hopeful that Germany can arrest its slide toward the abyss.

While the challenges ahead are daunting, Germany has recovered from worse. That resilience is due to the energy, creativity and steadfastness of its people, and we ultimately believe that these qualities will assert themselves once again. As former Chancellor Helmut Schmidt once said, *'In der Krise beweist sich der Charakter'* (character reveals itself in crisis).

Notes

EPIGRAPHS

Introduction	Hannah Arendt, *Men in Dark Times*, New York, 1968
Chapter 1	Thomas Mann, *Buddenbrooks: The Decline of a Family*, Berlin, 1901.
Chapter 2	Bertolt Brecht, 'Kinderhymne' *in Ausgewählte Werke in sechs Bänden,* Suhrkamp, Frankfurt am Main 1997.
Chapter 3	Friedrich Hebbel, *Tagebücher,* Walter de Gruyter, Berlin, 2017.
Chapter 4	Immanuel Kant, *Die Metaphysik der Sitten. Zweiter Teil. Metaphysische Anfangsgründe der Tugendlehre*, Felix Meiner Verlag, Hamburg, 2017.
Chapter 5	Heinrich Heine, *Der lyrische Nachlass*, Hoffmann und Campe, Hamburg, 1925.
Chapter 6	Friedrich Nietzsche, *Beyond Good and Evil*, Random House, New York, 1966.
Chapter 7	Peter Sirius, *Tausend und Ein Gedanken*, Carl Andelfinger, Munich, 1899.
Chapter 8	'Endgültiges amtliches Ergebnis der Bundestagswahl 2013', *Die Bundeswahlleiterin,* 9 October 2013. https://www.bundeswahlleiterin.de/info/presse/mitteilungen/bundestagswahl-2013/2013-10-09-endgueltiges-amtliches-ergebnis-der-bundestagswahl-2013.html.
Chapter 9	Speech to the Bundestag on the 65th anniversary of Germany's Basic Law, Berlin, 23 May 2015. https://www.bundestag.de/webarchiv/textarchiv/2014/280688-280688
Chapter 10	As quoted in *The Art of Looking Sideways* by Alan Fletcher, p. 129. Berlin, 2001. https://beruhmte-zitate.de/zit

NOTES

Closing Remarks   ate/1968971-walter-gropius-der-geist-ist-wie-ein-fallschirm-er-kann-nur-funk.
Stockholm International Peace Research Institute, n.d. '2. Trends in armed conflicts'. Sipri.org. Accessed 2 June 2024. https://www.sipri.org/yearbook/2023/02.

ONE: THE HOUSE IS CRUMBLING

1. Frank-Walter Steinmeier speech in Berlin on 23 May 2024. https://www.bundespraesident.de/SharedDocs/Reden/DE/Frank-Walter-Steinmeier/Reden/2024/05/240523-Staatsakt-75-Jahre-Grundgesetz.html.
2. See for instance a position paper from the AfD on the party's official website: https://www.afd.de/remigration, accessed 9 August 2024.
3. 'Zukunftserwartungen', Stiftung für Zukunftsfragen, 29 April 2021. https://www.zukunftserwartungen.de/immer-mehr-deutsche-fuehlen-sich-als-europaeer.
4. Jochen Roose, 'Begeistert, kritisch, unaufgeregt, resigniert: die Deutschen und Europa', Konrad-Adenauer-Stiftung, January 2024. https://www.kas.de/documents/252038/29391852/Begeistert%2C+kritisch%2C+unaufgeregt+resigniert+-+die+Deutschen+und+Europa.pdf.
5. Emal Atif, 'Euro-Symbol in Frankfurt droht erneut Versteigerung, hessenschau.de, June 2, 2023'. https://www.hessenschau.de/wirtschaft/sponsor-abgesprungen-euro-symbol-in-frankfurt-droht-erneut-versteigerung--vi,euro-zeichen-erneut-droht-versteigerung-100.html.
6. Bußgeldkatalog 2024, accessed 21 May 2024, https://www.bussgeldkatalog.org/wildpinkeln.
7. World Bank data for trade as a per cent of GDP. https://data.worldbank.org/indicator/NE.TRD.GNFS.ZS?locations=DE-US-GB-CN-JP-FR.
8. Petra Stanat et al., IQB-Bildungstrend 2022, Institut zur Qualitätsentwicklung im Bildungswesen, 13 October 2023, p. 66.
9. Ibid., p. 45.
10. Ibid., p. 67.
11. Ibid., p. 39.
12. 'Föderale Aufgabenteilung', Bundesamt für Verfassungsschutz, accessed 21 April 2024, https://www.verfassungsschutz.de/DE/verfassungsschutz/verfassungsschutzverbund/foederale-aufgabenteilung/foederale_aufgabenteilung_node.html.
13. 'Verfassungschutzbericht des Landes Brandenburg 2022', Ministerium des Innern und für Kommunales des Landes Brandenburg, accessed

21 April 2024. https://mik.brandenburg.de/sixcms/media.php/9/VS_Bericht_2022_Pressefassung_neu.pdf.
14 Press release from the federal interior ministry on 3 May 2024. https://www.bmi.bund.de/SharedDocs/pressemitteilungen/DE/2024/05/aktuelle-Cyberangriffe.html.
15 'BND-Spionageprozess vor dem KG: Plötzlich erscheint ein Angeklagter im Zeugenstand', *Legal Tribune Online*, 11 January 2024. https://www.lto.de/persistent/a_id/53617, accessed 8 May 2024.
16 'Ermittlungen zu Sabotageplänen in Deutschland', Tagesschau.de, 18 April 2024, https://www.tagesschau.de/investigativ/russland-sabotage-100.html.
17 'Fears German Military Leaks on Ukraine Are Just "tip of the iceberg"', *The Times*, 5 March 2024. https://www.thetimes.co.uk/article/ukraine-russia-war-secret-uk-operations-germany-9bprk29nl.
18 'Mieter soll nach 84 Jahren sein Haus verlassen', rbb24 Abendschau, 1.11.2023, 19.30 Uhr, https://www.rbb24.de/panorama/beitrag/2023/11/berlin-mieter-84-jahre-kleinkleckersdorf-anwohner-modernisierung.html.
19 Otto Langels, 'Ein Moped für Armando Rodrigues de Sá', *Deutschlandfunk*, 10 September 2014. https://www.deutschlandfunk.de/millionster-gastarbeiter-vor-50-jahren-ein-moped-fuer-100.html.
20 Kühn-Memorandum (September 1979), published in German History Intersections, https://germanhistory-intersections.org/de/migration/ghis:document-125.
21 Antifaschistisches Pressearchiv und Bildungszentrum Berlin e.V. https://www.apabiz.de/archiv/material/Profile/Heidelberger%20Kreis.htm.
22 The 1982 coalition agreement accessed at: https://web.archive.org/web/20150924040325/https://www.freiheit.org/files/288/IN5-304_Koalitionsvereinbarung_1982.pdf.
23 Unabhängige Kommission 'Zuwanderung', also known as the Süssmuth Commission, available at: http://www.archivportal-d.de/item/V4MDERIXRABJFXHXP2AH67DTYU7HVEJC.
24 See, for instance, Hubertus Knabe 'Wie sich die Grünen der deutschen Geschichte entledigen wollen', *Die Welt*, 3 May 2024. https://www.welt.de/debatte/kommentare/plus251265162/Claudia-Roth-Wie-sich-die-Gruenen-der-deutschen-Geschichte-entledigen-wollen.html.
25 For a rebuttal in the memory culture debate, see Jürgen Zimmerer, 'Warum Claudia Roth richtigliegt', *Der Spiegel*, 30 April 2024. https://www.spiegel.de/geschichte/erinnerungspolitik-warum-clau

NOTES

dia-roth-mit-ihrem-konzeptentwurf-richtigliegt-a-4a764
15f-6b43-4f6d-a892-201dcb9f43a8.

TWO: CODDLED CHILD

1. Willi Kammerer, *Narben bleiben: Die Arbeit der Suchdienste – 60 Jahre nach dem Zweiten Weltkrieg*, Berlin 2005.
2. Paul Celan, *Todesfuge*, 1948.
3. 'Directive to Commander-in-Chief of United States Forces of Occupation Regarding the Military Government of Germany; April 1945,' Department of State: Foreign Relations of the United States, 1945, vol. 3, European Advisory Commission; Austria; Germany, p. 484.
4. Ibid.
5. Stuttgart Speech ('Speech of Hope') by James F. Byrnes, United States Secretary of State, 6 Sept. 1946.
6. Office of The Historian, 2019. 'The Berlin Airlift, 1948–1949' State.gov, accessed 12 May 2024 https://history.state.gov/milestones/1945-1952/berlin-airlift.
7. 'Ernst Reuter's speech to the Reichstag on 9 Sept. 1948,' Berlin.de.
8. 'Airlift airport Tempelhof,' thf-berlin.de, accessed 12 May 2024, https://www.thf-berlin.de/en/history-of-location/symbol-of-freedom/airlift.
9. 'Interview with Gail Halvorsen, the Berlin Candy Bomber,' *Military History* magazine, published April 2009.
10. 'Audio: Former President Truman on the Berlin Blockade,' Trumanlibrary.gov, accessed 12 May 2024, https://www.thf-berlin.de/en/history-of-location/symbol-of-freedom/airlift.
11. 'Der Weg zum Grundgesetz – Teil 1 Der Parlamentarische Rat nimmt seine Arbeit auf,' Bundesregierung.de, accessed May 12, 2024, https://www.bundesregierung.de/breg-de/themen/75-jahre-grundgesetz/weg-zum-grundgesetz-1-1527924.
12. 'Germany and NATO,' Nato.int, accessed 12 May 2024, https://www.nato.int/cps/en/natohq/declassified_185912.htm.
13. Frauke Hachtmann, 'Promoting Consumerism in West Germany During the Cold War: An Agency Perspective.' Faculty Publications, College of Journalism & Mass Communications. 16, 2009.
14. Statistisches Bundesamt, accessed 12 May 2024. https://www.destatis.de/DE/Presse/Pressemitteilungen/2023/06/PD23_N041_31.html.
15. 'Pkw-Bestand in Deutschland 1950–2020,' Zahlenbilder.de, accessed 12 May 2024, https://zahlenbilder.de/deutschland/wirtschaft/verkehr/1029/pkw-bestand-in-deutschland-1950-2020.

NOTES

16 'John F. Kennedy: "Die Mauer ist keine sehr schöne Lösung",' MDR. de, 24 Aug 2018. https://www.mdr.de/geschichte/ddr/mauer-grenze/mauerbau-proteste-kennedy-chruschtschow-100.html
17 'The 1st Frankfurt Auschwitz Trial,' Landesarchiv Hessen.de, accessed 16 May 2024, https://landesarchiv.hessen.de/mow/chapters/chapter-5_en.
18 Sybille Steinbacher, 'NS-Verbrechen vor Gericht – Eine Online-Ausstellung,' fritz-bauer-der-staatsanwalt.de, accessed 16 May 2024, https://fritz-bauer-der-staatsanwalt.de/ed.
19 'Tonbandmitschnitte des Auschwitz Prozess (1963–65),' auschwitz-prozess.de, accessed 16 May 2024, https://www.auschwitz-prozess.de/zeugenaussagen/Schlussworte_der_Angeklagten/.
20 Tamar Zemach et al. 'Holocaust und NS-prozese: Die Presseberichterstattung in Israel und Deutschland Zwischen Aneignung und Abwehr,' Böhlau Verlag, 1995.
21 'Kniefall Angemessen Oder Übertrieben?,' *Spiegel*, 13 Dec. 1970.
22 Bundeszentrale für politische Bildung, 'Vor 50 Jahren: Unterzeichnung des Warschauer Vertrags,' bpb.de, accessed 16 May 2024, https://www.bpb.de/kurz-knapp/hintergrund-aktuell/322405/vor-50-jahren-unterzeichnung-des-warschauer-vertrags/.
23 Stefan Aust, *Baader Meinhof Komplex*, Hoffmann & Campe Verlag, p. 9
24 'Politische Überzeugung,' *Spiegel*, 25 July 1971.
25 'Zitate zur Deutschen Einheit von Helmut Kohl,' Bundesstiftung Helmet Kohl, accessed 16 May 2024, https://www.bundesstiftung-helmut-kohl.de/helmut-kohl/zitate/deutsche-einheit.
26 Jörg Roesler, 'Mass Unemployment in Eastern Germany: Recent Trends and Responses by Workers and Policy Makers.' *Journal of European Social Policy* 1 (2): 129–36. https://doi.org/10.1177/095892879100100204.
27 'Böse Blamage In Leuna.' *Spiegel*, 27 Feb. 1994. https://www.spiegel.de/wirtschaft/boese-blamage-in-leuna-a-ca977f17-0002-0001-0000-000013685025.
28 'Bevölkerungsentwicklung in Ost- und Westdeutschland zwischen 1990 und 2022: Angleichung oder Verfestigung der Unterschiede?' Statistisches Bundesamt. Accessed 31 May 2024 https://www.destatis.de/DE/Themen/Querschnitt/Demografischer-Wandel/Aspekte/demografie-bevoelkerungsentwicklung-ost-west.html.
29 'Ost- und Westregionen gleichen sich im Glück weiter an,' SKL Glücksatlas in Zusammenarbeit mit der Universität Freiburg.

Accessed 4 March 2024. https://www.skl-gluecksatlas.de/artikel/ost-west-vergleich-2023.html.
30 S. Buecker et al., 'In a Lonely Place: Investigating Regional Differences in Loneliness,' *Social Psychological and Personality Science*, 12(2), 2021. 147–155.
31 'Die Kosten und Erträge der Wiedervereinigung Deutschlands,' bpb.de, accessed 16 May 2024. https://www.bpb.de/themen/deutsche-einheit/lange-wege-der-deutschen-einheit/47534/die-kosten-und-ertraege-der-wiedervereinigung-deutschlandsNETZER.
32 'Elitenmonitor,' Ostbeauftragter.de, accessed 16 May 2024.
33 Denis Huschka, 'Fünf aus 54: So wenig Ostdeutsche sind in der neuen Bundesregierung,' *Berliner Zeitung*. 5 Jan. 2022.
34 'Netzer gegen Ballack: Der ewige Ossi,' FAZ, 18 Sept. 2003, https://www.faz.net/aktuell/feuilleton/netzer-gegen-ballack-der-ewige-ossi-1116225.html.
35 Cathrin Gilbert und Holger Stark, 'Aber das ist dennoch die einzige Chance, um den endgültigen Niedergang des Landes zu vermeiden,' *Zeit*, 13 April 2023. https://www.zeit.de/2023/16/mathias-doepfner-axel-springer-interne-dokumente
36 'Berlin: Wie geht es weiter mit dem Einheitsdenkmal?' Deutsche Welle, 2 Oct. 2023, https://www.dw.com/de/berlin-wie-geht-es-weiter-mit-dem-einheitsdenkmal/a-66916882
37 'The sick man of the euro,' *The Economist*, 3 June 1999, https://www.economist.com/special/1999/06/03/the-sick-man-of-the-euro
38 'CDU-parteitag: Was wir vorhaben, ist ein Befreiungsschlag zur Senkung der Arbeitskosten,' *Zeit Online*, 23 July 2003. https://www.zeit.de/reden/deutsche_innenpolitik/200349_merkelcduparteitag/komplettansicht
39 Luke Harding, 'Could Germany win?' *The Guardian*, 21 June 2006. https://www.theguardian.com/football/worldcup2006blog/2006/jun/21/couldgermanywin
40 Samuel Brittan, 'Almost a new economic miracle,' *Financial Times*, 12 April 2007, https://www.ft.com/content/290e5316-e920-11db-a162-000b5df1062
41 A. Blätte, Reduzierter Parteienwettbewerb durch kalkulierte Demobilisierung. In: Korte, KR. (eds) Die Bundestagswahl 2009. VS Verlag für Sozialwissenschaften, 2010. https://doi.org/10.1007/978-3-531-92494-6_14.

NOTES

42 Thilo Sarrazin, *Deutschland schafft sich ab*, Deutsche Verlags-Anstalt, 30 Aug. 2010.
43 Sunny Hundal, 'Angela Merkel Is Now the Leader of the Free World, Not Donald Trump', *Independent*, 1 February 2017. https://www.independent.co.uk/voices/angela-merkel-donald-trump-democracy-freedom-of-press-a7556986.html.

THREE: MYTH BUSTING

1 Matthias Wissmann, speech on the creation of Deutsche Bahn, Berlin, 12 January 1994. https://www.bundesregierung.de/breg-de/service/newsletter-und-abos/bulletin/die-bahnreform-als-entscheidender-schritt-hin-zu-einem-modernen-verkehrswesen-rede-von-bundesminister-wissmann-in-berlin-800844.
2 Deutsche Bahn, 'Netzzustandsbericht Fahrweg 2022', January 2024. https://www.dbinfrago.com/web/unternehmen/zielbild-infrastruktur/netzzustandsbericht-12636112.
3 'Helden der Digitalisierung: Deutsche Bahn sucht Admin für 30 Jahre altes Windows', *Focus*, 31 January 2024. https://www.focus.de/finanzen/news/stellenausschreibung-es-ging-1993-an-den-start-deutsche-bahn-sucht-mitarbeiter-fuer-uralt-windows_id_259618469.html.
4 Allianz pro Schiene, Das Schienennetz in Deutschland, https://www.allianz-pro-schiene.de/themen/infrastruktur/schienennetz.
5 Bundesrechnungshof, 'Bericht nach § 99 BHO zur Dauerkrise der Deutschen Bahn AG', 15 March 2023. https://www.bundesrechnungshof.de/SharedDocs/Downloads/DE/Berichte/2023/db-dauerkrise-volltext.pdf.
6 'Unruhegeist im Ruhestand – Hartmut Mehdorn wird 80', Deutsche Presse-Agentur, 25 July 2022. https://www.morgenpost.de/berlin/article235982433/Unruhegeist-im-Ruhestand-Hartmut-Mehdorn-wird-80.html.
7 Bericht des 1. Untersuchungsausschusses des Abgeordnetenhauses von Berlin, 14 June 2016. https://www.parlament-berlin.de/Ausschuesse/17-1-untersuchungsausschuss-ber.
8 Flughafen Berlin Brandenburg GmbH, Geschäftsbericht 2018. https://corporate.berlin-airport.de/content/dam/corporate/de/unternehmen-presse/newsroom/publikationen/geschaeftsbericht/2018-geschaeftsbericht.pdf.
9 Claudia van Laak and Axel Flemming, 'Das Scheitern des Hartmut Mehdorn', Deutschlandfunk, 7 March 2014. https://www.deutschl

NOTES

andfunk.de/berliner-flughafen-ber-das-scheitern-des-hartmut-mehdorn-100.html.

10 Nationaler Normenkontrollrat, Jahresbericht 2023. https://www.bmj.de/SharedDocs/Publikationen/DE/Fachpublikationen/2023_NKR_Jahresbericht.pdf.

11 Richard Arnold, Boris Palmer and Matthias Klopfer, Letter from Mayors of Schwäbisch Gmünd, Tübingen and Esslingen to Chancellor Olaf Scholz, 9 October 2023. https://www.tuebingen.de/Dateien/482_brief_buerokratie_scholz_anlage.pdf.

12 Deutscher Bundestag, Drucksache 20/11746, 10 June 2024. https://dserver.bundestag.de/btd/20/117/2011746.pdf.

13 'Umfrage zur Bürokratie in Deutschland', Civey for Initiative Neue Soziale Marktwirtschaft, 19 February 2024. https://www.insm.de/fileadmin/insm-dms/downloads/INSM-Umfrage_Buerokratie_in_Deutschland.pdf.

14 Data from Initiative Neue Soziale Marktwirtschaft Bundestag 'Nachhaltigkeit im Alltag der Bundesregierung', 15 December 2023. https://dserver.bundestag.de/btd/20/098/2009828.pdf.

15 OECD Digital Government Index. https://goingdigital.oecd.org/en/indicator/58.

16 'Agile Governance and Good Access to Markets Boost Citizens' Quality of Life', International Institute for Management Development, accessed 2 June 2024. https://www.imd.org/news/economics/agile-governance-and-good-access-to-markets-boost-citizens-quality-of-life.

17 Bundestag, 'Beschlussempfehlung und Bericht des 3. Untersuchungsausschusses der 19. Wahlperiode', pp. 1,892–4. https://dserver.bundestag.de/btd/19/309/1930900.pdf.

18 Sam Jones, 'Wirecard Fugitive Helped Run Russian Spy Operations Across Europe', *Financial Times*, 5 April 2024. https://www.ft.com/content/c3b50060-aa53-40fd-a698-579e8e1ae67d.

19 Bundestag investigative committee report, p. 1,647.

20 'Vertreter des Kanzleramts sagt zum Engagement für Wirecard in China aus', Bundestag, 12 January 2021. https://www.bundestag.de/dokumente/textarchiv/2021/kw02-pa-3ua-816148.

21 Wirecard-Untersuchungsausschuss, Bundestag, 17 December 2020. https://www.bundestag.de/dokumente/textarchiv/2020/kw51-pa-3ua-812244.

22 Bundestag, 'Scholz gelobt Schaffung einer schlagkräftigeren Finanzaufsicht', 22 April 2021. https://www.bundestag.de/dokumente/textarchiv/2021/kw16-pa-3ua-do-831934.

NOTES

23 Bundesverfassungsgericht, Urteil des Zweiten Senats, 15 November 2023. https://www.bverfg.de/e/fs20231115_2bvf000122.html.
24 Kathrin Mahler Walther and Helga Lukoschat, 'Bürgermeisterinnen und Bürgermeister in Deutschland 30 Jahre nach der Wiedervereinigung', EAF Berlin, 1 October 2020. https://www.eaf-berlin.de/fileadmin/eaf/Publikationen/Dokumente/2020_EAF_Berlin_Mahler-Walther_Studie_BuergermeisterInnen_Ost_West.pdf.
25 'Gleichstellung und Geschlechtergerechtigkeit', Hans-Böckler-Stiftung, 4 March 2024. https://www.boeckler.de/de/auf-einen-blick-17945-studien-zu-gleichstellung-und-geschlechtergerechtigkeit-21085.htm.
26 See the 2023 report at https://www.weforum.org/publications/global-gender-gap-report-2023.
27 'Gleichstellung und Geschlechtergerechtigkeit', Hans-Böckler-Stiftung, 4 March 2024.
28 'Typische Männer- und Frauenberufe', Institut der deutschen Wirtschaft, 3 April 2024. https://www.iwd.de/artikel/berufswahl-typisch-mann-typisch-frau-380726.
29 Clara Albrecht and Britta Rude, 'Wo steht Deutschland 2022 bei der Gleichstellung der Geschlechter?' Ifo Institut, 7 March 2022. https://www.ifo.de/DocDL/sd-2022-albrecht-rude-geschlechtergleichheit-deutschland.pdf.
30 Angela Merkel, Speech at ceremony for the 100th anniversary of women's right to vote, Berlin, 12 November 2018. https://www.bundeskanzler.de/bk-de/aktuelles/rede-von-bundeskanzlerin-merkel-bei-der-festveranstaltung-100-jahre-frauenwahlrecht-am-12-november-2018-1548938.
31 Reuters clip from the Düsseldorf event: https://www.youtube.com/watch?v=5PyrU3tkHQw&t=60s.
32 'Gewalt gegen Frauen in Deutschland 2022', UN Women Deutschland e.V., September 2023. https://unwomen.de/gewalt-gegen-frauen-in-deutschland.
33 'Nach rechtsextremen Vorfällen in Burg geht weitere Lehrerin', *RBB*, 24 April 2024. https://www.rbb24.de/panorama/beitrag/2024/04/brandenburg-burg-rechtsextremismus-schule-lehrerin-geht.html.
34 The letter was published by the teachers here: https://innn.it/brandbrief.
35 Benjamin Barthe, 'Ghassan Abu Sitta, le docteur qui répare les «gueules cassées» du Proche-Orient', *Le Monde*, 15 December 2015. https://www.lemonde.fr/proche-orient/article/2015/12/15/ghas

NOTES

san-abu-sitta-le-docteur-qui-repare-les-gueules-cassees-du-proche-orient_4832621_3218.html.

36 Nancy Faeser, post on social media site X, 12 April 2024. https://twitter.com/NancyFaeser/status/1778849826630734105.

37 Declaration of the Palestine Conference: https://palaestinakongress.de.

38 Salman Abu-Sitta, 'I could have been one of those who broke through the siege on October 7', *Mondoweiss*, 4 January 2024. https://mondoweiss.net/2024/01/i-could-have-been-one-of-those-who-broke-through-the-siege-on-october-7.

39 Interview with Al Jazeera on 13 April 2024. https://mediaview.aljazeera.com/video/OKxehcVPZV.

40 Slavoj Žižek, 'Beim Einreiseverbot gegen Yanis Varoufakis wird Deutschland autoritär', *Der Freitag*, Ausgabe 17/2024. https://www.freitag.de/autoren/slavoj-zizek/einreiseverbot-gegen-varoufakis-zizek-warnt-vor-autoritaerem-deutschland.

41 The response was posted on the Bavarian government's website: https://www.bayern.de/wp-content/uploads/2023/09/230903_FragenkatalogStMAiwanger.pdf.

42 'Hubert Aiwanger strebt nach Berlin', Interview with Michael Watzke, Deutschlandfunk Radio, 21 April 2024. https://www.deutschlandfunk.de/interview-aiwanger-hubert-bayer-wirtschaftsminister-bundesvors-freie-waehler-dlf-0e855257-100.html.

43 Press release from the US Securities and Exchange Commission, 15 December 2008. https://www.sec.gov/litigation/litreleases/lr-20829.

44 Carl Levin et al., 'Wall Street and the Financial Crisis: Anatomy of a Crisis', US Senate Permanent Subcommittee on Investigations, 11 April 2011, p. 10. https://web.archive.org/web/20110505035617/http://levin.senate.gov/newsroom/supporting/2011/PSI_WallStreetCrisis_041311.pdf.

45 Otfried Nassauer, 'Korruption bei deutschen Rüstungsexportgeschäften – Das Beispiel Griechenland', Berliner Informationszentrum für Transatlantische Sicherheit, 30 June 2015. https://www.bits.de/public/reden/red_150630.htm.

46 Christoph Twickel, 'Das System Kahrs', *Die Zeit*, 25 August 2022. https://www.zeit.de/2022/35/johannes-kahrs-spd-cum-ex.

47 Oliver Hollenstein und Oliver Schröm, 'Der Mann hinter der Cum-Ex-Masche', *Der Spiegel*, 26 March 2021. https://www.spiegel.de/

NOTES

wirtschaft/cum-ex-hanno-berger-ist-der-mann-hinter-der-steuerraub-masche-a-bde194f7-4865-4028-9e7c-b3795560c3a9.

48 'Cum-Ex Chefermittlerin spricht über ihre Kündigung', *NDR*, 22 April 2024. https://www.ardmediathek.de/video/wdr/exklusiv-interview-cum-ex-chefermittlerin-spricht-ueber-ihre-kuendigung/wdr/Y3JpZDovL3dkci5kZS9CZWlocmFnLTFiNDIzNDg5LTdjYjUtNGVkZS05ZGQ2LTg0OGI2ODdiMjA4Ng.

49 Post on social media platform X, 29 June 2021. https://x.com/GaryLineker/status/1409953095233290241.

50 Richard Rorty, 'The Unpatriotic Academy', *New York Times*, 13 February 1994. https://www.nytimes.com/1994/02/13/opinion/the-unpatriotic-academy.html.

FOUR: CRACKED PIPES

1 'Gas Leak in the Baltic Sea', *Danish Defence*, 27 September 2022, https://www.forsvaret.dk/en/news/2022/gas-leak-in-the-baltic-sea/a.

2 'Bundesnetzagentur-Chef fordert Deutsche auf, nicht so oft warm zu duschen', NordBayern.de, 13 April 2022, https://www.nordbayern.de/panorama/bundesnetzagentur-chef-fordert-deutsche-auf-nicht-so-oft-warm-zu-duschen-1.12029362.

3 Wilfried Eckl-Dorna, Jana Randow, et al., 'Germany's Days as an Industrial Superpower Are Coming to an End', *Bloomberg*, 10 February 2024. https://www.bloomberg.com/news/features/2024-02-10/why-germany-s-days-as-an-industrial-superpower-are-coming-to-an-end?sref=KeM3kOBb.

4 Link to debate: https://www.youtube.com/watch?v=GDtMvgpJUrI&t=2460s.

5 'Russia Preparing for Long-Term Confrontation with NATO, Including Baltics – Intelligence', *LRT*, 7 March 2024, https://www.lrt.lt/en/news-in-english/19/2216335/russia-preparing-for-long-term-confrontation-with-nato-including-baltics-intelligence.

6 BASF press release on 24 February 2023. https://www.basf.com/global/en/media/news-releases/2023/02/p-23-131.html.

7 Rasmus Buchsteiner and Christian Teevs,' Industrie könnte im großen Stil abwandern', *Der Spiegel*, 1 May 2024. https://www.spiegel.de/politik/deutschland/dgb-chefin-yasmin-fahimi-industrie-koennte-im-grossen-stil-abwandern-a-4ae0a9ca-27b5-4c8a-b53f-37d43e6aa605.

NOTES

8 'Nord-Stream-Pipeline eröffnet', NTV.de, 8 November 2011. https://www.n-tv.de/wirtschaft/Nord-Stream-Pipeline-eroeffnet-article4718011.html.
9 'Merkel und Medwedew drehen Gas auf', *Manager Magazin*, 8 November 2011. https://www.manager-magazin.de/politik/artikel/a-796460.html.
10 Daniel Friedrich Sturm, '"Launige Worte" von Kubicki im Borchardt: Schröder feierte seinen 80. mit Gabriel, Gysi und Lüpertz', *Tagesspiegel*, 28 April 2024. https://www.tagesspiegel.de/politik/launige-worte-von-kubicki-im-borchardt-schroder-feiert-seinen-80-mit-gabriel-gysi-und-lupertz-11585255.html.
11 'Structural Change and Industrial Politics in the Ruhr Region', Rosa Luxemburg Stiftung, September 2023. https://www.rosalux.de/fileadmin/rls_uploads/pdfs/engl/9-23_Onl-Publ_Structural_Change.pdf.
12 'Share of Global Cumulative CO_2 Emissions', Global Carbon Project, retrieved 6 May 2024 from https://ourworldindata.org/grapher/share-of-cumulative-co2.
13 'Ewigkeitsaufgaben', RAG Stiftung, accessed 6 May 2024. https://www.rag-stiftung.de/ewigkeitsaufgaben.
14 'Finanzierung des Kernenergieausstiegs'. Bundesministerium für Wirtschaft und Klimaschutz, accessed 31 May 2024. https://www.bmwk.de/Redaktion/DE/Artikel/Energie/kernenergie-stilllegung-rueckbau-kernkraftwerke.html.
15 'Deutsche wenden sich radikal von der Atomkraft ab', *Der Spiegel*, 15 March 2011. https://www.spiegel.de/panorama/umfragen-deutsche-wenden-sich-radikal-von-der-atomkraft-ab-a-750955.html.
16 'Greenhouse Gas Emission Intensity of Electricity Generation in Europe', European Environment Agency, 24 October 2023. https://www.eea.europa.eu/en/analysis/indicators/greenhouse-gas-emission-intensity-of-1?activeAccordion=309c5ef9-de09-4759-bc02-802370dfa366.
17 'Mehrheit ist gegen Atomausstieg', *Tagesschau*, 14 April 2023. https://www.tagesschau.de/inland/deutschlandtrend/deutschlandtrend-3357.html.
18 'Netzentwicklungsplan Strom 2012', 50Hertz Transmission GmbH et al., 15 August 2022, https://www.netzentwicklungsplan.de/sites/default/files/2022-12/nep_2012_2_entwurf_teil_1_kap_1_bis_8.pdf.

NOTES

19 'Fragen und Antworten zum Netzausbau', Bundesministerium für Wirtschaft und Klimaschutz, accessed 6 May 2024. https://www.bmwk.de/Redaktion/DE/FAQ/Netzausbau/faq-netzausbau.html.

20 'Neue Stromstrasse sind Falsches Zeichen', Bergrheinfeld Sagt Nein, accessed 7 May 2024, https://bergrheinfeld-sagt-nein.de/2024/02/24/uebertragungsnetzgausbau-in-der-kostenfalle-neue-stromtrassen-sind-falsches-zeichen.

21 'Energiewende: Netzausbau hätte vor 10 Jahren initiiert werden müssen', *Die Welt*, 28 April 2024, https://www.youtube.com/watch?v=v8lfF8DD55E.

22 'Fortschrittsmonitor 2024 Energiewende', BDEW, accessed 31 May 2024. https://www.bdew.de/media/original_images/2024/04/24/fortschrittsmonitor_2024_zCu1QX7.pdf.

23 'How Much Did the Apollo Program Cost?', The Planetary Society, accessed 6 May 2024. https://www.planetary.org/space-policy/cost-of-apollo.

24 'Public Electricity Generation 2023: Renewable Energies Cover the Majority of German Electricity Consumption for the First Time', Fraunhofer ISE, 15 January 2024. https://www.ise.fraunhofer.de/en/press-media/press-releases/2024/public-electricity-generation-2023-renewable-energies-cover-the-majority-of-german-electricity-consumption-for-the-first-time.html.

25 'Entwicklung der spezifischen Kohlendioxid-Emissionen des deutschen Strommix in den Jahren 1990–2020', Umweltbundesamt, May 2021. https://www.umweltbundesamt.de/sites/default/files/medien/5750/publikationen/2021-05-26_cc-45-2021_strommix_2021.pdf.

26 'Primärenergieverbrauch', Umweltbundesamt, accessed 6 May 2024, https://www.umweltbundesamt.de/daten/energie/primaerenergieverbrauch.

27 Christoph Rauwald, Wilfried Eckl-Dorna and Monica Raymunt, 'Germany's Dream of 15 Million Electric Vehicles Is Fading Away', *Bloomberg*, 3 February 2024. https://www.bloomberg.com/news/articles/2024-02-03/germany-s-dream-of-15-million-electric-vehicles-is-fading-away?sref=ttOZ5TVM.

28 'e.venture Zukunft des deutschen Strommarktes 2040 Perspektiven zur Energiewirtschaft', E.Venture, April 2023, https://e-vc.org/wp-content/uploads/e.venture_Point_of_View_Strommarkt_2040.pdf.

29 'Wie teuer Strom bis zum Endes des Jahrzehnts werden könnte | tagesschau.de', Tagesschau.de, 6 July 2023, https://www.tagesschau.de/wirtschaft/verbraucher/strompreis-2030-energie-100.html.

30 'Dunkle Zeiten für die Chemie', ChemieTechnik.de, 22 December 2023, https://www.chemietechnik.de/markt/dunkle-zeiten-fuer-die-chemie-159.html.
31 Jan Klauth, 'Industriegewerkschaft kritisiert Ampel scharf', *Die Welt*, 17 January 2024, https://www.welt.de/wirtschaft/article249543620/IGBCE-Irrlichtern-durch-die-Energiewende-Industriegewerkschaft-kritisiert-Ampel-scharf.html.
32 'Wasserstoff-Leitprojekte: H2Mare: Offshore-Technologien', Bundesministerium für Bildung und Forschung, accessed 6 May 2024. https://www.wasserstoff-leitprojekte.de/leitprojekte/h2mare.
33 'Krupp: A Century's History of the Krupp Works, 1812–1912', Krupp'sche Gussstahlfabrik, Essen, 1912, p. 15.
34 Lothar Gall, 'Krupp. Der Aufstieg eines Industrieimperiums', *Deutschlandfunk*, 26 March 2021. https://www.deutschlandfunk.de/lothar-gall-krupp-der-aufstieg-eines-industrieimperiums-100.html.
35 'Aufstieg zum größten Industriellen Europas', *Focus Online*, 25 August 2013. https://www.focus.de/wissen/mensch/geschichte/biografien/kanonen-koenig-krupp-portraet_id_2098265.html.
36 Hitler's speech to the Hitler Youth during the Nazi Party rally in Nuremberg on 14 September 1935.
37 Steel Statistical Yearbook 2011, World Steel Association, accessed 7 May 2024. https://worldsteel.org/wp-content/uploads/Steel-Statistical-Yearbook-2011.pdf.
38 'Ruhrbischof stellt sich drohender Zerschlagung von ThyssenKrupp entgegen', *Bistum Essen*, 20 July 2018. https://www.bistum-essen.de/pressemenue/artikel/ruhrbischof-stellt-sich-drohender-zerschlagung-von-thyssenkrupp-entgegen.
39 'Nach Bekanntgabe der Pläne von Thyssen Krupp Steel Europe: Betriebsbedingte Kündigungen vermeiden und Stahlstandort Duisburg sichern', Duisburg.de, accessed 7 May 2024. https://www.duisburg.de/guiapplications/newsdesk/publications/Stadt_Duisburg/102010100000244636.php.

FIVE: BUSTED BOILER

1 William Wilkes and Alexander Weber, 'The €650 Billion Exodus at the Heart of Germany's Political Turmoil', *Bloomberg*, 7 November 2024. https://www.bloomberg.com/news/articles/2024-11-07/germany-s-capital-exodus-is-at-the-heart-of-coalition-collapse?sref=KeM3kOBb.

NOTES

2 Steven Barrett et al., 'Impact of the Volkswagen Emissions Control Defeat Device on US Public Health', *Environmental Research Letters* 10, no. 11 (2015): 114005. https://iopscience.iop.org/article/10.1088/1748-9326/10/11/114005/pdf.

3 Guillaume P. Chossière et al., 'Public Health Impacts of Excess NOx Emissions from Volkswagen Diesel Passenger Vehicles in Germany', *Environmental Research Letters* 12, no. 3 (2017): 034014. https://iopscience.iop.org/article/10.1088/1748-9326/aa5987.

4 Henning Peitsmeier and Holger Appel, 'VDA-Präsident Wissmann: "Es gibt eine Anti-Diesel-Lobby"', *Frankfurter Allgemeine Zeitung*, 29 September 2015. https://www.faz.net/aktuell/wirtschaft/auto-verkehr/vda-praesident-wissmann-es-gibt-eine-anti-diesel-lobby-13830808.html.

5 Klaus Ott and Markus Balser, 'VW: So schützte Dobrindt VW vor einer Sammelklage', *Süddeutsche Zeitung*, 19 October 2016. https://www.sueddeutsche.de/wirtschaft/verbraucherschutz-so-schuetzte-der-verkehrsminister-vw-vor-einer-sammelklage-1.3210510.

6 Alexander Richter, 'Schramme-der Talk: 169 Jahre Haft? Ex-VW-Manager packt in Celle aus', 7 May 2023. YouTube. https://www.youtube.com/watch?v=CLcyzLCLaF0.

7 'How Many Semiconductor Chips in a Modern Car?', *DRex Electronics*, 15 May 2023. https://www.icdrex.com/how-many-semiconductor-chips-in-a-modern-car.

8 David Zax, 'Many Cars Have a Hundred Million Lines of Code'. *MIT Technology Review*, 2 April 2020. https://www.technologyreview.com/2012/12/03/181350/many-cars-have-a-hundred-million-lines-of-code.

9 Jens Dralle, 'VW ID.3 Pro Performance 1st Max im Test: Knapp daneben ist auch vorbei', *Auto Motor und Sport*, 27 September 2020. https://www.auto-motor-und-sport.de/test/vw-id-3-pro-performance-1st-max-test.

10 Susanne Preuß, 'Daimlers Wandel zur E-Mobilität hat einen Preis', *Frankfurter Allgemeine Zeitung*, 11 September 2017. https://www.faz.net/aktuell/wirtschaft/unternehmen/daimlers-wandel-zur-e-mobilitaet-hat-einen-preis-15193787.html.

11 Frik Els, 'Charts: China's Global Electric Car Dominance – Adamas Intelligence', *Adamas Intelligence*, 19 April 2024. https://www.adamasintel.com/charts-china-global-electric-car-dominance.

12 'One in Four EVs Sold in Europe This Year Will Be Made in China', *European Federation for Transport and Environment*, 7 May 2024. https://

www.transportenvironment.org/articles/one-in-four-evs-sold-in-europe-this-year-will-be-made-in-china-analysis.

13 Jennifer Mossalgue, 'BYD Overtakes VW's 15-Year-Run as Top Seller in China', *Electrek*, 24 January 2024. https://electrek.co/2024/01/23/byd-overtakes-vws-15-year-run-as-top-seller-in-china.

14 'BMW-Chef Zipse warnt Politik: "Man schießt sich ins Knie damit"', 9 May 2024. https://www.kleinezeitung.at/wirtschaft/18447769/bmw-chef-zipse-warnt-die-politik-man-schiesst-sich-ins-knie-damit.

15 'BYD Partners with Auto Nejma in Morocco', 22 April 2022. https://en.byd.com/news/byd-partners-with-auto-nejma-in-morocco.

16 'Automobile Production', *Verband der Automobilindustrie*, 17 May 2022. https://www.vda.de/en/news/facts-and-figures/annual-figures/automobile-production.

17 Regine Bönsch, 'Mehr deutsche Pkw in China als hierzulande gefertigt', *VDI nachrichten*, 12 May 2021.

18 'Beschäftigungszahlen und Beschäftigungsentwicklung', *Verband der Automobilindustrie*, 26 March 2024. https://www.vda.de/de/themen/automobilindustrie/marktentwicklungen/beschaeftigungszahlen-und-beschaeftigungsentwicklung.

19 'Merkel: "Mit Miele aufgewachsen"', Company press release from 10 July 2013. https://www.miele.de/de/m/merkel-mit-miele-aufgewachsen-1054.htm.

20 Eyk Hennig and Jan-Henrik Foerster, 'Germany's Backbone of Family-Owned Firms Is Up for Sale', *Bloomberg News*, 9 March 2024. https://www.bloomberg.com/news/articles/2024-03-09/germany-s-backbone-of-family-owned-firms-is-up-for-sale?sref=ttOZ5TVM.

21 'UK Trade: December 2023', UK Trade – Office for National Statistics, 2024. https://www.ons.gov.uk/economy/nationalaccounts/balanceofpayments/bulletins/uktrade/december2023.

22 Michael Schwartz, 'Nachfolge-Monitoring Mittelstand 2023: Trotz Nachfolgerengpass sind drei Viertel der Übergaben bis Ende 2024 geregelt', KfW, accessed 30 May 2024. https://www.kfw.de/PDF/Download-Center/Konzernthemen/Research/PDF-Dokumente-Fokus-Volkswirtschaft/Fokus-2024/Fokus-Nr.-450-Februar-2024-Nachfolge.pdf.

23 Anja Müller and Martin-W Buchenau, 'Arbeitsmarkt: Der große Stellenabbau droht auch Familienunternehmen zu erfassen', *Handelsblatt*, 12 March 2024. https://www.handelsblatt.com/unte

NOTES

rnehmen/mittelstand/familienunternehmer/arbeitsmarkt-der-grosse-stellenabbau-droht-auch-familienunternehmen-zu-erfassen-01/100018724.html.
24   Marcello De Cecco, *The Oxford Handbook of the Italian Economy since Unification*. Oxford: Oxford University Press, 2013, p. 153.
25   Letter reprinted by media including the *Berliner Morgenpost* on 21 March 2024. https://www.morgenpost.de/wirtschaft/article241935702/Der-Anti-AfD-Brief-des-Schraubenkoenigs-im-Wortlaut.html.
26   Facebook post from Anton Baron, a member of the state legislature in Baden-Württemberg, 18 March 2024. https://www.facebook.com/100057968382668/posts/809015324374073.
27   Sebastian Matthes and Martin-W. Buchenau, 'Reinhold Würth sorgt sich um Deutschland: "Leben in einer Vorkriegszeit"', *Handelsblatt*, 3 May 2024. https://www.handelsblatt.com/unternehmen/mittelstand/familienunternehmer/reinhold-wuerth-sorgt-sich-um-deutschland-leben-in-einer-vorkriegszeit-01/100035872.html.
28   Barbara Weiß, 'Personalnot: Pflegeheim muss schließen – 55 Bewohner müssen raus', *Bayerischer Rundfunk*, 11 December 2023. https://www.br.de/nachrichten/bayern/personalnot-pflegeheim-muss-schliessen-55-bewohner-muessen-raus,Txkw9jj.
29   'Personalmangel Pflege', Pflegenot Deutschland, accessed 28 May 2024. https://www.pflegenot-deutschland.de/ct/personalmangel-pflege.
30   Bündnis für gute Pflege, 'Pflege nicht gegen die Wand fahren', 15 November 2023. https://www.devap.de/fileadmin/Mediathek/02_Unsere_Positionen/pdf/2023_11_15_PM_Buendnis_Pflege.pdf.
31   Markus Klemm, 'Airbus steuert auf goldene Zeiten und Fachkräftemangel zu', *Die Welt*, 16 June 2022. https://www.welt.de/regionales/hamburg/article239399395/Airbus-steuert-auf-goldene-Zeiten-und-Fachkraeftemangel-zu.html.
32   'Fachkräfteengpässe gefährden Erfolg in wichtigen Schlüsseltechnologien', *Deutsche Industrie- und Handelskammer*, 29 March 2023. https://www.dihk.de/de/themen-und-positionen/fachkraefte/beschaeftigung/fachkraefteengpaesse-gefaehrden-erfolg-in-wichtigen-schluesseltechnologien-107880.
33   Filiz Koneberg, Anika Jansen and Vico Kutz, 'KOFA-Studie 3/2022: Energie aus Wind und Sonne – welche Fachkräfte brauchen wir?', Institut der deutschen Wirtschaft (IW), 2022. https://www.iwkoeln.de/studien/anika-jansen-energie-aus-wind-und-sonne-welche-fachkraefte-brauchen-wir.html.

NOTES

34 'Zukunftspanel Mittelstand 2023: Erhöhter Wettbewerbsdruck fordert die Unternehmen heraus', Institut für Mittelstandsforschung, Bonn, July 2023. https://www.ifm-bonn.org/fileadmin/data/redaktion/publikationen/chartbooks/Chartbook_Zukunftspanel_Mittelstand_2023.pdf.

35 Sabine Köhne, 'Berufe in der Halbleiterindustrie: Immer mehr Stellen können nicht besetzt werden', Institut der deutschen Wirtschaft, 2023. https://www.iwkoeln.de/studien/sabine-koehne-finster-immer-mehr-stellen-koennen-nicht-besetzt-werden.html.

36 Survey of 3,000 voting-age Germans was conducted on behalf of the Friedrich-Ebert-Stiftung from 15 November to 11 December 2018. https://www.fes.de/themenportal-flucht-migration-integration/umfrage-was-die-deutschen-ueber-migration-denken.

37 Alexander Hagelüken and Claus Hulverscheidt, interview with Monika Schnitzer, head of Germany's Council of Economic Advisers, *Süddeutsche Zeitung*, 2 July 2023. https://www.sueddeutsche.de/wirtschaft/zuwanderung-migration-heizungsgesetz-klimaschutz-fachkraeftemangel-1.5990360.

38 'Personen in Elternzeit', Statistisches Bundesamt, accessed 28 May 2024. https://www.destatis.de/DE/Themen/Arbeit/Arbeitsmarkt/Qualitaet-Arbeit/Dimension-3/elternzeit.html.

39 'Arbeitszeit von Männern und Frauen: Wunsch und Wirklichkeit klaffen auseinander', Bertelsmann Stiftung, 2021. https://www.bertelsmann-stiftung.de/de/themen/aktuelle-meldungen/2021/maerz/arbeitszeit-von-maennern-und-frauen-wunsch-und-wirklichkeit-klaffen-auseinander.

40 Stefan Fetzer, 'Mehr Nachhaltigkeit Wagen', Die Familienunternehmer, accessed 28 May 2024. https://www.familienunternehmer.eu/fileadmin/schnelluploads/240221_FamU_JungU_Gutachten_SozialeSicherung_WEB_DS.pdf.

41 Internet Use Statistics from Eurostat, accessed 29 March 2024. https://ec.europa.eu/eurostat/statistics-explained/index.php?title=Archive:Internet_use_statistics_-_individuals.

42 Odete Madureira, 'World Digital Competitiveness Ranking', IMD Business School for Management and Leadership Courses, 29 November 2023. https://www.imd.org/centers/wcc/world-competitiveness-center/rankings/world-digital-competitiveness-ranking.

NOTES

43 Country Wise Paper & Paperboard Production & Consumption Statistics, Paperonweb.com, accessed 29 March 2024. https://www.paperonweb.com/Country.htm.
44 'Germany: A Snapshot of Digital Skills', *Digital Skills and Jobs Platform*, 21 June 2023. https://digital-skills-jobs.europa.eu/en/latest/briefs/germany-snapshot-digital-skills.
45 '82 Prozent der deutschen Unternehmen faxen noch', Bitkom, accessed 29 March 2024. https://www.bitkom.org/Presse/Presseinformation/Digital-Office-Faxen-Unternehmen.
46 René Höltschi and Michael Rasch, Interview with Hasso Plattner, *Neue Zürcher Zeitung*, 29 January 2024. https://www.nzz.ch/wirtschaft/inte-hasso-plattner-ld.1775134.
47 Jan C. Breitinger, Benjamin Dierks and Thomas Rausch, 'Weltklassepatente in Zukunftstechnologien', Bertelsmann Stiftung, 3 June 2020. https://www.bertelsmann-stiftung.de/fileadmin/files/user_upload/BST_Weltklassepatente_2020_DT.pdf.
48 Data from Deutsches Patent- und Markenamt, 22 June 2023. https://www.dpma.de/english/our_office/publications/statistics/patents/index.html.
49 Ibid.
50 'Next Generation: Startup-Neugründungen in Deutschland', Startup Verband. https://startupverband.de/fileadmin/startupverband/mediaarchiv/research/Next_Generation_Report/Next_Generation_Startup-Neugruendungen_in_Deutschland_2023.pdf.
51 Data from Startup Ranking, accessed 29 May 2024. https://www.startupranking.com/countries
52 'Deutscher Startup Monitor 2023', PwC Deutschland, accessed 28 May 2024. https://www.pwc.de/de/branchen-und-markte/startups/deutscher-startup-monitor.html.
53 Georg Metzger, 'Grüündungsstandort Deutschland: Angst vor dem Scheitern mit besserer ökonomischer Grundausbildung kontern', *KfW*, 7 February 2019. https://www.kfw.de/PDF/Download-Center/Konzernthemen/Research/PDF-Dokumente-Fokus-Volkswirtschaft/Fokus-2019/Fokus-Nr.-242-Februar-2019-Gr%C3%BCndungsstandort-D-Angst-vor-dem-Scheitern.pdf.
54 Bloomberg Billionaires Index, data accessed 29 May 2024.
55 Stefan Wagner, Bürokratiekostenindex, ESMT Berlin, 9 April 2024. https://esmt.berlin/de/presse/esmt-berlin-neuer-index-belegt-zunehmende-buerokratie-deutschland.

56 Länderindex Familienunternehmen, Stiftung Familienunternehmen, accessed 29 March 2024. https://www.familienunternehmen.de/media/pages/publikationen/laenderindex-familienunternehmen-2023/3abc557b8d-1700136063/laenderindex-2022_studie_stiftung-familienunternehmen.pdf.
57 Holz et al., Instituts für Mittelstandsforschung, Bonn.
58 OECD Reviews of Innovation Policy: Germany 2022, OECD Publishing, Paris, https://doi.org/10.1787/50b32331-en.
59 'Startup Roadmap Ready: Federal Cabinet Adopts First Comprehensive Startup Strategy', *Bundesministerium für Wirtschaft und Klimaschutz*, 27 July 2022. https://www.bmwk.de/Redaktion/EN/Pressemitteilungen/2022/07/20220726-startup-roadmap-ready-federal-cabinet-adopts-first-comprehensive-startup-strategy.html.
60 Steffen Klusmann and Thomas Schulz. 2021. Interview with BioNTech-Gründer Özlem Türeci and Uğur Şahin, *Der Spiegel*, 1 January 2021. https://www.spiegel.de/wirtschaft/unternehmen/ biontech-gruender-oezlem-tuereci-und-ugur-sahin-deutschland- wird-genug-impfstoff-bekommen-a-00000000-0002-0001-0000-000174691195.

SIX: NEIGHBOURHOOD DECAY

1 'UN Report Details Summary Executions of Civilians by Russian Troops in Northern Ukraine', Office of the High Commissioner for Human Rights, 7 December 2022. https://www.ohchr.org/en/press-releases/2022/12/un-report-details-summary-executions-civilians-russian-troops-northern.
2 'Death at the Station', a Human Rights Watch and SITU Research investigation. https://www.hrw.org/video-photos/interactive/2023/02/21/death-at-the-station/russian-cluster-munition-attack-in-kramatorsk.
3 Melanie Amann and Veit Medick, 'Wie Steinmeier Selenskyj konfrontierte', *Der Spiegel*, 8 July 2022. https://www.spiegel.de/politik/deutschland/telefonat-von-steinmeier-und-selenskyj-a-00de121e-f18b-4cae-a4ea-6f690402e10f.
4 Katrin Bennhold, 'The Former Chancellor Who Became Putin's Man in Germany', *New York Times*, 24 April 2022. https://www.nytimes.com/2022/04/23/world/europe/schroder-germany-russia-gas-ukraine-war-energy.html.
5 Stefan Braun, 'Steinmeiers heikles Unterfangen', *Süddeutsche Zeitung*, 9 March 2014. https://www.sueddeutsche.de/politik/deutscher-aussenminister-in-der-krim-krise-steinmeiers-heikles-unterfangen-1.1908058.

NOTES

6 Frank-Walter Steinmeier, 'An einer gemeinsamen Zukunft mit Russland arbeiten', interview with *Kommersant*, 14 February 2014. https://www.auswaertiges-amt.de/de/newsroom/-/259876.
7 'Steinmeier stellt Sanktionen gegen Moskau infrage', *Der Spiegel*, 20 December 2014. https://www.spiegel.de/spiegel/vorab/russland-steinmeier-stellt-sanktionen-infrage-a-1009382.html.
8 Burkhard Uhlenbroich, 'Steinmeier kritisiert Nato-Manöver in Osteuropa', *Bild*, 18 June 2016. https://www.bild.de/politik/ausland/dr-frank-walter-steinmeier/kritisiert-nato-maneuver-und-fordert-mehr-dialog-mit-russland-46360604.bild.html.
9 Christoph Giesen and Julian Hans, 'Siemens und der Wolf', *Süddeutsche Zeitung*, 22 July 2017. https://www.sueddeutsche.de/wirtschaft/turbinen-auf-der-annektierten-krim-siemens-und-der-wolf-1.3598019.
10 Georg Ismar and Claudia von Salzen, 'Ukraine-Botschafter rechnet mit Steinmeier ab', *Tagesspiegel*, 2 April 2022. https://www.tagesspiegel.de/politik/ukraine-botschafter-rechnet-mit-steinmeier-ab--und-fordert-mehr-schwere-waffen-4320304.html.
11 Robert Roßmann, 'Steinmeier gesteht Fehler in Russland-Politik ein', *Süddeutsche Zeitung*, 4 April 2022. https://www.sueddeutsche.de/politik/steinmeier-selbstkritik-russland-1.5560571.
12 Christopher F. Schuetze, 'Germany Draws Mockery for Promising 5,000 Helmets to Help Ukraine Defend Itself', *New York Times*, 27 January 2022. https://www.nytimes.com/2022/01/27/world/europe/germany-5000-helmets-ukraine.html.
13 Josefine Fokuhl, 'Berlin Has a Surprising Soft Spot for Its Soviet Memorials', *Bloomberg*, 20 September 2022. https://www.bloomberg.com/news/features/2022-09-20/why-berlin-won-t-be-tearing-down-its-soviet-memorials?sref=KeM3kOBb.
14 Thomas Bagger, 'The World According to Germany: Reassessing 1989', *The Washington Quarterly*, 41:4, pp. 53–63.
15 Melissa Eddy, 'Pro-Nazi Soldiers in German Army Raise Alarm', *New York Times*, 10 May 2017. https://www.nytimes.com/2017/05/10/world/europe/germany-military-far-right-extremists-terror-plot-nazi.html.
16 https://www.tagesspiegel.de/politik/marine-hat-ihr-segelschulschiff-gorch-fock-wieder-4280860.html.
17 Stockholm International Peace Research Institute data accessed via the World Bank. https://data.worldbank.org/indicator/MS.MIL.XPND.GD.ZS?locations=DE.

NOTES

18 Olaf Scholz, Bundestag policy statement, Berlin, 27 February 2022. https://www.bundesregierung.de/breg-en/search/policy-statement-by-olaf-scholz-chancellor-of-the-federal-republic-of-germany-and-member-of-the-german-bundestag-27-february-2022-in-berlin-2008378.
19 Jake Sullivan, White House National Security Advisor, Interview by Martha Raddatz, *This Week*, ABC News, 26 February 2023. https://www.youtube.com/watch?v=TbItP5f4mg4&t=5s.
20 Anton Hofreiter and Norbert Röttgen, 'Der katastrophale Defätismus des Kanzlers', *Frankfurter Allgemeine Zeitung*, 11 March 2024.
21 Jens Plötner, 'Zur Zeitenwende', German Council on Foreign Relations, 21 June 2022. https://www.youtube.com/watch?v=HZc3Nxsaje4.
22 Simon Ziese, 'Erich Vad im Interview', *Berliner Zeitung*, 11 February 2024. https://www.berliner-zeitung.de/politik-gesellschaft/erich-vad-im-interview-ueber-das-schicksal-der-ukraine-wird-in-washington-und-moskau-entschieden-li.2185298.
23 See the letter at https://www.change.org/p/offener-brief-an-bundeskanzler-scholz, accessed 6 May 2024.
24 Eva Högl, '2022 Annual Report of the Parliamentary Commissioner for the Armed Forces', German Bundestag, 28 February 2023, p. 13. https://www.bundestag.de/resource/blob/949898/350e96fe32bce5146dbbf841d923c7eb/annual_report_2022_64th_report.pdf.
25 Ibid., p. 8.
26 Ibid., pp. 9, 17.
27 Sandra Ward, '"Arrogant, unfähig, nutzlos": CIA-Experte zerlegt deutsche Spione', *Focus*, 11 September 2022. https://www.focus.de/politik/ausland/interview-mit-geheimdienst-experte-arrogant-unfaehig-buerokratisch-nutzlos-cia-experte-zerlegt-deutsche-spione_id_141194052.html.
28 Alfons Mais, posted on LinkedIn on 24 February 2022. https://www.linkedin.com/posts/alfons-mais-46744b99_du-wachst-morgens-auf-und-stellst-fest-es-activity-6902486582067044353-RZky.
29 Högl, '2022 Annual Report of the Parliamentary Commissioner for the Armed Forces', p. 6.
30 Matthias Gebauer and Marina Kormbaki, 'Ein Minister zeigt Nerven', *Der Spiegel*, 15 May 2024. https://www.spiegel.de/politik/deutschland/boris-pistorius-unter-druck-ein-minister-zeigt-nerven-a-254048fe-9bec-4081-902f-6a34d59c4470.
31 Giovanni Sgaravatti et al., 'National Fiscal Policy Responses to the Energy Crisis', *Bruegel*, 26 June 2023. https://www.bruegel.org/dataset/national-policies-shield-consumers-rising-energy-prices.

NOTES

32 Jochen Roose, 'Enthusiastic, Critical, Unimpressed, Weary – the Germans and Europe', Konrad-Adenauer-Stiftung, 5 February 2024.
33 Alessandro Gasparotti and Matthias Kullas, '20 Years of the Euro: Winners and Losers', *Centre for European Policy*, February 2019. www.cep.eu/Studien/20_Jahre_Euro_-_Gewinner_und_Verlierer/cepStudy_20_years_Euro_-_Winners_and_Losers.pdf.
34 Patrick Donahue, 'Merkel Signals New Era for Europe as Trump Smashes Consensus', *Bloomberg*, 28 May 2017.
35 Donald Trump at a breakfast meeting with NATO Secretary-General Jens Stoltenberg on 11 July 2018. Clip from Associated Press. https://www.youtube.com/watch?v=9LLZBVTid4I&t=74s.
36 Jacob Poushter and Sarah Austin, 'The U.S.-German Relationship Remains Strong', Pew Research Center, 17 October 2022.
37 Robert Kagan, *Of Paradise and Power: America and Europe in the New World Order*. New York: Vintage, 2004.
38 'What's in the Inflation Reduction Act?' Committee for a Responsible Federal Budget, 7 September 2022. https://www.crfb.org/blogs/whats-inflation-reduction-act.
39 Christian Scheinert, 'EU's Response to the US Inflation Reduction Act', EU Parliament Policy Department for Economic, Scientific and Quality of Life Policies, 2 June 2023. https://www.europarl.europa.eu/RegData/etudes/IDAN/2023/740087/IPOL_IDA(2023)740087_EN.pdf.
40 Jannik Jansen, Philipp Jäger and Nils Redeker, 'For Climate, Profits, or Resilience?', *Hertie School*, 5 May 2023. https://www.delorscentre.eu/fileadmin/2_Research/1_About_our_research/2_Research_centres/6_Jacques_Delors_Centre/Publications/20230505_JDC_IRA.pdf.
41 Glenn Plaskin, 'The Playboy Interview with Donald Trump', *Playboy*, 1 March 1990. https://www.playboy.com/read/playboy-interview-donald-trump-1990.
42 'Kritik an Trump nach Bericht über Truppenabzugspläne', *Zeit Online*, 6 June 2020. https://www.zeit.de/politik/deutschland/2020-06/usa-truppen-abzug-deutschland-donald-trump-weckruf.
43 Frank Heindl, 'Donald Trump hat noch nicht angerufen', interview with Ralf Hechler, Mayor of Ramstein-Miesenbach, *Web.de*, 19 June 2020. https://web.de/magazine/politik/donald-trump-angerufen-ramstein-fuerchtet-abzug-amerikaner-34799464.
44 Stefan Nicola and Christoph Rauwald, 'Bosch Quits $2.6 Billion Solar Foray in Week of Suntech Failure', *Bloomberg*, 22 March 2013.

45   Irene Preisinger and Victoria Bryan, 'China's CATL to Build its First European EV Battery Factory in Germany', *Reuters*, 9 July 2018. https://www.reuters.com/article/idUSKBN1JZ160.
46   Jost Wübbeke et al., 'Made in China 2025: The Making of a High-Tech Superpower and Consequences for Industrial Countries', *Mercator Institute for China Studies*, December 2016.
47   'China Manufacturing 2025: Putting Industrial Policy Ahead of Market Forces', European Union Chamber of Commerce in China, 7 March 2017.
48   Jürgen Matthes, 'Gegenseitige Abhängigkeit im Handel zwischen China, der EU und Deutschland', Institut der deutschen Wirtschaft Köln, 13 June 2022.
49   William Wilkes, 'Germany Withdraws Approval of Chinese Takeover of Aixtron', *Wall Street Journal*, 24 October 2016.
50   Janosch Delcker, 'Sigmar Gabriel's Mission to Halt China's Investment Spree', *Politico*, 1 November 2016.
51   US Dept. of Justice press release, 19 May 2014. https://www.justice.gov/opa/pr/us-charges-five-chinese-military-hackers-cyber-espionage-against-us-corporations-and-labor.
52   US Trade Representative, 'Findings of the Investigation into China's Acts, Policies and Practices related to Technology Transfer, Intellectual Property and Innovations', 22 March 2018. https://ustr.gov/sites/default/files/Section%20301%20FINAL.PDF.
53   Lorand Laskai, 'Why Does Everyone Hate Made in China 2025?', Council on Foreign Relations, 28 March 2018. https://www.cfr.org/blog/why-does-everyone-hate-made-china-2025.
54   Max J. Zenglein and Anna Holzmann, 'Evolving Made in China 2025', *Mercator Institute for China Studies*, 2 July 2019. https://merics.org/en/report/evolving-made-china-2025.
55   Victoria Waldersee, 'Senior Staff at Auditing Firm Distance Themselves from Audit of VW's China Plant', *Reuters*, 13 December 2023. https://www.reuters.com/business/autos-transportation/auditing-firm-distances-itself-duos-work-vws-china-plant-2023-12-13.
56   Bruno Maçães, *Belt and Road: A Chinese World Order*. London: Hurst, 2018.
57   Martin Orth, 'Duisburg, die China-Stadt', deutschland.de, 22 November 2021. https://www.deutschland.de/de/topic/wirtschaft/duisburg-die-china-stadt.
58   'Elmos Chip Factory Cannot Be Sold to Chinese Investor – Cabinet Blocks Sale', Federal Ministry for Economic Affairs and Climate

Action, 1 November 2022. https://www.bmwk.de/Redaktion/EN/Pressemitteilungen/2022/11/20221109-elmos-chip-factory-cannot-be-sold-to-chinese-investor-cabinet-blocks-sale.html.

59 David Baqaee, Julian Hinz et al. 'What If? The Effects of a Hard Decouple from China on the German Economy', *Kiel Institute for the World Economy*, January 2024.

60 Speech by Foreign Minister Baerbock at MERICS on the future of Germany's policy on China, 13 July 2023. https://www.auswaertiges-amt.de/en/newsroom/news/policy-on-china/2608766.

61 Tom Hancock, 'German Direct Investment in China Rose to Record in 2023', *Bloomberg*, 16 February 2024.

SEVEN: BROKEN LADDER

1 'Vor 60 Jahren: Als in Bad Homburg ein ganzes Haus umzog', *Frankfurter Neue Presse*, 2 November 2018. https://www.fnp.de/lokales/hochtaunus/bad-homburg-ort47554/jahren-homburg-ganzes-haus-umzog-10439835.html.

2 Joachim Scholtyseck, *Der Aufstieg der Quandts*, C. H. Beck, 22 September 2011.

3 Eric Fiedler, dir., 'Das Schweigen der Quandts', *NDR*, 2007.

4 Data compiled by Bloomberg Billionaires Index. https://www.bloomberg.com/billionaires/?sref=KeM3kOBb.

5 Horst von Buttlar, 'Susanne Klatten übergibt Beteiligungen an ihre Kinder', *WirtschaftsWoche*, 6 June 2024. https://www.wiwo.de/unternehmen/dienstleister/skion-susanne-klatten-uebergibt-beteiligungen-an-ihre-kinder/29835398.html.

6 Christina Deckwirth, 'Fragwürdige Großspenden der BMW-Großaktionäre Quandt/Klatten', *Lobby Control*, 15 October 2013. https://www.lobbycontrol.de/parteienfinanzierung/grossspenden-der-bmw-grossaktionaere-quandtklatten-17123.

7 Data compiled from Bundestag records of donations over €50,000. https://www.bundestag.de/parlament/praesidium/parteienfinanzierung/fundstellen50000.

8 'Man fühlt sich grauenvoll und schämt sich', *WirtschaftsWoche*, 28 September 2011. https://www.wiwo.de/unternehmen/ns-vergangenheit-der-quandts-man-fuehlt-sich-grauenvoll-und-schaemt-sich/5222268-all.html.

9 'Das Schweigen der Quandts', Video, 11:06.
10 Dietmar Student and Martin Noé, 'Wer würde denn mit uns tauschen wollen?', *Manager Magazin*, 20 June 2019. https://www.manager-magazin.de/unternehmen/susanne-klatten-stefan-quandt-erstes-gemeinsames-interview-a-00000000-0002-0001-0000-000164471680.
11 Julia Friedrichs and Jochen Breyer, 'Die geheime Welt der Superreichen – Das Milliardenspiel', *ZDF*, 12 December 2023. https://www.zdf.de/dokumentation/zdfzeit/zdfzeit-die-geheime-welt-der-superreichen-100.html.
12 Christoph Neßhöver, 'Die Großaktionäre von BMW sind wieder die reichsten Deutschen', *Manager Magazin*, 9 November 2023.
13 Julia Jirmann and Christoph Trautvetter, 'Der Steuersatz des typischen Multimillionärs im Vergleich zum Durchschnittspaar', Arbeitspapier 1 zum Jahrbuch Steuergerechtigkeit 2023, 11 December 2023. www.netzwerk-steuergerechtigkeit.de/wp-content/uploads/2023/12/Steuersatz_Multimillionaer.pdf.
14 Michaela Alka and Christoph Trautvetter, 'Keine Angst vor Steuerflucht', Oxfam Deutschland and Netzwerk Steuergerechtigkeit, July 2024. https://www.oxfam.de/system/files/documents/oxfam_netzwerk_steuergerechtigkeit_2024_keine_angst_vor_steuerflucht_final.pdf.
15 Julia Jirmann, 'Der Weg zu einer gerechten Erbschafts – und Schenkungsteuer – ein Reformvorschlag', *Netzwerk Steuergerechtigkeit*, 10 October 2023. https://www.netzwerk-steuergerechtigkeit.de/der-weg-zu-einer-gerechten-erbschaftsteuer-reformvorschlag.
16 '29. Subventionsbericht des Bundes 2021–2024', Federal Finance Ministry, 6 September 2023.
17 Bundestag, 'Übersicht über das Lastenausgleichsgesetz', 26 September 2023. www.bundestag.de/resource/blob/974288/797ce8deed37cc0d7e6f229c4ba0383f/WD-3-107-23-WD-4-057-23-pdf.pdf.
18 Thilo N. H. Albers, Charlotte Bartels and Moritz Schularick, 'Wealth and its Distribution in Germany, 1895–2018', World Inequality Lab, June 2022, p. 4. https://wid.world/document/wealth-and-its-distribution-in-germany-1895-2018.
19 Albers et al., 'Wealth and its Distribution in Germany, 1895–2018'.
20 'A Broken Social Elevator? How to Promote Social Mobility', *OECD*, 15 June 2018. https://www.oecd.org/social/broken-elevator-how-to-promote-social-mobility-9789264301085-en.htm.

NOTES

21 Ludwig Erhard, 'Sonntagsreden', cited in n.d. https://www.ludwig-erhard.de/wp-content/uploads/2023/09/Ludwig-Erhard-Stiftung_2019_Wohlstand-fuer-alle_70-Jahre-Grundgesetz.pdf.
22 'House or Flat – Owning or Renting', n.d., European Commission, accessed 18 September 2024. https://ec.europa.eu/eurostat/cache/digpub/housing/bloc-1a.html.
23 'Household Wealth and Finances in Germany: Results of the 2021 Household Wealth Survey', n.d. Deutsche Bundesbank, accessed 18 September 2024. https://www.bundesbank.de/resource/blob/908924/3ef9d9a4eaeae8a8779ccec3ac464970/mL/2023-04-vermoegensbefragung-data.pdf.
24 Deutscher Bundestag, Parlamentsnachrichten, 25 September 2023. https://www.bundestag.de/presse/hib/kurzmeldungen-967750.
25 'Wohnungsnot in Deutschland – Zahlen, Fakten, Studien', n.d. Hans-Böckler-Stiftung, accessed 18 September 2024. https://www.boeckler.de/de/auf-einen-blick-17945-20782.htm.
26 '5 Jahre Mietpreisbremse: In nahezu allen Großstädten steigen die Preise weiter – plus 44 Prozent in Berlin', n.d. immowelt.de. https://www.immowelt.de/ueberuns/presse/pressemitteilungenkontakt/immoweltde/2020/5-jahre-mietpreisbremse-in-nahezu-allen-grosstaedten-steigen-die-preise-weiter-plus-44-prozent-in-berlin.
27 'Politik für bezahlbares Wohnen braucht Investitionen', 2024. Deutscher Mieterbund. https://mieterbund.de/aktuelles/meldungen/politik-fuer-bezahlbares-wohnen-braucht-investitionen.
28 'Schwangerenversorgung und Zugang zur Hebamme nach sozialem Status: Eine Analyse mit Routinedaten der BARMER', *NCBI*, 2021. https://www.ncbi.nlm.nih.gov/pmc/articles/PMC11248034.
29 'Sozioökonomischer Status und Gesundheit – Datenlage, Befunde und Entwicklungen in Deutschland', Robert Koch Institut. https://edoc.rki.de/bitstream/handle/176904/11674/0342-300X-2024-3-172.pdf?sequence=1&isAllowed=y.
30 Marcel Fratzscher, *Verteilungskampf: Warum Deutschland immer ungleicher wird*. Hanser: n.p., 2016.
31 Bertelsmann Stiftung, 'Ländermonitoring Frühkindliche Bildungssysteme 2023' https://www.bertelsmann-stiftung.de/de/themen/aktuelle-meldungen/2023/november/mehr-plaetze-und-bessere-qualitaet-in-kitas-bis-2030-wenn-jetzt-entschlossen-gehandelt-wird.
32 Amelie Knippert, 'Kita-Platz: 5 Tipps, die Ihre Chancen deutlich erhöhen', Praxistipps FOCUS, 2021. https://praxistipps.focus.de/kita-platz-5-tipps-die-ihre-chancen-deutlich-erhoehen_109000.

NOTES

33 Vogt, Sylvia. 2019. 'Betreuungskrise in Berlin: Warum ein Berliner Vater 5000 Euro für einen Kita-Platz geboten hat', tagespiegel.de. https://www.tagesspiegel.de/berlin/warum-ein-berliner-vater-5000-euro-fur-einen-kita-platz-geboten-hat-4641802.html.

34 'Studie: Kitas mit Kindern aus sozioökonomisch benachteiligten Familien sind vielfach mehrbelastet', 2024. Friedrich-Ebert-Stiftung. https://www.fes.de/presse/aktuelle-pressehinweise/studie-kitas-mit-kindern-aus-soziooekonomisch-benachteiligten-familien-sind-vielfach-mehrbelastet.

35 'Überlastung, Stress und Erschöpfung in vielen Kitas'. https://www.ash-berlin.eu/fileadmin/Daten/News/2024/2024_08_27_Aufruf_aus_der_Wissenschaft_zur_Kitakrise.pdf.

36 Jan Grossarth-Maticek, Kathrin Kann and Sebastian Koufen, 'Privatschulen in Deutschland – Fakten und Hintergründe', Federal Statistics Office, 10 August 2020. https://www.destatis.de/DE/Themen/Gesellschaft-Umwelt/Bildung-Forschung-Kultur/Schulen/Publikationen/Downloads-Schulen/privatschulen-deutschland-dossier-2020.pdf.

37 'INSM-Bildungsmonitor 2023: Die Qualität nimmt ab', Initiative Neue Soziale Marktwirtschaft, 12 Sept. 2023. https://www.iwd.de/artikel/bildungsmonitor-2023-die-qualitaet-nimmt-ab-596002.

38 'Der Lehrermangel in Deutschland verschärft sich', Institut der deutschen Wirtschaft, 31 May 2022. https://www.iwd.de/artikel/der-lehrermangel-in-deutschland-verschaerft-sich-546423.

39 '2021 kamen 4,3 Auszubildende auf 10 Studierende, 1950 waren es noch 75,5 Azubis', 2023. Statistisches Bundesamt. https://www.destatis.de/DE/Presse/Pressemitteilungen/2023/06/PD23_N036_12.html.

40 'Der Qualitätsreport Duales Studium 2023'. n.d. DGB-Jugend, accessed 18 September 2024. https://jugend.dgb.de/ueber-uns/meldungen/studium/++co++34bb137a-5871-11ee-b351-001a4a16011a.

41 Mathias Dolls, Florian Dorn et al., 'Gerechtigkeit für die Mitte?', Hanns-Seidel-Stiftung, 7 June 2023. https://www.hss.de/news/detail/neue-studie-gerechtigkeit-fuer-die-mitte-news10062.

42 Ibid.

43 OECD, 'Is the German Middle Class Crumbling? Risks and Opportunities', *OECD Publishing*, 1 December 2021. https://doi.org/10.1787/845208d7-en.

44 Oliver Nachtwey. 'Interview mit Oliver Nachtwey', Hans Boeckler Stiftung, n.d. https://www.boeckler.de/de/magazin-mitbestimmung-2744-oliver-nachtwey-ueber-schwieriger-gewordene-aufstiegschancen-6038.htm.

NOTES

45 Data from Bundesarbeitsgemeinschaft Wohnungslosenhilfe e.V. https://www.bagw.de/fileadmin/bagw/media/Doc/PRM/PRM_PM_BAG_W_Pressemappe_Hochrechnung_Zahl_der_wohnungslosen_Menschen.pdf.
46 OECD data on homelessness in Germany and the UK. https://webfs.oecd.org/Els-com/Affordable_Housing_Database/Country%20notes/Homelessness-GBR.pdf. https://webfs.oecd.org/Els-com/Affordable_Housing_Database/Country%20notes/Homelessness-DEU.pdf.
47 Facts and Figures at Deutsche Tafel eV, accessed 19 June 2024. https://www.tafel.de/fileadmin/media/Presse/Hintergrundinformationen/2024-06-26_TD_Faktenblaetter.pdf.
48 'Armut in der Inflation. Paritätischer Armutsbericht 2024', Deutscher Paritätischer Wohlfahrtsverband Gesamtverband e.V., March 2024. https://www.der-paritaetische.de/fileadmin/user_upload/Schwerpunkte/Armutsbericht/doc/Paritaetischer_Armutsbericht_2024.pdf.
49 Bundestag, 'Altersarmut in Deutschland', 4 May 2023. https://www.bundestag.de/presse/hib/kurzmeldungen-946652.
50 Guido Westerwelle, 'An die deutsche Mittelschicht denkt niemand', *Die Welt*, 11 February 2010. https://www.welt.de/debatte/article6347490/An-die-deutsche-Mittelschicht-denkt-niemand.html.
51 Katja Belousova, 'Sozialbetrug: Wie groß ist das Problem?', *ZDF*, 1 September 2023. https://www.zdf.de/nachrichten/wirtschaft/sozialbetrug-clans-ausmass-100.html.
52 Sebastian Dullien and Katja Rietzler, 'Die Mär vom aufgeblähten Sozialstaat', Böckler Impuls 4/2024, Hans Böckler Stiftung, pp. 6–7. https://www.boeckler.de/de/boeckler-impuls-die-mar-vom-aufgeblahten-sozialstaat-57956.htm.
53 Sebastian Weiermann, 'Thomas Wasilewski: Ein Bürgergeld-Empfänger wehrt sich', *ND*, 27 March 2024. https://www.nd-aktuell.de/artikel/1166430.armut-thomas-wasilewski-ein-buergergeld-empfaenger-wehrt-sich.html.
54 Benedikt Peters, 'Fünf Euro, drei Mahlzeiten – und jetzt die Inflation', *Süddeutsche Zeitung*, 9 May 2022. https://www.sueddeutsche.de/projekte/artikel/politik/leben-mit-hartz-iv-fuenf-euro-drei-mahlzeiten-und-nun-die-inflation-e259201.
55 Weiermann, 'Thomas Wasilewski,' *ND*, 27 March 2024.

56 Sanktionsfrei e.V., for instance, has distributed hundreds of thousands of euros to welfare recipients and also raises awareness over social inequality.

EIGHT: HOUSE DIVIDED

1. 'Europawahl 2014', *Die Bundeswahlleiterin*, accessed 11 April 2024. https://www.bundeswahlleiterin.de/europawahlen/2014/ergebnisse/bund-99.html.
2. 'AfD Sachsen: Wahlprogramm 2014, Langfassung', AfD, accessed 11 April 2024. https://programmarchiv.projekt-ergebnisse.info/media/files/sachsen-2014-.pdf.
3. 'A very British German', *Frankfurter Allgemeine Zeitung*, 21 September 2017. https://www.faz.net/aktuell/stil/mode-design/alexander-gaulands-kleidungsstil-a-very-british-german-15203166.html.
4. 'Alexander Gauland: Wir haben Russland falsch behandelt', *Zeit Online*, 11 September 2014. https://www.zeit.de/politik/deutschland/2014-09/alexander-gauland-afd-brandenburg-landtagswahl.
5. 'Interview mit Björn Höcke, Spitzenkandidat der AfD Thüringen', AfD Thüringen, accessed 11 April 2024. https://www.afd-thueringen.de/thueringen-2/2014/08/interview-mit-bjoern-hoecke-spitzenkandidat-der-afd-thueringen.
6. 'Erfurter Resolution', AfD Thüringen, March 2015.
7. 'AfD-Mann im Krankenhaus: Kalbitz verletzt Parteifreund mit Boxschlag zur Begrüßung', *RND*, 17 August 2020. https://www.rnd.de/politik/kalbitz-schlagt-afd-mann-hohloch-zur-begrussung-parteifreund-liegt-mit-inneren-verletzungen-im-krankenhaus-KFHXHWUUUZBG5BPLBNSAG2F6VM.html.
8. 'Erklärung im Wortlaut Bernd Lucke zu seinem Austritt aus der AfD', *Der Spiegel*, 8 July 2015. https://www.spiegel.de/politik/deutschland/bernd-lucke-erklaerung-zu-austritt-aus-der-afd-a-1042734.html.
9. 'Germany's Eurosceptic AfD Party Faces Split as Lucke Quits', *Financial Times*, 9 July 2015. https://www.ft.com/content/698b46fa-262b-11e5-bd83-71cb60e8f08c.
10. 'Why Germany Needs the Far Right', *Politico*, 5 November 2015. https://www.politico.eu/article/germanys-afd-fills-a-far-right-void-refugee-crisis-anti-immigrant-voters.
11. 'Migrationsbericht 2014', Bundesamt für Migration und Flüchtlinge, 6 January 2016. https://www.bamf.de/SharedDocs/Anlagen/DE/

Forschung/Migrationsberichte/migrationsbericht-2014.html?nn=447198.

12 'Syrien-Flüchtlinge dürfen in Deutschland bleiben', *Der Spiegel*, 25 August 2018. https://www.spiegel.de/politik/deutschland/syrien-fluechtlinge-deutschland-setzt-dublin-verfahren-aus-a-1049639.html.

13 'AfD-Vize Gauland sieht Flüchtlingskrise als Geschenk', *Der Spiegel*, 12 December 2015. https://www.spiegel.de/politik/deutschland/afd-alexander-gauland-sieht-fluechtlingskrise-als-geschenk-a-1067356.html.

14 'Paris Attack Terrorists Used Refugee Chaos to Enter France, Says PM Valls', *France 24*, 19 November 2015. https://www.france24.com/en/20151119-paris-attackers-slip-refugee-migrant-crisis-terrorism.

15 'Schlussbericht des Parlamentarischen Untersuchungsausschusses IV', Landtag Nordrhein-Westfalen, 16. Wahlperiode, 23 March 2017. https://www.landtag.nrw.de/home/der-landtag/ausschusse-und-gremien-1/untersuchungsausschusse/fruhere-untersuchungsausschus-1/16wp-pua-iv-abgeschlossen.html.

16 'Lehren aus der Kölner Silvesternacht', *Deutsche Welle*, 31 December 2020. https://www.dw.com/de/f%C3%BCnf-jahre-danach-lehren-aus-der-k%C3%B6lner-silvesternacht/a-55980209.

17 'Afghan Migrant Shot Dead After Hatchet Attack on German Train', *Wall Street Journal*, 18 July 2016. https://www.wsj.com/articles/attack-on-german-train-injures-multiple-people-1468876588.

18 'Anis Amri: Overview', Counter Extremism Project, accessed 11 April 2024. https://www.counterextremism.com/extremists/anis-amri.

19 'Rechtsextremismus und rechtsextremistischer Terrorismus', Bundesamt für Verfassungsschutz, accessed 11 April 2024. https://www.verfassungsschutz.de/DE/verfassungsschutz/der-bericht/vsb-rechtsextremismus/2022-vsb-rechtsextremismus_artikel.html.

20 Simon Schnetzer, *Jugend in Deutschland 2024*, Berlin, 23 April 2024.

21 'Das Umfragehoch der AfD: Aktuelle Erkenntnisse über die AfD-Wahlbereitschaft aus dem WSI-Erwerbspersonenpanel', Hans-Böckler-Stiftung, November 2023. https://www.boeckler.de/de/pressemitteilungen-2675-studie-leuchtet-anstieg-der-afd-wahlbereitschaft-aus-54087.htm.

22 A. Tutić, A. and H. von Hermanni, 'Sozioökonomischer Status, Deprivation und die Affinität zur AfD – Eine Forschungsnotiz', *Cologne Journal of Sociology and Social Psychology* 70 (2018), 275–94. https://doi.org/10.1007/s11577-018-0523-0.

23 Roberto Heinrich, 'AfD-Wähler: Herkunft, Profil und Motivation', Marktforschung.de, 15 February 2024. https://www.marktfo

rschung.de/marktforschung/a/afd-waehler-herkunft-profil-und-motivation.

24 'Joachim Gauck: Keine deutsche Identität ohne Auschwitz', Speech delivered in the Deutscher Bundestag, 27 January 2015. https://www.bundestag.de/webarchiv/textarchiv/2015/kw05_gedenkstunde-357044.

25 'The German Right Believes It's Time to Discard the Country's Historical Guilt', *Wall Street Journal*, 2 March 2017. https://www.wsj.com/articles/the-german-right-believes-its-time-to-discard-their-countrys-historical-guilt-1488467995.

26 YouTube video, accessed 30 May 2024. https://www.youtube.com/watch?v=eGFWIF34QqA.

27 Armin Pfahl-Traughber, 'Die Neue Rechte: ideologische Auffassungen & politische Wirkungen,' Stiftung Demokratie Saarland, June 29, 2023. https://www.youtube.com/watch?v=Y9ag879JL8A

28 'Secret Plan against Germany', *Correctiv*, 15 January 2024. https://correctiv.org/en/top-stories/2024/01/15/secret-plan-against-germany.

29 'Zufriedenheit mit dem Bundeskabinett: Habeck, Baerbock und Heil mit Zugewinnen', *Ipsos*, 12 March 2024. https://www.ipsos.com/de-de/zufriedenheit-mit-dem-bundeskabinett-habeck-baerbock-und-heil-mit-zugewinnen.

30 'Wer organisierte die Blockade gegen Habeck?' *Die Zeit*, 10 January 2024. https://www.zeit.de/politik/deutschland/2024-01/bauern-schluettsiel-habeck-rechte-demonstration.

31 'Staatsanwaltschaft ermittelt wegen Plakat auf Bauernprotest', *Stuttgarter Nachrichten*, 9 January 2024. https://www.stuttgarter-nachrichten.de/inhalt.pforzheim-staatsanwaltschaft-ermittelt-wegen-plakat-auf-bauernprotest.b23e9ddf-012b-40cc-9501-6340125b63c3.html.

32 'Verdächtiger Brief: Büro von Robert Habeck evakuiert', *Hamburger Abendblatt*, 3 February 2024. https://www.abendblatt.de/region/schleswig-holstein/article241570616/Verdaechtiger-Brief-Buero-von-Robert-Habeck-evakuiert.html.

33 'Jetzt äußert sich Habeck zum Vorfall an der Fähre', T-Online.de, 5 January 2024. https://www.t-online.de/nachrichten/deutschland/id_100314586/habeck-aeussert-sich-zu-vorfall-auf-faehre.html.

34 'Steinwurf auf Wahlkampfveranstaltung', *Polizei Bayern*, 17 September 2023. https://www.polizei.bayern.de/aktuelles/pressemitteilungen/055493/index.html.

35 'Aschermittwoch: Ricarda Lang in Schorndorf beschimpft und bei Abreise behindert', *SWR*, 15 February 2024. https://www.swr.de/

swraktuell/baden-wuerttemberg/stuttgart/stoerer-beschimpfen-ricarda-lang-nach-politischem-aschermittwoch-100.html.
36 'Ministerin erstattet Anzeige wegen Hausfriedensbruchs', Nds. Ministerium für Ernährung, Landwirtschaft und Verbraucherschutz, 19 December 2023. https://www.ml.niedersachsen.de/startseite/aktuelles/pressemitteilungen/ministerin-erstattet-anzeige-wegen-hausfriedensbruchs-228101.html.
37 'Angriffe auf Parteirepräsentanten im Jahr 2023', Deutscher Bundestag, Parlamentsnachrichten, 1 February 2024. https://www.bundestag.de/presse/hib/kurzmeldungen-988578.
38 'Söder: Die Grünen passen nicht zu Bayern', CSU.de, 4 September 2023. https://www.csu.de/aktuell/meldungen/august-2023/soeder-die-gruenen-passen-nicht-zu-bayern.
39 'Die Grünen sind ein Sicherheitsrisiko für das Land', *Focus*, 23 September 2023. https://www.focus.de/politik/deutschland/fdp-general-dringt-auf-umdenken-in-asyl-politik-die-gruenen-sind-ein-sicherheitsrisiko-fuer-das-land_id_211349750.html.
40 'Von wegen cool und öko – wie die Grünen Wirtschaft und Natur zerstören', Sahra Wagenknecht, YouTube, 20 October 2022. https://www.youtube.com/watch?v=bQNsHivR9AU&t=964s.
41 'Muss man die Deutschen vor dem Verfassungsschutz schützen, Herr Maassen? Der ehemalige Verfassungsschutz-Chef über eine Behörde ausser Rand und Band', *Die Weltwoche*, 13 April 2024. https://weltwoche.de/daily/muss-man-die-deutschen-vor-dem-verfassungsschutz-schuetzen-herr-maassen-der-ehemalige-verfassungsschutz-chef-ueber-eine-behoerde-ausser-rand-und-band.
42 'Baerbock drei Mal so oft wie Laschet von Hass überzogen', *Agence France-Presse*, 27 July 2021. https://www.merkur.de/politik/baerbock-annalena-gruene-hass-facebook-social-media-spiegel-bundestagswahl-2021-berlin-90880237.html.
43 'Neubauer sieht Hass gegen Aktivisten als Problem für Zivilgesellschaft', *Die Zeit*, 18 February 2024. https://www.zeit.de/gesellschaft/2024-02/klimaaktivistin-luisa-neubauer-hass-drohungen.
44 Petra Kelly, 'Reunification and the German Greens', *Capitalism Nature Socialism* 2, no. 2 (1991): 17–22.
45 '"Die kleinen Paschas" – Merz polarisiert und stellt konkrete Forderungen', *Die Welt*, 11 January 2023. https://www.welt.de/politik/deutschland/plus243139885/Friedrich-Merz-polarisiert-bei-Markus-Lanz-Die-kleinen-Paschas.html.

46 'Habeck will 500.000 Wärmepumpen jährlich', Tagesschau.de, 29 June 2022. https://www.tagesschau.de/wirtschaft/waermepumpen-offensive-101.html.
47 'Grüne versuchen seit Jahren vergeblich, eine Wärmepumpe in die Parteizentrale einzubauen', *Die Welt*, 9 June 2023. https://www.welt.de/politik/deutschland/article245770810/Gruene-versuchen-seit-Jahren-vergeblich-eine-Waermepumpe-in-die-Parteizentrale-einzubauen.html.
48 'Aufarbeitung und Verantwortung', *Die Grünen*, accessed 18 April 2024. https://www.gruene.de/artikel/aufarbeitung-und-verantwortung.
49 'Bundesweite Durchsuchungen und Festnahme Reichsbürger und Selbstverwalter Szene', Bundeskriminalamt, 8 December 2022.
50 'Unter Terrorverdacht stehender "Reichsbürger" suchte für Fluthilfe die Nähe zu "Querdenkern"', *Frankfurter Rundschau*, 12 July 2023. https://www.fr.de/politik/unter-terrorverdacht-stehender-reichsbuerger-suchte-fuer-fluthilfe-die-naehe-zu-querdenkern-92397875.html.
51 'Bundeswehrveteranen in zentraler Rolle bei Reichsbürger-Verschwörung', *Die Zeit*, 25 January 2024. https://www.zeit.de/politik/deutschland/2024-01/reichsbuerger-anklage-bundeswehrsoldaten-raedelsfuehrer-verdeckte-ermittler.
52 'Anklage gegen zehn Personen u.a. wegen Mitgliedschaft in oder Unterstützung einer terroristischen Vereinigung und Vorbereitung eines hochverräterischen Unternehmens vor dem Oberlandesgericht Frankfurt erhoben', Generalbundesanwalt, 12 December 2023.
53 'Festnahmen von 25 mutmaßlichen Mitgliedern und Unterstützern einer terroristischen Vereinigung sowie Durchsuchungsmaßnahmen in elf Bundesländern bei insgesamt 52 Beschuldigten', Generalbundesanwalt, 7 December 2022.
54 'Münchner Koch sollte offenbar "Reichsbürger"-Truppen verpflegen', *Süddeutsche Zeitung*, 9 December 2022. https://www.sueddeutsche.de/muenchen/muenchen-reichsbuerger-frank-heppner-koch-festnahme-1.5712872.
55 '"Grüße an dich und dein Seelentier": Wie das BKA drei verdeckte Ermittler in die Reichsbürger-Gruppe einschleuste', *Die Stern*, 25 January 2024. https://www.stern.de/politik/wie-das-bka-drei-verdeckte-ermittler-in-die-reichsbuerger-gruppe-einschleuste-34393538.html.
56 'Bundesweite Razzia gegen Reichsbürger: Durchsuchungen auch im Bodenseekreis', *Südkurier*, 8 December 2022. https://www.suedkurier.de/ueberregional/politik/festnahmen-bei-razzia-in-rei

NOTES

chsbuergerszene-gruppe-plante-offenbar-staatsumsturz;art410 924,11389332.

57 'Verfassungsschutzchef plädiert für Check bei Arbeit in Sicherheitsbehörden', *Der Spiegel*, 8 December 2022. https://www.spiegel.de/politik/deutschland/terrorrazzia-thomas-haldenwang-fuer-check-bei-arbeit-in-sicherheitsbehoerden-a-05e9fdc8-b6a8-4223-abf8-3d9210d44ddf.

58 'Reichsbürger und Selbstverwalter: Zahlen und Fakten', Bundesamt für Verfassungsschutz, accessed 27 April 2024. https://www.verfassungsschutz.de/DE/themen/reichsbuerger-und-selbstverwalter/zahlen-und-fakten/zahlen-und-fakten_node.html#:~:text=Jahr%202022%20an.-,Personenpotenzial,2021%3A%2021.000)%20Personen%20zuzurechnen.

59 'Kein Staat, meine Regeln', Konrad Adenauer Stiftung, March 2023. https://www.kas.de/documents/252038/22161843/Kein+Staat%2C+meine+Regeln.pdf/ff69929e-a26f-b199-4188-8645a9add2f6?

60 Matthes Haug, *Das Deutsche Reich 1871 bis heute*, Amadeus-Verlag, 2024.

61 'Alters- und Geschlechterstruktur unter Rechtsextremisten und Reichsbürgern', Landesamt für Verfassungsschutz Baden-Württemberg, 19 January 2021. https://www.verfassungsschutz-bw.de/,Lde/Alters-+und+Geschlechterstruktur+unter+Rechtsextremisten+und+_Reichsbuergern.

62 'Kein Staat, meine Regeln', Konrad Adenauer Stiftung, March 2023.

63 'Staatsgründung', *Königreich Deutschland*, accessed 28 April 2024. https://koenigreichdeutschland.org/de/rechtliche-grundlage-koenigreich-deutschland.html.

64 'Reichsbürger Peter Fitzek zu Haftstrafe verurteilt', *MDR*, 14 July 2023. https://www.mdr.de/nachrichten/sachsen-anhalt/dessau/wittenberg/reichsbuerger-fitzek-verurteilt-haftstrafe-102.html.

65 'Verfassung des Königreiches Deutschland', *Königreich Deutschland*, accessed 28 April 2024. https://koenigreichdeutschland.org/files/krd/rechtliches/Verfassung/PDF%20%20Version%20Verfassung.pdf.

66 'Video: Volkslehrer und Lichtwerk-TV auf der KRD-Messe 2020', *Königreich Deutschland*, accessed 28 April 2024. https://archiv.koenigreichdeutschland.org/de/neuigkeit/video-volkslehrer-und-lichtwerk-tv.html.

67 'Das "Königreich Deutschland" – Staatssimulation von Reichsbürgern und Selbstverwaltern', Bundesamt für Verfassungsschutz, accessed 28 April 2024. https://koenigreichdeutschland.org/de/verfassung.html.
68 'So trickst Reichsbürger Fitzek Deutschland aus', *MDR*, 22 August 2022. https://www.mdr.de/nachrichten/sachsen/reichsbuerger-fitzek-koenig-deutschland-sachsen-114.html.
69 Bundesamt für Verfassungsschutz, 'Islamistisches Personenpotenzial'. Verfassungschutz.de, accessed 31 May 2024. https://www.verfassungsschutz.de/DE/themen/islamismus-und-islamistischer-terrorismus/zahlen-und-fakten/zahlen-und-fakten_node.html#doc678982bodyText1.
70 'Demokratievertrauen in Krisenzeiten', Friedrich Ebert Stiftung, April 2023. https://library.fes.de/pdf-files/pbud/20287-20230505.pdf.
71 'Schweigende Mehrheit muss aufwachen', *ARD*, 11 January 2024. https://www.tagesschau.de/investigativ/kontraste/verfassungsschutz-haldenwang-rechtsextremismus-100.html.

NINE: ANGST AND ISOLATION

1 See the objectives of the *Verein Deutsche Sprache* at https://vds-ev.de/verein/leitlinien, accessed on 20 May 2024.
2 See the entry on 'Geschlechtergerechter Sprachgebrauch' in Duden's online version. https://www.duden.de/sprachwissen/sprachratgeber/Geschlechtergerechter-Sprachgebrauch.
3 Bayerisches Integrationsgesetz from 13 December 2016, accessed on 20 May 2024. https://www.gesetze-bayern.de/Content/Document/BayIntG.
4 OECD, *How's Life? 2020: Measuring Well-Being*. Paris: OECD Publishing, 9 March 2020. https://doi.org/10.1787/9870c393-en.
5 'Vertrauenskrise ohne Ende', Böckler Impuls, Hans-Böckler-Stiftung, July 2023. https://www.boeckler.de/de/boeckler-impuls-vertrauenskrise-ohne-ende-52385.htm.
6 Deutschland-Barometer Depression, Stiftung Deutsche Depressionshilfe und Suizidprävention, 7 November 2023. https://www.deutsche-depressionshilfe.de/forschungszentrum/deutschland-barometer-depression/einsamkeit.
7 Simon Schnetzer, Kilian Hampel and Klaus Hurrelmann, 'Trendstudie Jugend in Deutschland 2024', April 2024. https://simon-schnetzer.com/trendstudie-jugend-in-deutschland-2024.

8 The strategy paper was released on 13 December 2023 by the family ministry. https://www.bmfsfj.de/bmfsfj/service/publikationen/strategie-der-bundesregierung-gegen-einsamkeit-234582.

9 Data from Forschungsgruppe Weltanschauungen in Deutschland, accessed 24 May 2024. https://fowid.de/meldung/kirchenmitglieder-47%2C45-prozent.

10 Christian Wulff, 'Rede zum 20. Jahrestag der Deutschen Einheit ', 3 October 2020. https://www.bundespraesident.de/SharedDocs/Reden/DE/Christian-Wulff/Reden/2010/10/20101003_Rede.html.

11 'Gauck rückt von Positionen Merkels und Wulffs ab', *Die Zeit*, 31 May 2012. https://www.zeit.de/politik/deutschland/2012-05/bundespraesident-gauck-interview.

12 Lene Rock, *As German as Kafka: Identity and Singularity in German Literature around 1900 and 2000*. Leuven: Leuven University Press, 2019, pp. 31–66.

13 Friedrich Merz, 'Einwanderung und Identität', *Die Welt*, 25 October 2000. https://www.welt.de/print-welt/article540438/Einwanderung-und-Identitaet.html.

14 Thomas de Maizière, 'Leitkultur für Deutschland, was ist das eigentlich?', *Bild*, 29 April 2017. https://www.bild.de/politik/inland/thomas-de-maiziere/leitkultur-fuer-deutschland-51509022.bild.html.

15 Sajjan M. Gohel, 'Germany Increasingly a Center for Terrorism in Europe', *CTC Sentinel*, August 2011. https://ctc.westpoint.edu/germany-increasingly-a-center-for-terrorism-in-europe.

16 Email from Ibn Rushd-Goethe Mosque. https://mailchi.mp/93ebc1df665e/statement-der-ibn-rushd-goethe-moschee?e=e3082cdc1c.

17 Joel Waldfogel, 'Dining Out as Cultural Trade', *Journal of Cultural Economics* 44(2), June 2019, pp. 309–38. https://www.nber.org/papers/w26020.

18 Data stems from the EU's eAmbrosia register. https://ec.europa.eu/agriculture/eambrosia/geographical-indications-register.

19 In 2022, Germany spent €14.5 billion on culture, including €4.5 billion for music and theatre.

20 See for instance the 2022 annual report from Meldestelle für Diskriminierungsvorfällen im Fußball in NRW. https://medif-nrw.

de/de/aktuelles/medif-nrw-medif-veroeffentlicht-ersten-jahres bericht.

21 Jérôme Boateng, Post on X. 23 November 2023. https://x.com/JeromeBoateng/status/1727648639961518375.

22 Peter Schubert, Birthe Tahmaz and Holger Krimmer, 'Erste Befunde des ZiviZ-Survey 2023 Zivilgesellschaft in Krisenzeiten: Politisch aktiv mit geschwächten Fundamenten'. Berlin: ZiviZ im Stifter verband. https://www.ziviz.de/sites/ziv/files/ziviz-survey_2023_trendbericht.pdf.

23 Klaus D. Plümer, 'Obesity – An Increasing Public Health Problem in Germany', *Eurohealth* 25(1), 2019. https://iris.who.int/bitstream/handle/10665/332527/Eurohealth-25-1-14-16-eng.pdf.

24 OECD, 'The Heavy Burden of Obesity', 10 October 2019. https://www.oecd.org/germany/Heavy-burden-of-obesity-Media-country-note-GERMANY.pdf.

25 'Konzert mit Folgen – Die "GEMA-Vermutung", Kontrollkostenzuschlag und Lizenzgebühren', *Medien, Internet und Recht*, 29 May 2007. http://miur.de/1233.

26 Lars Haider, 'Hakenkreuz-Satz: Mercedes "fassungslos" über Precht-Äußerung', *Hamburger Abendblatt*, 14 November 2023. https://www.abendblatt.de/hamburg/altona/article240575856/Richard-David-Precht-der-Mercedes-Stern-und-das-Hakenkreuz.html.

27 Masha Gessen, 'In the Shadow of the Holocaust', *The New Yorker*, 9 December 2023. https://www.newyorker.com/news/the-weekend-essay/in-the-shadow-of-the-holocaust.

28 A public discussion with Gessen and the co-heads of the Heinrich Böll Foundation did take place on 18 December, two days later than scheduled after an uproar in social and traditional media. https://www.youtube.com/watch?v=Vb4yypPG-OE&t=595s.

29 Linda Mannheim, 'Germany's Theater of Memory: "Some People Already See the Flames. Others Don't Even Smell the Smoke"', *The Nation*, 29 December 2023. https://www.thenation.com/article/culture/max-czollek-germany-theater-memory-antisemitism-interview.

30 Hanno Hauenstein, 'Masha Gessen: "In Deutschland würde Hannah Arendt den Preis heute nicht erhalten"', *Frankfurter Rundschau*, 15 December 2023. https://www.fr.de/kultur/gesellschaft/journalistin-masha-gessen-deutschland-hannah-arendt-preis-eklat-92731175.html.

31 https://nothingchangeduntilfaced.com.

NOTES

32 Ilija Đurović, Interview with Bastašić, *Berliner Zeitung*, 25 September 2024. https://www.berliner-zeitung.de/open-source/bosnische-autorin-lana-bastasi-meine-vorstellung-vom-freien-berlin-war-zutiefst-naiv-li.2255502.
33 https://strikegermany.org.
34 Anna-Lena Scholz, 'Unease over Judith Butler', *Die Zeit*, 24 November 2023. https://www.zeit.de/kultur/2023-11/judith-butler-israel-hamas-university-english/komplettansicht.
35 Felix Klein, 'Hierarchien des Hasses', *Frankfurter Allgemeine Zeitung*, 19 February 2024. https://www.faz.net/aktuell/karriere-hochschule/akademischer-antisemitismus-hierarchien-des-hasses-felix-klein-19531381.html.
36 Timo Feldhaus, 'Susan Neiman: "Es ist falsch, alles nur im Licht deutscher Schuld zu betrachten"', *Berliner Zeitung*, 26 November 2023. https://www.susan-neiman.com/wp-content/uploads/2023/11/20231126_SN_BerlZ.pdf.

TEN: PATCHWORK

1 Magdalena Droste, *Bauhaus 1919–1933*. Cologne: Bauhaus-Archiv/Museum für Gestaltung, Taschen GmbH, 2023, p. 33.
2 Ibid., p. 38.
3 Stefan Bach, 'Grunderbe und Vermögensteuern können die Vermögenssungleichheit verringern', *DIW Wochenbericht* 50 (2021), pp. 807–15. https://www.diw.de/de/diw_01.c.831678.de/publikationen/wochenberichte/2021_50_1/grunderbe_und_vermoegensteuern_koennen_die_vermoegensungleichheit_verringern.html.
4 Gesellschaft für Informatik, 'Hessen – Informatik in der Schule bundesweit auf dem letzten Platz, muss das sein?' Accessed 31 May 2024. https://rg-rhein-main.gi.de/veranstaltung/hessen-informatik-in-der-schule-bundesweit-auf-dem-letzten-platz-muss-das-sein.
5 OECD, 'Number of Computers per Student (2022)', Education GPS, accessed 31 May 2024. https://gpseducation.oecd.org.
6 'Berufszufriedenheit/Schulleitung 2024 – Digitalisierung'. Verband Bildung und Erziehung, accessed 31 May 2024. https://www.vbe.de/service/meinungsumfragen/berufszufriedenheit-/-schulleitung-2024-digitalisierung.
7 'Neue Studie: Armut führt zu digitaler Ausgrenzung', Paritätischer Wohlfahrtsverband via Presseportal, 18 April 2023. https://www.presseportal.de/pm/53407/5487940.

NOTES

8. 'Mobiles Datenvolumen: Deutschland Im Europäischen Vergleich Überdurchschnittlich Teuer', Verbraucherzentrale Bundesverband, accessed 31 May 2024. https://www.vzbv.de/sites/default/files/2021-07/vzbv-MBD-Kurzpapier-Kosten%20f%C3%BCr%20mobiles%20Internet.pdf.
9. 'Galoppierende Digitalisierung grenzt ältere Menschen aus', Deutscher Familienverband, 28 April 2024. https://www.deutscher-familienverband.de/digitale-diskriminierung-galoppierende-digitalisierung-grenzt-aeltere-menschen-aus.
10. 'Projekthomepage Großschwabhausen', Energiequelle GmbH, accessed 30 May 2024. https://www.energiequelle.de/grossschwabhausen.
11. 'Energiegenossenschaften 2023', Deutscher Genossenschafts- und Raiffeisenverband e.V., accessed 30 May 2024. https://www.dgrv.de/news/energiegenossenschaften-2023.
12. 'Solaranlage mit Speicher: Darauf müssen Sie achten'. *ADAC*, accessed 30 May 2024. https://www.adac.de/rund-ums-haus/energie/versorgung/solaranlage-mit-speicher.
13. 'Klimakrise: Merz: Überbewertung des Themas Klimaschutz in der Politik', *Die Zeit*, 30 May 2024. https://www.zeit.de/news/2023-04/26/merz-ueberbewertung-des-themas-klimaschutz-in-der-politik.
14. 'AfD fordert Aufkündigung aller Klimavereinbarungen', Deutscher Bundestag, accessed 30 May 2024. https://www.bundestag.de/presse/hib/kurzmeldungen-966976.
15. Alice Weidel, '"Klimapolitik" geht immer zu Lasten der kleinen Leute'. afdbundestag.de, accessed 30 May 2024. https://afdbundestag.de/alice-weidel-klimapolitik-geht-immer-zu-lasten-der-kleinen-leute.
16. Video posted on X from 5 June 2024. https://x.com/harari_yuval/status/1798342553059893342?t=9UVFjCM423v1dxv8CoDEZA&s=08.

CLOSING REMARKS

1. European Parliament, 'The Concept of "climate refugee": Towards a Possible Definition'. europarl.europa.eu. Accessed 2 June 2024. https://www.europarl.europa.eu/RegData/etudes/BRIE/2021/698753/EPRS_BRI(2021)698753_EN.pdf.
2. 'Over one billion people at threat of being displaced by 20' (2020). Institute for Economics & Peace, accessed 2 June 2024. https://

NOTES

www.economicsandpeace.org/wp-content/uploads/2020/09/Ecological-Threat-Register-Press-Release-27.08-FINAL.pdf.

3 Thomas Mann, 'Germany and the Germans', Library of Congress, Washington, DC, 1945. https://babel.hathitrust.org/cgi/pt?id=uc1.b4153667&seq=5.

Index

Aachen 244
abortion 84
Abstiegangst (fear of decline) 186
Abu Sitta, Salman 87
Abu-Sittah, Ghassan 87
Adenauer, Konrad 36, 78n, 178
Adidas 239
Afghanistan 157–8, 201
Afrozensus 84–5
Ai Weiwei 61
Airbus 132
Aiwanger, Hubert 88–90, 210
Alliance 90, 211
Allianz 56
Allied occupation 31–2
Al-Qaeda 157
Altana 173
Alternative für Deutschland (AfD) 10–11, 15, 62, 81, 133, 144, 212, 214, 216, 238, 254–5, 266, 273
   and family businesses 129–30
   and gender equality 84
   and German language and culture 226, 235
   and Israel–Palestine conflict 241–2, 246–7
   Junge Alternative (JA) 203–4
   and Merkel's migration policy 59–60
   rise of 195–208
Amnesty International 247

Amri, Anis 201, 233
Ansbach 234
antisemitism 27, 86–8, 212, 219, 221, 241–8
   IHRA definition 245
ArcelorMittal 110
ARD 238
Arendt, Hannah 1, 240
Arnold, Karl 35
Arnstadt 160–1, 163–4
Arriva 68
Ateş, Seyran 234
Atta, Mohammed 233
Audi 118–20, 122
Augsburg 163, 180
Auschwitz 36, 44, 85, 88, 206, 244
   trial 40–2
austerity 9, 189–90, 192
Auto Motor und Sport magazine 120
Autobahn, speed limits on 106, 213

Baader, Andreas 44–5
Bach, Johann Sebastian 160, 231
Bad Homburg 171, 173, 177
Baden-Württemberg 102, 104, 217–19
Baerbock, Annalena 81, 166, 212
BaFin 74–5, 77–8
Ballack, Michael 51
Baltic Sea 63, 94, 96–7, 238
Baltic Youth Philharmonic Orchestra 99

INDEX

Bär, Dorothee 136
Barbarossa legend 16n
Baseballschlägerjahre (baseball-bat years) 49
BASF 18, 36, 97, 99, 114, 148, 162
Bastašić, Lana 244
Bauer, Fritz 40–2
Bauhaus 251–3, 259, 273
Bauhaus Museum 263
Bavaria 8, 12, 19–21, 89n, 103, 194, 202, 209–10, 214, 218, 225, 227, 250
  see also Christian Social Union (CSU)
Bavarian Radio Symphony Orchestra 236
Bayer 36
BDS movement 241–2, 244, 246
Beckenbauer, Franz 237n
Beckum 128
Beelitz 256
beer consumption 38, 235
Beethoven, Ludwig van 48, 63, 193
Benz, Bertha 113
Benz, Carl 113, 114n
Bergrheinfeld 103–4
Berlin
  airport 21, 70, 198
  Alexanderplatz 202
  AVUS racetrack 253
  Benderblock 62–3
  blockade and airlift 33–5, 156–7
  Borchardt restaurant 100
  Bornholmer checkpoint 47
  Brandenburg Gate 25, 54, 136, 157–8
  cabarets 253
  Charlottenburg 187
  Checkpoint Charlie 157
  childcare 182
  Christmas market attack 201
  Dreipfuhl 157
  election re-run 80, 86
  farmers' protest 208
  Glienicke Bridge 157
  Holocaust memorial 86, 206
  housing 179–80
  Ibn Rushd-Goethe mosque 234
  and Israel–Palestine conflict 244–6
  liberation and Red Army memorial 149
  Mädchenkammern 6
  Meyers Hof 5
  Oyoun cultural centre 244
  Palast der Republik 26, 49–50
  Palestine Congress 86–9
  Schöneberg district 5, 246
  Shah of Iran's visit 43
  Siegessäule 158
  Stadtschloss 50, 52, 187
  techno scene 236
  Tempelhof Airport 34
  Teufelsberg listening station 157
  Tiergarten park 31, 145
  Unter den Linden 25
Berlin Olympics (1936) 239
Berlin Wall 25–6, 39, 47, 52, 54, 136, 149, 156–7, 196, 237, 272
Bertelsmann Foundation 134
Beumer group 128
Beust, Ole von 76
Beutler, Ernst 30–1
Biden, Joe 97, 151, 158, 160
Bild 10, 211
billionaires 174–5
BioNTech 28, 140
Bismarck, Otto von 5, 76
Bitburg cemetery 46
Bitterfeld 106
Black Germans 84–5, 256
Blejerne Jahre (Years of Lead) 210
'blood and soil' nationalism 12, 15, 195, 207, 223, 255, 257, 269
  see also Volk, the
Bloomberg 75
Blume, Oliver 121
BMW 21, 57, 104, 121–5, 138, 156, 160, 164, 213
  and Quandt family 171–3

INDEX

Boateng, Jérôme 238
Bodemann, Y. Michal 243n
Boehringer family 175
Boger, Wilhelm 41–2
Böhmermann, Jan 60–1
Böll, Heinrich 44
Bornholm 95, 99
Borussia Dortmund 101
Bosch 104, 138, 161, 163
Bottrop 108
Brahim, Ihissou 124
Brandenburg 21, 70, 85, 198, 201, 227, 262
Brandmauer (firewall) 207, 254
Brandt, Willy 41, 43, 96, 145
Braun, Markus 74n
Brecht, Bertolt 29, 253
Bremen 20, 209, 243, 262
Brexit 60, 143, 247, 274
Brocken peak 268
Brorhilker, Anne 91
Brothers of Italy 129
Brown, Gordon 57
BSW party 134, 151, 195, 210, 214
Buback, Siegfried 44
Buchenwald concentration camp 86, 253
Buna 106
Bundesausgleichsamt (Federal Equalisation Office) 177
Bundesjugendspiele (federal youth games) 261
Bundeskriminalamt (Federal Criminal Police Office) 216
Bundesrechnungshof 69
Bundesverband der Deutschen Industrie (BDI, Federation of German Industries) 44, 200
Bundesverfassungsschutz (BND, domestic intelligence service) 21, 132, 197, 203, 211, 217, 221
Bundeswehr 150, 152, 217
bureaucracy 70–3, 133, 139
Bürgergeld 10, 189

Bush, George W. 157
Butler, Judith 245
BYD 122–5, 164
Byrne, James F. 32

Calw 217
care workers 131
Catholic Church 110, 113, 230
CATL 160–1, 164
Celan, Paul 31
Celonis 139
Chernobyl disaster 101
child abuse 213
childcare 132, 134, 182–3
China 16–18, 56–8
  auto industry 121–5, 162, 164–5
  Belt and Road Initiative 165
  and Covid-19 61
  and energy policy 99–100, 103–4
  espionage 152
  Ministry of State Security 21
  New Silk Road 165
  steel production 109–10
  threat to German economy 160–7
  and Wirecard scandal 76–7
Christian Democratic Union (CDU) 19, 42, 52–3, 57, 61–3, 80–1, 89, 102, 176, 189, 194, 254, 266
  and Constitution Day 267–8
  and German language and culture 227, 231–5
  and Israel–Palestine conflict 241–2, 245
  Junge Union 204n
  and migration 59, 133–4
  and political violence 210
  Quandt family donations 173
  and rise of AfD 198, 200, 202, 204–5, 207
  and rise of greens 212–14
Christian Social Union (CSU) 19, 59, 89, 136, 205, 207, 212, 214, 225, 241
Christmas markets 239–40

INDEX

Christmas trees 232–3, 239
climate crisis and action 23, 28, 79, 100–5, 111, 132–3, 135, 166–7, 205, 212, 257, 264–6, 272–3
Clinton, Bill 129
CNC machines 152n
coal mines 100–1, 107
Cold War 19, 29, 32, 127, 144, 150, 157
Cologne 1, 21, 24, 31, 83, 153, 180, 232
    central train station 201
    DITIB-Central Mosque 232
colonies, German 27, 256
Commerzbank 56, 155
Correctiv 207
Council of Economic Experts 134
Covid-19 pandemic 28, 61, 65, 79, 140, 154–5, 196, 218, 236
Crimea, Russian annexation 60, 96, 146–8, 152
cuisine, German 235–6, 256–7
Cum-Ex scandal 90–1
Czollek, Max 243

Dachau 86, 88
Daimler, Gottlieb 137
Daimler 148
Daimler-Benz 172
Daleel, Mohammad 234
Damascus 83
DAX index 74–5, 77, 137
Day X 216–17
de Maizière, Thomas 233–4
De Sutter, Petra 247
debt ratios 198, 212
Demjanjuk, John 59
demographic decline 58, 131–5
Der III. Weg 197
Der Spiegel 43, 211
de-risking 18
Dessau 253
Deutsche Bahn 66–70
Deutsche Bank 56, 90, 171
Deutsche Bundesbank 58, 115
Deutsche Herbst (German Autumn) 44

Deutsche Mark 33, 48, 198
Deutsche Post 69
Deutsche Telekom 69
Deutsche Welle 256
Deutscher Gewerkschaftsbund (German Trade Union Confederation) 99
Deutscher Werkbund 252
DFB football association 238
Diaby, Karamba 210
Die Heimat 197
Die Mädels vom Immenhof (*The Immenhof Girls*) 37
Die Rechte 197
Die Zeit 209
Diesel, Rudolf 114
Diess, Herbert 121
Digital Riser Report 136
digitalisation 16, 53, 58, 72, 135–7, 185, 261–3
DIW research institute 260
Djir-Sarai, Bijan 84, 210
Dobrindt, Alexander 116
Döner Kebabs 232
Döpfner, Mathias 51
Dortmund 244
Dotan-Dreyfus, Tomer 244
Dow Chemical 106
Dresden 31, 145n, 180, 210, 250
Duden dictionary 226
Duisburg 110–11, 165, 236
Düren 1–2, 249
Düsseldorf 108, 110
Dutschke, Rudi 43

EagleBurgmann 128
Eckhart, Meister 271
education 20, 182–4, 261–2, 274
    see also vocational training
Eichmann, Adolf 41
Einstein, Albert 73
Einstein Forum 248
electric heat pumps 105, 133, 212–13
electric home furnaces 211
Elizabeth II, Queen 217

INDEX

Energiewende 16, 103–5, 264–5
Enlightenment 31, 231, 233, 251
Ensslin, Gudrun 44
E.ON 99
Erdoğan, Recep Tayyip 61
Erfindergeist (spirit of invention) 114
Erfurter Kreuz 160–1
Erfurter Resolution (Erfurt Resolution) 199
Erhard, Ludwig 13–14, 33, 38, 175, 178–9, 254
Erinnerungskultur (memory culture) 205
Ersol Solar Energy 161
Esken, Saskia 81
ESMY Management School 139
Essen 107–8, 110, 199
ESTA 20n
Etdorf Museum 63
European Central Bank 11
European Chamber of Commerce in China 162
European Coal and Steel Pact 109
European Institute for Gender Equality 81
European Parliament 154n, 197–8
European Union 10–11, 60, 81, 109–10, 147, 151, 154–5, 212, 236, 262
    relations with US 158–9
Eurovision Song Contest 59, 236
eurozone debt crisis 10, 87, 90
EVG union 69
Ewigskeitaufgaben (eternity tasks) 101

Faeser, Nancy 87
Fahimi, Yasmin 99
farmers' protests 208–10
FBI 21, 115, 216
FC Schalke 04, 101
Federal Audit Office 79n
Federal Constitutional Court 188–9
Federal Ministry for Family Affairs 84
Federal Statistics Office 70
federal system 19–22, 72

feminism 83, 211
Fichtelgebirge 216
Financial Reporting Enforcement Panel (FREP) 77–8
Financial Times 55, 73–5
Fischer, Joschka 157, 211–12
Fitzek, Peter 219–20
Flaschensammler (bottle collectors) 188
Flick, Friedrich 172
Focus magazine 10
food banks 187, 190
Franconians 250
Franco-Prussian War 108
Frank, Peter 219
Frankfurt 11, 180, 187, 191, 255, 261
    Auschwitz trial 40–2
    counter-terrorism operation 215
    Goethe Haus 30–1, 38, 40
Frankfurt Book Fair 88
Frankfurt School 253
Fraser, Nancy 244
Fratzscher, Marcel 182
Frauengold (Women Gold) tonic 37
Fraunhofer Institutes 139, 164
Free Democrats (FDP) 24, 53, 58–9, 78–80, 154, 189, 194, 208, 210, 212
    and Israel–Palestine conflict 241, 246
    Quandt family donations 173
Freie Wähler (Free Voters) 89, 214
Freiheitsfonds 188n
Friedliche Revolution (Peaceful Revolution) 47, 52
Friedrich, Caspar David 231
Friedrich Evert Stiftung 221
Fritsche, Klaus-Dieter 76
fuel inequality 129
Fujian Grand Chip Investment Fund 163
Fukushima disaster 98, 102
Fukuyama, Francis 150, 272

Gabriel, Sigmar 163
Gandhi, Mahatma 52

INDEX

Gastarbeiter (guest workers) 23–4, 36, 238
Gauck, Joachim 205–6, 232
Gauland, Alexander 198–9, 201, 206, 238
Gazprom 17, 95, 148
Geibel, Emanuel 229n
Geissner, Wilhelm 38
Gelowicz, Fritz 233
Gelsenkirchen 108, 238
GEMA 240
gender equality 20, 80n, 81–4
gendern 226
Generationenkapital (generations capital) 135
Genscher, Hans-Dietrich 154
Georgia, Russian invasion 146
German Agency for Transfer and Innovation 140
German Council on Foreign Relations 153
German Empire 8, 27, 215–17
German Institute for Economic Research 182
German language 224–9
German Renters Federation 181
GermanDream initiative 273–4
Gessen, Masha 242–4
Gestapo 21
Gini coefficient 174
Gläsker, Horst 265
global financial crisis 55–6, 65, 79
globalisation 17, 53, 123, 129, 141, 143, 162, 167, 199, 212, 218, 226, 235
Goebbels, Magda 172
Goerke, Björn 120
Goethe, Johann Wolfgang von 30, 32, 66, 227, 231, 233, 252, 263
Gorbachev, Mikhail 46, 157
Gorch Fock 150
Great Depression 49, 191
Great Replacement theory 202, 206
Greece 10–11, 56, 58, 87, 198
green hydrogen 106–7, 265

Green Party 78–9, 81, 154, 194
and energy policy 95, 101–2
and *gendern* 226
and Israel–Palestine conflict 241–2
rise of 208–15
Greifswald 99, 238
Gropius, Walter 249, 251–3, 259
Groβschwabhausen 263–5
Grunderbe (universal inheritance) 260
Gründerzeit 5–6, 127, 175, 251–2, 273
Grundgesetz (Basic Law) 7–9, 19, 22, 35, 49, 57, 186, 233, 247, 254
Gütersloh 126–7, 209

H2 Mare plan 106
Habeck, Robert 95, 97, 165–6, 208–9, 211–12
Habermas, Jürgen 45–6
Haftpflichtversicherung (personal liability insurance) 13
Hage, Ghassan 244
Hagen, Nina 63
Haldenwang, Thomas 217, 221
Halle 247
Halligen islands 208
Halvorsen, Gail 34, 156
Hamburg 20, 50, 93, 110, 132, 180, 199, 250
container terminal 165–6
Elbphilharmonie concert hall 143–4, 165
Hanau 234
Hannah Arendt Prize for Political Thought 242
Hannover 172
Hanson, Erin 80
Harari, Yuval Noah 269
Hartmann, Gustav 268
Hartz IV welfare reforms 185, 188–9
Harz mountains 268
Hasso Plattner Institute 137
Haug, Matthes 216–17
Haus am Horn 252, 273
healthcare 181–2, 185

328

INDEX

Hebbel, Friedrich 65
Hefets, Iris 245
Heidelberg 250
Heidelberger Manifest 24
Heimatfilme (homeland films) 37
Heine, Heinrich 113
Heinrich Böll Stiftung 242–4
Hellma Materials 126
Helmholtz Association 164
Helsinki Accords 148
Henkel, Hans-Olaf 200
Heppner, Peter 223
Herbert Quandt Stiftung 173n
Herero and Nama people 27
Herrhausen, Alfred 171
Hesse 40, 261
Hessians 250
Heuberg concentration camp 40
Heuss, Theodor 40
Historikerstreit (historians' dispute) 46
Hitler, Adolf 27, 31, 36, 38, 43, 56, 63, 109, 114n, 223, 240
Hitler salute 85
Höcke, Björn 84, 195, 206, 239
Högl, Eva 153
Holocaust 26–7, 29–30, 41, 44, 46, 87, 174, 206, 220, 243–5, 248, 275
  Berlin memorial 86, 206
homelessness 33, 181, 187, 249
Honeker, Erich 47
Hooge island 208
Höss, Rudolf 40
housing 15, 38, 132, 178–81, 185, 257–60
Hülkenberg, Nico 239
Hussein, Saddam 157

I. G. Farben 36, 127
Identitarian Movement (Austria) 204
Industrie 4.0 concept 161–2
inequality 6, 11, 14, 169–70, 174–8, 188, 192, 218, 220, 257–8, 260
Infineon 133

inflation 33, 56, 74, 170, 187, 190, 205, 213, 220, 252
Institut für Staatspolitik (IfS, Institute for State Policy) 206
International Holocaust Remembrance Alliance 245
Iraq war 157–8
Iron Curtain 39, 50, 101, 123, 145, 150
Islam 232, 197, 199, 203, 232–4, 241n
Islamic Jihad Union 233
Islamic State 201, 234
Islamists 221
Israel–Palestine conflict 27, 81, 86–8, 241–7

Jäger, Harald 47
Jagschloss Waidmannsheil 215, 216n
Japan 17, 98, 102, 139, 159
Jewish Voice for a Just Peace in the Middle East 86
Jews 12, 27, 29, 31, 40, 46, 88, 171–2, 233, 240–8, 250, 267
  see also antisemitism
job losses 9, 14, 128
  with reunification 48–9
Joplin, Janis 124
Judaism 232, 240
Junkers-Werke 253

Kaeser, Joe 148
Kalbitz, Andreas 199
Kant, Immanuel 31, 66, 240
Karikó, Katalin 140
Karneval 8
Kartoffelsuppe (potato soup) 55
Kassel, *Documenta* art exhibition 244
Kaufland 175
Kennedy, John F. 39, 156
Kiesinger, Kurt Georg 42
Kirchensteuer (church tax) 230
Kissinger, Henry 77, 166
Klein, Felix 246–7
Klose, Miroslav 238
Klum, Heidi 236

Koch, Wilhelm 63–4
Koduk, Oswald 40
Kohl, Helmut 24, 46, 48–9, 52, 60, 171, 194, 227, 266
Kommersant newspaper 147
Königreich Deutschland (Kingdom of Germany) 219
Königsberg 31
Konrad Adenauer Stiftung 11
Kraftwerk 93
Kramp-Karrenbauer, Annegret 62, 81
Kreditanstalt für Wiederaufbau 32
Kristallnacht 267
Kroos, Toni 238
Krupp, Alfred 108–9
Krupp, Friedrich 107
Krupp company 107–11, 127
  see also ThyssenKrupp
KSK special forces unit 216, 219
Kubitschek, Götz 206
Kühn, Heniz 24
KUKA 163
Künzelsau 130
Kurzarbeit (furlough programme) 56

Laban, Rudolf 254n
Labour Day 268
Lahm, Philip 238
Lambrecht, Christine 81
Lampertheim 256
Land der Dichter und Denker (land of poets and thinkers) 31, 66
Landstuhl military hospital 158
Lang, Fritz 36, 169, 253
Lang, Ricarda 81, 209, 213
Langheinrich, Franz 195
Laschet, Armin 51, 62
Lavrov, Sergey 81, 146
Le Pen, Marine 197
Lebensreform (life reform) movement 211, 231
Leergut (deposit packaging) 188
Lehman Brothers 56, 68
Lehnert, Erik 206

Leipzig 46–7, 52, 209
Leisten, Anna 204
Leitkultur debate 233–5, 240–1
Leuna 49, 106
Li Keqiang 161
Lidl 175
Lindner, Christian 193–4
Lineker, Gary 65, 92
Link, Sören 110
Litvinenko, Alexander 146
Lower Saxony 118, 210, 225
Lübcke, Walter 210
Lucke, Bernd 198–200
Ludwig II, King of Bavaria 175
Ludwigshafen 97, 99, 162
Lusatia 110
Luther, Martin 219

Maas, Heiko 97
Maaßen, Hans-Georg 210
McCrum, Dan 74n, 75
Magnitz, Frank 210
Mais, General Alfons 152
Malaysia Airlines Flight 17, 96
Malsack-Winkemann, Birgit 216
Mammen, Jeanne 36–7
Manager Magazin 175
Mann, Thomas 5, 36, 169, 275
Mannheim 113, 255
Marsalek, Jan 74n, 75
Marshall Plan 32–3
Marx, Karl 169
Massachusetts Institute of Technology 262
Max Planck Institute for Social Anthropology 244
Max Planck Society 139, 164
Maxima, Queen of the Netherlands 83
Maybach, Wilhelm 137
Mbembe, Achille 244, 246
Medvedev, Dmitry 99
Mehdorn, Hartmut 69–70
Meinhof, Ulrike 44

INDEX

Mercedes-Benz 14, 45, 57, 65, 102, 116, 119, 121–2, 124–5, 160, 164, 185
Merkel, Angela 10–11, 26, 52–64, 74, 76–7, 80, 87, 143, 146, 154, 161, 163, 189, 227
   and digitalisation 136–7, 139
   and energy policy 97–9, 101–2, 111, 147, 264
   and gender equality 80n, 82–3
   and German culture 232
   and housing policy 180–1
   and manufacturing industry 114, 126
   mobile phone surveillance 158
   and refugee crisis 201–2
   relations with US 155–6, 158
   and rise of far-right 193–4, 196, 198, 200, 202
   and rise of Greens 213–15
   and Volkswagen scandal 116
Merkel, Ulrich 83n
Merz, Friedrich 189, 207, 212, 227, 232, 234, 239, 266
Messi, Lionel 238
Metropolis 36, 169–70, 192
Meyer, Hannes 253
Meyer-Landrut, Lena 59
Michael, Theodor Wonja 256
middle class, decline in 186
Midea 163
Miele 126–7
Mies van der Roher, Ludwig 253
Mietpreisbremse (rental price brake) 181
migration 24–5, 58–9, 63, 84, 132–4, 200–2, 260–1, 271
   and German colonies 255–6
   and German culture 232–5
   'remigration' plans 207
military spending 150, 160
minimum wages 79
Minsk agreements 147
Mischkultur (mixed culture) 250
Mitbestimmung 7
Mittelstand 125–30, 133, 138, 163, 185

Mönchengladbach 190
Monday demonstrations 47
Monroe, Marilyn 37
Morocco 124–5
Moslehner, Manfred 23
Mossad 41
motor racing 239
MS *Hillegenlei* 208
Mülheim an der Ruhr 110
Müller, Axel 242
Müller, Ernst and Yvonne 1–2, 249
Munich 83, 111, 131, 155, 179, 188, 237, 255
   welcome for refugees 201
Munich Olympics (1972) 239
Musk, Elon 122, 125
Muslims 12, 58, 232–4, 241–2, 248–9
Mustermann, Erika 83

N26 bank 139
Nachtwey, Oliver 186
national anthem 49
National Democratic Party (NPD) 203n
National Socialist Underground 59, 234
NATO 36, 95–6, 147, 150, 153, 156, 159, 212
Nazism 3, 11–12, 26, 28–31, 40–2, 45–6, 48, 52, 72, 84, 191, 231, 251, 275
   and antisemitism 241–4, 247–8, 267
   Bertha Benz and 114n
   and German culture 36–7, 231–2, 239–40, 251–3, 256
   and military spending 150
   and *Mittelstand* 127
   and Quandt family 171–2
   remembering Nazi past 85–90, 223–4
   and rise of AfD 195, 199, 204–6, 208
Neiman, Susan 248
Nelly Sachs Prize for Literature 244
Nena 101
neo-Nazis 59, 199, 210, 234

INDEX

Netzer, Günter 51
Netzwerk Steuergerechtigkeit (tax justice network) 175
Neubauer, Luisa 211
Neue Rechte (New Right) 206
Neue Sachlichkeit (New Objectivity) 36, 274
New Year's Eve 240
New Yorker 242
Nickel, Laura 85
Niersbach, Wolfgang 237n
Nietzsche, Friedrich 143, 227
Nolte, Ernst 46
Nord Stream pipelines 58, 95–100, 146–8
North Sea 97, 208
Northern League 129
Nouripour, Omid 84, 213
nuclear power 98, 101–3
Nuremberg trials 29

Obama, Barack 135–6, 158
Oberhausen 108
obesity 239
Obrigkeit (imperiousness) 229
Oetker, Rudolf-August 32
Ohnesorg, Benno 43
Oktoberfest 8
Olearius, Christian 91
Olympic Games 239
Ostalgie 26
Ostpolitik 145
Otto, Nicolaus 137
Overbeck, Bishop Franz-Josef 110
Owens, Jesse 239
Oxfam Deutschland 176
Özdemir, Cem 84, 209
Özil, Mesut 238

pacifism 17, 65, 150
Papandreou, George 57
Paris climate agreements 100–1, 212
patent applications 138

Patriotische Union (Patriotic Union) 215
Pegida 199, 206
pensions 22–3, 55, 134–5, 190
Perestroika 46
Petry, Frauke 198–200, 202–3
Pfizer 140
Pforzheim 113
Piëch, Ferdinand 121
Pilates, Joseph 254n
Pilates 253–4
Pistorious, Boris 153
Plattner, Hasso 137
Plötner, Jens 151
Podolski, Lukas 238
Politkovskaya, Anna 146
Ponto, Jürgen 44
Popular Front for the Liberation of Palestine 45
populism 6, 11, 15, 106, 111, 115, 129, 134, 155, 191, 197, 199–200, 233, 255, 260, 264, 266, 273–4
Porsche, Ferdinand 32, 38, 117–18, 137
Porsche 14, 102, 118, 120–1, 125, 213
Potsdam 207, 248
poverty 14, 22n, 23, 170, 182, 184, 186, 188, 191
Precht, Richard David 240
proportional representation system 198n, 221
Prussia 12, 37
Prussians 250
public service broadcasting 236–7
Putin, Vladimir 2, 97–100, 143, 146, 148–9

Qatar 95, 97, 118, 153
Quandt family 171–5
Querdenker 220

R&D 139–41
Raad, Walid 244
racism 84–5
  see also Black Germans; migration

INDEX

Ramstein airbase 159, 233
Rat für deutsche Rechtschreibung (Council for German Orthography) 224, 225n, 226
Reagan, Ronald 46, 136, 157
Red Army Faction (RAF) 44–5, 171, 210
Red Brigades 44
Reformation 231, 251
Reformhaus chain 231
Reichsbürger movement 215–19, 235
Reichsmark 33
Reinheitsgebot (beer purity law) 235
renewable energy 79, 103–7, 111, 162, 264–6
reunification 7, 19, 25–7, 30, 48–52, 55, 63, 66, 68, 123, 145, 149, 160, 171, 180, 186, 211–12, 214, 232, 235, 239, 242, 250
 and national commemorations 266–7
Reuss, Heinrich XIII. Prinz 215–17, 219
Reuter, Ernst 34
Rheinmetall 153
Richter, Gerhard 46
Risikphobie (fear of risk) 138
Rodrigues de Sá, Armando 23–4
Rohwedder, Detlev Karston 49
Röller, Lars-Hendrik 77
Romanticism 211, 231, 256
Rorty, Richard 92
Rosberg, Nico 239
Roth, Claudia 26–7
Ruhrkohle AG 190
Rumsfeld, Donald 157
Ruppert, Stefan 246
rural populations, declining 218
Rüsen, Tom 129
Russia
 espionage and sabotage 21, 75
 and German far-right 195, 199, 205, 207
 German relations with 16–17, 60, 81, 94–100, 103, 128, 144–56, 159–60, 162, 167, 212
 see also Nord Stream gas pipelines; Ukraine war
RWE 264

Saarland 110
Şahin, Uğur 140
St Josefs-Heim 131
Salvini, Matteo 129
same-sex marriage 198
SAP 137
Sarrazin, Thilo 58
Saudi Arabia 107, 153, 159
Sauer, Joachim 83n
Sauerland 233
Saxony 20, 198, 250
 tech cluster 133
Saxony-Anhalt 207, 219
Schäuble, Wolfgang 11, 56
Schenker-Stinnes 68
Schiller, Friedrich 31, 66, 227, 252, 263
Schleswig-Holstein 37
Schleyer, Hanns Martin 45
Schlüttsiel 208
Schmidt, Helmut 45
Schmidt, Oliver 115–17
Schneider, Daniel 234
Schnellroda 206–7
Scholz, Olaf 2–3, 51, 57, 62, 71, 78–9, 81, 91, 130, 135, 154, 165, 180, 190
 assassination plan 216
 and coalition collapse 193–5
 and energy policy 97, 100–1, 111, 147
 and rise of AfD 204
 and rise of Greens 210, 213–14
 and Ukraine war 17, 145, 150–3
 Unity Day speech 267
Scholzing 151–2
Schröder, Gerhard 24, 52–5, 146, 211
 and energy policy 96, 100, 102, 274
 welfare reforms 185, 188–9

Schuld ('guilt') 69
Schumacher, Michael 239
Schützenfest 269
Schwarz, Dieter 175
Schwarzer, Alice 151
Schwetzingen 256
Sellner, Martin 204, 207
Sesselmann, Robert 196
Sezession 206
SGL Carbon 173
Shamsie, Kamila 244
Siebenkotten, Lukas 181
Siemens, Werner von 114
Siemens 45, 56, 90, 104, 115, 148, 185
Sirius, Peter 169
Sochi Olympics 147
Social Democratic Party (SPD) 21, 42, 52–3, 57–8, 62, 78, 81, 146n, 176, 194
  and Cum-Ex scandal 91
  and energy policy 100, 102
  and Israel–Palestine conflict 241
  and rise of AfD 202, 204, 207
  and rise of Greens 211–14
social market economy 14, 177, 182
social spending 11, 15, 189–90
'social tourism' 198
social withdrawal 229–30
Söder, Markus 89, 210, 226
SolarWorld 163–4
Sondervermögen (special assets) 57
Sonneberg 196–7, 205
South Korea 139, 159
Soviet Union 31–2, 43, 46, 136, 153, 157, 253, 267
Spargelzeit (asparagus season) 256–7, 268–9
Sparkassen 86, 155
Spielberg, Steven 157
Spreewald 85
Spremberg 227n
Springer media group 43–4, 51
Staatsräson (state's reason for being) 243

staff shortages 132–3
Stalin, Josef 33–5, 156
Stasi 37–8, 47
Stauffenberg, Colonel Claus von 62–3
Steigerlied (miner's song) 101
Steinhaus, Helena 274
Steinmeier, Frank-Walter 9, 58, 144–9, 151
Stolpersteine ('stumbling stones') 86
Strauss, Franz-Josef 202
Strike Germany 245
Stuttgart 21 rail project 67, 111
Süddeutsche Zeitung 190
SüdLink transmission line 104
Sundays 230
Swabian housewife legend 57, 79
Syrian civil war 59, 200

Tatort 237
Taunus mountains 171
taxation 82, 175–7, 179
Tekkal, Düzen 273
Teske, Max 85
Tesla 21, 121–2, 125
Teutoberg Forest, Battle of the 250
Teyssen, Johannes 99
Thunberg, Greta 211, 245
Thuringia 194–6, 198–9, 215, 217
ThyssenKrupp 93, 109–10
Tibi, Bassam 233
Tillschneider, Hans-Thomas 207
Toyota 116, 122
Trabant cars 26, 48
Transparency International 91n
Treaty of Warsaw 43
Treuhandanstalt (trust agency) 48–9
Truman, Harry S. 35, 156
Truman Doctrine 158
Trümmerfrauen (rubble women) 31
Trump, Donald 2–3, 60, 96, 143–4, 150, 152, 155–6, 158–61, 165, 193, 204, 271, 274
Tschentscher, Peter 91
TSMC 133

INDEX

Tübingen 71
Tugenden (virtues) 65–6
Türeci, Özlem 140–1
Turkish Grey Wolves 221

Ukraine war 2, 17, 81, 94–8, 103, 110, 141, 143–5, 147–53, 166, 170, 193, 205, 212, 220
Ukrainian refugees 28, 133, 153, 189
Ulbricht, Walter 35, 39
Ulrichs, Karsten 69
unemployment 49, 52, 55–6, 237, 267
unemployment benefits 134
UNESCO 236
unicorns 139
union membership, decline in 185–6
United States, relations with Germany 155–60
US Department of Justice 163
US Environmental Protection Agency 116
University of Cologne 244

Vad, Erich 151
Vallourec 110
Valls, Manuel 201
van de Velde, Henry 252
van Dyk, Paul 223
Varoufakis, Yanis 87–8
Vassiliadis, Michael 106
Verein Deutsche Sprache (German Language Association) 225–6
Verfassungspatriotismus (constitutional patriotism) 8, 45
Vergangenheitsbewältigung (coming to terms with the past) 42
Viessman 126
Villa Hügel 108
violence against women 83–4
vocational training 7, 184–5
Volk, the 3, 15, 26, 30, 197, 216, 250, 272
Völkerschauen (human zoos) 256
Volkswagen 18, 36, 38, 45, 50, 56–7, 90, 115–23, 148, 160, 162, 164

Cariad division 119–21
emissions cheating scandal 90, 115–17
von der Leyen, Ursula 81

Wadden Sea 208
Wagenkecht, Sahra 134, 195, 210, 214, 266
Wagner, Richard 175, 234
Wallace, Ben 21
Walpurgisnacht 268
Wan Gang 122
Wandel durch Handel (change through trade) 18, 98, 153, 162
Warburg bank 91
Warsaw ghetto 43
Warsaw Pact 47
Wasilewski, Thomas 190–1
Wefa Inotec 126
wefox 139
Wegner, Kai 86
Weidel, Alice 130, 203, 266
Weimar Republic 11, 36–7, 76, 130, 169, 191, 252–4
Weizsäcker, Richard von 45
Welt am Sonntag 219
Wende (transformations) 16
WerteUnion (Values Union) 207, 211, 214
Westerwelle, Guido 189
Weyel, Harald 206–7
whistleblowers 129
Wilder, Billy 37
Wildpinkeln (urinating in public) 13
Wilhelm I, Kaiser 171
Wilhelm II, Kaiser 108, 171
Wilkommenskultur (welcoming culture) 133, 235
Winterkorn, Martin 117, 121–2
Wirecard scandal 73–8
Wirtschaftswunder 13, 23, 33, 38, 42, 52, 127–8, 138, 172, 178, 250, 256, 261
Wissmann, Matthias 67

INDEX

Witten Institute for Family Business 129
Wohlstand für Alle (prosperity for all) 13, 38, 40, 51, 53, 114, 170, 186, 207, 223, 254
Wolfratshausen 128
Wolfsburg 38, 111, 117, 119
Wolfsgrün 220
work–life balance 132
World Cup football 8, 14, 38, 54, 59, 65, 68, 232, 237–9
World Economic Forum 81
World Trade Organisation 109
Wulff, Christian 231–2
Würde (dignity) 22

Würth, Reinhold 130
Würzburg 201

Yugoslav wars 200

Zapatero, José Luis Rodríguez 57
Zeitenwende 17, 150, 152, 154
Zelensky, Volodymyr 149
ZF Friedrichshafen 138
Zimmerman, Olaf 52
Zipse, Oliver 123
Žižek, Slavoj 87
Zollverein colliery 100
zu Guttenberg, Karl-Theodor 76–7
Zuständigkeit (area of responsibility) 78

A Note on the Authors

After studying international relations and political philosophy in Washington, DC and in the UK, **Chris Reiter** has worked as a journalist covering economics, politics and business. For more than twenty years, he has been based in Berlin where he has chronicled Germany's ups and downs. He is a senior editor for Bloomberg after previously reporting for Reuters and Dow Jones Newswires. While born and raised in the US, he learned to love Knödel, Leberkäse and Fußball from his German father.

Will Wilkes studied German and Italian in London and Rome. Now based in Frankfurt, he has spent his working life writing about Germany, travelling across the country to talk with politicians, executives, union leaders and workers. From terrorism to economic crises to the resurgence of the far right, he has reported on the country's mounting challenges and fraying social cohesion. He is currently a reporter for Bloomberg and has previously written about Germany for Market News International and the *Wall Street Journal*. He appreciates Germany's rich music culture – less so the national aversion to queuing.

A Note on the Type

The text of this book is set in Bembo, which was first used in 1495 by the Venetian printer Aldus Manutius for Cardinal Bembo's De Aetna. The original types were cut for Manutius by Francesco Griffo. Bembo was one of the types used by Claude Garamond (1480–1561) as a model for his Romain de l'Université, and so it was a forerunner of what became the standard European type for the following two centuries. Its modern form follows the original types and was designed for Monotype in 1929